BUROS DESK REFERENCE

ASSESSMENT OF SUBSTANCE ABUSE

BUROS
Desk Reference

BUROS DESK REFERENCE

ASSESSMENT OF SUBSTANCE ABUSE

Edited by Linda L. Murphy
and James C. Impara

Preface by
Jane Close Conoley

User's Guide by
Peter E. Nathan

Compiled from the *Mental Measurements Yearbook* series

The Buros Institute of Mental Measurements
The University of Nebraska-Lincoln
Lincoln, Nebraska

1996
Distributed by The University of Nebraska Press

ISBN 910674-42-6

Manufactured in the United States of America.

The paper used in this publication meets the minimum requirements of American National Standard for Information Sciences—Permanence of Paper for Printed Library Materials, ANSI Z39.48-1984.

Note to Users

The staff of the Buros Institute of Mental Measurements has made every effort to ensure the accuracy of the test information included in this work. However, the Buros Institute of Mental Measurements and the Editors of the *Buros Desk Reference: Assessment of Substance Abuse* do not assume, and hereby expressly and absolutely disclaim, any liability to any party for any loss or damage caused by errors or omissions or statements of any kind in the *Buros Desk Reference: Assessment of Substance Abuse*. This disclaimer also includes judgments or statements of any kind made by test reviewers, who were extended the professional freedom appropriate to their task; their judgments and opinions are their own, uninfluenced in any way by the Buros Institute or the Editors.

All material included in the *Buros Desk Reference: Assessment of Substance Abuse* is intended solely for the use of our readers. None of this material, including reviewer statements, may be used in advertising or for any other commercial purpose.

TABLE OF CONTENTS

PREFACE

by

Jane Close Conoley

The successful treatment of substance abuse and dependence remains illusive in the majority of clinical cases. Millions of lives are touched by the negative effects on health, family functioning, and work success caused by alcohol and other substance abuse.

There are many obstacles to successful treatment. These include abusers' tendency to deny the seriousness of problems, the often long-standing/chronic history of the abuse making intervention especially difficult, the psychological and physical predispositions that may make substance abuse more likely among some people, and the difficulty of mapping treatment approaches that match particular characteristics of the client.

These and other difficulties have spurred the development of many approaches to assessment of substance abuse. Counselors and researchers have hoped to screen for early warning signs of abuse, verify abuse that was being denied by the client, measure the effectiveness of educational programs, and gain information about the individual that would allow for prescriptive tailoring of treatment strategies.

As the prevalence, diversity, and intensity of abuse problems have intensified more tests and interviews have appeared in the literature and been adopted by alcohol counselors and other helping professionals. These measures vary widely in format, supporting evidence, use, and application. The need for informed decision making regarding substance abuse assessment grows more important as more instruments are made available.

The Buros Institute has a long history of attempting to fill exactly this need—valid information for consumer use to inform the choice and use of assessment devices. This Buros Desk Reference is likely to have a wide audience and fill a compelling need. Drug abuse threatens the lives of abusers, those who care for them, and the welfare of society. This is high stakes assessment because of the ecology of concerns that surround accurate identification of an abusive problem with substances and the monitoring of treatment success.

The assessment of substance abuse is also a particular scientific and clinical problem that makes the right choice of instruments very important. Clearly, no single instrument can provide definitive diagnosis. Experienced counselors know, however, that drug abuse is enabled, in part, by intricate webs of rationalizations and denials perpetrated by abusers and their significant others. Powerful tools are necessary to confront these obstacles and facilitate full responsibility for the disordered behavior and commitment to a difficult treatment regimen. Although no single test can accomplish this, valid and reliable measurement is an ally for the client and the service provider.

Once again, the Buros Institute has been successful in bringing together an array of reviews that will inform the careful practitioner. Some of the reviews contained in this volume will challenge conventional wisdom among counselors. I urge an open mind, remembering that assessment and diagnosis is based on a multimodal process and even the most accurate therapist is probably somewhat unaware of all the data used to make a diagnosis. The reviews are meant to enhance our decision making by illuminating the real structure of tests and the actual data that support their use.

The historic mission of the Institute continues with the publication of this volume. This convenient compilation of tests related to a single content area will be a great resource to busy practitioners who remain committed to scientifically guided practice.

Jane Close Conoley
Dean
College of Education
Texas A&M University

ACKNOWLEDGEMENTS

With the publication of this, the second in the Buros Desk Reference series, we are grateful both to those individuals who were instrumental in developing the idea of the *BDR* and those who were helpful in the completion of the current volume. Richard M. Jaeger, a former member of the Buros National Advisory Committee first suggested the production of a new publication series that would include relatively small numbers of reviews focused on special topics. The *BDR: Psychological Assessment in the Schools* was thus developed and published and has met with sufficient enthusiasm that it seemed appropriate to continue the series.

Our current National Advisory Committee, including Larry Rudner, Anthony Nitko, Frank Schmidt, Gary Melton, and Charles Peterson, suggested that we also include a user's guide or "how to" chapter in our next *BDR* to enhance its usefulness. We are grateful to Peter Nathan for understanding what we wanted and doing a splendid job of writing such a chapter for this *BDR*.

We are grateful to Jane Close Conoley for her suggestions on important tests to be included and appropriate individuals to prepare reviews. The decision to publish a *BDR* for professionals working in the area of substance abuse assessment came from her earlier workshops for these individuals. We also thank Jane for her continuing interest and for writing the Preface for this volume after she left the Buros Institute and the University of Nebraska to take up her new position as Dean of Education at Texas A&M.

A publication such as this would not be possible without the support and commitment of the other members of the Buros team. We are grateful to Barbara Plake, the director of both the Buros Center for Testing and the Buros Institute of Mental Measurements, for her vision and leadership and her wonderful enthusiasm and support for the project and for us personally. We also thank her for pitching in and helping with editing tasks at the end of the project.

Gary Anderson, editorial assistant, quietly and competently kept track of the process of inviting and receiving reviews for the many tests requiring reviews before this *BDR* could be published. We thank him for his cheerful attitude while proofreading manuscripts and page proofs. We are also grateful to Rosemary Sieck, word processing specialist, for typing the test descriptions and reviews and for all her help in preparing indexes. Jane Gustafson, marketing coordinator, receives our thanks for her friendly nudging of us to complete this publication and for her creative ideas for marketing it. Janice Nelsen, secretary at the Buros Institute, can never be thanked enough for dealing with phones and mail and the millions of things we do not have to worry about because she does.

Again we thank all the reviewers who donate their time and expertise to reviewing the tests included in the *MMY* and this *BDR*. Our work would be impossible without their continuing support. We are also grateful to all those editors before us who have established the Buros tradition of excellence. Following in the footsteps of such individuals as Oscar Buros, James Mitchell, Jack Kramer, and Jane Conoley is a privilege and a responsibility that we do not take lightly.

We are also grateful to our colleagues at Printing Services at the University of Nebraska for their efficient printing and binding of this volume and for their friendliness and helpfulness. We also appreciate the efforts and attitude of Kirt Card and his staff in customer service at the University of Nebraska Press for their patience and helpfulness as they distribute and help to promote the publications of the Buros Institute.

Linda L. Murphy
James C. Impara
December 1996

INTRODUCTION

BUROS DESK REFERENCE ASSESSMENT OF SUBSTANCE ABUSE

This is the second volume in a new series of books introduced by the Buros Institute of Mental Measurements in 1994 with the publication of the *Buros Desk Reference: Psychological Assessment in the Schools* (Impara & Murphy, 1994). We hope you will find this volume and this series useful. This book is designed to bring together reviews of many of the tests used by clinicians and others involved in the assessment and treatment of substance abuse. This is meant to be a comprehensive collection of all reviews of commercially available tests relating to the assessment of substance abuse.

The first *BDR* did not include information about every test a school psychologist or counselor might use. Because hundreds of tests exist in that area, it was based in part on a survey that identified the 100 tests used most frequently by school psychologists. Although many tests exist for the assessment of substance abuse, the number of commercially available tests in this area is limited and so we have attempted to make this *BDR* as comprehensive as possible.

SOURCES OF REVIEWS

The reviews in this book have been drawn from *Mental Measurements Yearbooks* as early as *The Seventh Mental Measurements Yearbook* (1972) and some are from yearbooks as recent as *The Twelfth MMY* (1995). Some of the reviews are so current that they are appearing in print for the first time in this book. They will also be in a future Yearbook; either *The Supplement to the Twelfth Mental Mea-*surements Yearbook* (in press), or in *The Thirteenth MMY* is scheduled for publication in early 1998. All of the *Mental Measurements Yearbooks* are included in the references list at the end of this introduction so the reader may determine the year of publication of the reviews. Reviews from older *Yearbooks* have been included as they originally appeared with no editing to conform to the current *APA Style Manual*. Grammar and syntax may occasionally seem archaic and the references appear in the style of the times.

Unlike the *Mental Measurements Yearbooks*, this book contains reviews of tests that have been published across several years. The *Yearbooks* are hierarchical and include only tests published or revised since the previous yearbook, or the occasional re-review of an older test that meets certain criteria. Like the *Yearbooks*, this book includes reviews only of commercially available (i.e., published) tests in the English language. So informal tests, tests developed for research purposes, or other tests that are not commercially available are not reviewed in this book or in any of the *Yearbooks*.

PURPOSE OF THIS BOOK

This book brings together reviews from many *Yearbooks* within a single source document. Reviews are written by individuals who have expertise in the content area of the test and who have some training in psychometrics. The reviews are intended to be helpful in identifying the strengths and weaknesses of the tests. This information is intended to help you, the test user, better understand the limitations of the test and to inform you what cautions you might need to take when using a particular test. We also hope the test author and publisher benefit by taking the reviews into consideration when revising the test or the manual.

We hope this book will provide you with information helpful in making informed decisions about the quality and utility of measures you are using, or might consider using. The decision to publish this *BDR* was based in part on a series of workshops presented by our former colleague, Jane Close Conoley, to clinicians involved in the identification and treatment of substance abuse. They were eager to learn how to use instruments available to them and also to learn about additional instruments that might serve their purposes more effectively.

A special "user's guide" chapter by Peter E. Nathan is included in this *BDR*. This chapter is intended as a practical and prescriptive aid to provide individuals who are involved in assessing clients who are substance abusers with specific guidelines about why this book will be valuable to them and how they can best use it in dealing with their clients. It is our hope that Nathan's chapter will serve to increase the usefulness of this *BDR* as a personal reference book and as a resource for future workshops.

INCLUSION CRITERIA

We have attempted to include reviews of all commercially available tests intended for the purpose of identifying or treating substance abuse as well as those tests intended for other purposes but including a score relating to the assessment of substance abuse. A few tests thus identified have not been reviewed for previous or upcoming *Mental Measurements Yearbooks*. In those cases we have included a description of the test with a notation that a review is not available. Only commercially available tests are reviewed in *The Mental Measurements Yearbooks* and it has come to our attention that several tests currently in use for the assessment of substance abuse are not commerically available. Some of the most important instruments in this category have been mentioned and referenced by Peter Nathan in his chapter.

We have made a concerted effort to be comprehensive in this volume and have identified new and revised tests using several sources while preparing this *BDR*. Jane Conoley was very helpful in making us aware of important tests we might have missed. Philip Ash not only served as a reviewer for several instruments but was also helpful in making us aware

of some tests. The National Institute on Alcohol Abuse and Alcoholism publication, *Assessing Alcohol Problems: A Guide for Clinicians and Researchers* (Allen, 1995) was a valuable resource in helping us identify commercially available tests. We recommend it to users of this *BDR* because it also includes information (and selected reproductions) of several tests that are well known in this area but are not commercially available.

ORGANIZATION OF THIS BOOK

The reviews are organized into two sections. The first section includes tests with a primary focus on assessing substance abuse. The second section includes additional tests having a secondary focus on assessing substance abuse. Within each category the tests are listed alphabetically.

INCLUDED REVIEWS

Some of the tests reviewed in this book have been available for many years and have undergone several revisions or have several editions. In such cases, both the current versions of the test and the earlier versions or editions may have been reviewed. We have included only the most recent reviews in these cases. Earlier reviews are noted in the Cross References field of the test description.

A few of the recently revised tests have only one review completed at this time, although eventually a second review might be completed and included in *The Thirteenth MMY*. A special third review, not included in any *MMY*, was completed for this *BDR* for the Minnesota Multiphasic Personality Inventory-2 to concentrate specifically on the use of the MMPI-2 for the assessment of substance abuse.

The reviews are in the same format as those in the *MMY*. The test entries (i.e., the descriptive information that precedes the test review) includes such information as the population for which the measure is designed, scores produced, price, publisher, and the *MMY*s where the included review plus any previous reviews were published.

One component of the original *MMY* listing not included in this book is the references. Included in each *MMY* is a list of references or citations associated with many of the tests reviewed. These references are instances when the test has been used in a research study of some sort. These references may be obtained by going back to the original review in the *MMY* as indicated in the

Cross References field in the entry information. Reviewers frequently include citations in their reviews and these reviewer references have been reproduced in this volume.

HOW TO USE THE BUROS DESK REFERENCE

As indicated above, the tests and reviews in this volume are presented in alphabetical order within each of the two categories. The sections are numbered as Section 1 and Section 2. Each test within a section is also numbered (e.g., Adolescent Drinking Index is 1.3 and is the third test listed in Section 1; Millon Adolescent Clinical Inventory is 2.22 and is the 22nd test listed in Section 2). The page heading of the left-hand page cites the number and title of the first test listed on that page, and the page heading of the right-hand page cites the number and title of the last test listed on that page. All numbers presented in the various indexes are test numbers, not page numbers. Page numbers are important only for the Table of Contents and are indicated at the bottom of each page.

The *Mental Measurements Yearbooks* include several indexes to assist the user in locating a test. The following four indexes have been created for the *Buros Desk Reference*: Index of Titles, Index of Acronyms, Publishers Directory and Index, and Score Index. Additional comment on these indexes is presented below.

Index of Titles. Because this volume is ordered by category, the Index of Titles is helpful in locating a test by title name. It is important to keep in mind that the numbers in this index, and all the indexes, are test numbers and not page numbers.

Index of Acronyms. Some tests seem to be better known by their acronyms than by their full titles. The Index of Acronyms can help in these instances; it refers the reader to the full title of the test and to the relevant descriptive information and reviews.

Publishers Directory and Index. The Publishers Directory and Index includes the names and addresses of the publishers of all in-print tests included in the *Buros Desk Reference* plus a listing of test numbers for each individual publisher. This index can be particularly useful in obtaining addresses for specimen sets or catalogs after the test reviews

have been read and evaluated. It can also be useful when a reader knows the publisher of a certain test but is uncertain about the test title, or when a reader is interested in the range of tests published by a given publisher (limited in this volume, but appropriate for use with *TIP* and the *MMY*).

Score Index. The Score Index is an index to all scores generated by the tests in the *BDR*. Test titles are sometimes misleading or ambiguous, and test content may be difficult to define with precision. But test scores represent operational definitions of the variables the test author is trying to measure, and as such they often define test purpose and content more adequately than other descriptive information. A search for a particular test is most often a search for a test that measures some specific variables. Test scores and their associated labels can often be the best definitions of the variables of interest. It is, in fact, a detailed subject index based on the most critical operational features of any test—the scores and their associated labels.

Making Effective Use of the Test Entries. The test entries include extensive information. For each test, descriptive information is presented in the following order:

a) TITLES. Test titles are printed in boldface type. Secondary or series titles are set off from main titles by a colon.

b) PURPOSE. For each test we have included a brief, clear statement describing the purpose of the test. Often these statements are quotations from the test manual.

c) POPULATION. This is a description of the groups for which the test is intended. The grade, chronological age, semester range, employment category, or other population descriptor is usually given.

d) PUBLICATION DATE. The inclusive range of publication dates for the various forms, accessories, and editions of a test is reported.

e) ACRONYM. When a test is often referred to by an acronym, the acronym is given in the test entry immediately following the publication date.

f) SCORES. The number of part scores is presented along with their titles or descriptions of what they are intended to represent or measure.

g) ADMINISTRATION. Individual or group administration is indicated. A test is considered a group test unless it may be administered *only* individually.

h) FORMS, PARTS, AND LEVELS. All available forms, parts, and levels are listed.

i) MANUAL. Notation is made if no manual is available. All other manual information is included under Price Data.

j) RESTRICTED DISTRIBUTION. This is noted only for tests that are put on a special market by the publisher. Educational and psychological restrictions are not noted (unless a special training course is required for use).

k) PRICE DATA. Price information is reported for test packages (usually 20 to 35 tests), answer sheets, all other accessories, and specimen sets. The statement "$17.50 per 35 tests" means that all accessories are included unless otherwise indicated by the reporting of separate prices for accessories. The statement also means 35 tests of one level, one edition, or one part unless stated otherwise. Because test prices can change very quickly, the year that the listed test prices were obtained is also given. Foreign currency is assigned the appropriate symbol. When prices are given in foreign dollars, a qualifying symbol is added (e.g., A$16.50 refers to 16 dollars and 50 cents in Australian currency). Along with cost, the publication date and number of pages on which print occurs are reported for manuals and technical reports (e.g., '85, 102 pages). All types of machine-scorable answer sheets available for use with a specific test are also reported in the descriptive entry. Scoring and reporting services provided by publishers are reported along with information on costs. In a few cases, special computerized scoring and interpretation services are given in separate entries immediately following the test.

l) FOREIGN LANGUAGE AND OTHER SPECIAL EDITIONS. This section concerns foreign language editions published by the same publisher who sells the English edition. It also indicates special editions (e.g., Braille, large type) available from the same or a different publisher.

m) TIME. The number of minutes of actual working time allowed examinees and the approximate length of time needed for administering a test are reported whenever obtainable. The latter figure is always enclosed in parentheses. Thus "50(60) minutes" indicates that the examinees are allowed 50 minutes of working time and that a total of 60

minutes is needed to administer the test. A time of "40–50 minutes" indicates an untimed test that takes approximately 45 minutes to administer, or—in a few instances—a test so timed that working time and administration time are very difficult to disentangle. When the time necessary to administer a test is not reported or suggested in the test materials but has been obtained through correspondence with the test publisher or author, the time is enclosed in brackets.

n) COMMENTS. Some entries contain special notations, such as: "for research use only"; "revision of the ABC Test"; "tests administered monthly at centers throughout the United States"; "subtests available as separates"; and "verbal creativity." A statement such as "verbal creativity" is intended to further describe what the test claims to measure. Some of the test entries include factual statements that imply criticism of the test, such as "1990 test identical with test copyrighted 1980."

o) AUTHOR. For most tests, all authors are reported. In the case of tests that appear in a new form each year, only authors of the most recent forms are listed. Names are reported exactly as printed on test booklets. Names of editors generally are not reported.

p) PUBLISHER. The name of the publisher or distributor is reported for each test. Foreign publishers are identified by listing the country in brackets immediately following the name of the publisher. The Publishers Directory and Index must be consulted for a publisher's address.

q) FOREIGN ADAPTATIONS. Revisions and adaptations of tests for foreign use are listed in a separate paragraph following the original edition.

r) SUBLISTINGS. Levels, editions, subtests, or parts of a test available in separate booklets are sometimes presented as sublistings with titles set in small capitals. Sub-sublistings are indented and titles are set in italic type.

s) CROSS REFERENCES. For tests that have been listed previously in a Buros Institute publication, a test entry includes—if relevant—a final paragraph containing a cross reference to the reviews, excerpts, and references for that test in those volumes. In the cross references, "T4:467" refers to test 467 in *Tests in Print IV*, "9:1023" refers to test 1023 in *The Ninth Mental Measure-*

ments Yearbook, "7:637" refers to test 637 in *The Seventh Mental Measurements Yearbook*.

SUMMARY

This volume in the *BDR* series includes reviews of 78 tests used for assessing substance abuse in clinical settings. Most of these tests have been reviewed in previous volumes of the *Mental Measurements Yearbooks* and are brought together in a single book for the first time. The content of the reviews is the same as that found in the *MMY* in which the review originally appeared. This volume is organized such that test reviews are listed alphabetically within the two categories of tests. There are several indexes available to help users find specific tests or tests that provide specific scores. Each entry contains information about the test including such things as the Title, Acronym, Scores, Price, and Publisher.

REFERENCES

Allen, J. P. (Ed.). (1995). *Assessing alcohol problems: A guide for clinicians and researchers*. Bethesda, MD: National Institute on Alcohol Abuse and Alcoholism.

Buros, O. K. (Ed.). (1938). *The nineteen thirty eight mental measurements yearbook*. New Brunswick, NJ: Rutgers University Press.

Buros, O. K. (Ed.). (1941). *The nineteen forty mental measurements yearbook*. Highland Park, NJ: Gryphon Press.

Buros, O. K. (Ed.). (1949). *The third mental measurements yearbook*. Highland Park, NJ: Gryphon Press.

Buros, O. K. (Ed.). (1953). *The fourth mental measurements yearbook*. Highland Park, NJ: Gryphon Press.

Buros, O. K. (Ed.). (1959). *The fifth mental measurements yearbook*. Highland Park, NJ: Gryphon Press.

Buros, O. K. (Ed.). (1965). *The sixth mental measurements yearbook*. Highland Park, NJ: Gryphon Press.

Buros, O. K. (Ed.). (1972). *The seventh mental measurements yearbook*. Highland Park, NJ: Gryphon Press.

Buros, O. K. (Ed.). (1978). *The eighth mental measurements yearbook*. Highland Park, NJ: Gryphon Press.

Conoley, J. C., & Impara, J. C. (Eds.). (1994). *The supplement to the eleventh mental measurements yearbook*. Lincoln, NE: Buros Institute of Mental Measurements.

Conoley, J. C., & Impara, J. C. (Eds.). (1995). *The twelfth mental measurements yearbook*. Lincoln, NE: Buros Institute of Mental Measurements.

Conoley, J. C., & Kramer, J. J. (Eds.). (1989). *The tenth mental measurements yearbook*. Lincoln, NE: Buros Institute of Mental Measurements.

Impara, J. C., & Conoley, J. C. (Eds.). (in press). *The supplement to the twelfth mental measurements yearbook*. Lincoln, NE: Buros Institute of Mental Measurements.

Impara, J. C., & Murphy, L. L. (Eds.). (1994). *Buros desk reference: Psychological assessment in the schools*. Lincoln, NE: Buros Institute of Mental Measurements.

Kramer, J. J., & Conoley, J. C. (Eds.). (1992). *The eleventh mental measurements yearbook*. Lincoln, NE: Buros Institute of Mental Measurements.

Mitchell, J. V., Jr. (Ed.). (1985). *The ninth mental measurements yearbook*. Lincoln, NE: Buros Institute of Mental Measurements.

Murphy, L. L., Conoley, J. C., & Impara, J. C. (Eds.). (1994). *Tests in Print IV*. Lincoln, NE: Buros Institute of Mental Measurements.

ASSESSING SUBSTANCE ABUSERS

by
Peter E. Nathan
The University of Iowa

Even if you haven't worked with substance abusers and know little about them, if you are a helping professional, you will almost certainly be called upon at one time or another to assess persons suspected of substance abuse. Not only is substance abuse extremely common (its lifetime prevalence among American citizens approaches 20%; Robins et al., 1984), it affects virtually every facet of the life of the abuser. So it is the rare psychologist or counselor who will not have to identify, assess, diagnose, and/or treat a substance abuser—or many more than one—during his or her career.

This chapter is designed to aid the helping professional who is not an expert on the assessment and diagnosis of substance abuse to get the most from this volume. Although persons experienced in working with substance abusers will also find useful assessment instruments here with which they are not familiar, much of what is in this volume will be well known to those who spend most of their days working with persons with alcohol and drug abuse and dependence. Nonetheless, because of the ubiquity of these problems, and the fact that no one has all the answers to the problems posed by substance abuse, most helping professionals who find themselves called upon to assess persons with alcohol or drug problems, either regularly or only occasionally, will doubtless welcome some help in doing so. That's the purpose of this chapter.

The chapter begins with a brief recounting of the settings in which the psychological assessment instruments reviewed here might be used. The instruments are quite diverse, largely because substance abusers seek help in virtually the entire spectrum of helping settings, from junior high school and high school guidance offices to college counseling centers, from mental health centers and community agencies to the private offices of psychologists and psychiatrists, from the emergency rooms of general hospitals to most of the wards of those hospitals. As well, of course, many of this volume's instruments play important roles in epidemiological surveys or clinical research.

The chapter turns first to brief screening and assessment instruments designed to identify persons who may have substance-related problems. Once a screening instrument alerts the clinician or counselor to the possibility of substance abuse, a more definitive diagnostic study is in order. Accordingly, the chapter next considers the structured and semi-structured diagnostic interviews and self-report questionnaires that are intended to diagnose substance abuse and, in so doing, illuminate the array of psychological, psychiatric, interpersonal, and physical problems commonly associated with it. The chapter concludes with a discussion of the diverse assessment instruments and procedures to plan effective treatment for substance abuse as well as to assess the outcomes of its treatment.

The assessment instruments that are both reviewed in this volume and discussed in this chapter are highlighted in **bold** type and their authors, publisher, and date of publication are indicated. Additional valuable assessment methods, some available only from their developers, others only from one or another of the federal agencies, are also mentioned in order to provide the fullest possible coverage of potentially useful instruments, interviews, and techniques for the assessment of the substance abuser.

Many of the instruments included in this volume focus specifically on persons with alcohol abuse or dependence. The preponderance of assessment instruments for alcoholics reflects both the substantial length of time psychologists—and society—have been concerned about alcohol problems, as well as the fact that many more Americans abuse alcohol than drugs (NIAAA, 1993). Readers will also observe that about half the instruments reviewed in the volume directly assess substance-related behaviors, whereas the other half more broadly assess and diagnose a range of personality factors and psychological conditions and disorders and thereby indirectly reflect on substance-related matters. Both kinds of instruments are useful to those who need to screen, diagnose, and plan treatment for substance abusers.

IN WHAT SETTINGS AND UNDER WHAT CIRCUMSTANCES ARE THESE INSTRUMENTS USED?

Helping and health professionals, whether they work in public mental health treatment centers, college counseling centers, general hospitals, or private practice settings, will be called upon both to identify persons with substance abuse problems and, when appropriate, to assess the severity of the problem. Does it require treatment? If so, is detoxification—withdrawal from the substance—in an inpatient setting indicated before "talking" therapy can begin? Does the patient suffer as well from other psychological or psychiatric conditions—depression, anxiety, or one or more of the personality disorders typically accompany substance abuse—that require concurrent treatment? These questions must be answered before treatment for substance abuse begins or referral is made. The instruments in this volume are designed to provide the answers.

High school and junior high school guidance counselors, for whom alcohol and drug abuse are pressing problems, need to be able to identify those of their students who are at risk to abuse substances or have begun to do so. Some of the instruments included in this volume could be of help in this regard.

Physicians and other health care personnel who work in settings to which persons with substance abuse problems in need of immediate treatment commonly come—hospital emergency rooms, for example, or the admissions units of psychiatric facilities—will also find measures in this volume designed to permit the rapid identification of these persons and their problems. Important as well is having the capacity to identify these persons when they come to a physician's office for the first time, especially if they seek treatment for a physical condition that might be caused or exacerbated by alcohol or drug abuse. A number of studies suggest the difficulty of identifying substance abusers solely from behavioral observation or medical history. A number of the assessment instruments in this volume represent useful means of supplementing these traditional methods of inquiry.

Mental health research workers will also find some of the instruments in this volume invaluable. Research workers undertaking substance abuse prevalence surveys of a community, a college campus, or an age or occupational cohort will find most useful the measures that permit rapid, accurate screening for substance abuse and/or one or more of the structured or semi-structured diagnostic instruments, whereas those planning to evaluate substance abuse treatment outcomes who need to ensure that they have assembled diagnostically homogeneous groups of subjects will want to use one or another of the instruments in the volume capable of ruling in substance abusers and, if desired, ruling out persons with other *DSM-IV* diagnoses.

Once appropriate groups for treatment outcome research have been assembled, a number of the instruments in the volume will track short-term treatment gains—changes in quantity and frequency of alcohol and drug consumption, for example, as well as changes in affective and interpersonal behavior. Other instruments reflect indices of longer-term outcomes, including marital and vocational status and length and quality of sobriety.

Although the instruments discussed in this chapter and this volume will not meet every substance abuse assessment need, there is clearly an instrument here—or several—for most applications.

IDENTIFYING THE SUBSTANCE ABUSER

Identifying potential or actual substance abuse requires that persons at normal or heightened risk for substance abuse be screened by assessment instruments sensitive to behavioral indicators of abuse. The aim of a substance abuse screening is to identify as many potential or actual abusers as early in their use or abuse history as possible. Because missing a potential or actual abuser can have substantially more negative consequences than pinpointing a person who turns out later not to be either an actual abuser or at risk to become one, most screens for substance abuse are designed to reduce false negatives to the extent possible, while allowing for some number of false positives, to be ascertained more carefully with more detailed diagnostic instruments.

Substance abusers can be identified from behavioral observation, collateral informants, laboratory tests, and self-report measures.

Behavioral Observation

It is very difficult to identify alcoholics or drug addicts, sober or intoxicated, just by watching and talking to them.

When they are sober, substance abusers tend not to behave very differently from nonabusers, especially if they are young and at the beginning of their abuse. Although substance abusers are substantially more likely than nonabusers to experience depression, anxiety, and other common psychological symptoms, even early in their abuse, nonabusers experience the same symptoms often enough that they are of limited value for diagnostic purposes (Skinner, Holt, Allen, & Haakonson, 1980).

Even when substance abusers are intoxicated, identifying them as abusers is not easy, primarily because the behavioral tolerance their abuse produces tends to attenuate their intoxication and make it indistinguishable from that of nonabusers. Moreover, because intoxication is a high-frequency phenomenon, just because someone has had too much to drink or has ingested another intoxicating substance is no guarantee he

or she is an alcoholic or a drug addict. Adding to the difficulty of using intoxicated behavior to diagnose substance abusers is the fact that, despite widespread belief to the contrary, it is extremely difficult to detect intoxication in a person one does not know well (Langenbucher & Nathan, 1983).

Collateral Informants

Friends, family, and co-workers are a reasonable source of information on a person's drinking and substance use or history of involvement in treatment or with the criminal justice system, although in many school, college, and work settings, asking friends or co-workers about these matters is inappropriate. However, if drug or alcohol use is suspected and family members or friends have expressed concerns about it, their suspicions probably justify more detailed inquiry, because they often represent an accurate initial screen for substance dependence or abuse.

Laboratory Tests

Emergency health facilities rely on laboratory tests of urine, blood, or breath samples as screens for recent evidence of alcohol or drug use. By reflecting the metabolic products of alcohol or drug use, these tests indicate whether an individual has used alcohol or another drug in the recent past (Hawks & Chiang, 1986). Because most substances disappear from the body relatively quickly, however, it is rarely possible to detect drugs ingested more than a day or two previously from laboratory tests (Chiang & Hawks, 1986). Moreover, assessing the level of alcohol in the blood to determine whether and how much a person has been drinking is only possible before all the alcohol that has been consumed has been metabolized. Because most of us metabolize about one drink an hour, the blood of a person who has consumed half a bottle of wine or two six packs of beer will no longer test positive for alcohol 12 hours or so after he or she stops drinking (Nathan, 1993).

Certain biochemical tests can reflect the physical consequences of prolonged drinking (Schottenfeld, 1995). The most useful of them signal alcohol-induced liver damage by showing increases beyond normal levels in one or more liver enzymes (e.g., SGOT, GGT, LDH, AST, and GHD). However, because the levels of these enzymes also increase when blood mean corpuscular volume (MCV) or high density lipoproteins (HDL) increase (the latter increases are not caused by abusive drinking), elevations in these liver enzymes do not always indicate prolonged alcohol consumption.

Self-Report Measures

Unless they are markedly impaired cognitively, most substance abusers know about how much alcohol or drugs they are using. As a result, it makes sense to ask possible substance abusers to complete one or more of the brief self-report measures that screen for drinking and drug problems. Of course, persons concerned about legal or other consequences of their drinking or drug use might well decline to complete a self-report measure of consumption or might choose to give invalid responses to them. There is not a great deal that can be done to reduce either behavior, especially because it isn't easy to disguise the intent of a substance abuse screening instrument.

Self-report screening measures typically ask about quantity and frequency of drug and alcohol consumption, as well as attitudes toward and the impact of alcohol and drug use, especially any negative consequences of use (e.g., legal difficulties, job or school problems, interpersonal problems, and the like).

The two most widely used self-report screening instruments are the 4-item CAGE (Mayfield, McLeod, & Hall, 1974) and the 25-item **Michigan Alcoholism Screening Test (MAST;** Selzer, 1971). The **MAST** also comes in shorter 13-item (Selzer, Vinokur, & van Rooijen, 1975) and 10-item (Pokorny, Miller, & Kaplan, 1972) formats. Both the CAGE and the MAST solicit yes-no responses to questions about common consequences of alcohol misuse; cutoff scores (e.g., scores above a certain level) signal the probability of an alcohol-related disorder. These instruments are widely used because they combine brevity with sensitivity, although they are of limited usefulness with persons who do not want their abusive drinking known.

The **Alcohol Use Inventory (AUI:** Horn, Wanberg, & Foster, National Computer Systems, Inc., 1987) is another widely used screening instrument for adults suspected of problem drinking. A self-report instrument designed to assess 24 different behaviors, feelings, and attitudes associated with the use and abuse of alcohol, the **AUI** calls on an extensive empirical research base on the behavior of persons with alcohol problems. Although the **AUI**

does not yield a tentative diagnosis as do some screening instruments, it does give the clinician extensive information on the behaviors, feelings, and attitudes most affected by the individual's drinking, as well as an indication of the extent to which the individual's drinking has become problematic. Because the instrument focuses on problematic drinking, it is not suitable for persons who are unable or unwilling to acknowledge existing drinking problems.

This volume also reviews three substance abuse assessment instruments designed primarily to screen for adolescent substance abuse. The **Adolescent Drinking Index (ADI:** Harrell & Wirtz, Psychological Assessment Resources, Inc., 1985-1989) asks 24 questions tapping four common consequences of abusive drinking in the effort to reflect the severity of the drinking problems of young persons aged 12-17. The **Personal Experience Screening Questionnaire (PESQ:** Winters, Western Psychological Services, 1991) is a 40-item questionnaire designed to screen youth 12 to 18 years of age; it provides information on the severity of alcohol and drug problems, as well as on defensiveness and infrequency (both of which reflect the validity of the respondent's self-report). The **PESQ** also inquires about the respondent's alcohol and drug use history, as well as when he or she first began abusing drugs. The **Substance Abuse Screening Test (SAST:** Hibpshman & Larson, Slosson Educational Publications, Inc., 1993) focuses on adolescents and young adults, both those at risk for substance abuse and those who are not. The **SAST** is a 30-item questionnaire; some items ask directly about alcohol or drug use and others reflect loneliness, family conflict, and mood states, all of which are associated with increased risk of substance abuse.

All three of these instruments are designed to screen groups of adolescents for substance abuse. The young people could be enrolled in junior high school or high school health or biology classes, involved in clubs or other social groups concerned about health-related issues, new patients of family practice physicians or family doctors, or referrals to school guidance counselors or community counseling or mental health centers because of a suspicion of or heightened risk for emotional or substance abuse problems. Of course, because all the three measures call for self-reports, they can be answered torted to "fake good" and deny substance abuse, they are clearly less effective as screening devices than self-report instruments completed by respondents who have no need to deny problems that may exist.

Two other screening instruments reviewed in this book, although not specifically designed to screen for substance abuse, have reasonable psychometric properties and contain scales or provide scores that alert examiners to possible substance abuse problems. The two are the **College Adjustment Scales (CAS:** Anton & Reed, Psychological Assessment Resources, Inc., 1991) and the **Personality Assessment Inventory (PAI:** Morey, Psychological Assessment Resources, Inc., 1991). Both are so new that little has been reported to date about their sensitivity to substance abuse problems.

DIAGNOSING THE SUBSTANCE ABUSER

Once a screening device, an interview, or a family member or friend has identified a person—or the person has identified him- or herself—as a possible substance abuser, the clinician, counselor, or family physician will want to turn to a diagnostic interview to determine whether and to what extent the individual's substance use satisfies established criteria for abuse or dependence. In so doing, the examiner will also want to explore for the presence of other psychopathological conditions. Substance abuse is often accompanied by comorbid psychiatric conditions, which can play a role in its etiology and tend to make its treatment substantially more difficult (Nathan, 1993).

The diagnostic interviews discussed here are all based on the *Diagnostic and Statistical Manual of Mental Disorders,* either *DSM-III* (APA, 1980) or *DSM-III-R* (APA, 1987). Diagnostic interviews based on the newest *Diagnostic and Statistical Manual of Mental Disorders, DSM-IV* (APA, 1994) are currently being developed.

Over the years, some alcoholism workers have tended to question the relevance of diagnosis for alcoholics, in the belief that comorbid psychopathology simply disappears when the alcoholism had been treated successfully. Now that it has become clear that alcohol dependence and the depression, anxiety, personality disorder, bipolar disorder, or schizophrenia that so often accompany it must both be treated, often by different means,

diagnosis of substance abuse and concurrent psychopathology is recognized as of crucial importance before effective treatment can begin.

Structured Interviews

Structured diagnostic interviews provide a prearranged sequence of questions that permit paraprofessional interviewers to diagnose quite reliably. Because these interview protocols, which adhere closely to *DSM* operational criteria, require minimal professional judgment, they are a cost-efficient way to gather large amounts of epidemiological data. As individual diagnostic instruments, the structured interviews have a drawback, however. Although they yield reliable diagnoses, they do not provide as much information for treatment planning and exploration of causes as do the semi-structured interviews, which rely more heavily on the interviewer's expertise and professional background, training, and experience.

The *Diagnostic Interview Schedule* (*DIS:* Robins, Helzer, Croughan, & Ratcliff, 1981) is the most widely used structured diagnostic interview. Based on *DSM-III* and covering the full range of DSM disorders, it has been used extensively in major epidemiological studies, including the NIMH Epidemiologic Catchment Area (ECA) Study (Regier et al., 1984). As a consequence, extensive data attest to the instrument's excellent reliability and validity. The ongoing effort to revise the *DIS* to make it fully reflect *DSM-IV* diagnostic criteria will enable the *DIS* to continue to be the structured diagnostic interview of choice for epidemiological research.

The **Composite International Diagnostic Interview (CIDI:** World Health Organization, American Psychiatric Press, Inc., 1993), like the *DIS,* is a comprehensive, structured diagnostic interview for adults. It was created by the World Health Organization explicitly to diagnose conditions included in both *ICD-10* (WHO, 1992) and *DSM-III-R* (APA, 1987), according to diagnostic criteria structured to allow clinicians from many different cultures to use the instrument. Although the **CIDI** was designed for cross-cultural epidemiological research, it has also been used in clinical settings. As a result, a very substantial clinical literature supports its reliability and validity, increasing its value to potential users. One drawback, however, is the extensive training in its administration that its creators strongly urge.

torted to "fake good" and deny substance abuse, they are clearly less effective as screening devices than self-report instruments completed by respondents who have no need to deny problems that may exist.

Two other screening instruments reviewed in this book, although not specifically designed to screen for substance abuse, have reasonable psychometric properties and contain scales or provide scores that alert examiners to possible substance abuse problems. The two are the **College Adjustment Scales (CAS:** Anton & Reed, Psychological Assessment Resources, Inc., 1991) and the **Personality Assessment Inventory (PAI:** Morey, Psychological Assessment Resources, Inc., 1991). Both are so new that little has been reported to date about their sensitivity to substance abuse problems.

DIAGNOSING THE SUBSTANCE ABUSER

Once a screening device, an interview, or a family member or friend has identified a person—or the person has identified him- or herself—as a possible substance abuser, the clinician, counselor, or family physician will want to turn to a diagnostic interview to determine whether and to what extent the individual's substance use satisfies established criteria for abuse or dependence. In so doing, the examiner will also want to explore for the presence of other psychopathological conditions. Substance abuse is often accompanied by comorbid psychiatric conditions, which can play a role in its etiology and tend to make its treatment substantially more difficult (Nathan, 1993).

The diagnostic interviews discussed here are all based on the D*iagnostic and Statistical Manual of Mental Disorders,* either *DSM-III* (APA, 1980) or *DSM-III-R* (APA, 1987). Diagnostic interviews based on the newest *Diagnostic and Statistical Manual of Mental Disorders, DSM-IV* (APA, 1994) are currently being developed.

Over the years, some alcoholism workers have tended to question the relevance of diagnosis for alcoholics, in the belief that comorbid psychopathology simply disappears when the alcoholism had been treated successfully. Now that it has become clear that alcohol dependence and the depression, anxiety, personality disorder, bipolar disorder, or schizophrenia that so often accompany it must both be treated, often by different means,

diagnosis of substance abuse and concurrent psychopathology is recognized as of crucial importance before effective treatment can begin.

Structured Interviews

Structured diagnostic interviews provide a prearranged sequence of questions that permit paraprofessional interviewers to diagnose quite reliably. Because these interview protocols, which adhere closely to *DSM* operational criteria, require minimal professional judgment, they are a cost-efficient way to gather large amounts of epidemiological data. As individual diagnostic instruments, the structured interviews have a drawback, however. Although they yield reliable diagnoses, they do not provide as much information for treatment planning and exploration of causes as do the semistructured interviews, which rely more heavily on the interviewer's expertise and professional background, training, and experience.

The *Diagnostic Interview Schedule* (*DIS*: Robins, Helzer, Croughan, & Ratcliff, 1981) is the most widely used structured diagnostic interview. Based on *DSM-III* and covering the full range of DSM disorders, it has been used extensively in major epidemiological studies, including the NIMH Epidemiologic Catchment Area (ECA) Study (Regier et al., 1984). As a consequence, extensive data attest to the instrument's excellent reliability and validity. The ongoing effort to revise the *DIS* to make it fully reflect *DSM-IV* diagnostic criteria will enable the *DIS* to continue to be the structured diagnostic interview of choice for epidemiological research.

The **Composite International Diagnostic Interview (CIDI:** World Health Organization, American Psychiatric Press, Inc., 1993), like the *DIS,* is a comprehensive, structured diagnostic interview for adults. It was created by the World Health Organization explicitly to diagnose conditions included in both *ICD-10* (WHO, 1992) and *DSM-III-R* (APA, 1987), according to diagnostic criteria structured to allow clinicians from many different cultures to use the instrument. Although the **CIDI** was designed for cross-cultural epidemiological research, it has also been used in clinical settings. As a result, a very substantial clinical literature supports its reliability and validity, increasing its value to potential users. One drawback, however, is the extensive training in its administration that its creators strongly urge.

The **Psychiatric Diagnostic Interview—Revised (PDI-R**: Othmer, Penick, Powell, Read, & Othmer, Western Psychological Services, 1989) is a structured diagnostic interview designed to evaluate 17 basic psychiatric syndromes and four derived syndromes. The instrument was originally developed to operationalize the Feighner diagnostic criteria (Feighner et al., 1972), which anticipated many of the diagnostic advances of *DSM-III* (1980). Like the Feighner criteria, the diagnostic criteria in the **PDI-R** are arranged hierarchically, so that highest frequency diagnoses are explored first. The result is an efficient diagnostic instrument, as well as one with satisfactory reliability and validity. However, the instrument is designed to be administered by a trained interviewer, because it requires clinical experience and judgment to assess patients' self-reports of psychopathology. The instrument's other principal shortcoming is that it confers diagnoses based on the 1980 edition of the *DSM* rather the new, 1994 edition of the nomenclature.

The **Comprehensive Assessment of Symptoms and History (CASH**: Andreasen, author and publisher, 1987) is a structured diagnostic interview designed specifically for subjects in research studies of the major psychoses and affective disorders. Because the instrument is still under development, is best administered by a trained interviewer, and is restricted to diagnoses within the psychotic spectrum, it is of less value to readers of this volume than other more comprehensive diagnostic interviews.

The **Schedule for Affective Disorders and Schizophrenia, 3rd edition (SADS**: Spitzer et al., Department of Research Assessment and Training, New York State Psychiatric Institute, 1977-1988), like the **CASH**, is a research instrument designed to assemble diagnostically homogeneous patient groups for research on the major psychoses. The **SADS** was originally created to reflect diagnoses based on the Research Diagnostic Criteria (Spitzer, Endicott, & Williams, 1979), which were developed from the Feighner criteria (Feighner et al., 1972) and, hence, anticipated development of *DSM-III* (1980). That the instrument confers diagnoses based on the diagnostic cues included in the 1980 nomenclature dates the **SADS** and, for that reason, reduces its usefulness.

Two structured diagnostic interviews reviewed in this volume were designed specifically to diagnose alcohol abuse. The **Comprehensive Drinker Profile (CDP**: Marlatt & Miller, Psychological Assessment Resources, Inc., 1984-1987) is a structured interview lasting between 1 and 2 hours designed to provide detailed information on the interviewee's demographics, drinking history, and level of motivation to change his or her drinking behavior. The very extensive information the **CDP** elicits has value for both diagnostic and treatment-planning purposes. One of the instrument's most interesting aspects is the set of six cards given the interviewee that describe "drinker types," ranging from the nonalcoholic to the alcohol dependent person. The respondent is asked to choose the card that best describes father, mother, partner, and spouse. A similar forced-choice format elicits information on where and with whom drinking typically takes place, beverage(s) preferred and other drugs used, and effects of drinking and alcohol-related life problems. If the clinician wishes only to generate a diagnosis to confirm (or disconfirm) an initial impression of alcohol abuse, then the effort to complete this instrument is probably unwarranted; a briefer interview designed only to provide a *DSM* diagnosis of alcohol abuse or dependence makes more sense. If, however, substantially greater information on the range of behaviors that typically surround and interact with an alcohol abuse problem is desired, the **CDP**, used in conjunction with the *DIS* or the *SCID-P* (reviewed below), makes excellent clinical sense.

The **Adolescent Diagnostic Interview (ADI**: Winters & Henly, Western Psychological Services, 1993) is a structured interview to diagnose substance abuse problems in adolescents according to *DSM-III-R* (1987) diagnostic criteria. The **ADI** also explores the psychosocial stressors mediating the interviewee's substance abuse, his or her substance use history, level of functioning with friends and family and in school and at leisure, and his or her legal and psychiatric status. The instrument is currently being revised to conform to the 1994 *DSM-IV* diagnostic criteria for substance abuse.

Semi-Structured Interview

Semi-structured diagnostic interviews are designed to guide trained mental health professionals in conducting detailed diagnostic examinations of psychiatric patients. Because they typically provide greater depth of diagnostic detail than structured diagnostic interviews, they are useful for both diagnostic and treatment-planning purposes,. The best-known—and most current—of these instruments is the Structured Clinical Interview for *DSM-IV* (SCID: First, Spitzer, Gibbon, & Williams, 1995).

A recent validation study employing an earlier version of the SCID (which yielded *DSM-III-R* diagnoses) found that the instrument was more accurate in identifying substance abusers in a hospitalized population of acute psychiatric patients than either several biochemical tests or admission and discharge diagnoses given by experienced clinicians (Albanese, Bartel, Bruno, Morgenbesser, & Schatzberg, 1994).

PLANNING EFFECTIVE TREATMENT AND ACCURATELY ASSESSING TREATMENT OUTCOMES

A number of assessment instruments have been developed to aid clinicians in planning—and assessing the effectiveness of—treatment for substance abuse. These instruments typically seek information quite different from that sought by screening and diagnostic instruments, because the data required to determine whether a person meets diagnostic criteria for substance abuse are not sufficient to plan or evaluate treatment. To plan effective treatments and accurately assess their results, detailed knowledge of patients' alcohol and drug use patterns before, during, and after treatment, the life problems associated with patients' substance use and abuse, and the settings in which patients drink and are at risk for relapse is essential. The assessment instruments described here provide this kind of information.

Readers who wish to read current reviews of empirically valid treatments for substance abuse and dependence should refer to Finney and Moos (1997), Kleber & Galanter (1995), Miller et al. (1995), and Moos, Finney, and Cronkite (1990).

Substance Use Patterns

Knowing a substance abuser's pretreatment consumption or use pattern, typically described in terms of quantity and frequency of consumption (as, for example, an average of four to six beers or glasses of wine an evening an average of three times a week), is an aid to predicting the likelihood that treatment will be effective. In general, the heavier a person's abusive consumption or use pattern is, and the longer he or she has abused alcohol or drugs, the less likely he or she is to benefit from treatment. Similarly, knowing as much as possible about the success or failure of the patient's previous efforts to stop using alcohol or drugs, and whether such efforts were independent of or involved formal treatment or self-help groups helps the clinician gauge the patient's level of motivation to change abusive consumption patterns and decide which treatments might work best.

Once treatment has begun, knowing whether the patient is continuing to consume alcohol or use drugs is an obvious measure of the patients' motivation to reduce or stop his or her drug or alcohol abuse, and an excellent predictor of ultimate treatment outcome. As well, once intensive treatment has ended, having a pretreatment drug or alcohol consumption pattern against which to compare a nonabstinent treatment outcome allows the clinician to judge the extent to which treatment has had an impact on drug or alcohol usage and whether continued treatment is indicated and would have a reasonable chance of leading to further gains.

Two of the most widely used methods for assessing substance use patterns focus on alcohol consumption. One of the oldest and still one of the best is the Quantity-Frequency-Variability (QFV) Index of Cahalan, Cisin, and Crossley (1969). Developed for the first national study of drinking practices in the United States, the QFV Index asks for a summary self-report of drinking, most often during an average week. Although an efficient means of gathering consumption data in epidemiological surveys of the general population, the QFV is less useful with alcoholic patient populations, in which some patients will be unwilling or unable to provide accurate self-reports on their drinking.

The more recently developed Timeline Followback Procedure (TLFP: Sobell & Sobell, 1992) has been used by clinical researchers to assess quantity and frequency of alcohol consumption. It is a semi-structured interview designed to elicit patient self-reports of alcohol consumption over discrete time periods, which can range from 30 days to a year. (The shorter the span of recall, the more reliable the resultant consumption data.) The TLFP helps patients reconstruct consumption patterns by prompting them to remember drinking tied to special days, like birthdays, anniversaries, and holidays, occasions on which they are especially likely to remember what and how much they drank.

As important as data are on the quantity and frequency of drinking for treatment planning and outcome assessment, information on binge periods and periods of abstinence—when and under what circumstances they occurred and how long they lasted—is just as valuable. The TLFP is one of the few methods to measure alcohol consumption that captures both binge and abstinence periods.

Although self-report data on drinking patterns are clearly subject both to intentional modification and to forgetting, especially following periods of prolonged, abusive drinking, much of the extensive research on the reliability of self-report data suggests that when patients are sober and there are no negative consequences of accurate self-reports, they are likely to provide accurate information (Sobell & Sobell, 1992). Nonetheless, it is still worth trying to supplement self-reports of drinking by seeking corroboration from others, like friends, parents, a spouse or a partner, who know the patient well.

This volume contains information about a number of other instruments and procedures for gathering information on consumption patterns. The best known is the **Comprehensive Drinker Profile** (CDP: Marlatt & Miller, Psychological Assessment Resources, 1984-1987). As indicated above, the **CDP** is a structured interview for diagnosing alcohol abuse and dependence; its detailed coverage of drinking history provides the clinician a great deal of material on which to base a diagnosis. But the **CDP** can also help in planning and assessing treatment. The information on drinking history it provides can help clinician and patient together decide on foci for treatment (for example, the development of ways, using cognitive-behavioral techniques, to deal with high-stress situations, which have been associated in the past with abusive drinking). As well, the motivational information provided by the **CDP** helps the clinician decide when and whether the patient can sustain the emotional and interpersonal rigors of both treatment and an alcohol-free post-treatment return to family and friends—how motivated he or she is learn to handle stress, anxiety, depression, and the like—without self-medicating with alcohol to blur their impact. The information the **CDP** provides on motivation also helps the clinician assess the effectiveness of treatment: if motivation to reduce or stop drinking does not increase during treatment, treatment is unlikely to be effective.

The **Personal Experience Inventory** (PEI: Winters & Henly, Western Psychological Services, 1988-89) and the **Personal Experience Inventory for Adults** (PEI-A: Winters, Western Psychological Services, 1995-1996), both self-report inventories, and **A Structured Addictions Assessment Interview for Selecting Treatment** (ASIST: Addiction Research Foundation, author and publisher, 1984-1990), a structured interview, are all designed to yield detailed information on drinking histories and current drinking behavior as well as on life problems associated with abusive drinking.

The **PEI** is designed for adolescents aged 12-18; the **PEI-A** is an extension of the **PEI** for adults. Both are self-report measures of drug and alcohol use which elicit detailed information on the onset, duration, and frequency of use of alcohol and drugs from each of the major drug categories and provide usage norms for both clinical and nonclinical samples. These norms are likely to prove useful, especially for the guidance counselor or school social worker or psychologist who wants to know how a particular student's alcohol or drug use compares to the normative samples of adolescents (chosen from a drug clinic and a high school).

At the same time, it sometimes makes sense for the counselor to develop his or her own school's alcohol and drug use norms. If school norms are developed and their relation to outcomes tracked, they might be of considerable help to the counselor called upon to make referral decisions. These will range from no referral, because the problem is minor and seems unlikely to progress, to an outpatient treatment program for a definite problem that has nonetheless not caused significant academic, interpersonal, or family problems, to an intensive outpatient program or an inpatient program for a problem that has progressed substantially and does not appear likely to lessen without strong intervention.

Life Problems Associated with Substance Use and Abuse

The easiest way to assess life problems associated with substance use and abuse is to use a simple problem checklist like the Drinking Problem Scales developed by Cahalan more than 25 years ago (DPS: Cahalan, 1970) for his groundbreaking study of American drinking practices. The various forms of the **MAST** (discussed previously on p. xx) are also commonly used for this purpose, because the instrument judges the presence and severity of alcohol problems from the number of positive items describing common adverse consequences of alcohol abuse. Knowing the kind and degree of substance-related problems afflicting a substance abuser enables the clinician to gauge level of motivation for change (if the problems are minimal, chances are the patient will not be terribly highly motivated to lessen or stop the abuse), as well as to plan treatment (if the problems are primarily physical, treatments designed to relieve serious psychological and psychiatric consequences of abuse are less likely to be seen as useful).

One of the most widely used instruments specifically designed to assess the severity of life problems associated with alcohol dependence is the **Alcohol Dependence Scale (ADS:** Skinner & Horn, Addiction Research Foundation, 1984), a 25-item self-report derived from the **Alcohol Use Inventory,** previously discussed on pp. xx. The strengths of the **ADS** are its brevity, empirical base, and theoretical grounding in the alcohol dependence syndrome, which was the basis for the *DSM-III-R* concept of alcohol dependence. Accordingly, the instrument assesses such consequences of alcohol dependence as compulsive drink seeking, loss of behavioral control over alcohol use, and physical and perceptual sequelae of alcohol withdrawal. Four groups of alcoholics seeking treatment at the Addiction Research Foundation in Toronto constituted the measure's normative sample. The substantial empirical foundation of the **ADS** and an excellent normative process are real strengths. However, because the instrument taps only a portion of the life problems associated with alcohol dependence, it would probably be wise to use it in conjunction with instruments designed to reflect other of those problems, such as the **MAST** and the Addiction Severity Index.

The Addiction Severity Index (ASI: MacLellan et al., 1992) is a structured interview designed to gather a comprehensive array of information on a client's alcohol and drug use and consequent life problems. It includes a section specifically designed to assess the severity of problems related to abuse that merit focused intervention. Because the ASI can be given several times over the course of treatment, it is especially well-suited both to assess treatment gains as it proceeds and as an outcome measure.

Both the **PEI** and **PEI-A,** previously considered on pp. xxv, assess "the rewards, consequences, and social effects of alcohol and drug use." The principal advantage of the **PEI** is that it was constructed specifically to tap the kinds of life problems adolescent alcohol and drug abusers tend to experience when they have begun to misuse substances. Accordingly, the Psychosocial section of the instrument assesses eight personal and four environmental "risk factors" which include Negative Self-Image, Social Isolation, Peer Chemical Environment, Family Pathology, and Sexual Abuse, along with other serious life problems. Presumably, adolescents whose life histories or current circumstances include one or more of these risk factors are at higher risk both to experiment with alcohol and drugs and to progress from experimentation to abuse once use has been established. The Chemical Involvement section of the instrument includes five "basic" and five "clinical" scales designed to evaluate the severity of substance abuse by assessing its consequences. Knowledge of the severity of the abuse problem, in conjunction with the information gained from the instrument about quantity and frequency of use, should help the clinician make an appropriate referral for treatment. A range of validity indicators are also built into the **PEI,** making it possible for the examiner to detect "faking good" or "faking bad" by the respondent.

Although the **PEI-A** shares some of the strengths of the **PEI**'s model for delineating crucial life problems associated with alcohol and drug abuse, it competes with quite a number of other instruments designed to assess the extent, severity, and consequences of drug abuse in adults. In this competition, it has one major drawback, the fact that it was developed and normed on white males attending a drug clinic. Accordingly, the instrument will have substantially less utility with women and minorities, both of whom are substantially represented among populations of alcohol and drug abusers.

A Structured Addictions Assessment Interview for Selecting Treatment (ASIST: Addiction Research Foundation, author and publisher, 1984-1990), as its name suggests, is a structured interview to help clinicians plan treatment as a function of the severity of the patient's alcohol and drug abuse problems. Its inquiry into life problems associated with substance abuse extends to physical and emotional health as well as other life areas, including living situation, family issues, social issues, education/training, work, financial issues, leisure-time activities, and legal concerns: there are few problems precipitated by substance abuse not covered in this interview. A unusual feature is a set of open-ended questions likely to elicit useful responses (e.g., "What concerns do you have?", "Do you feel that you need help?", "What behavioral disturbances do you experience?", and "How important now is help to you?"). This information, in turn, flows into a detailed model of a treatment plan, to guide the clinician in specifying appropriate therapeutic goals, recommended interventions, and client, therapist, and, if appropriate, case manager responsibilities. Although of less value for experienced clinicians, this template for developing and implementing a treatment plan will certainly be most helpful to newly trained clinicians. Even though one of the instrument's reviewers in this volume is concerned about the regional and national specificity of some of the instrument's references (it was produced in Canada), I would guess that most clinicians will find it relatively easy to translate these concepts to the U.S. More significant is another concern expressed by the same reviewer: After 12 years, no empirical data on the practical utility of the instrument appear to have been reported. The absence of such reports is troubling. At best, it suggests the interview has not generated much research; at worst, it could mean it has not proven useful enough to be used in research.

Antecedents and Consequences of Substance Use and Abuse

Prior to treatment, clinician and patient together should undertake a careful behavioral analysis of the biological, social, and emotional anteced-

ents and consequences of the patient's abusive drinking and/or drug consumption. This information is essential to treatment planning, because effective treatment, including relapse prevention (Marlatt & Gordon, 1985), typically requires that alternative ways be found for substance abusers to access a suitable range of reinforcers to replace those previously available only from substances.

Over the past decade, several different questionnaires have been developed that provide detailed information on expectations of both the positive and negative consequences of drinking. A large and still-growing body of literature on what have come to be termed alcohol expectancies now makes clear that these expectations strongly affect drinking behavior. Expectancies can be assessed in children before drinking begins, appear to interact with personality risk factors to predict drinking behavior, and seem to mediate the impact of other early risk factors, including family history of alcoholism, on subsequent alcohol consumption (Goldman, Brown, Christiansen, & Smith, 1991; Smith, 1994).

The alcohol expectancies most predictive of heavy drinking by high school students (Smith, Goldman, Greenbaum, & Christiansen, 1995), college students (Carey, 1995; Wood, Sher, & Strathman, 1996), and young males aged 21 to 25 (Deckel, Hesselbrock, & Bauer, 1995) have also recently been identified. As a result, assessment of the alcohol expectancies of a high school or college student suspected of abusive drinking should be determined in order to evaluate his or her risk for continued abusive drinking and to better plan treatment. The two alcohol expectancy questionnaires in current widest use have been developed by Brown and her colleagues (Brown, Goldman, Inn, & Anderson, 1980; Brown, Christiansen, & Goldman, 1987) and by Leigh and her associates (Leigh & Stacy, 1993).

The Inventory of Drinking Situations (IDS: Annis, Graham, & Davis, Addiction Research Foundation, 1987) and the associated Situational Confidence Questionnaire (Annis & Graham, Addiction Research Foundation, 1987-88) provide detailed information on drinking and relapse antecedents and consequences. As with alcohol expectancies, knowing where abusive drinking has taken place and what the environmental, interpersonal, and emotional stimuli associated with it are is essential to effective treatment planning.

The **Inventory of Drinking Situations** is a self-report instrument "designed to assess situations in which a client drank heavily over the past year." It contains 100 items describing specific aspects of eight different situations in which drinking is likely to take place. The eight situations, derived from Marlatt and Gordon's (1985) taxonomy of potential relapse determinants, include Unpleasant Emotions, Physical Discomfort, Pleasant Emotions, Testing Personal Control, Urges and Temptations, Conflict with Others, Social Pressure to Drink, and Pleasant Times. The patient is to indicate in which situations he or she drank heavily *almost always, frequently, rarely,* or *never* during the year preceding treatment.

Knowledge of these situations by the clinician who is planning treatment can help structure an intervention that focuses on the situations and associated emotional states and interpersonal settings most consistently related to the patient's drinking. In addition, as treatment proceeds, patient and clinician can return to the patient's **IDS** responses to consider whenever they wish the emotional and interpersonal circumstances surrounding the patient's most recent abusive drinking.

Designed to be used in conjunction with the **IDS,** the **Situational Confidence Questionnaire** is a self-report measure that aims to assess the patient's sense of self-efficacy to control his or her drinking in each of the eight situations detailed in the **IDS.** Anticipating the kinds of stresses to which the patient will be exposed following treatment—and his or her response to them—clearly helps both patient and therapist to plan treatment. Knowledge of **SCQ** responses also gives the clinician information on the success of treatment that has already begun: If the patient has low self-efficacy for successfully confronting stressful situations without returning to alcohol abuse, treatment to date has probably not been very successful. In such an instance, the therapist probably needs to refocus on efforts to build the patient's confidence in his or her ability successfully to confront high risk drinking situations.

The **Substance Abuse Relapse Assessment** (**SARA:** Schonfeld, Peters, & Dolente, Psychological Assessment Resources, Inc., 1993) is a

structured interview, which a clinician familiar with the theory and practice of relapse prevention (Marlatt, 1985) would administer. The **SARA** is designed to reflect the extent to which a patient will achieve and maintain abstinence by means of relapse prevention strategies. These strategies comprise an array of largely cognitive-behavioral techniques designed to help newly abstinent alcoholics anticipate the inevitable challenges they will experience during the early months of their sobriety. Experiencing intense craving without giving in to it and recommencing drinking, interacting with still-drinking friends and family without joining them, even recovering from a "slip"—a brief return to drinking—without quickly falling into an abusive drinking pattern, all these challenges to abstinence are grist for the therapeutic mill during relapse prevention training. The **SARA** interview is designed to help the behavioral clinician who plans to teach his or her newly abstinent patient relapse prevention techniques and procedures by alerting him or her to especially high risk situations for the patient. For clinicians who have incorporated relapse prevention into their therapeutic armamentarium, the **SARA** interview is essential.

SUMMARY AND CONCLUSIONS

This brief overview of substance abuse assessment methods surveys instruments designed to identify and diagnose substance abuse, as well as to plan its effective treatment and accurately assess the outcomes of that treatment.

The methodological rigor of the processes by which many of these instruments were developed, especially those appearing more recently, along with the voluminous data now in the literature attesting to their usefulness encourage us to believe that this volume contains a wealth of valuable interviews and questionnaires for a broad range of clinical and research applications.

REFERENCES

Albanese, M. J., Bartel, R. L., Bruno, R. F., Morgenbesser, M. W., & Schatzberg, A. F. (1994). Comparison of measures used to determine substance abuse in an inpatient psychiatric population. *American Journal of Psychiatry, 151,* 1077-1078.

American Psychiatric Association. (1980). *Diagnostic and statistical manual of mental disorders* (3rd ed.). Washington, DC: Author.

American Psychiatric Association. (1987). *Diagnostic and statistical manual of mental disorders* (3rd ed., rev.). Washington, DC: Author.

American Psychiatric Association. (1994). *Diagnostic and statistical manual of mental disorders* (4th ed.). Washington, DC: Author.

Brown, S. A., Goldman, M. S., Inn, A., & Anderson, L. R. (1980). Expectations of reinforcement from alcohol: Their domain and relation to drinking patterns. *Journal of Consulting and Clinical Psychology, 43,* 419-426.

Brown, S. A., Christiansen, B. A., & Goldman, M. S. (1987). The Alcohol Expectancy Questionnaire: An instrument for the assessment of adolescent and adult alcohol expectancies. *Journal of Studies on Alcohol, 48,* 483-491.

Cahalan, D. (1970). *Problem drinkers.* San Francisco: Jossey-Bass.

Cahalan, D., Cisin, I. H., & Crossley, H. M. (1969). *American drinking practices: A national study of drinking behavior and practices.* New Brunswick, NJ: Rutgers Center of Alcohol Studies.

Carey, K. B. (1995). Alcohol-related expectancies predict quantity and frequency of heavy drinking among college students. *Psychology of Addictive Behaviors, 9,* 236-241.

Chiang, C. N., & Hawks, R. L. (1986). Implications of drug levels in body fluids: basic concepts. In R. L. Hawks & C. N. Chiang (Eds.), *Urine testing for drugs of abuse* (NIDA Research Monograph 73) (pp. 62-83). Rockville, MD: National Institute of Drug Abuse.

Deckel, A. W., Hesselbrock, V., & Bauer, L. (1995). Relationship between alcohol-related expectancies and anterior brain functioning in young men at risk for developing alcoholism. *Alcoholism: Clinical and Experimental Research, 19,* 476-481.

Finney, J. W. & Moos, R. H. (1997). Psychosocial treatments for alcohol use disorders. In P. E. Nathan & J. M. Gorman (Eds.), *Treatments that work.* New York: Oxford University Press.

Feighner, J. P., Robins, E., Guze, S. B., Woodruff, R. A., Winokur, G., & Munoz, R. (1972). Diagnostic criteria for use in psychiatric research. *Archives of General Psychiatry, 26,* 57-63.

First, M. G., Spitzer, R. L., Gibbon, M., & Williams, J. B. W. (1995). *Structured clinical interview for DSM-IV—Patient version (SCID-I/P,* version 2.0). New York: Biometrics Department, New York State Psychiatric Institute.

Flynn, P. M., McCann, J. T., & Fairbank, J. A. (1995). Issues in the assessment of personality disorder and substance abuse using the Millon Clinical Multiaxial Inventory (MCMI-II). *Journal of Clinical Psychology, 51,* 415-421.

Goldman, M. S., Brown, S. A., Christiansen, B. A., & Smith, G. T. (1991). Alcoholism etiology and memory: Broadening the scope of alcohol expectancy research. *Psychological Bulletin, 110,* 137-146.

Gripshover, D.L., & Dacey, C.M. (1994). Discriminative validity of the MacAndrew Scale in settings with a high base rate of substance abuse. *Journal of Studies on Alcohol, 55,* 303-308.

Hawks, R. L., & Chiang, C. N. (1986). Examples of specific drug assays. In R. L. Hawks & C. N. Chiang (Eds.), *Urine testing for drugs of abuse* (NIDA Research Monograph 73) (pp. 84-112). Rockville, MD: National Institute of Drug Abuse.

Kleber, H. D., & Galanter, M. (Eds.). (1995). Substance-related disorders. In G. O. Gabbard (Ed.), *Treatments of psychiatric disorders* (2nd ed.; pp. 635-939). Washington, DC: American Psychiatric Press.

Langenbucher, J. W., & Nathan, P. E. (1983). Psychology, public policy, and the evidence for alcohol intoxication. *American Psychologist, 38,* 1070-1077.

Leigh, B. C., & Stacy, A. W. (1993). Alcohol outcome expectancies: Scale construction and predictive utility in higher-order confirmatory models. *Psychological Assessment, 5,* 216-229.

MacAndrew, C. (1965). The differentiation of male alcoholic outpatients from nonalcoholic psychiatric outpatients by means of the MMPI. *Quarterly Journal of Studies on Alcohol, 26,* 238-246.

MacLellan, A. T., Kushner, H., Metzger, D., Peters, R., Smith, I., Grissom, G., & Pettinati, H. (1992). The fifth edition of the Addiction Severity Index: Historical critique and normative data. *Journal of Substance Abuse Treatment, 9,* 199-213.

Marlatt, G. A. (1985). Situational determinants of relapse and skill training interventions. In G. A. Marlatt & J. R. Gordon (Eds.), *Relapse prevention: Maintenance strategies in the treatment of addictive behaviors* (pp. 77-127). New York: Guilford.

Marlatt, G. A., & Gordon, J. R. (1985). *Relapse prevention: Maintenance strategies in the treatment of addictive behaviors.* New York: Guilford Press.

Mayfield, D., McLeod, G., & Hall, P. (1974). The CAGE questionnaire: Validation of a new alcoholism screening instrument. *American Journal of Psychiatry, 130,* 1121 1123.

Miller, W. R., Brown, J. M., Simpson, T. L., Handmaker, N. S., Bien, T. H., Luckie, L. F., Montgomery, H. A., Hester, R. K., & Tonigan, J. S. (1995). What works? A methodological analysis of the alcohol treatment outcome literature. In R. K. Hester & W. R. Miller (Eds.), *Handbook of alcoholism treatment approaches: Effective alternatives* (pp. 12-44). Boston: Allyn and Bacon.

Millon, T. (1983). Millon Clinical Multiaxial Inventory manual. Minneapolis, MN: National Computer Systems.

Moos, R. H., Finney, J. W., & Cronkite, R. C. (1990). *Alcoholism treatment: Context, process, and outcome.* New York: Oxford University Press.

Nathan, P. E. (1993). Alcoholism: Psychopathology, etiology, and treatment. In P. B. Sutker & H. E. Adams (Eds.), *Comprehensive textbook of psychopathology* (2nd ed.; pp. 451-476). New York: Plenum Press.

National Institute on Alcohol Abuse & Alcoholism (NIAAA). (1993). *Eighth special report to congress on alcohol and health.* Washington, DC: U.S. Department of Health and Human Services.

Pokorny, A. D., Miller, B. A., & Kaplan, H. A. (1972). The Brief MAST: A shortened version of the Michigan Alcoholism Screening Test. *American Journal of Psychiatry, 129,* 342-345

Regier, D. A., Myers, J. K., Kramer, M., Robins, L. N., Blazer, D. G., Hough, R. L., Eaton, W. W., & Locke, B. Z. (1984). The NIMH Epidemiologic Catchment Area program. *Archives of General Psychiatry, 41,* 934-941.

Robins, L. N., Helzer, J. E., Croughan, H., & Ratcliff, K. S. (1981). National Institute of Mental Health Diagnostic Interview Schedule: Its history, characteristics, and validity. *Archives of General Psychiatry, 38,* 381-389.

Robins, L. N., Helzer, J. E., Weissman, M. M., Orvaschel, H., Gruenberg, E., Burke, J. D., & Regier, D. A. (1984). Lifetime prevalence of specific psychiatric disorders in three sites. *Archives of General Psychiatry, 41,* 949-958.

Saunders, J. B., Aasland, O. G., Babor, T. F., De La Fuente, J. R., & Grant, M. (1993). Development of the Alcohol Use Disorders Identification Test (AUDIT): WHO Collaborative Project on early detection of persons with harmful alcohol consumption. *Addiction, 88,* 791-804.

Schottenfeld, R. S. (1995). Assessment of the patients. In G. O. Gabbard (Ed.), *Treatment of psychiatric disorders* (2nd ed.; pp. 652-660). Washington, DC: American Psychiatric Press, Inc.

Selzer, M. L. (1971). The Michigan Alcoholism Screening Test: The quest for a new diagnostic instrument. *American Journal of Psychiatry, 127,* 1653-1658.

Selzer, M. L., Vinokur, A., & van Rooijen, L. (1975). A self-administered Short Michigan Alcoholism Screening Test (SMAST). *Journal of Studies on Alcohol, 36,* 117-126.

Skinner, H. A., Holt, S., Allen, B. A., & Haakonson, N. H. (1980). Correlation between medical and behavioral data in the assessment of alcoholism. *Alcoholism: Clinical and Experimental Research, 4,* 371-377.

Smith, G. T. (1994). Psychological expectancy as mediator of vulnerability to alcoholism. *Annals of the New York Academy of Sciences, 708,* 165-171.

Smith, G. T., Goldman, M. S., Greenbaum, P. E., & Christiansen, B. A. (1995). Expectancy for social facilitation from drinking: The divergent paths of high-expectancy and low-expectancy adolescents. *Journal of Abnormal Psychology, 104,* 32-40.

Sobell, L. C., & Sobell, M. B. (1992). Timeline followback: A technique for assessing self-reported alcohol consumption. In R. Litten & J. Allen (Eds.), *Measuring alcohol consumption.* Totowa, NJ: Humana Press.

Spitzer, R. L., Endicott, J., & Williams, J. B. W. (1979). Research Diagnostic Criteria. *Archives of General Psychiatry, 36,* 1381-1382. New York: Biometrics Research, New York State Psychiatric Institute.

Weed, N. C., Butcher, J. N., & Williams, C. L. (1994). Development of MMPI-A Alcohol/Drug Problem Scales. *Journal of Studies on Alcohol, 55,* 296-302.

Wood, M. D., Sher, K. J., & Strathman, A. (1996). Alcohol outcome expectancies and alcohol use and problems. *Journal of Studies on Alcohol, 57,* 283-288.

World Health Organization. (1992). *International classification of diseases* (10th edition). Geneva: World Health Organization.

1

TESTS WITH PRIMARY FOCUS ON ASSESSING SUBSTANCE ABUSE

[1.1]
Addiction Research Center Inventory.

Purpose: Designed to measure subjective effects of drugs and various dimensions of psychiatric disorders.
Population: Drug addicts.
Publication Dates: 1961–1967.
Acronym: ARCI.
Scores: 29 scales: Carelessness, General Drug, Psychopathic Deviate, Alcohol Withdrawal, Opiate Withdrawal, 7 empirical drug scales (Alcohol, Amphetamine, Chlorpromazine, LSD, Morphine, Pentobarbital, Pyraphexyl), 7 group pattern scales (Alcohol, Amphetamine, Chlorpromazine, LSD, Morphine, Morphine—Amphetamine, Pentobarbital—Chlorpromazine—Alcohol), 10 factor scales (Reactivity, Efficiency, Patience—Impatience, Sentimental, Uncritical, Immaturity, Masculinity—Femininity, Inadequacy, Impulsivity, Neurotic Sensitivity vs. Psychopathic Toughness).
Administration: Group.
Price Data: Available from publisher.
Time: Administration time not reported.
Comments: Test booklet title is The ARC Inventory; IBM computer scoring program available.
Authors: Harris E. Hill, Charles A. Haertzen, and Richard E. Belleville.
Publisher: NIDA Addiction Research Center (Attn. Charles A. Haertzen, Ph.D.).
Cross References: See T3:113 (4 references); T2:1093 (8 references), and P:3 (15 references).

This test has not been reviewed in *The Mental Measurements Yearbook*.

[1.2]
Adolescent Diagnostic Interview.

Purpose: "Assesses psychoactive substance use disorders."

Population: Ages 12–18.
Publication Date: 1993.
Acronym: ADI.
Scores: 8 sections to indicate presence or absence of a DSM-III-R diagnosis of psychoactive substance use disorder: Sociodemographic Factors, Psychosocial Stressors, Substance Use/Consumption History, Alcohol Use Symptoms, Cannabis Use Symptoms, Additional Drug Use Symptoms, Level of Functioning Domains, Orientation and Memory Screen; plus 8 psychiatric status screens: Depression, Mania, Eating Disorder, Delusional Thinking, Hallucinations, Attention Deficit Disorder, Anxiety Disorder, Conduct Disorder.
Administration: Individual.
Price Data, 1995: $75 per complete kit including 5 administration booklets and manual (46 pages); $32.50 per 5 administration booklets; $45 per manual.
Time: (45–55) minutes.
Comments: Structured interview for use with adolescents.
Authors: Ken C. Winters and George A. Henly.
Publisher: Western Psychological Services.
Cross References: Reviews by Tony Toneatto and by Logan Wright, Donna Ford, and Karyll Kiser originally appeared in 12:16.

Review of the Adolescent Diagnostic Interview by TONY TONEATTO, Scientist, Addiction Research Foundation, Toronto, Ontario, Canada:

The Adolescent Diagnostic Interview (ADI) is a structured interview designed to diagnose psychoactive substance use disorders. In addition to providing diagnoses of abuse/dependence the ADI also assesses Psychosocial Stressors, Substance Use/Consumption History, Level of Functioning Domains (i.e., peer and opposite-sex relations, school social functioning, academic

1

functioning, leisure activities, home behavior, home environment, psychiatric status, legal status), and screens for orientation and memory problems.

Developing valid instruments to assess adolescent substance use is certainly a useful endeavor. However, the ADI does not appear to meet the criteria for such an instrument. One limitation is the congruence of the ADI with the *DSM* criteria. The materials provided this reviewer were consistent with the *DSM-III-R* criteria, but not with the *DSM-IV*. Although the publisher mentioned no plans to revise the ADI to reflect anticipated changes in diagnostic criteria (Grant, 1993), revisions of the ADI are now in place.

The authors also fail to establish how the ADI improves upon competing diagnostic instructions such as the Structured Clinical Interview for DSM-III-R (SCID; Williams, Gibbon, First et al., 1992) and the Diagnostic Interview Schedule (DIS; Robins, Helzer, Croughan, & Ratcliff, 1991), both of which can also be used with adolescents.

The authors also do not clarify the utility of formal diagnoses. As the authors themselves state, meeting criteria for dependence rarely impacts upon the nature or course of treatment, which is frequently a function of treatment philosophy, theoretical orientation, waiting list, etc. Although the primary interpretive value of an ADI diagnosis is the determination of the general level of the need for drug treatment no more than one paragraph is allotted to interpreting ADI diagnoses. It can be argued that treatment need is determined by the individual, not diagnoses of dependence. Thus, the ADI is an instrument that will shortly be outdated, has yet to be demonstrated to have value over existing instruments, and which yields diagnoses for which there are limited treatment implications.

There are many problems with the ADI itself. For example, the authors stress that the ADI is a highly structured instrument that excludes clinical intuition (similar to the DIS). Yet, this kind of inference is critical in making a valid diagnosis. In contrast, the SCID, also structured, permits the clinician to score an item as positive if the individual's pattern of responses and nonverbal behavior contradict their response to a specific item (e.g., denial of sadness despite evidence of clinical depression).

Identifying all of the stressful life events that have occurred within the past 12 months seems to be of dubious value. If an adolescent endorses even a few items (not an unlikely occurrence given the turbulence of adolescence in general) the interview will quickly extend beyond the 45–55-minutes administration time. Would not the issues identified in such an exercise, especially important ones surrounding family relations and abuse, be better, and more sensitively, assessed within the framework of a clinical interview? Furthermore, although the ADI searches for evidence of disorder and stress, social supports, coping skills, and positive values are not assessed. These domains of functioning are at least as crucial for treatment planning and referrals as problem identification.

The screening for other psychiatric disorders is very poorly developed, highly selective and inconsistent in the choice of screening questions, and frequently outright inaccurate. To screen for depression an item on crying is included although this is not part of the DSM diagnosis for depression but resembles grief or an adjustment disorder. The question on sleep problems asks only about insomnia and neglects hypersomnia. Two of the three questions under the category of delusional thinking clearly apply to schizophrenia yet no mention of this disorder is made. The questions for auditory hallucinations confuses imagination and hallucinations. Among the anxiety disorders, social phobia and post-traumatic stress disorder, certainly potentially common among adolescents, are not inquired about whereas questions for which a "yes" might be normal (i.e., concern about peer relations and the future) are taken to be indicants of a possible anxiety disorder. Given that serious errors of inference are possible on the basis of this selective solicitation of psychiatric symptomatology it would have been preferable had existing psychiatric screens been used or to have omitted this section altogether.

The assessment of alcohol and drug information is inconsistent and confusing. For example, quantity is assessed only for alcohol. Questions specific to alcohol or cannabis are frequently redundant with each other (asking separate questions for frequency of intoxication in the lifetime and in the past year). With the burgeoning interest in nicotine addiction, especially in treatment of other substance abuse, tobacco use should have been included.

Interrater reliability is favorable for the ADI based on a sample of 72 adolescents who were administered the test. Kappas for diagnosis of dependence/abuse for all substances was quite high (ranging from .53–1.00 with the majority >.75). High kappas were also reported for individual symptoms of alcohol/cannabis dependence (ranging from .66–.97 with most >.80) as well as for the screens for other psychiatric disorders, ranging from .58–.98 but with most kappa values >.85. A one week test-retest assessment of reliability for assessment of alcohol/cannabis abuse and dependence, and individual symptoms of dependence for these two substances, although lower, was marginally acceptable with values ranging from .52–.83; 6 out of 20 comparisons fell between .65 and .75. Reliability data for the other components of the ADI were not reported.

Assessment of the validity of the ADI is very limited. Data are presented only for criterion validity which uses another test developed by the authors (the Personal Experience Inventory). No assessment of the ADI's predictive or construct validity is presented although such work is reported to be underway.

Finally, very limited data on norms for the various domains of functioning are provided. With such incomplete data it is impossible to know whether or not the adolescent falls within the range of normal development. The authors assign evaluative scores (i.e., good—average—poor) to the individuals' responses but do not provide a compelling empirical base to support the descriptions.

The limited evidence for the validity of the ADI, the limited norms, and the limitations in the rationale, conceptualization, and actual content of the ADI enumerated above cast serious doubt on the value of this instrument as a whole. The authors attempt to do too much by screening for psychiatric disorders, assessing stress, levels of functioning, etc., and consequently the entire instrument suffers. Should a diagnosis of dependence be required a well-validated instrument such as the SCID will certainly suffice.

REVIEWER'S REFERENCES

Robins, L. N., Helzer, J. E., Croughan, J., & Ratcliff, K. S. (1981). *NIMH Dianostic Interview Schedule: Version III*. Rockville, MD: National Institute of Mental Health.

Williams, J. B., Gibbon, M., First, M. B., Spitzer, R. L., Davies, M., Borus, J., Howes, M. J., Kane, J., Pope, H. G., Rounsaville, B., & Wittchen, H. U. (1992). The Structured Clinical Interview for DSM-III-R (SCID): II. Multisite test-retest reliability. *Archives of General Psychiatry, 49*, 630–636.

Grant, B. F. (1993). ICD-10 and proposed DSM-IV harmful use of alcohol/ alcohol abuse and dependence, United States 1988: A nosological comparison. *Alcoholism: Clinical and Experimental Research, 17*, 1093–1101.

Review of the Adolescent Diagnostic Interview by LOGAN WRIGHT, Associate Professor of Psychology, and DONNA FORD and KARYLL KISER, Research Assistants, University of Central Oklahoma, Edmond, OK:

The Adolescent Diagnostic Interview (ADI) is designed to assess psychoactive substance abuse disorder in adolescents aged 12 to 18 years. The ADI is a criterion-referenced diagnostic instrument, in which the individual is "evaluated against a specific set of standards or criteria" (manual, p. 23). These diagnostic criteria are taken from the *Diagnostic and Statistical Manual of Mental Disorders, Third Edition, Revised* (*DSM-III-R*; American Psychiatric Association, 1987). The ADI is one of three instruments comprising the Minnesota Chemical Dependence Adolescent Assessment Package (MCDAAP). This package also contains the Personal Experience Screening Questionnaire (PESQ; 286) and the Personal Experience Inventory (PEI; T4:1971). It is recommended that the ADI be used in conjunction with other MCDAAP instruments; however, it can be used independently.

The ADI is individually administered, follows a structured interview protocol, and consists of 306 possible items. The eight sections of the ADI require approximately 45 minutes to complete when the client's psychoactive substance use is restricted to alcohol and/or cannabis. Administration time increases with the number of additional drugs involved. The following nine classes of substance abuse and dependency can also be evaluated: amphetamines, barbiturates, cocaine, opioids, hallucinogens, PCP, inhalants, unspecified or combination drug use, and polysubstance. The ADI is hand scored rather than machine scored.

The ADI is based entirely on the self-reports of the adolescents, and the instrument has been field tested on only white English-speaking individuals. In addition to the diagnostic evaluation of psychoactive substance use disorder of the ADI, its Psychiatric Status Screens section is designed as a screening tool for: affective, anxiety, psychotic, eating, attention deficit, and conduct disorders. Clients are assigned a Global Severity Rating for psychosocial stressors. The ADI also assesses additional variables that may be related to substance abuse (e.g., peer relations, opposite sex relations, home behaviors, academics, etc.).

Items for each interview section of the ADI were generated from: (*a*) a review of existing structured interviews for children and adolescents, (*b*) existing substance abuse interviews, and (*c*) items suggested by an unspecified number of "chemical dependence counselors, clinicians, and experts" (manual, p. 23). Items were also generated from the description of substance abuse in the *DSM-III-R* of the American Psychiatric Association and from the diagnostic categories in the International Classification of Diseases of the World Health Organization. Finally, items were generated based on the authors' impressions of "the essential features of psychoactive substance abuse and dependence disorders" (manual, p. 2) prevailing in the mental health field.

The ADI manual authors refer to an initial item pool; however, it appears that all items in the original pool were retained. If, in fact, some items were discarded, nothing on the nature of the items retained versus discarded, or the basis for such decisions, is provided.

Details of the test construction, reliability, and validity are described in the test manual and in a related study by Winters, Stinchfield, Fulkerson, and Henly (1993). Reliability of the ADI was assessed for both interrater agreement and test-retest stability. No internal consistency information is available for the 15 ADI categories or its Psychiatric Status Screens or the Psychosocial Stressors Global Severity Rating.

To assess interrater reliability, initial interviews were recorded and subsequently rated by four judges. Interrater reliability for the 15 dependence and abuse categories was estimated for 72 subjects. The resulting kappas for the 15 categories, using Cohen's (1960) percentage of agreement technique to correct for the degree of agreement which might be expected by chance alone, fell between .53 to 1.00.

Estimates of interrater reliability for the Psychiatric Status Screen and the Psychosocial Stressors Global Severity Rating segments of the ADI are described only as having "exceeded chance expectations" (manual, p. 26). Interrater reliability for these segments of the ADI was also estimated using *T* indices, to indicate the actual magnitude of agreement when greater than chance-expected agreement is found. The degrees of agreement on these latter two segments ranged from .58 to .98. Agreement or disagreement on the Psychiatric Status Screens was based on a 3-point scale for *no indication, some indication,* or *strong indication* of psychiatric disorder. Interrater agreement for the Psychosocial Stressors Global Severity Rating was based on a 5-point scale of stressor severity.

Test-retest reliability for the ADI is estimated for only two (alcohol and cannabis) of the substance categories. No test-retest reliability data are available for the abuse components of the 10 substance categories. Likewise, no test-retest reliability data are available for the Psychiatric Status Screens or Psychosocial Stressors Global Severity Ratings components.

Test-retest reliability for alcohol dependence and cannabis dependence was estimated using a different sample of 49 adolescent drug users. The subjects were retested by the same interviewer one week following an initial administration using a simple binomial (yes/no) scale. Observed agreement between first and second interviews, again employing Cohen's kappa, was .83 for alcohol and .80 for cannabis. Percent of agreement for the alcohol and cannabis dependence and abuse symptoms ranged from 78 to 92%, whereas the resulting kappas ranged from .52 to .79. The short interval between test-retest may have inflated these test-retest results. The authors suggest that future test-retest studies include longer intervals between the initial and second administrations.

Validity of the ADI was evaluated by correlating ratings for the ADI substance use disorder groups with staff ratings for Heilman's (1973) warning signs of addiction, using 278 subjects recruited from an outpatient adolescent substance abuse evaluation center, residential evaluation centers, and aftercare programs. The resulting correlations of .72 and .78 were significant at $p < .001$.

In summary, the interrater and test-retest reliability of the ADI appear to have been established, at least to a minimal degree. However, the ADI's validity remains essentially undetermined, as does its advantage over other available instruments in the area of substance abuse diagnosis. Additional validity studies are certainly in order. In the meantime, the ADI may serve as a useful clinical tool, but should not be regarded as a validated research or clinical instrument.

REVIEWER'S REFERENCES

Cohen, J. (1960). A coefficient of agreement for nominal scales. *Educational and Psychological Measurement, 20*, 37–46.

Heilman, R. O. (1973). *Early recognition of alcoholism and other drug dependence.* Center City, MN: Hazelden Educational Materials.

American Psychiatric Association. (1987). *Diagnostic and statistical manual of mental disorders* (DSM-III-R; rev. 3rd ed.). Washington, DC: Author.

Winters, K. C., Stinchfield, R. D., Fulkerson, J., & Henly, G. A. (1993). Measuring alcohol and cannabis use disorders in an adolescent clinical sample. *Psychology of Addictive Behaviors, 7*(3), 185–196.

[1.3]
Adolescent Drinking Index.

Purpose: Constructed to screen for alcohol abuse.
Population: Ages 12–17.
Publication Dates: 1985–1989.
Acronym: ADI.
Scores, 3: Self-Medicated Drinking (MED), Aggressive/Rebellious Behavior (REB), Total.
Administration: Group or individual.
Price Data, 1994: $47 per complete kit including manual ('89, 34 pages) and 25 test booklets.
Time: (5) minutes.
Comments: Test booklet title is Drinking & You.
Authors: Adele V. Harrell and Philip W. Wirtz.
Publisher: Psychological Assessment Resources, Inc.
Cross References: Reviews by Thomas F. Donlon and by Kevin J. McCarthy and Penelope W. Dralle originally appeared in 12:17.

Review of the Adolescent Drinking Index by THOMAS F. DONLON, Director, Office of Test Development and Research, Thomas Edison State College, Trenton, NJ:

The Adolescent Drinking Index (ADI) is a 24-item scale that attempts to measure the severity of any drinking problem that an adolescent may have. The Index is based upon a conceptual framework that delineates four domains or facets of developmentally dysfunctional drinking: (*a*) loss of control over drinking, so that there is drinking at inappropriate times, places, or in inappropriate amounts; (*b*) interference with significant interpersonal relationships through drinking; (*c*) drinking to alter mood or state of relaxation; and (*d*) physical changes through drinking: memory losses or increased tolerance for alcohol.

Two of these four domains are important enough in their own right to be assessed by a subscale: The Self-Medicated Drinking (MED) scale is a four-item indicator of drinking to alter mood, and the Rebelliousness (REB) scale is a seven-item index of aggressive, rebellious behavior, interfering with interpersonal relationships.

The purposes of the ADI are assisting in identifying issues to be addressed in treatment, in clarifying differences in male and female adolescent base rates for alcohol use, and in reducing the tendency to overlook problem drinking in self-medicating adolescents whose drinking problem is unobtrusive. The instrument is described as "*not designed to serve as a school-wide screening instrument for the detection of alcohol abuse among adolescents in general*" (manual, p. 3). However, one part of its validation is based on data collected from a sample selected "to represent a general population of adolescents," and the normative data for these 583 subjects is presented first in the appendices. It was not clear to this reviewer what specific limitations were seen by the authors to rule out its use among adolescents in general.

The content of the 24 questions calls for very direct self-reports, through simple Likert scales indicating the extent to which the statement provided is valid for the subject: *like me a lot* to *not like me at all*, and, for frequency data: *4 or more times* to *never*. The four-item MED scale asks about motivation for drinking in order to counter anger, loneliness, sadness, and tension. The seven-item REB scale asks about "fighting" and "getting into trouble"; however, there is some logical overlap between its questions: One question asks "how often in the past year did you get into a fight over drinking," and another asks "how often in the past year did you fight with your parents about your drinking." The two frequencies reported could obviously be the same events for some students and different events for others, depending on the interpretation of the language. "Get into a fight" may not mean a physical fight to every student.

The manual authors present substantial data on the psychometric characteristics of the instrument, including a confirmatory factor analysis of the scale structure, an analysis of variance testing the age by gender interaction, and the use of a sequence of discriminant analyses in the service of deriving cutoff scores. These analyses are conducted on three samples: the 583-person "school sample" from the general population; the 233-person "treatment sample" consisting of adolescents actively under treatment for alcohol abuse; and the 261-person "validation sample" consisting of adolescents referred to clinicians for some psychological, emotional, or behavioral problem.

Some of these psychometric analyses, however, are based upon complex logical edifices that make them unconvincing. Thus, the confirmatory factor analysis tested the probability that the three hypothesized scales were not perfectly identical. Such statistical significance, even though demonstrated, may not support any practical significance. Given the small numbers of items in the two scales, and the inclusion of these items in the total score (referred to as the primary scale, severity of drinking), it is doubtful that the subscales have useful meaning. Of the seven REB scale items, for example, only one shows a higher correlation with its scale total than with the ADI total in the validation sample; only two of these items show such a higher correlation in the treatment sample. The subscales are called "research scales," and their suggested use is in "generating hypotheses about potential forms of treatment and further methods of evaluation." However, they appear to this reviewer to be somewhat oversold in the manual.

The authors note that "in general, male adolescents ... have higher rates of alcohol abuse" (p. 13). However, females aged 16–17 show higher ADI total scores than males in the validation sample (20.39 vs. 16.98), and in the treatment sample (32.19 vs. 31.76), and a similar pattern is observed for females and males ages 12–15. Only the school sample showed data conforming to the expectation (females 16–17 averaging 8.11 vs. comparable males 11.84, and females 12–15 averaging 5.63 vs. males 5.92). An analysis of variance testing age-gender interactions, performed *only* on the school sample, is interpreted as "consistent with the general finding of increased alcohol use by males" (p. 13). There was a need for a fuller and more detailed analysis to clarify these results.

A cutoff score of 15 was derived by drawing a series of 25 random samples of 130 subjects (50% of the group sampled) from the validation sample. A discriminant analysis was used to establish in each sample the cutoff score that would best differentiate the severe drinkers from the others in this group. The modal value of the distribution of such cutoffs was 15, and this was chosen as the operational cutoff value. These procedures seem rational, but the cutoff so determined will identify a large proportion of persons whose drinking problem is "moderate." The average score for the 65 "moderate" drinkers in the validation sample was 15.42. There are obviously some choices to be made in devising the cutoff. The use of the cutoff in the other samples showed that 17% of the school sample would demonstrate scores above the cutoff, whereas 78% of the treatment sample would demonstrate such scores. The index seems likely to err in the direction of overidentifying problem drinkers.

The ADI appears to be a commonsense way of screening adolescents in order to identify those with a severe drinking problem. It requires a cooperating subject, and it could be easily manipulated by anyone who wished to conceal a problem. It seems well designed for its intended function as an aid to clinicians making a judgment as to needed additional referral. Although it obviously offers information as to a complex framework with respect to aggressivity and the use of alcohol to control mood, the data do not support the use of the two research scales for anything more than just that: research.

Review of the Adolescent Drinking Index by KEVIN J. McCARTHY, Ph.D Candidate, Associate in Psychology Department, E. Hunt Correctional Center, St. Gabriel, LA, and PENELOPE W. DRALLE, Associate Professor of Psychiatry, Louisiana State University School of Medicine, New Orleans, LA:

The Adolescent Drinking Index (ADI) is a four-page booklet consisting of 24 questions about alcohol usage among teenagers. The assessment instrument is simple and direct. The Index can be self-administered in a few minutes and uses a format that divides the instrument into two component scales. Questions 1–10 address the issue of alcohol use and emotions. Data are collected on a modified 3-point Likert-type scale with answers ranging from *like me a lot* to *not like me at all*. Questions 11–24 focus on the issue of behaviors while under the influence of alcohol. It uses a modified 4-point Likert-type scale with answers ranging from *never* to *4 or more times*. This straightforward approach to drinking practices permits the client to focus on the issue of severity of use and subsequent behavioral problems and minimizes resistance commonly associated with longer instruments.

The Index's two subscales focus on Self-Medicated Drinking (MED) and Aggressive/Rebellious Behavior (REB) related to the use of alcohol. The authors caution that "the MED and REB subscales are research scales, their use should be restricted to generating hypotheses about potential forms of treatment and further methods of evaluation" (manual, p. 6).

The ADI manual authors state the instrument is not designed "to serve as a school-wide screening instrument for the detection of alcohol abuse among adolescents in general" (manual, p. 3). Also the authors state in the manual that "In no case will ADI data be sufficient in making a formal diagnosis of an alcohol abuse disorder" (p. 3). Thus, it has a rather limited primary function, to assess the severity of an adolescent's drinking problems. However, because the treatment study sample consisted of several groups of adolescents hospitalized for alcohol abuse and included several programs offering treatment for substance abuse without treatment differentiation between alcohol and other drugs usage, there is some confusion regarding whether the ADI assesses alcohol use or polysubstance use. The authors report that "Some of the subjects in this sample, therefore, may not have had drinking problems" (p. 9).

The majority of adolescents hospitalized for substance abuse are usually involuntarily admitted by a parent or guardian secondary to some precipitating event involving the use of alcohol or other drugs. Frequently, newly admitted patients minimize their using behaviors or deny the existence of an alcohol abuse problem. Because the ADI contains no measure of test-taking attitude, its usefulness seems to be restricted to those patients who have overcome denial about their drinking behaviors. The manual authors do not report which phase of treatment patients in the normative population were in at the time of assessment.

Substantive data regarding reliability and validity are provided in the manual. The ADI, developed from an item pool of 40 questions, went through pilot testing including qualitative and quantitative item analysis. This yielded an internal

consistency reliability alpha coefficient of .92 for the final version, whereas analysis of the three samples comprising the normative population yielded an alpha coefficient exceeding .90. The authors report test-retest reliability at .78.

Convergent validity was assessed using the Michigan Alcoholism Screening Test (MAST) as an indicator yielding a correlation of $r = .60–.63$ for scores 2 and 1. Discriminant validity data suggest this index is a measure of alcohol abuse among adolescents, but some question remains regarding polysubstance abuse. The manual authors note that analysis of variance was used to conduct criterion group comparisons focusing on severity of adolescent drinking problems. The analysis revealed significant difference among three groups, ranging from minor to no problems to substantial problems.

The fact the ADI's REB subscale is designed to assess drinking behaviors over the last 12 months limits analysis of the data to recent past and current levels of using behaviors while avoiding the complexities of a more longitudinal perspective. This time frame permits the clinician to focus upon those behaviors that are currently problematic. The generalizability of the instrument is enhanced by including in the validation study data from six different sites in five different states tapping many of the regional differences found within the country. However, the regional utility of the instrument would be increased by including sites with larger representations of African-American youth and by specifying the composition of the "other" category.

The questions have not been counterbalanced, which may enhance response set bias. Alternating the social desirability of the items might increase the likelihood the client would read each item before responding. In the manual, the authors note that "The administrator should be available during testing to answer questions concerning test administration or the meaning of items" (p. 5), but they have not provided guidelines for standardized responses to such inequities.

In addition, the authors choose to break their sample into two age groups: 12–15-year-olds and 16–17-year-olds. There are significant developmental differences between 12-year-olds and 15-year-olds. Data presented in this format might be more effectively reorganized into three developmentally equitable groups (i.e., 12–13-year-olds,

14–15-year-olds, and 16–17-year-olds). This grouping would also correspond to the peer groups commonly found in local school districts (i.e., middle school, early and late high school).

The manual layout was rather difficult to follow. Matching data presented in graphs and charts to contextual components was difficult and frequently cumbersome.

In summary, the Adolescent Drinking Index's primary focus is limited to assessing the severity of drinking behaviors among a population of adolescents "referred for emotional or behavioral disorders" (p. 3). Its principal advantage is its brevity and succinctness as well as its ease of administration. When used in conjunction with historical and familial data, the ADI may aid the clinician in assessing drinking problems among receptive patients.

[1.4]
The Alcadd Test, Revised Edition.

Purpose: "Designed to: a) provide an objective measurement of alcoholic addiction that could identify individuals whose behavior and personality structure indicated that they were alcoholic addicts or had serious alcoholic problems; b) identify specific areas of maladjustment in alcoholics to facilitate therapeutic and rehabilitation activities; and c) obtain better insight into the psychodynamics of alcoholic addiction."

Population: Adults.

Publication Dates: 1949–1988.

Scores, 6: Regularity of Drinking, Preference for Drinking over Other Activities, Lack of Controlled Drinking, Rationalization of Drinking, Excessive Emotionality, Total.

Administration: Individual or group.

Editions, 2: Paper-and-pencil, microcomputer.

Price Data, 1993: $55 per complete kit including 25 AutoScore test booklets ('88, 4 pages) and manual ('88, 24 pages); $29.50 per 25 AutoScore test booklets; $27.50 per manual; $125 per microcomputer edition (IBM) including diskette (tests up to 25) and user's guide; $9.50 or less per mail-in answer sheet.

Time: (5–15) minutes.

Comments: Self-administered.

Authors: Morse P. Manson, Lisa A. Melchior, and G. J. Huba.

Publisher: Western Psychological Services.

Cross References: Reviews by William L. Curlette and Paul Retzlaff originally appeared in 11:12 (1 reference); see also T3:152 (3 references), T2:1098 (1 reference), and P:7 (3 references); for a review by Dugal Campbell, see 6:60 (6 references); for reviews by Charles H. Honzik and Albert L. Hunsicker, see 4:30.

Review of The Alcadd Test, Revised Edition by WILLIAM L. CURLETTE, Professor of Educational Foundations, Georgia State University, Atlanta, GA:

According to the revised edition of The Alcadd Test manual (1988), the purposes of The Alcadd Test are threefold: namely, to "provide an objective measurement of alcoholic addiction," to "identify specific areas of maladjustment," and to "obtain better insight into the psychodynamics of alcoholic addiction." These objectives are accomplished by having respondents answer yes or no to 65 items resulting in scores on the following five subscales: Regularity of Drinking (12 items), Preference for Drinking Over Other Activities (11 items), Lack of Controlled Drinking (20 items), Rationalization of Drinking (20 items), and Excessive Emotionality (20 items). The test and the manual are produced with an attractive format.

The original Alcadd Manual (1965, 1978) provided by Western Psychological Services consisted of only two pages and one-paragraph descriptions of validity, reliability, and administration. Thus, the revised manual with 19 pages of text and 4 additional pages for test form and profile form samples represents a substantial revision.

Previous reviewers of the test (Campbell, 6:60; Hunsicker, 4:30) have commented on the lack of a theoretical support for the dimensions used in the test. The revised manual reports a factor analysis of the five Alcadd subscales; hence, providing through empirical research some basis for the total score. Ultimately, however, the meaningfulness and usefulness of the subscales come from the studies employing the Alcadd. The revised manual reports a number of studies.

As the previous reviews of the Alcadd and the test manual indicate, scores on the test could be influenced by the response set of social desirability. This occurs because the responses to the items are obvious if a person desires to fake a nonalcoholic response. Furthermore, there is no social desirability subscale to measure faking on the test. The manual suggests the MMPI validity scales or the Social Desirability Scale by Crowne and Marlowe (1960) may be used in conjunction with the Alcadd if there is concern about faking. The discussion of this issue in the test manual is brought to a close by stating that the use of the Alcadd in voluntary treatment settings should not be a problem.

Based on information in the previous manual, scoring has improved with the new revision. Previously, scoring was done by hand using a template (or sheet next to the person's responses). Now scoring is done on a form having carbon paper underneath the sheet on which the examinee takes the test. The carbon paper eliminates one step in the hand-scoring process. Also included in the test booklet are profile sheets that convert raw scores to centiles and T-scores, and the probability of being an alcoholic. In addition, the manual states that a microcomputer disk (IBM 5 1/4-inch or 3 1/2-inch) is available to administer, score, and print a report (two pages long) for The Alcadd Test.

Two key aspects for using any test are the amount of time required to administer the test and its reading level. On both accounts the Alcadd appears very good. The test manual reports that it requires between 5 and 15 minutes to take the 65 items in the test. Although there are many readability formulas and approaches, there are several ways to obtain a quick estimate of the grade level for reading. The Flesch-Kincaid, as calculated by the RightWriter computer program for the first 99 words and the last 101 words of the Alcadd, was 3.0. Using the SMOG index on the same selections, the reading was at the 4.7 grade level. Thus, reading level appears low enough to be used with most populations. The manual also suggests it is appropriate to read the items to examinees.

Two bothersome technical aspects are overlapping items between subscales and 40-year-old norms. A technical aspect of the test, which may be a limitation for the use of the test in research, is the assignment of some items to more than one subscale (although many tests do this). In fact, there are 23 items that are scored on more than one subscale. Even though it may reduce test-taking time, the effect of overlapping items between subscales is to induce spurious correlation between subscales. This means the correlation between subscales sharing items may be artificially inflated unless statistical adjustments are made. Whether due to overlapping items or not, the intercorrelation (.81) between two subscales (Rationalization of Drinking and Excessive Emotionality) seems high, if only from the perspective that subscales on a test battery are typically created to measure distinct attributes and, thus, would not be expected to correlate highly.

The norms shown in a sample 1988 score report in the test manual are based on a 1949 sample. Subsequent research on norms by Dunlop is reported in the manual; however, the results do not appear to provide direct support for the 1949 norms. More recent norms are needed for score interpretation.

There is a lack of information in the test manual on topics considered necessary (primary standards) in the Standards for Educational and Psychological Testing (AERA, APA, & NCME, 1985). Missing from the manual are standard errors of measurement, reliabilities for the subscales, and cultural fairness research information.

A unique aspect of the test is translating an examinee's total test score into the probability of being an alcoholic. Interestingly, for both males and females in any preassigned risk group, a total raw score of exactly 22 or higher yields a .99 probability of being in the alcoholic group. This observation might be helpful as a benchmark for quickly interpreting test scores.

On a PsychALERT and PsychINFO computer literature search run during Fall 1989, two citations (not listed in the test manual) (Ramsay, 1979; Zeh, 1985) were found. Ramsay (1979) administered the Alcadd, the MMPI, and the 16PF to patients suffering from alcoholism. Zeh (1985) compared scores on the Michigan Alcoholism Screening Test, the MacAndrew Alcoholism Scale, and the Alcadd in a sample of 80 incarcerated male adolescent felons. An Educational Resources Information Center (ERIC) literature search on Alcadd using SilverPlatter V1.5 for 1/83 to 6/89 did not provide any citations.

In conclusion, the concerns of previous reviewers regarding the lack of control of social desirability and the potential to fake scores on the Alcadd still limit the use of the Alcadd. Disregarding this concern, the Alcadd does approach all three of its objectives. Additional work is needed, however, to bring the Alcadd manual into closer agreement with basic test standards.

REVIEWER'S REFERENCES

Crowne, D. P., & Marlowe, D. A. (1960). A new scale of social desirability independent of psychopathology. Journal of Consulting Psychology, 24, 349-354.

Ramsay, S. A. (1979). Statistical information on three personality measures used with alcoholics. National Institute for Personnel Research, Johannesburg, South Africa (Afrikaans Abstract).

American Educational Research Association, American Psychological Association, & National Council on Measurement in Education. (1985). Standards for educational and psychological testing. Washington, DC: American Psychological Association, Inc.

Zeh, R. S. (1985). Alcoholism and incarcerated adolescent males: Knowledge and testing (Doctoral Dissertation, The University of Akron, 1985). Dissertation Abstracts International, 45, 3593A. (ISSN: 04194209)

Review of The Alcadd Test, Revised Edition by PAUL RETZLAFF, Assistant Professor of Psychology, University of Northern Colorado, Greeley, CO:

This 65-item (60 items scored) inventory of obvious yes/no alcohol-related behaviors purports to "identify" alcoholics. Its scoring results in a total score and five subscales: Regularity of Drinking, Preference for Drinking over Other Activities, Lack of Controlled Drinking, Rationalization of Drinking, and Excessive Emotionality. It was originally developed in 1949 and remains substantially unchanged in its 1988 revision.

It is brief and easy to administer, score, and determine sophisticated hit rate statistics. The new Autoscore multipart test forms and scoring sheets are particularly noteworthy. Finally, the adoption of positive and negative predictive power statistics is found in few other tests.

There are a number of problems with the test, however. First, all items, norms, and hit rates are from the original 1949 development. The test was developed via empirical group separation at an item level. The problem with this is that empirical group separation results in poorer operating characteristics than domain theory test construction. Further, in the last 40 years it is very likely that different items would be better and that "alcoholics" as a group may have changed. This is particularly true in light of the relatively low N employed in the original study–282 split four ways, male-female and alcoholic-nonalcoholic. The reliability and validity statistics are also disturbing. Although the test as a whole has an internal consistency of .92 and .96, there are no reliabilities for the five subscales reported in the manual. There is also a problem with the independence of the five subscales. They were subjectively derived and as such have no empirical basis. Further, the manual attempts to put a positive face on their very high intercorrelations by saying this proves high internal consistency. Finally, although the test as a whole has been examined for validity indices, there are no validity estimates reported for any of the five subscales.

The most positive aspects of the test are the hit rate statistics integrated into the scoring process. The test publisher is applauded for adopting the operating

characteristics of positive and negative predictive powers. The reliance on the 1949 norms, however, greatly reduces the validity of these data.

In summary, The Alcadd Test is substantively unchanged from 1949 and as such is limited by its construction, norms, and other developments. A better test is probably the Alcohol Use Inventory (AUI) (Horn, Wanberg, & Foster, 1987). Its subscales were empirically derived, have high reliabilities, and add additional dimensions. The most recent revision of the AUI has added scales, items, and norms. Although longer than the Alcadd, it is a far superior test.

REVIEWER'S REFERENCE

Horn, J. L., Wanberg, K. W., & Foster, F. M. (1986). Alcohol Use Inventory. Minneapolis, MN: National Computer Systems.

[1.5]
Alcohol Clinical Index.

Purpose: "To identify alcohol problems among patients."
Population: Adults at-risk for alcohol problems.
Publication Date: 1987.
Administration: Individual.
Price Data, 1990: $9.75 per user's booklet (31 pages); $9.95 per 50 questionnaires (specify test).
Time: Administration time not reported.
Authors: Harvey A. Skinner and Stephen Holt.
Publisher: Addiction Research Foundation [Canada].
    a) CLINICAL SIGNS.
    Scores, 6: Hand, Head, Abdomen, Body, Locomotor Function, Total.
    b) MEDICAL HISTORY.
    c) ALCOHOL USE.
    d) RISK FACTORS.
    Scores, 2: Early Indicators, Risk Factors.
Cross References: Reviews by Steven I. Pfeiffer and William I. Sauser, Jr. will appear in the 13th MMY.

Review of the Alcohol Clinical Index by STEVEN I. PFEIFFER, Professor, Graduate School of Education, Kent State University, Kent, OH:

The Alcohol Clinical Index (ACI) was designed as a brief and economic screening instrument for use by physicians and allied health care professionals to identify alcohol use problems among patients in primary care settings. The ACI consists of two components: a 17-item clinical signs checklist (CSC) and a 13-item Medical History Questionnaire (MHQ).

The test authors, Drs. Skinner and Holt, advocate administering laboratory tests (e.g., serum gamma-glutamyl-transferase and mean corpuscular volume) and brief alcohol questionnaires (e.g., CAGE questionnaire, Alcohol Dependence Scale) to corroborate a positive finding on the ACI.

The ACI was derived from a comprehensive set of 108 clinical indicators of alcohol abuse (Skinner, Holt, Sheu, & Israel, 1986; also test manual). It is recommended that the 17 clinical signs should be elicited by a physician or nurse as part of a physical examination (illustrative items: "rhinophyma-varying degrees of epithelial thickening, dilation of sebaceous follicles and bluish-red discoloration of the distal portion of the nose"; "gynecomastia-male only, glandular and fatty tissue enlargement of both breasts").

The 13 Medical History items can either be self-completed by the patient or administered by the physician or nurse. Illustrative items include: "Do you often wake up with headache?" and "Do you find it hard to remember recent events?"

The manual reports the diagnostic rule that if either clinical signs or Medical History is greater than or equal to four then there is a "high likelihood of alcohol abuse or dependence" (p. 6). The manual recommends, however, as mentioned above, corroboration using laboratory tests and alcohol questionnaires. Although a decision rule is provided, the manual offers no evidence to support the diagnostic sensitivity, specificity, or predictive power of the ACI.

Similarly, the manual includes no information to suggest that any estimates of reliability or validity were obtained. Also, it is uncertain what type, if any, of pilot testing or validation was undertaken, and basic information on the sample used for test development is sorely missing. There are no norms in the manual, and one has no idea if the test or test items are biased across different racial, ethnic, or geographic regional groups.

A study by Skinner and Holt, along with two coinvestigators, reports a higher predictive power for the ACI than with laboratory tests in distinguishing an outpatient group with alcohol problems from social drinkers (Skinner, Holt et al., 1986). This same investigation provides the data that led to the diagnostic rule reported in the test manual (88%–90% accuracy was achieved by the decision rule of clinical signs or medical history of four or more).

However, a recently published validity study with lower socioeconomic alcohol-dependent men

obtained overall predictive values for the ACI not nearly as favorable as those reported by the test authors. For example, The Clinical Signs Checklist yielded 70% accuracy regardless of cutoff point (ranging from 1 through 5). The Medical History questionnaire generated somewhat better outcomes, with an overall accuracy of 84% (Alterman, Gelfund, & Sweeney, 1992).

The ACI is a brief, economical, and easy-to-administer screening instrument to identify primary care patients with alcohol problems. The authors appropriately recognized the need for future investigators to evaluate the diagnostic sensitivity and specificity of the index (Skinner, Holt et al., 1986). Research is also needed to evaluate sources of measurement error and estimates of reliability, content and construct validity, and possible test and item bias (e.g., one item on the clinical signs checklist inquires about tattoos). Until these much needed reliability, validation, and norming steps are undertaken, the ACI should be restricted to use as a research tool and not in individual clinical decision making.

REVIEWER'S REFERENCES

Skinner, H. A., Holt, S., Sheu, W. J., & Israel, M. (1986). Clinical versus laboratory detection of alcohol abuse: The Alcohol Clinical Index. *British Medical Journal, 292,* 1703–1708.

Alterman, A. I., Gelfund, L. A., & Sweeney, K. K. (1992). The Alcohol Clinical Index in lower socioeconomic alcohol-dependent men. *Alcoholism: Clinical and Experimental Research, 16,* 960–963.

Review of the Alcohol Clinical Index by WILLIAM I. SAUSER, JR., Professor and Executive Director for Outreach, College of Business, Auburn University, Auburn, AL:

The Alcohol Clinical Index consists of 13 objective medical history questions that can be answered "yes" or "no," plus 17 observable clinical signs that could be recognized easily by trained health care professionals. According to the manual, it is intended for use as a low-cost screening device, administered by primary care physicians or nurses, "to identify patients who drink excessively but who do not consider themselves 'alcoholics.' The basic strategy is to intervene with brief counseling before the patient has developed major symptoms of alcohol dependence" (p. 2).

In the manual, the test developers cite epidemiological evidence from the U.S.A. and Canada indicating that roughly 5% of North American adults are alcoholics, 20% are problem drinkers, 60% are social drinkers, and 15% abstain from consuming alcohol. There are a number of clinical assessment devices available to identify alcoholics (Ingram, Sauser, & Owens, 1989); a purpose of the Alcohol Clinical Index, however, is to distinguish between social drinkers and problem drinkers, the latter group being defined in the manual as those individuals who "do *not* show major symptoms of alcohol dependence … [but] drink at levels that have increased health risk and … may have accrued some consequences related to drinking in the recent past" (p. 1).

It is these problem drinkers who the test developers view as a rich target audience for early detection and intervention programs. They argue that such early detection and intervention might curb the incidence of alcohol-related problems, which have staggering economic and social-psychological costs. Skinner, Holt, and Israel (1981) note that in the United States "alcohol-related problems cost nearly $43 billion in 1975 as a result of lost production, motor vehicle accidents, crime, social problems, and demands for health care services. Indeed, over 12% of the total expenditure on health care for adults … was for alcohol-related medical service" (p. 1142).

The Alcohol Clinical Index is very simple and straightforward. Literate patients could complete the medical history in a matter of minutes; illiterate or visually impaired patients would have no difficulty responding to the questions administered orally. Similarly, a medical professional could easily detect the presence or absence of the clinical signs during the course of a routine physical examination. The Alcohol Clinical Index, when administered alongside other simple questionnaires recommended by the test developers (and included within the manual), appears to be effective for use as a screening device for identifying problem drinkers.

Despite its simplicity, the Alcohol Clinical Index is built upon significant scientific research. The authors cite 11 of their published research articles (readily available in most medical libraries) substantiating the effective use of the Alcohol Clinical Index in the manner they recommend. Most impressive is a study of 131 outpatients with alcohol problems, 131 social drinkers, and 52 patients from family practice (Skinner, Holt, Sheu, & Israel, 1986), which found "a probability of alcohol abuse exceeding 0.90 … if four or more clinical

signs or four or more medical history items from the index were present" (p. 1703). This study serves as the basis for the diagnostic rule given in the manual, "If Clinical Signs ≥4 or Medical History ≥4 then there is a high likelihood of alcohol abuse or dependence. Investigate further using the laboratory tests and alcohol questionnaires" (p. 6).

One warning is in order: personnel specialists and human resource managers must recognize that the Alcohol Clinical index is a medical examination that leads to medical diagnosis and intervention. It should *not* be used as a routine employment screening device lest the potential employing organization run afoul of the Americans with Disabilities Act (Veres & Sims, 1995).

In summary, the Alcohol Clinical Index is a short, easily administered medical screening device that may be used by primary care physicians and nurses to detect problem drinkers, who may be further examined and targeted for early intervention programs. Although presented in a simple, easy-to-understand manual, the Alcohol Clinical Index is the product of rigorous scientific study.

REVIEWER'S REFERENCES

Skinner, H. A., Holt, S., & Israel, Y. (1981). Early identification of alcohol abuse: I. Critical issues and psychosocial indicators for a composite index. *Canadian Medical Association Journal, 124,* 1141–1152.
Skinner, H. A., Holt, S., Sheu, W. J., & Israel, Y. (1986). Clinical versus laboratory detection of alcohol abuse: The Alcohol Clinical Index. *British Medical Journal, 292,* 1703–1708.
Ingram, J. J., Sauser, W. I., Jr., & Owens, C. A. (1989). Assessment: Determination of client needs and progress. In D. R. Self (Ed.), *Alcoholism treatment marketing: Beyond TV ads and speeches* (pp. 207–223). New York: Haworth.
Veres, J. G., III, & Sims, R. R. (Eds.). (1995). *Human resource management and the Americans with Disabilities Act.* Westport, CT: Quorum.

[1.6]

Alcohol Dependence Scale.

Purpose: "Provides a brief measure of the extent to which the use of alcohol has progressed from psychological involvement to impaired control."

Population: Problem drinkers.

Publication Date: 1984.

Acronym: ADS.

Scores: Total score only.

Administration: Group.

Price Data, 1990: C$6.50 per 25 questionnaires; $14.25 per user's guide (41 pages); $15 per specimen set.

Foreign Language Edition: Questionnaire available in French.

Time: (5–10) minutes.

Comments: Test booklet title is Alcohol Use Questionnaire.

Authors: Harvey A. Skinner and John L. Horn.

Publisher: Addiction Research Foundation [Canada].

Cross References: Reviews by Robert E. Deysach and Nick J. Piazza originally apperared in 10:12 (1 reference).

Review of the Alcohol Dependence Scale by ROBERT E. DEYSACH, Associate Professor of Psychology, Department of Psychology, University of South Carolina, Columbia, SC:

The theoretical context in which the Alcohol Dependence Scale (ADS) is set reflects the practice (i.e., exercised by the World Health Organization and others) of separating primary alcohol dependence from alcohol-related physical, psychological, and social disabilities stemming from alcohol dependence. According to this formulation, levels of alcohol dependence (including characteristics of drinking pattern disturbance) can be independently identified and placed on a continuum of severity. Recently, DSM III-R (APA, 1987) has acknowledged the centrality of an alcohol-dependence syndrome by broadening the definition introduced in DSM III, by limiting the importance of the dependence/abuse distinctions and by reducing "abuse" to a "residual" status.

The ADS is a 25-item self-report derivative of the Alcohol Use Inventory (AUI), a scale that has enjoyed long service as a research tool and comprehensive clinical device. The ADS is limited to measuring those behaviors specifically linked to reports of compulsive drink seeking, to loss of behavioral control with alcohol use, and to physical and perceptual disturbances associated with withdrawal. A major advantage of the ADS is its brevity and ease of administration. Adaptable for use in either an interview or questionnaire format, the authors recommend the economy of a self-administered questionnaire. Although a clinical interview may afford opportunity to challenge deceptive responses, direct examiner contact may further lower a client's threshold for defensiveness. The ADS questionnaire requires approximately 10 minutes to complete.

Scoring is based on a 2- or 3-point scale with resulting raw scores ranging from 0 to 47. The higher scores describe greater reported levels of dependence. Available in the manual are percentile and standard scores generated on normative data from four clinical samples of clients seeking treatment. The samples (with Ns ranging from 70 to 225) were taken from admissions to the Clinical Institute of Addiction Research Foundation in Toronto. The ADS manual provides tentative interpretative guidelines in the form of brief characterizations of patients in each quartile together with a promise for inclusion of additional material as more research is conducted with the questionnaire. The authors promise to update interpretative material as a result of future research investigations.

Reported reliabilities of the ADS are in the low .90s and appear acceptable. These reliabilities, however, seem to be drawn primarily from a single large sample of moderate problem drinkers admitted to a short term treatment facility and are based on data gathered with the parent instrument and utilizing a slightly altered set of ADS items. (The authors report that after research conducted in 1982 three more discriminating items were introduced to replace seven less discriminating ones from the AUI, reducing the items from 29 to the present number of 25). Initial comparisons between the two data sets indicate the original and revised ADS share common properties and are considered by the authors to be "operationally equivalent."

At all levels of analysis of the ADS, concern must be directed toward the accuracy of the self-reported symptoms. Analysis of the internal structure of the ADS suggests that it serves best as a measure of the signs of perceived physical disability resulting from alcohol use and withdrawal and concomitant psychological distress. However, high correlations between self-reported drinking behavior and behavioral control and independent measures of Social Desirability suggest that patients are routinely less candid on these items. Although the authors acknowledge that use of the ADS "demands caution" because of the correlations with Social Desirability, they conclude that such effects are inevitable if items are going to retain content validity.

Additional validational efforts undertaken in Toronto have raised similar concern regarding the adequacy of patient report as a measure of private perceptions. Although the authors do cite evidence for a solid relationship between alcohol dependence as measured by the ADS and alcohol-related disabilities (i.e., with correlations approximating .70), the scale appears less adequate as an index of perceived psychological and social disabilities than of physical ones. Such a finding might be better accounted for in terms of patients' greater facility in externalizing responsibility for ill health than in admitting limited self-control or emotional difficulties.

The most encouraging signals for the utility of the ADS appear to be found in the authors' claims of its ability to successfully predict patterns of help-seeking behavior among a "socially stable" sample of problem drinkers. The authors found that those problem drinkers who report high levels of alcohol dependence are more willing to admit a need for a firm, restrictive treatment program than are a similarly constituted group of drinkers who report lower levels of alcohol dependence. Unfortunately, the tenuous relationship between insight and behavior may account for the increased tendency for self-reported highly alcohol-dependent patients to fail to keep their initial treatment appointments.

On the other hand, problem drinkers reporting low to moderate levels of alcohol dependence are more likely to deny the need for programs of abstinence in favor of a controlled drinking approach to treatment. Among this sample, however, it is those who acknowledge moderate dependence who appear more likely to demonstrate sustained motivation to comply with controlled drinking programs (i.e., compared to those acknowledging only low levels of dependence). The authors report these effects to be present in follow-up assessments of up to 2 years.

Overall, the ADS offers an opportunity to sample an array of physical, social, and psychological consequences reported by problem drinkers. However, it is clear from the research that this self-report measure is limited in its ability to depict actual behavior or private perceptions of such behavior. In point of fact, the ADS seems to accurately depict only perceived physical symptoms and disability. The authors' contentions aside that examiner skill can limit patient deceptiveness, the private beliefs of problem drinkers regarding social, behavioral, and psychological consequences of drinking are heavily masked by social demand characteristics when they are asked to make their beliefs public on the ADS.

While validity of the scale as a measure of the alcohol dependence construct remains largely undemonstrated, the ADS' ability to predict motivation for treatment and treatment response is encour-

aging. It is a frequently offered speculation that degree of motivation is associated with alcohol treatment outcome. Equally common, however, are disagreements regarding identifying the best measure of motivational level. To the extent the ADS depends on the willingness of the problem drinker to acknowledge a number of the consequences of alcohol abuse, it may serve as a vehicle by which a patient may "project" his/her level of openness to treatment. In combination with other data about an individual's drinking history, environmental determinants, and therapist and treatment attributes, the ADS may well serve as a useful component of a multifaceted assessment of alcoholism.

REVIEWER'S REFERENCE

American Psychiatric Association. (1987). Diagnostic and statistical manual of mental disorders (3rd ed. rev.). Washington, DC Author.

Review of the Alcohol Dependence Scale by NICK J. PIAZZA, Department of Counselor Education, The University of Toledo, Toledo, OH:

The Alcohol Dependence Scale (ADS) was derived from the larger Alcohol Use Inventory. The Alcohol Use Inventory is based on a "multidimensional" conceptualization of alcoholism that includes many different types or styles of alcoholic drinking behavior. One such type of alcoholic use identified in the Alcohol Use Inventory was the alcohol dependence syndrome, which is characterized by impaired control over alcohol consumption, increased tolerance for the effects of alcohol, presence of withdrawal symptoms when alcohol consumption is discontinued, compulsion to drink excessively, and alcohol-seeking behavior. The ADS was developed to provide a brief, yet "psychometrically sound measure of this syndrome."

Skinner and Horn (1984) complain that too often alcohol dependence is thought of as a dichotomous condition, that is, either someone is alcohol dependent or they are not. The ADS is designed to reflect the authors' contention that the alcohol-dependence syndrome exists in "degrees rather than as an all-or-none state." The authors cite numerous research articles to support their belief that alcohol dependence is developmental and that it progresses from the merely "psychologically involved" to impaired control over alcohol use. Consequently, the authors intend for the ADS to be used not only to identify the presence of the alcohol-dependence syndrome, but also to provide a "brief measure of the extent to which the use of alcohol has progressed from psychological involvement to impaired control."

Skinner and Horn attribute much of the theoretical foundation for the alcohol-dependence syndrome to work done initially by Edwards and Gross, and the authors appear to have made every effort to develop items that reflect this theoretical orientation. Concurrent validity seems adequate, with the authors reporting a correlation of .69 with scores on the Michigan Alcoholism Screening Test (MAST). This finding strongly suggests that the items on the ADS are, in fact, a measure of problematic drinking.

The authors report very favorable reliabilities for their instrument. They report an internal-consistency (alpha) reliability of .92 and test-retest reliability of .92 as well. Based on these reliability coefficients, the authors claim that "one may have considerable confidence that the ADS will exhibit substantial reliability with individuals who are seeking treatment for their alcohol-related problems."

While the authors identify several uses for the ADS, it is obvious they foresee its greatest use in predicting "compliance with abstinence versus controlled drinking goals." Skinner and Horn cite ample research data to indicate that persons scoring in the low to moderate ranges on the ADS would be more likely to accept and comply with controlled-drinking goals and reject treatments based on total abstinence than persons who score in the higher ranges. The results reported by the authors would appear to support using the ADS in differential diagnosis and treatment planning.

Since Skinner and Horn intend for the ADS to be used in a variety of treatment settings with persons presenting a range of alcohol dependence, they recognize that no single norm group would be sufficient. Consequently, they provide normative data on both outpatient and inpatient groups as well as samples of individuals assigned to both controlled drinking and abstinence-oriented treatment conditions. Consistent with their intent that the instrument be used to determine appropriate treatment goals based on degree of measured dependence, the authors provide an ADS interpretation guide to assist the professional in using the results obtained.

The ADS consists of a 25-item Alcohol Use Questionnaire and a User's Guide. The items, which are multiple forced-choice, are easy to read, have from two to four alternatives, and come in a booklet with clear instructions. Administration is estimated to take about 10 minutes. The questionnaire could be given to groups or individuals and could just as easily be given as an oral interview. The questionnaires appear to be relatively inexpensive and would fit easily into a client or patient record.

The documentation provided in the User's Guide consists of background information on the ADS and on the concept of alcohol dependence as well as all the necessary information to score and interpret the instrument. The materials are clear, and pertinent information is easy to find. Procedures for scoring the questionnaire and for scaling the raw scores are fairly straightforward and adequately documented. Scaled scores are presented as percentiles, z scores, and T scores.

Skinner and Horn claim several advantages to using the ADS: (a) The ADS is well-grounded theoretically, (b) the ADS gives an index of the degree of alcohol dependence, (c) the ADS is brief and easy to administer and interpret, (d) the ADS appears to possess high reliability and validity, and (e) the ADS is useful as both a diagnostic and a research tool.

There are, however, several limitations inherent in the questionnaire. Limitations would include: (a) The items on the questionnaire seem to be vulnerable to deception or poor recall, (b) too much emphasis may be given to the instrument in treatment planning or in setting treatment goals, and (c) research does not yet seem to be adequate to support any rules for making treatment-planning decisions.

Overall, the ADS appears to be a sound instrument to use clinically as part of a more complete survey of drug and alcohol use. It would also appear to be very useful in evaluating the appropriateness of treatment referrals and program effectiveness with different types of clients. Having instruments such as the ADS available will become increasingly important in determining which groups of individuals respond best to which treatments and in justifying admissions to very expensive and restrictive programs.

[1.7]
Alcohol Use Disorders Identification Test.

Purpose: A screening procedure "to identify persons whose alcohol consumption has become hazardous or harmful to their health."
Population: Adults.
Publication Date: 1992.
Acronym: AUDIT.
Scores, 2: Core, Clinical.
Administration: Individual or group.
Price Data, 1996: Test and manual (33 pages) are free; $75 per training module.
Time: [2] minutes.
Comments: Developed by World Health Organization and validated on primary care patients in six countries; available in English, Japanese, Spanish, Norwegian, and Romanian.
Authors: Thomas F. Babor, Juan Ramon de la Fuente, John Saunders, and Marcus Grant.
Publisher: World Health Organization [Switzerland]; also available from Thomas F. Babor.

This test has not been reviewed in *The Mental Measurements Yearbook.*

[1.8]
Alcohol Use Inventory.

Purpose: "To assess the nature of an individual's alcohol use pattern, and problems associated with that pattern."
Population: Adults suspected of problem drinking.
Publication Date: 1987.
Acronym: AUI.
Scores, 24: Social Improvement, Mental Improvement, Manage Moods, Marital Coping, Gregarious, Compulsive, Sustained, Loss of Control, Role Maladaptation, Delirium, Hangover, Marital Problems, Quantity, Guilt and Worry, Help Before, Receptivity, Awareness, Enhanced, Obsessed, Disruption 1, Disruption 2, Anxious Concern, Receptive Awareness, Alcohol Involvement.
Administration: Group.
Price Data, 1991: $18.85 per 10 reusable test booklets; $21.95 per hand-scoring key; $5.65 per 25 hand-scored answer sheets; $6.95 per Profile Report; $13.50 per Interpretive Report; $5.45 per 25 profile sheets; $11.95 per manual ('87, 95 pages); $8.50 per Interpretive Report User's Guide.
Time: (35–60) minutes.
Comments: Reports are available via immediate on-site microcomputer scoring as well as through a mail-in scoring service.
Authors: John L. Horn, Kenneth W. Wanberg, and F. Mark Foster.
Publisher: National Computer Systems, Inc.
Cross References: Reviews by Robert J. Drummond and Sharon McNeely originally appeared in 12:25 (3 references).

Review of the Alcohol Use Inventory by ROBERT J. DRUMMOND, Professor of Counselor Education, University of North Florida, Jacksonville, FL:

The Alcohol Use Inventory (AUI) is a self-report inventory designed to assess patterns of behavior, attitudes, and symptoms pertaining to the use of alcohol of individuals 16 years of age or older who drink to some extent. It was developed for use with individuals admitted to an alcoholism treatment program. The AUI is not appropriate for use with individuals who do not drink. The AUI reflects the multiple condition theory about drinking problems and has evolved from numerous research studies originally begun in the 1960s and from previous instruments such as the Alcohol Use Questionnaire (Horn, Skinner, Wanberg, & Foster, 1984) and the Alcohol Use Inventory (Horn, 1974) known as the Drinking History Questionnaire.

The current (1987) edition of the AUI has several new features. There are three new scales: RECEPTIVE, AWARENESS, and RECPAWAR. The scale concerning the use of nonalcohol drugs was deleted. The arrangements of the scales have been altered and some of the scales renamed. Some experimental items that have been added for research purposes are not utilized in the scoring of any of the scales. Different norms are also mentioned as a new feature. Overall, there are 24 scales that assess dimensions of behavior at three different levels: primary, second-level, and third-level.

The scales appear to be reasonably associated with problem drinking. The Primary Scales focus on the "benefits," "styles," "consequences," and "concerns and acknowledgments" of drinking; for example, SOCIALIM (drink to improve sociability), MENTALIM (drink to improve mental functioning), MANGMOOD (drink to manage mood), MARICOPE (drink to deal with marital problems), GREGARUS (drink in bars, parties, with friends) and the like. There are six second-level scales derived from factor analysis of the relationships among the primary scales; for example, OBSESSED (obsessive, compulsive, sustained drinking).

Factor analysis was used to construct the scales of the AUI. The authors, however, do not present the results of the factor analysis in the manual or provide a matrix of the intercorrelations among the items or primary scales.

The AUI presents internal consistency reliabilities and test-retest information on the scales from a number of different years and groups. The third-level scale and second-level scales have higher coefficients than the primary scales as expected. Of the Primary Scales, QUANTITY has the lowest coefficient. Most of the reliability coefficients range from .65 to .80 for the scales.

Point-biserial correlations are presented to report gender and age differences rather than the more traditional T or F comparisons. A review of the data suggests there should be separate sex norms and norms by age levels. Comparisons are presented among Native Americans, White, African Americans, and Hispanic groups with F ratios given but no multiple comparison results presented to show between which groups the differences were found. There is not a good demographic description of the makeup of the norming group. No standard errors of measurement are given for the scales. The manual authors provide the user with salient information on interpreting the scale and on the BSCS approach (Benefits, Styles, Consequences, and Concerns) associated with the use and abuse of alcohol. A sample computerized report is also presented. The manual is not especially user friendly. There are a number of gaps in the information presented in the manual as previously indicated. The information in the manual is a justification of the approaches used rather than a translation of the information in a way counselors and psychologists could use to better understand the concepts.

Overall, the AUI has as its aim "to obtain measurements that are useful with different kinds of people (are hardy), have satisfactory breadth (bandwidth), adequate internal consistency (fidelity), genuine independence and appropriate stability over time" (manual, p. 22). The AUI appears to have made good progress in meeting these goals and is based on sound research and development. Counselors will find this a useful assessment tool when working with individuals with alcohol problems.

REVIEWERS REFERENCES

Horn, J. L. (1974). Alcohol Use Inventory. Washington, DC: U.S. Patent Office.

Horn, J. L., Skinner, H. A., Wanberg, K. W., & Foster, F. M. (1984). Alcohol Use Questionnaire (AUQ). Toronto, Canada: Addiction Research Foundation.

Review of the Alcohol Use Inventory by SHARON McNEELY, *Associate Professor of Educational Foundations, Northeastern Illinois University, Chicago, IL:*

The Alcohol Use Inventory (AUI) evolved out of research that sought to provide a multiple-condition assessment of alcohol-related problems. The AUI is designed to provide operational indicators to describe patterns of alcohol use, allowing mental health workers to identify and understand different kinds of alcoholics.

The AUI has 24 scales, three new to this edition. Sixteen of the 17 primary scales rely on responses to less than 10 items (range 3–9) for analysis. The six second-level scales have 11 to 21 items each. The third (broad) scale relies on responses to 40 items. In all, there are 228 self-report items which are answered "Yes" or "No" or with selected frequencies of behaviors.

The primary scales provide four separate domains related to drinking behaviors. The benefits domain provides explanations as to why the respondent drinks. The styles domain shows where and when drinking occurs. The consequences domain presents results the drinker faces. The concerns and acknowledgements domain allows the respondent to admit to feelings associated with the drinking and ways help has been sought and is currently desired.

The second-level scales are not merely combinations of the primary scales, but are derived from factor analysis of the primary scales' relationships. The ENHANCED scale represents benefits of using alcohol. The OBSESSED scale presents the general drinking style of the respondent. The DISRUPT1 scale presents the consequences of drinking in terms of disruptions. Most of the items in this scale are frequently measured indicators of signs of alcoholism. The respondent may recognize and lie about these items so to not seem alcoholic. The DISRUPT2 scale also indicates uncontrolled life disruption. It provides less typical indicators of alcoholism and thus may provide more honest responses. The ANXCONCN scale measures fears and other feelings about drinking. The RECPAWAR scale shows self-awareness of drinking problems.

The third-level factor measures broad involvement with alcohol on the ALCINVOL scale. This may be used as a general indicator of alcohol-related problems.

The manual authors state that most people 16 years of age or older can read and understand the language of the test. Ideally the respondent should be alcohol-free for 8 hours or more before test administration. The respondent should be able to complete the items in 35–60 minutes. With careful reading, the instruction page may take a couple of minutes to read. Although most of the items may be readable for those 16 years and older, they require absolute honesty and a good memory for completion. If the respondent ponders items or has difficulty in reading, completion may take longer than one hour.

Because so many of the items clearly define alcohol as a problem in the item stem, the respondent may be hesitant to answer honestly for fear of being portrayed as a chronic alcoholic. Some of the items also have problems in that the possible responses do not agree with the stems, (e.g., some items should begin with "How often" instead of "Have you").

The AUI is clearly labeled as a test in bold on the cover and title pages, which may lead some respondents to believe there is a best or correct answer. The title page descriptor does not clarify this, for those who may, having taken other tests, skip the instructions page.

The internal consistency reliabilities and test-retest reliabilities are both good across all but two scales (QUANTITY—amount consumed, and MARIPROB—marital problems resulting from drinking). In addition to the scales being fairly stable as long as the respondent's circumstances remain relatively the same, the scales also have good operational independence.

The authors suggest the AUI has strong content validity because only content relevant for decision making in treatment programs was included. The lack of further clarification as to types of treatment programs and types of decisions that relate to the content raise questions about the appropriateness of this validity for decision making. The criterion validity (criterion of alcohol dependence) is also supported. Correlates with the Michigan Alcoholism Screening Test (Selzer, 1971) vary considerably by scale, as would be expected. The manual author provides information for hand scoring and guidelines for interpretation and clinical use. The interpretations are provided in general only for high scale scores, thereby limiting other interpretations and clinical uses. Most of the

norming and supportive studies have involved primarily Caucasians, possibly limiting applicability to other groups.

In summary, the AUI is one way for a clinician to obtain information about the multiple dimensions of alcoholism in clients who are fairly capable, honest, and cooperative. The AUI seems to have good reliability and validity, and to be appropriate for use with Caucasian populations. Lack of information about use with other populations should encourage cautious use and interpretation until further studies are undertaken.

REVIEWER'S REFERENCE

Selzer, M. L. (1971). The Michigan Alcoholism Screening Test: The quest for a new diagnostic instrument. *American Journal of Psychiatry, 127,* 1653–1658.

[1.9]
The American Drug and Alcohol Survey.

Purpose: Designed to estimate levels of drug use in schools.
Population: Schools and school districts.
Publication Dates: 1989–1990.
Scores: Item scores only.
Administration: Group.
Levels, 2: Grades 4–6, Grades 6–12 and college.
Price Data: Available from publisher.
Time: (20–30) minutes.
Comments: Results tabulated by publisher.
Authors: Eugene R. Oetting, Frederick Beauvais, and Ruth Edwards.
Publisher: Rocky Mountain Behavioral Science Institute, Inc.
Cross References: See T4:155 (1 reference); reviews by Jeffrey Jenkins and Steven Schinke originally appeared in 12:27.

Review of the American Drug and Alcohol Survey by JEFFREY JENKINS, Attorney, Narvaez & Jenkins, P.A., Albuquerque, NM:

The American Drug and Alcohol Survey (ADAS) was developed to identify the nature and extent of substance abuse among children and adolescents, and is intended for use by communities and local school districts. Different forms are available for children (grades 4–6) and adolescents (grades 6–12). In addition to the questionnaire itself, the publisher of the ADAS provides analysis and reporting of the results, as well as considerable support for public presentation and dissemination of the results. As a survey, the ADAS is not intended to provide a measure of an individual's drug or alcohol use, but an overall picture of the patterns of substance abuse within a local community.

The adolescent form of the ADAS consists of 57 multipart items in a Likert scale or yes/no format. The items are presented on an easy-to-read four-page computer-scannable form. The form collects some demographic information on each respondent (grade, age, sex, ethnicity) for use in reporting categorical results. The first 15 items request information about alcohol use, including how often alcohol was used and where such use occurred. Questions on the extent of alcohol use are also included, as well as whether drinking ever caused the respondent any of a series of problems, including legal, financial, school, or family problems. The remainder of the items address drug use. The items progress from questions about marijuana and inhalants to stimulants, narcotics, and steroids. Several questions also ask about the use of specific drugs such as amphetamines, crack, LSD, and heroin. Three items address tobacco usage.

The children's form of the ADAS consists of 39 items on both sides of a single computer-scannable form. The items are stated clearly in language appropriate for children, and address the use of alcohol, marijuana, inhalants, tobacco, and crack. Several items on the children's form, as well as on the adolescent form, deal with peer issues, such as "How much would your friends try to stop you from getting drunk?"; "How many of your friends use marijuana?"; and "How often have your friends asked you to sniff something to get high?"

The ADAS provides users with extensive analysis and reporting services. The results for the adolescent survey are delivered in a three-ring binder with tabbed sections labeled Executive Summary, Detailed Reports, Media Kit, Resource Guide, and Survey. The results of the survey are reported in descriptive text, tables of percentage breakdowns, and pie charts, and are presented in three parts. The first part is a brief overview of drug and alcohol use among respondents, addressing how many students have tried drugs, what drugs they have used, and the extent or amount of such use. Students at each grade level are also classified at "High Risk," "Moderate Risk," or "Low Risk" from their drug or alcohol use. The second part summarizes students' "experiences and attitudes regarding drugs and alcohol" (manual, p.

15) and analyzes the availability and opportunity for drug use, and the attitudes of students about the harmfulness and problems involved in drug use. Part 3 discusses the use of individual drugs, and provides a brief description of the various drugs surveyed. The report for the children's form follows a different, somewhat simplified format, but provides similar information.

The Media Kit is also a useful part of the report. It includes a presentation script that can be adapted for presentation of the results in a local community, and provides transparencies of pie charts and bar graphs summarizing the results.

The report binder for the ADAS briefly described the reliability and validity of the survey. The publishers generally report performing approximately 40 "consistency checks" among pairs of items in the survey to detect random or otherwise inaccurate responses. They also report an internal consistency coefficient to be approximately .80 "for the 12 major drug categories" (p. 2, Survey section of manual). Although the publishers correctly note that .80 is satisfactory for this type of measure, it is not clear how the coefficient is arrived at or what the reliability of the discrete areas of the survey are. Given the generally responsible and professional manner in which the survey appears to have been developed, this shortcoming in accurately reporting separate reliability estimates as well as a reliability coefficient for the full survey should be remedied. The publisher also addresses the validity of the ADAS by discussing protections taken against false responses, an area of clear concern in a survey of this type. These protections include listing a "fake drug" on the survey, as well as flagging unusual patterns of reported drug use. The publisher also states that "extensive research" has been done "on the relationships of the drug use questions to the questions on student characteristics and attitudes" (p. 3, Survey section of the manual). The publisher should summarize some of this research and make available any technical reports or papers resulting from this work. In addition, the publisher notes that results obtained from the ADAS are similar to those obtained from other drug and alcohol surveys, including the University of Michigan National Senior Survey. No specific comparative data are reported, however. Without more information about these studies, it is not possible to make a conclusive determination about the validity of the ADAS.

Despite these shortcomings in ascertaining the technical characteristics for the ADAS, the survey appears to be a well-constructed and useful tool for assessing the drug and alcohol use of students. A particular strength of the survey is its clear and understandable analysis and summary of the results. School districts should find the ADAS beneficial in assessing the extent of substance abuse among young people in their local communities.

Review of the American Drug and Alcohol Survey by STEVEN SCHINKE, Professor, Columbia University School of Social Work, New York, NY:

The American Drug and Alcohol Survey is a self-report, paper-and-pencil questionnaire intended for anonymous administration to students in the 4th through 12th grades. Survey items ask students about their drug and alcohol use and the frequency and intensity of their current drug and alcohol use. With the responses to the survey's questions, it is possible to describe the adolescents' drug-use type (multi-drug user, occasional drug user, etc.) and to determine their risk level for future drug use. Other questions help determine when students are first experimenting with substances and where students are using substances most frequently (school, parties, home). This information is critical for intervention. Data gleaned by the survey also help drug and alcohol programs determine the nature and extent of substance use in the schools and community. Such knowledge is necessary for successful community campaigns against adolescent substance abuse.

The American Drug and Alcohol Survey has for years effectively measured substance abuse among children and adolescents. Chief among the strengths of the survey are its ease of delivery, conciseness, and documented reliability and validity. The authors validate consistency in survey responses by asking about each drug several different times. Consistency checks are made 40 times during data analyses; students who report two or more inconsistencies are deleted from the report data.

Other safeguards in the survey detect erroneous or exaggerated responses. For example, the survey includes "fake" drugs to detect exaggeration. The authors found that on average only 1.2% of 12th

graders and 3.6% of 8th graders indicated that they used these "fake" drugs. Surveys are also checked for implausible responses, such as the student who reports heroin use but not marijuana use. Reliability coefficients for the drug use scales average around .90. The internal consistency reliability index for the 12 major drug categories is about .80. Further testifying to the reliability of the survey is its production of data that bear a strong similarity to data found in other national surveys.

Besides the actual surveys, the American Drug and Alcohol Survey kit provides tabulation analyses and interpretation of results, multicolored overhead transparencies, press releases, and other user-friendly materials. Such a turn-key operation has obvious advantages. Professional, factual reporting of reliable survey results helps ensure attention to the community-wide problem of adolescent substance abuse. This survey is an excellent measure for assessing substance abuse among adolescents.

[1.10]
ASIST: A Structured Addictions Assessment Interview for Selecting Treatment.

Purpose: To assess alcohol and drug use for the purpose of selecting treatment.
Population: Adults.
Publication Dates: 1984-1990.
Acronym: ASIST.
Scores: 12 sections: Identifying Information, Basic Information, Alcohol Use, Psychoactive Drug Use, Health Screening, Other Life Areas, Previous Treatment, Client Preference for Treatment, Treatment Assessment Summary, Treatment Plan, Actual Referrals, Assessment Worker's Observation.
Administration: Individual.
Price Data, 1994: $25 per 10 questionnaires; $35 per Assessment Handbook ('90, 200 pages).
Foreign Language Edition: Questionnaire available in French.
Time: Administration time not reported.
Author: Addiction Research Foundation.
Publisher: Addiction Research Foundation [Canada].
Cross References: Reviews by Wesley E. Sime and by Nicholas A. Vacc and Gerald A. Juhnke will appear in the 13th MMY.

Review of the ASIST: A Structured Addictions Assessment for Selecting Treatment by WESLEY E. SIME, Professor, University of Nebraska-Lincoln, Lincoln, NE:

The ASIST is a structured interview designed to aid therapists and administrators in determining the severity of need and the best treatment intervention for individuals who exhibit alcohol and/or drug abuse symptoms. The ASIST is more than an instrument, rather it includes a very comprehensive manual that could serve as a procedures model for developing a new program for establishing a community-based referral system.

The instrument itself assesses four different categories that include alcohol use, drug use, physical and emotional health, and "other life" areas. Other life areas include accommodation, family issues, social issues, education/training, work, financial, leisure, and legal concerns. Each of these four areas contains a standard sequence of inquiry that includes questions about "what concerns do you have," "do you feel that you need help" in order to control this area, "what behavioral disturbances do you experience," "how important now is help to you," and finally "what is the severity of the rating" as viewed by the therapist (p. 23). It also includes a determination of all previous treatment, specifically defining which was most helpful. A treatment assessment form elicits the client's preference for treatment compared with the assessment worker's preference for treatment followed by the agreed upon treatment plan (usually a compromise).

The treatment plan contains an assessment of the problem, the goals to be accomplished, the recommended interventions, a specific section for client responsibility and therapist or assessment worker responsibility, and finally, case manager responsibilities. In comparison to other similar instruments, the last three items (listed above) seem to be the most salient elements in structuring a viable treatment plan.

The physical health screening questions include a variety of medical disorders of which two (rheumatic fever and tuberculosis) seem to be irrelevant to substance abuse and others such as the pulmonary disorders related to smoking and/or infectious diseases and the neurological disorders related to long-term substance abuse are notably absent. Certainly this part of the instrument could be more useful if it included a more comprehensive and relevant list of medical disorders related to substance abuse.

The procedural manual for this instrument includes a thorough description of intake assessment references in the community, treatment guidelines, case management, a clinical procedural policy regarding crisis emergencies, withdrawal, and security issues. It also provides an interesting and useful procedure for developing a community resource directory.

The appendix includes three articles on substance use, all of which were published by the Addiction Research Foundation 10–15 years ago, making them somewhat outdated.

My major concern about this instrument is its general utility for others in the field. Unfortunately, the instrument is regionally and nationally specific. The manual is prepared in accordance with statutes from the province of Ontario and the Ministry of Health for Canada. The Ontario Health Insurance program (OHIP) requirements punctuate the entire document and specific terms such as "are useful only in Canada" appear frequently. The spelling of terms (e.g., centre) is generic to the King's English and terms such as HMRI (Health Ministries Regional District Codes) and HSC (homes for special care) in the Ministries of Health and Victorian Order of Nurses are applicable only for current Canadian and/or Ontario users. Standards for blood alcohol content (.08) at the legal limit may not be uniform across other provinces or in some U.S. states where the legal limit is .10. In addition, the limit for percent of alcohol in beer in Ontario is known to be 5% whereas many of the U.S. beers are 3.2%. Finally, there is reference to Canadian laws on patient records.

Demographic questions specify two alternative language response options (French and English only). For more universal usage, Spanish language options should be included. It is unfortunate that the authors did not take the time to prepare a separate version of the workbook and the instrument, which would be applicable to other populations beyond those in Ontario or Canada.

A more serious issue of attending to detail is noted in two sections of the ASIST where typographical errors have apparently persisted throughout the past 10 to 12 years of usage (this instrument came out in 1984 and was edited again in 1989). The word aggressive is misspelled in Section 3.12, and the term "now" was misspelled as "know" in Section 5.6 under physical health. [Editor's note: Both of these errors have been corrected in the most recent printing of the revised version.]

I am very concerned that no data are reported regarding the functional utility of this instrument after 10–12 years of usage. In the ASIST, client recommendations are found on a risk-o-graph (p. 8), which defines the amount of drinks per day against body weight for males and females. There is a criterion line for three different levels of risk, but these have not been defined nor data provided supporting the validity of such criteria. It should also be noted that there are no measures of reliability regarding the instrument and no assessment of the instrument's predictive or construct validity to make appropriate referrals of treatment outcome based on those referrals.

This instrument is hand scored with no extra provision for machine scoring. There is no description of how the instrument was formulated and how it has been revised over the years. Although the validity remains essentially undetermined and there is no way of assessing the advantage of this instrument over other available options in the area of substance abuse, it is, however, a very practical tool for identifying the severity of symptoms for clients. It should be noted that the instrument is designed for case managers and administrators who need a relatively simple and nonclinical device for assessing need for therapy. By using this instrument to make client needs assessments, it would appear that trained and experienced clerical workers could function as well as mental health counselors.

Review of the ASIST: A Structured Addictions Assessment Interview for Selecting Treatment by NICHOLAS A. VACC, Professor and Chairperson, and GERALD A. JUHNKE, Assistant Professor of Counseling and Educational Development, School of Education, The University of North Carolina at Greensboro, Greensboro, NC:

A Structured Addictions Assessment Interview for Selecting Treatment (ASIST) was designed to structure the assessment and referral process for alcohol- and drug-abusing clients and to propose a treatment selection. The ASIST is a structured interview, which includes recommendations at specific points in the interview for possibly administering the Alcohol Dependence Scale (ADS; T4:145) and the Drug Abuse Screening Test (DAST; see the Drug Use Questionnaire, 1.19 this volume), respectively. Also available is an Assessment Handbook, which is equivalent to a technical manual, that includes procedures for addictions assessment/referral services including ASIST.

The interview format provides data relating to 12 areas: Identifying Information (e.g., client name, address), Basic Information (e.g., date of birth, referral source), Alcohol Use (e.g., family drinking history, personal drinking history), Psychoactive Drug Use (e.g., drug types and amounts used), Health Screening (e.g., medical history), Other Life Areas (e.g., relationship, employment, or legal problems), Previous Treatment, Client Preference for Treatment (e.g., client-identified goals), Treatment Assessment Summary, Treatment Plan, Actual Referrals, and Assessment Workers' Observation Form. The same format is used for both males and females. No indication is given within the ASIST or the Assessment Handbook concerning the average completion time for the interview.

The ADS and DAST are independent instruments and are recommended as an element of the ASIST assessment and referral process; these instruments are not included in the ASIST booklet. However, the Assessment Handbook provides both scoring and interpretation guidelines for the use of the ADS and DAST. The instruments appear integral to the ASIST interview process, and they are also available from the agency, Addiction Research Foundation, which produced the Assessment Handbook and the ASIST.

The ADS has 25 questions presented in a multiple-choice self-report format (Personal communication, Linda Omerea, May 17, 1996). Although the purpose of the ADS is not clearly indicated within the Assessment Handbook or the ASIST, it seems to reflect the respondent's alcohol use. The Handbook includes an ADS scoring key and interpretation guide. The ADS score is determined by first matching the client's responses to the respective item scores indicated in the ADS scoring key, and then summing the matching scores to provide an ADS score, which is interpreted using the ADS interpretation guide. This guide is broken into four quartiles and provides a suggested interpretation of alcohol dependence (i.e., low, moderate, substantial, severe) and general clinical guidelines (e.g., "Abstinence is probably the only reasonable treatment goal" [p.H.3.8]).

The DAST is a 20-question screening instrument presented in a dichotomous, yes-no, self-report format. Although the purpose for the administration of the DAST is not specifically stated within the Assessment Handbook of the ASIST, directions given to the client suggest that the instrument will reflect the client's current involvement with drugs other than alcohol. The Handbook contains a sample of the DAST, a scoring scheme, and a DAST scoring table that reports drug-abuse severity ranging from 0 for "None Reported" to 20 for "Severe Level." The score is obtained by summing the number of client scores that correspond with the scoring scheme.

The Assessment Handbook indicates that formal validity studies regarding the ASIST interview procedure have been conducted only on the ADS and DAST, but information regarding these studies is not provided. However, Skinner and Allen (1982) and Ross, Gavin, and Skinner (1990) reported validity and reliability data for the ADS, and Skinner (1983) and Saltstone, Halliwell, and Hayslip (1994) presented validity and reliability estimates for the DAST. Validity estimates range between .06 and .86 for the ADS and the Alcohol-Related Measures items (Horn, Wanberg, & Foster, 1974), and were found to be .69 (Skinner & Allen, 1992) and .79 (Ross, Gavin, & Skinner, 1990) for the ADS and the Michigan Alcoholism Screening Inventory (MAST; 1.24 this volume). Validity estimates range from -.38 to .55 for the DAST and a variety of relevant indices (Skinner, 1983), and a correlation of .41 was found for the DAST and the MAST (Saltstone, Halliwell, & Hayslip, 1994). Reliability estimates for the DAST and ADS are high with both being above .90. Subjects initially used for the development of the DAST (i.e., 223 subjects [Skinner, 1983]) and the ADS (i.e., 225 subjects [Skinner & Allen, 1982]) were volunteers who sought help at the Clinical Institute of the Addiction Research Foundation in Toronto, Canada. The subjects were overwhelmingly male (72% and 80%, respectively); no indications were noted as to ethnic or racial distributions.

The Assessment Handbook was designed for the Canadian Ministry of Health Addictions Services, and a substantial amount of the information and forms included were intended to match the services requirement format of the Canadian Ministry of Health Information Services, thus having limited utility outside such governmental agencies. In general, some sections of the handbook are elementary and limited in usefulness to all but the least experienced addictions professionals. The Assessment Handbook includes suggestions regarding topics such as client cancellations, no-shows, subpoenas, and evening appointments. Yet, omitted in the Assessment Handbook are important topics such as information about the age range and needed reading competencies of clients completing the DAST and ADS.

The authors have attempted to create a broad-spectrum alcohol and other drug-intake procedure to accommodate the assessment of all clients. However, the proposed clinical guidelines are very general and too nonspecific to be of substantial value to most addiction professionals. Also, the print quality of the ASIST is lower than expected for a commercial instrument. Despite these many limitations, the ASIST has some qualities that make it a useful instrument. First, it provides a thorough intake format that requires the joint identification of specific client goals. Second, basic life needs related to health, food, shelter, and social interactions are identified. Third, the treatment assessment summary provides the addictions professional and the client with an "urgency rating." Based upon the client's self-report, this rating indicates the most pressing issues facing the client. Thus, counselor and client can rank order the immediacy of presenting concerns. Fourth, the ASIST provides the client and counselor with a list of identified goals and their corresponding responsibilities. The DAST and ADS appear to hold clinical merit as brief initial assessment tools to provide a measure of alcohol and drug misuse.

In summary, the ASIST interview has some merit, particularly because it addresses a population for which comprehensive instruments are needed. However, it is impossible to judge adequately the potential value of the instrument because of the lack of sufficient information. This instrument could best be classified as being in the research or developmental stage. As an "in-house" procedure to aid an agency in the assessment and referral process for alcohol- and drug-abusing clients, the ASIST offers some promise. Yet, much needs to be done before it reaches the criterion of *The Standards for Educational and Psychological Testing* (American Educational Research Association, American Psychological Association, & National Council on Measurement in Education, 1985).

REVIEWER'S REFERENCES

Horn, J. L., Wanberg, K. W., & Foster, F. M. (1974). The Alcohol Use Inventory. Denver, CO: Center for Alcohol Abuse Research and Evaluation.

Skinner, H. A. (1983). The Drug Abuse Screening Test. *Addictive Behaviors, 7,* 363-371.

Skinner, H. A., & Allen, B. A. (1982). Alcohol dependence syndrome: Measurement and validation. *Journal of Abnormal Psychology, 91,* 199-209.

American Educational Research Association, American Psychological Association, & National Council on Measurement in Education. (1985). *Standards for educational and psychological testing.* Washington, DC: American Psychological Association, Inc.

Ross, H. E., Gavin, D. R., & Skinner, H. A. (1990). Diagnostic validity of the MAST and the Alcohol Dependence Scale in the assessment of DSM-III alcohol disorders. *Journal of Studies on Alcohol, 51,* 506-513.

Saltstone, R., Halliwell, S., & Hayslip, M. A. (1994). A multivariate evaluation of the Michigan Alcoholism Screening Test and the Drug Abuse Screening Test in a female offender population. *Addictive Behaviors, 19,* 455-462.

[1.11]
Assessment of Chemical Health Inventory.

Purpose: "Designed to evaluate the nature and extent of adolescent and adult chemical use and associated problems."

Population: Adolescents, adults.

Publication Dates: 1988–1992.

Acronym: ACHI.

Scores: 9 factors (Chemical Involvement, Alienation, Family Estrangement, Personal Consequence, Depression, Family Support, Social Impact, Self Regard, Family Chemical Use) yielding Total score.

Administration: Individual.

Price Data, 1993: $179.95 per starter set including microcomputer disk containing 25 administrations and user manual ('92, 119 pages); $9 per 10 response forms; $5.75 (sold in multiples of 50) per microcomputer disk to administer and score ACHI; $29.95 per manual.

Time: (15–25) minutes.

Comments: Requires 4th grade reading level; may be taken and scored on computer (or administered on paper); mail-in service available.

Authors: Daniel Krotz, Richard Kominowski, Barbara Berntson, and James W. Sipe.

Publisher: RENOVEX Corporation.

Cross References: Reviews by Philip Ash and Betsy Waterman will appear in the 13th MMY.

Review of the Assessment of Chemical Health Inventory by PHILIP ASH, Director, Ash, Blackstone and Cates, Blacksburg, VA:

The Assessment of Chemical Health Inventory is a 128-item self-administered computer-based instrument intended to assist chemical dependency counselors in evaluating the nature and extent of adolescent and adult substance (alcohol and other drugs) abuse. Both an adolescent form and an adult form are available; both come on disk for computer administration and in a paper-and-pencil machine-scannable version that must be entered into a computer for scoring and analysis. Most of the items in the two versions are identical; a few reflect adolescent/adult differences (e.g., among the biodata items, the adolescent version asks "With whom do you live?" whereas the adult version asks for level of educational attainment).

The first six items inquire as to biographical data (e.g., age, ethnicity, religion, sex, and living arrangements or educational level). The remaining 122 items are cast in a Likert-type five-choice response format (*Strongly Agree* to *Strongly Disagree*), scored in ascending or descending order so that the highest weight is assigned to the most negative or pathological response, yielding higher scores for the more serious abusers. In obtaining composite (factor or subtest) scores, however, each item is differentially weighted, and the factor scores are also differentially weighted to obtain the overall assessment score (user manual, p. 4). The source or method of arriving at these differential weights is not described. The resultant factor scores and the ACHI Assessment Score are transformed to standard scores, which are presented in the Assessment Report.

The computer-generated Assessment Report yields means and standard deviations for the standard scores for 11 measures: ACHI Assessment Score [total], Berntson Social Desirability Scale, and nine "factor" scores including Use Involvement, Personal Consequences, Family Estrangement, Alienation, Social Impact, Family Chemical Use, Self Regard/Abuse, Depression, and Family Support, as well as a Validity Check, a list of Critical Life Items if any of a particular subset of items is responded to in a significantly deviant fashion, a discussion ("ASSESSMENT SCORE") of the meaning of the respondent's ACHI Assessment Score, and a RECOMMENDATION as to further work with the respondent.

According to information received from Dr. James W. Sipe, one of the main authors of the instrument and a member of the staff of RENOVEX, which distributes the inventory, the ACHI is no longer advertised nor included in any catalog, and the company that developed the software is no longer in business. RENOVEX sells copies of administration materials to previous and current users, but apparently no new customers are added.

The main and probably only source of information about the Inventory is contained in the user manual. A computer-based search of the psychological and social sciences literature (January 1974—September 1995) failed to reveal a single reference to the ACHI, or to a book or paper authored by any of the named authors of the Inventory, or even to any reference in which any of them were cited.

For purposes of administration, use, and interpretation, the main parts of the manual include a summary "Characteristics of ACHI" (p. 1); "ACHI: Abstract and Review" (pp. 2–7), outlining general measurement principles with limited reference to any characteristics of the ACHI itself; "ACHI: The Development Stages" (pp. 8–11); "Validation Protocols," describing four "validation" projects (pp. 13–15); "Research and Design" (pp. 16–41); and six sections dealing with actual application: "ACHI Installation," "Administrative Guidelines," "ACHI Tutorial," a sample Assessment Report, "Clinical Interpretation," and "Clinical Applications" (pp. 42–88). The first four sections were apparently written by Dr. Sipe. The "Research and Design" chapter was written by Barbara and Bruce Berntson and Bryan Davis. No authorship is given for the applications sections or chapters.

Overall, the manual is not very well written, including misspellings (e.g., "expirimental" is repeatedly used; "randon" for "random"; "compromising" for "comprising"), and apparent typographical or clerical errors. More importantly, however, there are significant inconsistencies both within the sections authored by Drs. Sipes and by Drs. Berntson et al., and among the differently authored sections.

ITEM SOURCES. We are told (Validation Project 1, p. 13) that "Subject matter experts from Minnesota identified 508 questions assumed to have value in distinguishing among chemical use, abuse, and dependency" *or* that "this study was designed to identify …items, taken from four existing questionnaires consisting of 255 items" (Research and Design, p. 16). Validation Project I involved the

administration of the 508 items to two adolescent samples ($N = 416$), on the basis of which 255 items were selected to have "good construct validity" (p. 13) "through face validation" (p. 9) decided upon by the participating substance abuse counselors.

FACTOR ANALYSES. At least two factor analyses are reported. The first, based upon the 255 items selected by face validity analysis of the original pool of 508 items, yielded (principal components analysis with varimax rotation) 30 (or 29, depending upon who wrote the sections) composites. This was apparently followed by a principal components with varimax rotation of 100 items (how selected?). It should be noted, however, the output of "merely a numerical technique with no direct clinical or substantive significance" (p. 20) was "scrutinized from a clinical perspective in an attempt to achieve composite indices that, while being empirically verified, were also meaningful and of clinical usefulness" (p. 20)! These procedures "culminated in ten composites" (p. 20). However, detailed data are provided for only eight (pp. 22–26), and only nine are included in the assessment report printout.

ITEM DISTRIBUTION. The final instrument contains 128 items on the paper-and-pencil forms, as indicated in the summary sheet. It should be noted, however, that in the Research and Design (R&D) chapter the ACHI is referred to as "a 100 item questionnaire" (p. 16). The item content (of only eight) of the nine "factors," of the Berntson Social Desirability Scale, and of the Critical Life Items, are given in the R&D chapter. Analysis of the list found that at least *26* item numbers did not occur in any of the lists (although some may belong in Factor 7 [Self Regard/Abuse], for which item data were missing). About 80 items were each included in only one of the lists, and about 19 items were each included in two lists. The list for Factor 3 (Family Estrangement) was obviously in error, with the array "8, 23, 26, 27, 30, 21, 23, 27 …." Item 6, a biodata item (adult/Educational Level; adolescent/Family Living Arrangement) was also included in the group of items for Factor 2 (Personal Consequences). To add to the confusion, the factor numbers given with the factor definitions (pp. 40–41) are different from the factor numbers assigned to the "Composite Characteristics" table (Table II, pp. 22–26).

NORMS. The summary (p. 1) indicates case numbers for the samples used: adults/150 nonclinical, 100 clinical; adolescents/1,288 nonclinical, 688 clinical. All the adults came from one (Minneapolis) sample, and the summary agrees with the text. However, the numbers for adolescents came from three samples. Adding the sample numbers for adolescents in these three studies (no study involved both adults and adolescents) yields totals discrepant with those given in the summary: 1,088 nonclinical, 619 clinical. Where the higher numbers in the summary came from is not explained. Furthermore, the user manual contains no norms tables of any sort.

RELIABILITY. The reliabilities reported in the summary are coefficient alpha internal consistency estimates (.74–.94), and based upon data from Validation Research Project II—Salt Lake City (pp. 13–14), which involved administration of a prior 255-item questionnaire to 981 adolescents (851 control and 130 exp*i*rimental [*sic*]). Alpha coefficients were also reported (Table II, pp. 22–26) for eight of the nine factors for a combined sample derived from Validation Project II (Salt Lake City) plus Validation Project III (Detroit, or Michigan). These factor alphas were in about the same range as reported in the summary.

No coefficient alpha data were presented for the adult sample. Furthermore, no other reliability measures (test-retest, alternate forms) are reported in the user manual.

VALIDITY. At least four approaches to validation are claimed in the manual.

The first is "concurrent validity" based on a correlation between a score (ACHI Assessment Score?) and "staff assessment" (p. 1), with $r = .82$. This is mentioned in one line on the summary (p. 1), but not referred to or elaborated upon anywhere else in the manual.

The second is "face validity," apparently based upon the item selection and reduction from 508 to 255 items in Validation Project I (p. 13).

The third is discriminant analysis, done on 29 (p. 14) or 30 (p. 18) "composites," in which percent of correct identification as between clinical and nonclinical samples yielded "hit" rates usually above 90% in Validation Projects II, III, and IV. Discriminant function analysis, however, is a suboptimal approach to validation. As Tatsuoka and

Tiedeman (1954) point out, discriminant function analysis may be used to (a) identify group differences, (b) study and understand such differences, and (c) classify people. There is nothing in the technique that implies prediction, such as a statement that a person with this score will, if untreated, exhibit substance abuse behavior. Rulon (1951) presents a satirical fable about classifying a hexagon as a square or a circle. For most psychological testing purposes, regression equations against appropriate criteria provide a more effective technique (Anastasi, 1988, p. 191). Other substance abuse scales have reported criterion-related validities based upon number of different substances used, frequency of use, incidence of hospitalization or legal offenses while "under the influence," and similar measures. What the summary describes as "concurrent validity" (p. 1) would probably qualify as a criterion-based approach, but no information on the claim cited is available.

The fourth approach to validity claimed by the authors is by way of canonical correlations. Typically, in canonical correlation a correlation matrix of predictors (e.g., test scores) is correlated with a matrix of quantified criteria (observed or rated behaviors) for a defined sample of subjects. The manual authors nowhere describe the input to the canonical correlations reported for Validation Projects III and IV (pp. 14–15), and no mention is made of canonical correlation in the summary. It is this reviewer's understanding, however, that the two correlation matrices used were (a) the correlation matrix among the item responses for the clinical sample and (b) the item intercorrelation matrix for the nonclinical sample. Unlike in its usual application, therefore, the two matrices each consisted of the same variables, but based upon different human samples. The very high (above .90) resulting canonical correlations would therefore be expected, and would not reflect any aspect of the *validity* of the instrument. In fact, it seems to be a methodologically inappropriate use of canonical correlation.

In short, evidence supporting the validity of the ACHI for assessing substance abuse seems to be thin to negligible. The manual contains a Level of Care guide (pp. 82–82), based primarily upon the ACHI Assessment Score, providing "rules of thumb" (p. 82) that range from in-patient candidacy; through out-patient candidacy; to education, counseling, and contracting, but without any explicit data showing why the recommendations move by standard deviations above and below the mean.

In summary, since its inception as a 508-item experimental inventory much effort seems to have been expended in collecting and analyzing sample data on abusers and nonabusers. However, the user manual is poorly organized, carelessly written, and afflicted with many internal inconsistencies. The data supporting reliability and validity concerns are, at best, weak. As noted above, although the summary provides number of cases for norms, no tables of norms are presented in the manual. Self-administration of the ACHI by computer is not difficult, although a couple of glitches were noted in the program as this reviewer took it. The format of the printed assessment report is not easy to follow and far from optimum in design. In this reviewer's opinion current users should take the time to evaluate the instrument again, and possibly consider other inventories such as the Personal Experience Inventory (PEI; T4:1971) (Winters & Henly, 1989), the Chemical Dependency Assessment Survey (Oetting, Beauvais, Edwards, & Waters, 1984), and the Drug Use Screening Inventory (Tarter, 1990).

REVIEWER'S REFERENCES

Rulon, P. J. (1951). The stanine and the separile: A fable. *Personnel Psychology, 4*, 99–114.

Tatsuoka, M. M., & Tiedeman, D. V. (1954). Discriminant analysis. *Review of Educational Research, 24*, 402–420.

Oetting, E., Beauvais, F., Edwards, R., & Waters, M. (1984). The Drug and Alcohol Assessment System. Fort Collins, CO: Rocky Mountain Behavioral Sciences Institute.

Anastasi, A. (1988). *Psychological testing* (6th ed.). New York: Macmillan Publishers.

Winters, K. C., & Henly, G. A. (1989). Personal Experience Inventory. Los Angeles: Western Psychological Services.

Tarter, R. (1990). Evaluation and treatment of adolescent drug abuse: A decision-tree method. *American Journal of Drug and Alcohol Abuse, 16*, 1–46.

Review of the Assessment of Chemical Health Inventory by BETSY WATERMAN, Assistant Professor, Counseling and Psychological Services Department, State University of New York at Oswego, Oswego, NY:

The Assessment of Chemical Health Inventory (ACHI) was developed to assess chemical misuse among adolescents and adults. This instrument is designed to be self-administered and is an attempt to provide a more objective look at chemical use than many other current measures provide. The 128 test items were developed from within a Disease Model theoretical orientation and reflect the criterion outlined in the *DSM-III-R.* It appears there are two forms, one for adolescents and one for adults, although this is not clearly stated in the manual. The authors indicate that approximately 20 minutes is required for administration. Reading level is reported to be at the fourth grade level. Use with special populations (e.g., poor or nonreaders) is discussed briefly and the authors indicate the items can be read aloud to those who cannot read adequately.

Administration procedures are outlined in the manual, including standardized verbal instructions. The inventory can be administered on a computer or by having the individual fill in the appropriate circles on a response form. There are opportunities for practice trials to familiarize the respondent with the computerized format. The manual also includes instruction for using the software program. Testing administration is generally straightforward and requires individuals to respond to a statement, such as, "I use drugs or alcohol to change the way I feel" (p. 35), by selecting from among five choices (*Strongly Disagree, Disagree, No Opinion, Agree,* or *Strongly Agree*). The computer format allows for immediate scoring. The printed profile presents client identifying information, demographic data, and validity checks including "paired opposites" (p. 52) items and the Berntson Social Desirability Scale.

ACHI scores range from 1.00 to 9.00. They are presented on a graph and compared with the means of chemically dependent individuals. "Levels of care" (e.g., inpatient treatment) are suggested in the manual as they relate to the score earned. Scores between 1.00 and 5.07 are considered to be typical ranges of substance use and scores above 6.08 indicate possible need for treatment. Nine factor scores are presented in a profile (Chemical Involvement, Alienation, Family Estrangement, Personal Consequences, Depression, Family Support, Social Impact, Self-Regard, and Family Chemical Use) and compared to the means of nonclinical groups. Critical items (e.g., suicidal ideation) that may require immediate attention are also identified on the printout.

The ACHI was constructed and validated in four separate phases and in four locations: Minnesota, Salt Lake City, Detroit, and Minneapolis, respectively. During Phase I, 508 original items were identified by experts in the chemical dependency field. Subjects ranged in age between 14 and 20 years and were in outpatient (N = 116) or inpatient (N = 300) treatment programs. Of the original 508 items, 255 were identified by the authors as having good "construct" validity, although it appears they are actually referring to face validity in this case.

In Phases II to IV, validity studies were conducted in which the ACHI was used to distinguish between users and nonusers of chemical substances. A total of 981 adolescents between the ages of 13 and 18 provided the sample in Phase II. It was not clear how gender and racial groups were reflected in experimental and control samples. Three hundred and ten adolescents, aged 13 to 18, served as the sample in Phase III with equal numbers of white and black subjects reflected in the pool. Two hundred and fifty adults participated in Phase IV. It should be noted that the control sample in this final phase included 150 individuals attending a community college. No age range or mean was given for this group of individuals. This sample may not be very different in age than the upper end of the previous adolescent group samples. The ACHI was reported as able to classify correctly 94% to 99% of nonusers and 74% to 88% of those who were chemically dependent.

Data from both Salt Lake City and Michigan were combined and analyzed, and, according to the authors, resulted in 10 composites or factors. Only 8 were reported in the validation study itself: Chemical Use Involvement, Social Impact, Personal Consequence, Family Chemical Use, Family Estrangement, Depression, Alienation, and Family Support. A ninth factor is reported elsewhere in the manual as Self Regard/Abuse. Cronbach alphas and standardized item alphas for the ACHI ranged between .74 and .94 across items within factors. There was no information about test-retest reliability in the manual.

The ACHI is an instrument designed to identify individuals who are chemically dependent. It is easy to administer and can be taken on a computer allowing for quick scoring and interpretation. Although the instrument appears to have an adequate ability to discriminate substance users from nonusers, a number of annoying problems exist. The manual is difficult to use and appears to have been constructed in a fragmented way. Information regarding the norming samples was extremely hard to follow and terms such as face validity and construct validity appear incorrectly used. The manual is not integrated into a coherent format, omits key pieces of information (such as the years when the validation studies were completed), and includes conflicting pieces of information. Numbers do not add up and clear explanations regarding missing data are not included. Although not conceptually problematic, numerous misspellings and typographical errors are distracting.

The computer-assisted feature is appealing but the software is outdated. The software included with the instrument was available on a 5.25-inch floppy disk that will run only on older IBM or compatible PCs. Most 486 and Pentium computers cannot use the current disk included in the package. The directions assume that the computer boots up on a floppy drive, which is not consistent with most modern computers and, overall, instructions were not easily generalizable to different computer setups. The authors would be encouraged to include both size disks (3.5-inch and 5.25-inch) with the test manual and it would be useful to have Windows, DOS, and Macintosh versions available.

In spite of the annoying problems related to this instrument the instrument appears to have been reasonably well constructed. Although norming information is confusing, it does seem that the instrument is effective in discriminating between users and nonusers a majority of the time. Problems related to "faking good" exist with this instrument as they do with other measures of this type, and it is unlikely that the ACHI has overcome this difficult problem. Overall, this instrument appears to have value in identifying those who are chemically dependent as well as determining possible family, social, or emotional factors that may be negatively impacting upon the individual. Revising the manual, integrating and extending the norming information, and updating the computer software would enhance this instrument's utility.

[1.12]
The Child "At Risk" for Drug Abuse Rating Scale.

Purpose: "Seeks to assess risk factors for later drug abuse."

Population: Preschool–grade 6.
Publication Date: 1990.
Acronym: DARS.
Scores, 4: Developmental History, Family Relations, Child Behavior Pattern, Total.
Administration: Individual.
Price Data, 1990: $11 per manual (20 pages); $25 per program with diskette.
Time: (15) minutes.
Comments: Program designed to run on PC XT-like computer with a minimum of 256K of memory.
Author: Russell N. Cassel.
Publisher: Psychologists and Educators, Inc.
Cross References: Reviews by Ernest A. Bauer and Richard B. Stuart originally appeared in 12:70.

Review of The Child "At Risk" for Drug Abuse Rating Scale by ERNEST A. BAUER, Research, Evaluation and Testing Consultant, Oakland Schools, Waterford, MI:

The Child "At Risk" for Drug Abuse Rating Scale (DARS) "seeks to assess risk factors for later drug abuse" (p. 3). The "manual" presents a series of largely unsubstantiated assertions ("Timing of corrective action in relation to hazards from development and family relations is the most critical for fostering success"), circular arguments ("Drug abuse and deviant behavior are so closely allied, that when one predicts for one, it serves as an equally valid prediction for the other. It is not conceivable that one could be involved in drug abuse, and still not be involved in deviant behavior"), seemingly pointless analogies ("By the same logic, one would not say that a person born with a crippled hand is unable to type"), and philosophical meanderings ("The best way to deal with any problem, to be sure, is to prevent it from happening"). At one point, under the side-head "Drug Using Society," the reader is asked, "Could you be this kind of role model as a parent?" On page 15, the manual completely loses the at-risk for drug abuse theme and begins discussing language disorder clinics and never returns to the original theme. Two poems are printed on the inside and outside of the back cover, "Myself," and "Cocaine," respectively.

The "rating scale" is administered via a microcomputer. The approach is archaic, the entry redundant and irritating. Putting this rating scale on a microcomputer did nothing to improve it.

The rating scale contains 60 items that reflect developmental history, family relations, and behavior pattern. Each area is represented by 20 yes-no questions. Many of the "items" are standard sociological questions about family structure and relationships (divorce, separation, abuse, etc.) and developmental items about complications at delivery, development of bladder and bowel control, walking, talking, etc. Others seem idiosyncratic. "Were child's teeth scrubbed regularly?" "Did mother often hug and even kiss child?" "Did child dislike father?"

Several items try to deal with both school age and preschool age children in a unique way. For example, "Did child dislike school, if under 6 dislike home?" "Did child fail kindergarten or 1st grade? (retained in grade) if under 6, did child fight going to sleep?" "Does child fail to complete homework for school, or if under 6, refuse to play by self?" "Does child dislike arithmetic, if under 6, refuse to play with other children?" The user has entered the child's age, the computer program could easily ask the appropriate question, but, more importantly, one is left wondering if these alternative questions are "equivalent." "Six different levels of at risk for drug abuse serve as the norm reference, ranging from 'low risk level' to 'Crisis State'" (pp. 6–7). There may be some kind of "norms," because the scales are reported as "T-like" scores that range from approximately 10 through 100. This reviewer entered fake data that reached these extremes; however, the scale on the margin of the computer generated report ranges from 20 to 80. The program offers reports that purport to use general, female, male, "professional," and "Hispanic" norms, although neither the professional nor the Hispanic norms would function on the disk the reviewer received. There are absolutely no data about the norm groups or the distributions of scores. One cannot tell if there are age or grade norms within the sets of norms offered. There is no information about how the bounds of the "six at risk levels" were determined. There is no mention of reliability. There are no data about predictive or concurrent validity. There is not a single correlation coefficient or other descriptive statistic in the entire "manual." In short, there appears to be absolutely no attempt to assure potential users that the collection of items has any psychometric properties whatsoever.

The author describes the current version as "experimental." Given the complete lack of information available about the psychometric characteristics of the rating scale, it should not be used in its present form.

Review of The Child "At Risk" for Drug Abuse Rating Scale by RICHARD B. STUART, Professor Emeritus, Department of Psychiatry and Behavioral Sciences, School of Medicine, University of Washington, Seattle, WA:

The Child "At Risk" for Drug Abuse Rating Scale (DARS) is a risk assessment tool intended for use by adults who are interested in assessing the risk of drug use by school-age children, essentially in kindergarten through sixth grade. It contains 60 true/false items accessible on a 5.25-inch floppy drive which can be run on XT or later model IBM-compatible computers. The questions pertain to various aspects of the parents' demographic characteristics (e.g., married at time of child's birth, prison records, etc.), the circumstances of the subject child's delivery (e.g., prematurity) and development (e.g., walking, toilet training landmarks), aspects of the child's habit patterns (e.g., nailbiting), and aspects of the child's interaction with each parent during early developmental years (e.g., hugged by father and/or mother). Most of the answers to these questions require data from the parent who, along with professionals, are the intended users of this instrument. The 60 items are equally divided between three subscales: Developmental History, Family Relations, and Behavioral Pattern, although the specific items assigned to each category are not identified. A printout in the form of a histogram provided a "t-like score" (p. 20) description of the level of risk in the three categories, as well as yielding an overall risk rating. Risks are assigned one of six levels, from low through "crisis state," although the cutoff points for three of the levels are somewhat overlapping.

The manual stipulates that this instrument (published in 1990) is in "experimental form" (p. 5). As such, it must be assessed as an instrument in process rather than as a finished tool. A great many flaws mar the DARS, all of which would require correction before its use can be recommended.

The 20-page typescript manual is flawed by a great many omissions. After a cursory review of the nature of preventive programming, the manual identifies "gate-way drugs" including coffee, ciga-

rettes, tea, and chocolate as well as marijuana, which is identified as a "hard-core" drug. Drugs are dichotomized between stimulants and depressants, with hallucinogens presumably, but not explicitly, classified in one of these categories. As an even more serious omission, alcohol is not mentioned in this manual.

As is true throughout this manual, research findings are not cited to justify the inclusion or exclusion of various risk factors, or the weights, if any, assigned to each factor. Those for whom psychodiagnosis is a concern will find difficulty with the author's discussion of "character disorders," not in Axis II terms as one might expect, but in such categories as "disturbed home conditions" and "inability to use leisure time." In addition, the utility of assignment to one of the six risk levels is compromised by the fact that the highly general action recommendations suffer from considerable overlap.

The manual contains no data pertaining to the statistical stability or clinical utility of the DARS. Data are not presented to support the factorial independence of the three clusters of risk factors. Alpha coefficients are not presented to support the internal consistency of each class of risk factors. Neither test-retest and related forms of reliability nor validity (as in demonstrating the accuracy with which subsequent drug use is predicted by the risk levels assigned) are addressed as a means of assessing the coherence of the subscales.

The absence of appropriate statistical evaluation is sufficient reason to discourage use of the DARS. But other problems should be mentioned. The manual contains undocumented lists of apparent signs of drug abuse, a great many of which might as likely be symptoms of physical or psychological illness, posing the risk that serious physical illnesses might be overlooked. In addition, parents are perhaps the primary end-users of this product. Equipped with this apparently professional diagnostic information, they may take useful preventive steps. But they are also at risk of taking highly unproductive actions based upon inferences with unproven diagnostic or therapeutic value. For example, although the manual stipulates that risk level does not equate with use level, this qualification is apt to be overlooked by concerned parents. Because of the fact that access to the DARS is unrestricted, great care should have been taken to guard against misinterpretation by nonprofessionals, a risk that appears high in this instrument.

The manual does not contain explanations for the use of the software, requiring either considerable computer sophistication or concerted attempts to reach the author to obtain instructions. Although the disk is essentially user friendly once the program is accessed, it does contain a few bugs (e.g., drives must be designated as A, B, or C, not A:, B:, or C: per instructions, and the program also fails to reject data on subjects who fall outside the age spectrum of the program).

In conclusion, it is strongly advised that use of the DARS be restricted to efforts to evaluate its statistical properties and clinical utilities. Its use in educational or drug treatment programs is unwarranted due to its highly speculative nature.

[1.13]
Children of Alcoholics Screening Test.

Purpose: Measures children's and adults' attitudes, feelings, perceptions, and experiences related to their parents' drinking behavior; also identifies probable children of alcoholics (CoAs) and adult children of alcoholics (ACoAs).
Population: School-age children through adults.
Publication Dates: 1981–1993.
Acronym: CAST.
Scores: Total score only.
Administration: Group or individual.
Price Data, 1993: $30 per Clinician/Researcher set including manual ('93, 106 pages), research abstracts, and 50 test forms.
Time: (5–10) minutes.
Comments: Reduced rate is available for additional forms used in research or mass testing.
Author: John W. Jones.
Publisher: Camelot Unlimited.
Cross References: Reviews by Stuart N. Hart and Steven P. Schinke originally appeared in 10:52; for reviews by Susanna Maxwell and Barrie G. Stacey, see 9:217.

Review of The Children of Alcoholics Screening Test by STUART N. HART, Associate Professor of Educational Psychology, Indiana University-Purdue University at Indianapolis, Indianapolis, IN:

The Children of Alcoholics Screening Test (CAST) is intended for use (a) in identifying children in schools and clinics who are "at risk" due to having adult caretakers (e.g., parents) who are alcoholics, (b) to assist in the diagnosis of a parent's alcoholism, (c) as a clinical counseling tool for children of alcoholics, and (d) for research on children of alcoholics. The CAST consists of 30 one-sentence items designed to measure "children's attitudes, feelings, perceptions, and experiences related to their parents' drinking behavior." Children are instructed to answer yes or no to items about "(a) psychological distress (of child) associated with a parent's drinking," "(b) perceptions (of child) of drinking-related marital discord between their parents," "(c) attempts (by child) to control a parent's drinking," "(d) efforts (by child) to escape from the alcoholism," "(e) exposure (of child) to drinking-related family violence," "(f) tendencies (of child) to perceive their parents as being alcoholic," and "(g) desire (of child) for professional counseling."

The Ninth Mental Measurements Yearbook contained two reviews of the CAST (Maxwell, 1985; Stacey, 1985). At that time a preliminary manual was available. A test manual, presented as in nonpreliminary form, was available for my review. No substantive changes appeared to have been made that would justify modification of the major findings of the previous reviews. The major findings reaffirmed by this review and additional comments follow.

The rationale for the test remains strong, although it has not been updated with support more recent than 1983 references. The administration, indicated to require 5-10 minutes, seems simple enough, but information/instructions have not been modified to adequately address the appropriateness of the test and procedures for children under 9 years of age. The manual (copyright 1983, fifth printing 1987), presents an order of instructions for the tester which must be in error (i.e., first administer, secondly read the instructions, page 6).

Reliability support is limited to the split-half internal consistency findings previously available (Spearman Brown coefficient of .98), leaving questions about stability of findings over time unanswered. Validity support is limited to face validity of items as judged by an undisclosed number of alcoholism counselors and grown-up children of alcoholics, and the findings of two validity studies previously available, one study of latency-age and adolescent children and one of adult children of alcoholics. The findings for latency-age and adolescent children are interpreted by the author to support the following cutoffs for decision making: With possible scores ranging from 0-30, 6 or higher identifies children of alcoholics, 2-5 identifies the children of problem drinkers, and 0-1 identifies children of nonalcoholics. The 6 or higher cutoff identified 100% of those who were known to be children of alcoholics accurately, and 23% of those in the control group, presumed but unsubstantiated to have nonalcoholic parents, as false positives. The grown-up children of alcoholics (5 of the 81 subjects) scored significantly higher than the grown-up children of nonalcoholics and scores on the CAST were positively correlated with children's judgment of the quantity of alcohol consumed by their parents. The relevance of false positives and the possibilities for "faking good" were recognized but not clarified in these studies, while no consideration was given to sex, ethnic background, and age/developmental stage differences. Additionally, the new manual contained three sections describing procedures for intervention/treatment programs which did not further clarify the psychometric qualities of the instrument.

Information, not included in the manual, was available for this review from 11 studies incorporating the CAST (published 1984-86). They provided no evidence to further clarify CAST reliability and validity, or the relevance of specific examinee factors. Most of these studies applied the CAST to sort groups into those who were and were not children of alcoholics, assuming adequate reliability and validity, for the purposes of investigating presumed associated characteristics (e.g., personality, adjustment, role in family). The majority (7 of 11) of the studies were dissertation projects.

At this time the CAST should be considered to be an experimental instrument appropriate for carefully designed use in research and in therapeutic relationships where problem drinking is likely to be a factor for individuals or families. Its use to identify children at risk within schools appears to represent an inappropriate invasion of privacy, especially in consideration of the high levels of false positives it produces. Its use to diagnose or validate the drinking problem of a parent may create substantial child-adult relationship problems unless handled very carefully. Though the author pre-sents interesting case study information in the manual, he does not address special administration strategies that would reduce the dangers for these last mentioned two uses. The potential application strengths of this instrument are significant; for example, the CAST might be useful in the study of "stress-resistant" or "invulnerable" children. However, the instrument's reliability and validity, with consideration of special factors (e.g., age, sex, race, ethnicity), require much more research and are presently overstated in the CAST manual. Most of these concerns were raised in previous reviews and appear not to have been addressed during the intervening period.

REVIEWER'S REFERENCES

Maxwell, S. (1985). Review of the Children of Alcoholics Screening Test. In J. V. Mitchell, Jr. (Ed.), The ninth mental measurements yearbook, (pp. 307-308). Lincoln, NE Buros Institute of Mental Measurements.
Stacey, B. G. (1985). Review of the Children of Alcoholics Screening Test. In J. V. Mitchell, Jr. (Ed.), The ninth mental measurements yearbook, (pp. 308-309). Lincoln, NE Buros Institute of Mental Measurements.

Review of The Children of Alcoholics Screening Test by STEVEN P. SCHINKE, Professor, School of Social Work, Columbia University, New York, NY:

STRENGTHS. The Children of Alcoholics Screening Test (CAST) offers a clinically helpful means for determining how children will respond to questions and items concerning their parents' drinking. As such, the CAST seems most profitably used to stimulate discussions and interventions with children and families where drinking is an issue. The CAST represents a pioneer effort to assess and quantify what children think about their parents and alcohol and to confront parents about the effects of their drinking behavior on their children.

WEAKNESSES. Despite its potential value, the CAST has several flaws. Together, these flaws indicate that the CAST is more fittingly used as a therapeutic process than as a diagnostic, evaluation, or research tool. For example, the CAST manual is accompanied by two treatment programs. One program is for children of alcoholics and the other is for marital group therapy for alcoholics and their spouses. Because these manuals are included with the CAST manual, the test is placed in the context of a therapeutic tool. Further expressing the therapeutic use of the CAST are the many anecdotes in the manual describing how the administration of the measure led to clinically significant insights among the target family members and alcohol abusers.

The potential for confusing clinical assessment, research data collection, and program evaluation baseline development tasks with treatment and therapy weakens the CAST as a stand-alone psychometric device. Added to this weakness are rather vague and undocumented statements about the construction and application of the CAST. For instance, on page four of the CAST manual, the author states "All items [on the CAST] were judged to be face valid by a number of alcoholism counselors and grown-up children of alcoholics."

The author of the CAST grounds the measure in publications that are largely outside of the peer-reviewed, scientific literature. Of the three cited papers he has written on the measure, one is an earlier version of the screening manual, one is a conference paper, and one is a technical report from the company that produces the CAST.

Finally, the author of the CAST overstates the instrument's value, and deemphasizes its possible problems. Illustrative is the statement on page 14 of the CAST manual, "The CAST can then be used to gain an objective measure of alcoholism from the viewpoint of the children." Yet, on an earlier page (12), the author says, "When using the diagnostic criteria, remember that some children might have been motivated to 'fake good' on the CAST. Interpret with caution." Though not entirely contradictory, these statements express opinions that seem inappropriate for the process of instrument development, testing, and dissemination.

RELIABILITY, VALIDITY, NORMATIVE DATA. Internal consistency scores reported for the CAST show Spearman-Brown coefficients of .98 based on samples of children and adults. Validity data on the CAST also support the measure's psychometric properties. From information provided in the manual, sufficient numbers of children have taken the CAST to yield adequate normative data.

SUMMARY. Due to its psychometric properties, the potential contribution of the CAST to clinical activities with children of alcoholic parents cannot be discounted. Still, the confusing presentation of treatment and therapeutic guidelines along with instrumentation data call into question the authors' understanding of the purposes and applications of a diagnostic, evaluation, and research tool. Furthermore, the CAST manual's lack of published, peer-reviewed scientific support for the instrument,

combined with the anecdotal and therapeutic tone of the accompanying materials, put doubt on the instrument's research grounding. In sum, the CAST seems more fitting to therapy and treatment settings than to research, diagnosis, or evaluation tasks.

[1.14]
Children's Role Inventory.

Purpose: "A measure assessing the roles played by children in their alcoholic families."
Population: Adult children of alcoholics.
Publication Date: 1988.
Acronym: CRI.
Scores: 4 role categories: Hero, Mascot, Lost Child, Scapegoat.
Administration: Group.
Manual: No manual.
Price Data: Available from publisher.
Time: Administration time not reported.
Authors: Ann E. Potter and Dale E. Williams.
Publisher: Dale E. Williams (the author)
Cross References: Reviews by Stephen N. Axford and Kathleen D. Paget will appear in the 13th MMY.

Review of the Children's Role Inventory by STEPHEN N. AXFORD, Psychologist, Pueblo School District No. 60, Pueblo, CO, and University of Phoenix, Southern Colorado Campus, Colorado Springs, CO:

The Children's Role Inventory (CRI), as described by its authors, is a "measure assessing the roles played by children in their alcoholic families" (p. 71). In fact, the instrument, contrary to what its name may convey, is apparently designed to be used with adult children of alcoholics rather than juveniles. This assumption is based on the fact that all subjects used in the validation of the instrument were self-reported adult children of alcoholics. The CRI specifically is designed to measure self-esteem and use of social support. The authors suggest that the CRI may have utility in "isolating those [adult] children who may be at risk for developing esteem and alcohol-related problems" (p. 77).

The group-administered CRI comprises 60 items employing a 5-point Likert scale. Materials include: a research article (Potter & Williams, 1991) describing the construction and validation of the instrument; the scale or protocol sheet used by the examinee to rate items (e.g., "When I was a child, I … was an achiever"); and a scoring key with items arranged in four categories: Hero, Mascot,

Lost Child, and Scapegoat. Administration instructions are limited to a brief statement on the single-page scale, simply stating, "Circle the number that best fits how each word or phrase describes how you were or how you acted in the family in which you were raised."

Although no technical manual currently exists for the CRI, the authors, in personal correspondence with the Buros Institute, indicated that development of such a manual is a goal of theirs. Nevertheless, normative scores are not provided. Also absent, outside the limited information provided in the research article, are instructions for interpreting data. Of course, this places limitations on the CRI for clinical use at the present time.

Three studies are reported by the authors, related to the development and validation of the CRI. In general, the authors were diligent and appropriately cautious in terms of attention to issues related to theoretical conceptualization, research design and methodology, and interpretation of results. The authors are off to a good start in developing and validating the CRI.

The first of the studies focused on item development and selection. The authors employed children of alcoholics to generate items. Subjects were 140 self-declared adult children of alcoholics participating in a support group, Adult Children of Alcoholics (ACA). Five psychologists specializing in alcohol addiction reviewed the 100 items generated and employed a rating system for assigning items with "best" fit to categories. Eighty-two items were selected for the first version of the CRI. Adequate levels of internal consistency (Cronbach's alpha ranged from .89 to .95) were observed.

The second study focused on cross-validating the internal consistency and construct validity of the first study. Subjects included 142 ACA members, 28 men and 114 women. Ranging from .90 to .95, internal consistency was observed to be within quite acceptable limits. However, given that all subjects were members of a support group, although "data were collected anonymously and within a 2-week time span," there does seem to be the potential of cohort contamination of results. In any case, through item analysis/item deletion, employing a rank-ordering system using corrected item-total correlation, 15 items for each subscale or category were retained.

The third study was conducted to: "(1) obtain convergent and discriminant validity evidence for the CRI and (2) compare the responses of self-identified adult children of alcoholics with a control sample" (p. 71). One-hundred-thirty-eight ACA subjects (27 men, 111 women) were employed. As acknowledged by the authors, these subjects were not screened and thus there was the possibility that subjects may have participated in the previous two studies. All ACA subjects chosen for participation "scored above the recommended cut off indicative of parental drinking problems on the Children of Alcoholics Screening Test" (pp. 73–74). A comparison sample of 105 adult subjects (24 men, 81 women) denying parental alcoholism and scoring below the recommended cutoff on the Children of Alcoholics Screening Test was employed. For both the clinical and comparison samples, "CRI subscales were differentially predictive of self-esteem as well as size of and satisfaction with one's social support network" (p. 70). Also, reliability results were replicated for both samples. Internal consistency for both samples was observed to be adequate (with correlations ranging from .89 to .92).

The authors acknowledge several limitations related to their research: In completing the inventory, subjects were required to recall childhood memories; the clinical samples were all solicited from the ACA support group (thus, it is uncertain as to whether the obtained results can be generalized to the larger population of children of alcoholics); and subjects were not screened for prior participation, which may have contaminated results for the second and third studies. In addition, all subjects were recruited from a limited geographic region (Omaha/Council Bluffs metro area, and Lincoln, NE). Ethnicity is not addressed. Nevertheless, the authors appear to have conducted their research carefully. The results from the studies reported are encouraging and warrant continued research using the CRI.

In summary, the initial research in developing and validating the CRI is encouraging. However, as the authors seem to acknowledge, additional research is needed before interpretive results can be generalized beyond the clinical sample (i.e., ACA support group members) used in the study, in terms of differential diagnosis and preventative care. Thus, it is not recommended that the CRI be used as a primary method, within a clinical context, for gathering diagnostic information regarding children of alcoholics. The CRI may be useful, however, as an adjunct or supplementary measure when working with children of alcoholics. However, the CRI does seem to possess ample technical merits to be used in research. Also, with additional validation and standardization, the CRI has potential to be used as an important clinical tool.

REVIEWER'S REFERENCE

Potter, A. E., & Williams, D. E. (1991). Development of a measure examining children's roles in alcoholic families. *Journal of Studies on Alcohol, 52,* 70–77.

Review of the Children's Role Inventory by KATHLEEN D. PAGET, Division Director, The Center for Child and Family Studies, College of Social Work, University of South Carolina, Columbia, SC:

The Children's Role Inventory (CRI) is an adult self-report scale designed to measure the roles played by children in their families. Comprising 60 adjectives, the measure requires respondents to rate themselves retrospectively on a Likert scale from 0 ("Strongly disagree or very unlike me") to 4 ("Strongly agree or very like me"). The scale is based on the popular conceptualization that children growing up in families affected by alcoholism assume "roles or defensive behavior patterns in response to the parental alcoholism and the imbalanced family system" (Potter & Williams, p. 70). The four roles that form the foundation for the measure were described more than 10 years ago as the Hero, Mascot, Lost Child, and Scapegoat (Black, 1981; Wegscheider, 1981). According to the test developers, "all children of alcoholics are thought to assume one or more of these roles" (Potter & Williams, p. 70).

The genesis of the scale suggests that it was developed as a tool for research purposes rather than as an instrument to be marketed for use by practitioners. No manual accompanies the scale; instead, supporting documentation results from three studies conducted by the test developers and published in the same article (Potter & Williams, 1991). In the first study, items were generated and responded to by adult children of alcoholics, and their responses were used to refine the measure. The second study incorporated a refined measure to cross-validate internal consistency findings. The third study resulted in convergent and discriminant validity evidence through a comparison of self-iden-

tified adult children of alcoholics with a comparison sample. In reporting the results of these studies, the test developers used scoring procedures that compiled items into the four categories, but they did not detail how specific numerical ratings were incorporated into the final scores. Thus, in contrast to many measures marketed for practical use and supported by extensive supporting documentation, the CRI is in the very early stages of development, a reality that results in more questions than answers about its practical use. In addition to the basics of scoring, questions arise about administration, norming, and interpretation when the measure's accompanying materials are perused.

Administration procedures appear to be very easy, and the time period to complete the items is very short, possibly as short as 5 minutes. The procedures are based on certain assumptions, however, that leave the user unguided about some important aspects of the measure. Instructions are as follows: "The following words or phrases describe behaviors and characteristics of children. Circle the number that best fits how each word or phrase describes how you were or how you acted in the family in which you were raised." The lack of a more circumscribed frame of reference leaves respondents struggling to define their own temporal and relational context: Some will focus on their memories as young children whereas others will reflect more on their adolescence; some will emphasize interactions with an adult family member and others will think more often of sibling interactions. In addition, the assumption that people grow up in one family ignores the increasing number of adults who, as children, experienced multiple-family situations as a result of foster care and divorce. Moreover, although the directions ask for how the respondent "acted in the family," some respondents will extend the context to include situations outside the family. Despite the range of contexts that respondents may create for themselves when completing the items, this information is not known because the directions do not request it. In short, the vagueness of the measure's directions combine with the general scope of the trait-based adjectives to cry out for more situational specificity to the items. Information on the consistency of results across time and respondents would help temper these concerns, but at the present time, test-retest and interrater reliability coefficients are missing from the materials that accompany the measure.

Specific information about the measure's validity also is missing. Before results from the CRI can be interpreted to support the four roles that it purports to measure, more work must be done to collect construct validity information. The interitem and inter-subscale reliability coefficients provided by the test developers are a necessary but not sufficient prerequisite to empirically derived construct validity. This is especially true because the sample used to generate items comprised individuals ("adult children of alcoholics") who had begun counseling and may have been exposed to information regarding the four roles. A factor analysis based on a priori questioning of the original clustering of items is needed. Through the use of a comparison sample and a discriminant analysis, the test developers are beginning to address the important issue that some individuals who do not grow up in families characterized by alcoholism may exhibit behavioral patterns similar to those who do. Also, in studying convergent and predictive validity, they have begun to address possible gender differences in response patterns on the CRI. Missing from published information, however, is the consideration of possible racial/ethnic differences in response patterns on the CRI. In describing the four samples used across the three published studies, no mention is made of the racial composition of the samples. Given the diversity of the American population, such information is sorely needed.

Although increased psychometric documentation has been collected and recorded over time by the developers of the CRI, the instrument is not ready for application and public use. If the developers wish for it to be, then continued refinement of the measure is needed with respect to administration, scoring, validation, and interpretation prior to the preparation and printing of a manual.

REVIEWER'S REFERENCES

Wegscheider, S. (1981). *Another chance: Hope and health for the alcoholic family.* Palo Alto, CA: Science and Behavior Books, Inc.

Black, C. (1981). *It will never happen to me.* Denver, CO: MAC Publishing.

Potter, A. E., & Williams, D. E. (1991). Development of a measure examining children's roles in alcoholic families. *Journal of Studies on Alcohol, 52,* 70–77.

[1.15]

Clinical Support System Battery.

Purpose: "Designed for use with the potential school dropout student, and/or with chemical dependency rehabilitation programs."

Population: High school–adult.
Publication Dates: 1990–1991.
Administration: Individual.
Time: Administration time not reported.
Comments: May be used with or without biofeedback equipment. Programs designed as a companion piece to the initial Life Style Analysis Test.
Author: Russell N. Cassel.
Publisher: Psychologists and Educators, Inc.

a) LIFE STYLE ANALYSIS TEST.
Purpose: To assess one's degree of wellness in relation to one's emotional stress.
Acronym: LFSTYLE.
Scores, 10: Positive Life Style (Self-Esteem, Satisfaction, Assertiveness, Involvement, Total Ego Strength), Negative Life Style (Loneliness, Anxiety, Health Worry, Depression, Total Stress Load).
Price Data, 1990: $11 per manual ('90, 38 pages); $25 per program diskette; $11 per added diskette.

b) NEURAL FUNCTIONING ASSESSMENT.
Purpose: To assess anxiety level.
Scores, 5: Relax, Disproof [guided imagery dissonance profile], Neural [neural personality cluster], Emote [unconscious need presence], Riskage [estimated coronary age].
Price Data: $11 per manual ('91, 36 pages); $25 per program diskette; $11 per added diskette.
Comments: Requires TRI-BI-SENSOR with 4 biofeedback units (price data available from publisher).

c) THE NEED GRATIFICATION ASSESSMENT TEST.
Purpose: "To assess level of need status."
Scores, 12: Home and Family, Religion and Inner Development, Affiliation and Social, Law and Security, School and Learning, Romance and Psychosexual, Sports and Risk Taking, Health and Safety, Travel and Relaxation, Aesthetic and Beauty, Money and Productivity, Survival and Pollution.
Price Data: $11 per manual ('90, 11 pages); $25 per program diskette; $11 per added diskette.

d) THE IDENTITY STATUS TEST.
Purpose: Assesses perception of "to love and to be loved."
Scores, 7: Intimate and Private, Heart and Soul, Committed Fully, Personal Acceptance, Compassion and Forgiveness, Romanticism, Total.
Price Data: $11 per manual ('91, 16 pages); $25 per program diskette; $11 per added diskette.

e) THE INDEPENDENCE VERSUS REGRESSION TEST.
Purpose: Assesses perception of unlicensed freedom in relation to perception of exaggerated constraints.

Scores, 8: Freedoms (Coping Style, Conforming, Sympathetic, Locus of Control), Constraints (Rationalization, Regression, Repression, Escapist).

Price Data: $11 per manual ('91, 14 pages); $25 per program diskette; $11 per added diskette.

f) THE COSMIC CONSCIOUSNESS TEST.

Purpose: Measures freedom to "escape earthly bounds and achieve cosmic consciousness."

Scores, 7: Mutuality and Synergy, Spirituality and Love, Loyalty and Pride, Caring and Commitment, Depersonalization and Reward, Parent/Child Role, Total.

Price Data: $11 per manual ('90, 7 pages); $15 per program diskette; $11 per added diskette.

Cross References: Reviews by William L. Curlette and Mary Lou Kelley originally appeared in 12:82.

Review of the Clinical Support System Battery by WILLIAM L. CURLETTE, Professor of Counseling and Psychological Services, Professor of Educational Policy Studies, and Director of the Educational Research Bureau, Georgia State University, Atlanta, GA:

The Clinical Support System Battery by Russell N. Cassel consists of a series of computerized tests to assess aspects of an individual's holistic health status. Actually, there are six different batteries of tests within the Clinical Support System, all of which relate to the underlying theme of holistic health. These batteries are Life Style Analysis, Neural Functioning Assessment, Need Gratification Assessment, Identity Status, Independence versus Regression, and Cosmic Consciousness. Given the extensive number of tests and subtests in each battery, the reader is referred to the listing that accompanies this review for the names of tests and subtests within a battery. Each battery is described in its own manual and also discussed in an overall manual for the Clinical Support System.

To obtain an understanding of this system, consider the first battery listed in the Clinical Support System, the Life Style Analysis Battery consisting of two tests: Positive Life Style and Negative Life Style. The four subtests for the Positive Life Style Test (Self-Esteem, Satisfaction, Assertiveness, and Involvement) are combined to yield a total score for Positive Life Style, described as "Ego Strength to handle problems" (Life Style Analysis Test manual, p. 1). It is suggested that this score be compared with the Negative Life Style Test score that measures "stress load being carried" (Life Style Analysis Test manual, p. 1). The Negative Life Style test also is the sum of four other subtests (Loneliness, Anxiety, Health Worry [or Negative Attitude], and Depression). Each of these subtests as well as the two test scores are reported as "T-like score" ranging from 20 to 80 with a mean of 50 on a one-page computer generated profile report for the examinee. Percent correct scores are also printed on the report below the bar representing the normalized T-scores. For the T-scores or percent correct scores, no standard errors of measurement are presented. When discussing the use of this battery with drug abusers, Cassel (Life Style Analysis Test manual, p. 3) says that "Whenever the Stress Load is greater than Ego Strength, a significant at risk is depicted." In contrast, "An ideal life style is where the ego strength is two times or more than as much as the stress load" (Life Style Analysis Test manual, Figure 1, p. 35).

Besides having an examinee answer questions presented on the computer screen, three of the "Holistic Health" modules obtain data from an examinee through biofeedback devices (electromyograph, galvanic skin response, peripheral temperature, and pulse rate). These three modules are dissonance assessment using guided imagery and neural personality cluster, assessment of self-control in relaxation, and non-dominant brain need-presence assessment.

To illustrate how a module is used, consider the non-dominant need-presence assessment (EMOTE) module in the Need Gratification Battery. The EMOTE module employs "from one to four different biofeedback instruments interfaced with a computer to measure neural functions in response to your bodily changes in connection with view of the 96 slides" (Neural Harmony Essential for Global Functioning manual, p. 32). The examinee responds to each slide on a scale of 1 to 10 depending on its appeal. The 96 slides cover 12 different areas of life (e.g., Home and Family, Religion and Inner Development, Survival and Pollution) during a 16-minute period. These assess need-presence in the "non-dominant" or unconscious brain areas. The examinee also responds to 20 true/false items on each of the same 12 areas of life in order to assess the needs in the conscious person or "dominant" brain. Contrasting the bio-feedback data with the test data on the 12 life areas provides an indication of the disparity between conscious and unconscious need-presence. Not addressed in the manual is research on a possible order effect for presentation of the slides; however, the manual does note that EMOTE is still considered to be experimental.

The theory underlying the Clinical Support System Battery is based on the concept of wellness in contrast to fighting sickness. A fundamental aspect of this concept is the idea of "global functioning" and the connection of one's mind and body (psychoneroimunology). Furthermore, according to Cassel, "The notion underlying the holistic series is that no person is ever living as well as it is possible to live, and that the six different programs provide guidance for improved quality of life and greater life expectancy" (The Identity Status Test manual, p. 7). Although the number of references supporting the theory and tests in the seven manuals range from 9 to 51, more specific linking of the existing literature with the particular choice of tests or subtests in the various batteries is needed.

The development, administration, and interpretation of the six different batteries share many common features. Even though the manuals cite studies which support the general notion of measuring particular aspects of health, there is a lack of tables of specifications and/or outlines to operationally define the areas measured. Furthermore, there is no information on how the items were generated. Interjudge agreement studies regarding the placement of items on scales are not reported. The factor analyses which are reported appear to have factored the subtests as variables and consequently do not show loadings for items on scales. Incidentally, in one instance where the cutoff value for the eigenvalues in the factor analyses are reported, it was .5 (Neural Harmony Essential for Global Functioning manual, p. 8). This value is much lower than the recommended value of 1 in the literature.

Construct validity is obtained by using the group difference approach. Cassel correctly states that the "Validity begins with determining the discerning power of a psychological instrument" (Neural Harmony Essential for Global Functioning manual, p. 13). To validate the batteries,

therapy and no-therapy groups are compared using discriminant analyses. Cassel points out that individuals who spend money and time for health services present "prima facie evidence of 'non-wellness'" (The Life Style Analysis Test manual, p. 6) leaving the wellness group to be defined by default. Not procuring health services could be due to factors such as lack of disposable income, lack of knowledge regarding symptoms, and non-availability of transportation. Hence, it may have been better to obtain additional information to more clearly define both the therapy and the no-therapy groups.

In addition to the problem of group definition, the reporting of the discriminant analyses is incomplete. Missing are statistics usually reported related to how well the discriminant function separated the groups, such as Bartlett's Chi-Squared for the overall model, discriminant function coefficients, and partial Wilks' Lambdas for each variable in the model. When hit-miss classification tables are reported, it is not clear whether the calibration samples were reclassified tending to result in a slight overestimation of the proportion of correct classifications or whether another procedure such as the holdout sample or jackknife technique was employed.

Essentially, the group difference approach reported in most of the manuals amounts to t-tests for the subtest means of the therapy and no-therapy groups. The results are often statistically significant lending some validity to the subtests, conditional to some extent on the quality of the therapy and no-therapy group definitions.

In regard to risk, one interesting possibility presented in the Life Style Analysis Battery is using the notion that an ideal profile has a Positive Life Style score at least twice the Negative Life Style score. By analogy, the physical body has many redundancies and strengths beyond what is normally required in everyday life. Perhaps then, the usual statement in the stress literature of resources just exceeding stressors as not inducing the stress response needs elaboration. A contribution of Cassel is that he has moved us in the direction of wanting more resources, although the 2:1 ratio as a minimum may need additional justification.

As an aside, it may be noted that when concerned with risk, the statistical analysis often seen in the medical journals is logistic regression. For the two-group problem, both discriminant analysis and logistic regression can be computed but interpretation of results may differ (Hosmer & Lemeshow, 1989). A difference between the analyses is that in logistic regression the coefficients provide an estimate of the log odds adjusting for other variables in the model and may approximate a quantity called the relative risk.

Missing from the manuals is criterion-related validity information which shows the correlations of the tests or subtests in the Clinical Support System with other measures of similar constructs. For example, correlations of Cassel's measure of depression could be reported with other measures of depression such as the Beck Depression Inventory (T4:268). Also, the usefulness of tests in the Cosmic Consciousness Battery could be shown by correlations with other variables or their incremental validity in a regression equation.

Reliability is supported by test/retest correlations, subtest intercorrelations, and subtest with test correlations. For the Life Style Analysis scale, the test and subtest test/retest correlations for the no-therapy group ($n = 143$) ranged from .86 to .54, whereas for the therapy group ($n = 78$) they varied from .81 to .22. The manuals for the other scales did not report test/retest reliability. There are no KR-20s, KR-21s, or coefficient alphas given in the manuals for internal consistency reliability. Furthermore, there are no standard errors of measurement reported in the manuals or presented in the profile reports to aid in score interpretation.

The intercorrelation of the subtests is discussed from the viewpoint of factorial validity which, according to Cassel, "is a quasi-reliability measure; since it deals with the structure of the instrument" (The Life Style Analysis manual, p. 9). The intercorrelations of most subtests seem to be in line with what is to be expected—low to moderate correlations within a battery. Furthermore, reliability is discussed in terms of the number of behaviors (items) sought. For many subtests, the number of true/false items is 25, which typically is more than sufficient to measure most constructs.

There is no research reported in the manuals on item bias. More specifically, there are no statistical analyses for item bias or sensitivity reviews of the items for possible ethnic or gender differences.

The issue of various groups responding differently to items on the test is handled by using different norm groups. Various norm groups are available in the computer programs for the different batteries to help interpret an examinee's scores. For example, the Life Style Analysis Battery first asks the person scoring the profile to select between the Adult Norm and the Youth Norm (under 22 years of age). Then the person scoring the profile selects from among the General Norm, Female Norm, or Male Norm. Frequently, norms and data analyses involve samples from the United States, New Zealand, and Australia. Most manuals do include t-tests for mean differences of males and females on many of the tests and subtests for various data sets. For some tests and subtests there are statistically significant differences.

The administration of the true/false items in a test is done on the computer with one item appearing on the screen at a time. The software, written in the BASIC computer language, ran without problems. It can be copied over to a hard disk and executed from there. The user is given the choice of from which drive to execute the program and on which drive to store the results. The programs do not require very much storage space if copied over to a hard drive. The Clinical Support System disk used 319 K bytes and the largest space requirement for any of the six separate disks for each of the batteries was 287 K bytes.

The items are presented on the screen in white characters against a black background. The same set of items is presented to every examinee. Although the initial screen of instructions tells the respondent how to go back and change an answer (down arrow key), this instruction does not appear on each screen and a respondent may forget how to go back and change answers. The program does not store changes regarding the drives and they must be entered each time at startup. There are no provisions to skip items or to exit the battery early and save item responses.

Two practical concerns for using any test are the amount of time required to administer the test and its reading level. On both accounts the Clinical Support System appears good. Typically a battery has between 120 and 200 items and takes about 20 minutes to administer. According to the SMOG reading formula, the first 100 words in the items at the beginning of the Life Style Analysis Battery were at approximately the 7th grade reading level.

In summary, the strengths of the instrument are that it furthers support for some newer ideas such as a higher ratio of resources to stressors, measuring cosmic consciousness, and biofeedback related to 12 life situations. It also provides ease of administration and immediate profile generation. However, the Clinical Support System could be improved by reporting standard errors of measurement and concurrent validity studies with other instruments designed to measure similar constructs. Overall, this test battery represents a starting point in the assessment of holistic health.

REVIEWER'S REFERENCE

Hosmer, D. W., Jr., & Lemeshow, S. (1989). *Applied logistic regression*. New York: John Wiley & Sons.

Review of the Clinical Support System Battery by MARY LOU KELLEY, Professor of Psychology, Louisiana State University, Louisiana State University Medical Center, Baton Rouge, LA:

The Clinical Support System is intended for assessing the lifestyle and health-related behavior of adolescents and adults. The battery consists of six computer-administered multiple-choice tests assessing a variety of personality traits that the author purports are related to health from a holistic perspective. Using the author's descriptors, the battery includes tests measuring ego strength, neural functioning, need gratification, identity status, balance of control, and cosmic consciousness. The test packet consists of a manual providing an overview of the battery and separate manuals for each of the tests. The tests are on 5.25-inch PC format floppy computer disks, which present individual items and which print a profile subsequent to administration. Unfortunately, when I attempted to complete one of the tests, which contained over 170 items, I encountered a "fatal flaw," which prevented the scoring of my test responses. A message instructed me to contact the author in California and listed two numbers, which apparently identified the nature of the "fatal flaw." The author provides an overview of the test battery and its intended uses. The battery is very ambitious and creative and attempts to incorporate numerous psychodynamic and psychological tenets into the test content. For example, the Life Style Analysis

Test measures ego strength, defined by the author as the "ability to cope with problems in one's life space" (Life Style Analysis Test manual, p. 2) and compares ego strength to the individual's perceived stress load. Thus, the lifestyle test compares positive and negative areas of one's life. The Positive Life Style component (ego strength), consists of four separate components (Self-Esteem, Satisfaction, Involvement, Assertiveness) each containing 25 true/false items. The Negative Life Style component (stress load), also consists of four components measuring Loneliness, Anxiety, Negative Attitude, and Depression. The other tests of the battery are also centered around various broad concepts with item selection apparently based on the author's intuition.

The author makes a very substantial effort to explain the philosophy and scholarly foundation of the constructs measured and to relate test purposes to a psychological theory perceived as important to health maintenance. Each test in the battery is accompanied by a fairly extensive explanatory manual. In spite of the author's ambitious efforts, the descriptions are highly jargonistic and esoteric. For example, the Cosmic Consciousness Test manual relates the test to tenets of transpersonal psychology and "is intended for use with persons who desire to escape the worldly bonds and soar into the heavens in mind and in spirit" (The Life Style Analysis Test manual, p. 2). Furthermore, some constructs for which there is a substantial literature are defined in an idiosyncratic manner without apparent consideration for other research. For example, the author states that "A comparison of the ego strength and stress load present serves as an effective means for depicting the 'TYPE-A Proneness' of an individual. Where the stress load of an individual is high in comparison to one's ego strength, TYPE-A proneness is the more likely to be present" (The Life Style Analysis Test manual, p. 2). The author cites his own research almost exclusively in support of this assertion.

Reliability data are provided for only some of the many constructs measured. Where reliability is addressed, the rationales and data presented are neither clear nor impressive. Measures of internal consistency (e.g., inter-item correlations) are not presented for any test. The author does provide data on the factor structure of each test in the battery as well as data on its use with clinical and nonclinical samples. Each test apparently is normed on male and female samples. However, very little information is provided on the standardization sample or the norming process. Moreover, data are not presented on the relationship of any of the tests to any external criterion other than sex, age, marital status, and therapy/nontherapy status.

In summary, the Clinical Support System is an ambitious effort aimed as assessing the author's theory of psychological factors related to health maintenance. In the absence of a thorough rewrite of the manual and the inclusion of extensive reliability and validity data documenting the psychometric soundness and criterion-related validity of the battery, I cannot recommend its use for any applied purpose. Further, anyone who intends to conduct research on the tests must contend with reading manuals that are heavy on theory and light on practical information about test administration and interpretation.

[1.16]
Comprehensive Drinker Profile.

Purpose: To provide "an intensive and comprehensive history and status of the individual client with regard to his or her use and abuse of alcohol."
Population: Problem drinkers and alcoholics.
Publication Dates: 1984–1987.
Acronym: CDP.
Scores: Problem drinking indices.
Administration: Individual.
Price Data, 1994: $63 per complete kit including 25 interview forms, 8 card sets, and manual ('84, 81 pages); $42 per 25 forms; $14 per set of cards; $14 per manual.
Comments: 3 adjunct instruments available as separates.
Authors: G. Alan Marlatt and William R. Miller.
Publisher: Psychological Assessment Resources, Inc.
a) BRIEF DRINKER PROFILE.
Publication Date: 1987.
Acronym: BDP.
Price Data: $38 per 25 forms; $11 per CDP manual supplement (54 pages).
Time: 50 minutes.
Comments: Abbreviated version of the Comprehensive Drinker Profile; CDP manual and card sets required for administration and interpretation.
b) FOLLOW-UP DRINKER PROFILE.
Publication Date: 1987.
Acronym: FDP.
Price Data: $22 per 15 forms; $11 per CDP manual supplement.

Time: (30–50) minutes.
Comments: To be used in conjunction with the CDP or BDP; CDP manual and card sets required for administration and interpretation.
c) COLLATERAL INTERVIEW FORM.
Purpose: To provide information not available from the client.
Population: Friends and family of the client.
Publication Date: 1987.
Acronym: CIF.
Price Data: $22 per 15 forms; $11 per CDP manual supplement.
Time: Administration time not reported.
Comments: CDP manual required.
Cross References: Reviews by Robert R. Mowrer and Nick J. Piazza originally appeared in 10:70 (1 reference).

Review of the Comprehensive Drinker Profile by ROBERT R. MOWRER, Assistant Professor of Psychology and Sociology, Angelo State University, San Angelo, TX:

The term "comprehensive" is certainly applicable to this extensive instrument intended to address the diagnosis and treatment of alcoholism and problem drinking. In addition, there are also related materials available to assess the efficacy of treatment (Follow-up Drinker Profile, FDP) and the Collateral Interview Form (CIF), which allows for information from friends and relatives. Finally, there is a shorter version available that is an abbreviation of the Comprehensive Drinker Profile (CDP). An examination of these materials indicates the combination of these measures is unique in its purpose.

The full-length CDP is divided into three main sections: demographics, drinking history, and motivational information. It is intended for use in a structured interview setting and requires 1 to 2 hours to complete (the shorter version, the Brief Drinker Profile [BDP], requires approximately 1 hour).

An especially interesting aspect of the drinking history section is the use of a set of six cards describing "drinker types" ranging from nonalcoholic to alcoholic. The client is then asked to choose which card best describes the drinking habits of various significant others (mother, father, spouse, partner). This type of forced-choice procedure is used also with regard to drinking location, social situation (who you drink with), other drugs used, and beverage preference. In the motivational section, this procedure is used to determine effects of drinking, other life problems, and drinker type.

I think this approach may be especially useful and effective in reducing the ambiguity of an interview. A second plus is the incorporation of aspects of the Michigan Alcoholism Screening Test (MAST) into this instrument. Third, several sections of the CDP are converted into quantitative indices increasing the reliability of the instrument (similar quantitative indices are derived in the abbreviated version). All four instruments (CDP, BDP, FDP, and CIF) are logically structured into major sections, another advantage in terms of consistency. In sum, I like the forced-choice cards, the incorporation of the MAST, the quantitative indices, and the consistency of the instrument.

On the negative side, although this instrument clearly has face validity, it is difficult to see how it could be incorporated with something such as the MMPI (as the MacAndrew [1965] can be). A second potential weakness is its psychometric characteristics. The normative sample was small and no attempt was made to obtain a cross-validation sample. The normative sample consisted of 103 problem drinkers at a University-related clinic. I think it is important that additional normative data be obtained especially from a sample of "social," nonproblem drinkers to show this set of instruments can differentiate problem drinkers from those not identified as problems. Further supportive data could be obtained from a "normal" sample, randomly selected without regard to drinking behavior. The research potential of this instrument is extremely rich and strongly merits pursuit.

Some other minor problems with the CDP involve its administration. Although the CDP manual is fairly extensive, it is clear that competent administration will require quite a bit of practice. The entire manual is 79 pages long with the "instruction" portion garnering 41 of these pages. The manual points out that style and consistency are extremely important.

All in all, I feel this is an extremely important and promising diagnostic tool. With further validation studies this may become the instrument of choice for family systems therapists and practitioners due to its emphasis on functional impairments within the examinee's various systems. The idea of a comprehensive set of inventories is a very good one with significant advantages over other assessment approaches.

REVIEWER'S REFERENCE

MacAndrew, C. (1965). The differentiation of male alcoholic outpatients from nonalcoholic psychiatric outpatients by means of the MMPI. *Quarterly Journal of Studies on Alcohol, 26,* 238–246.

Review of the Comprehensive Drinker Profile by NICK J. PIAZZA, Assistant Professor, Department of Counselor Education, The University of Toledo, Toledo, OH:

The Comprehensive Drinker Profile (CDP) is not so much an assessment device as it is a structured interview. As such, the CDP is able to provide the clinician or researcher with a structured data base. However, the consumer should be aware that the CDP offers little that is not already available or that could not be easily duplicated with materials produced locally.

The CDP interview consists of a sequence of questions encompassing three different areas: demographics, drinking history, and motivation. Materials necessary for the interview include the manual, an interview booklet, and numerous color-coded cards that are to be sorted by the client. The authors suggest that the CDP be administered in one session approximately 1 to 2 hours in length. The authors also recommend that the CDP not be administered to persons who are withdrawing from alcohol or who have blood alcohol concentrations exceeding .05%.

The CDP, because of its comprehensive nature and complexity of administration, should only be administered by a trained interviewer. Training to use the CDP could be done quickly with someone with good basic interviewing skills and should not need to consist of more than a few practice administrations.

Much of the interview consists of eliciting information from the interviewee and then recording it into the CDP booklet. With several items, however, there is the need to present the client with a series of cards that are arrayed on the table before the interviewee. The interviewee is then asked, depending on the nature of the information needed, to either select the appropriate card or to sort the cards into an order that represents the interviewee's drinking experiences or feelings.

Several problems were immediately apparent with the card-sort technique as suggested by the authors of the CDP. First, using this technique adds greatly to the time needed to conduct the interview. Second, the card-sort technique makes it impossible to administer the interview in more efficient group settings. This could be an important limitation when the CDP is employed in research or assessment situations. Third, there is an obvious alphanumeric identification number on the face of the cards that could influence the interviewee as he or she sorts the cards. An interviewee might use these identification numbers in an effort to "second guess" the purpose of the interview. Fourth, the identification numbers do not correspond to the item and section numbers within the interviewer's booklet. Consequently, the identification numbers do not contribute to the ease of training or administration of the CDP. Fifth, having the interviewee sort cards requires the interviewer to transcribe the results into the booklet later. It would seem much more efficient to merely give the interviewee a set of forms to fill out that could then be inserted into the booklet. Such forms could be given to the interviewee either before or after the interview for completion outside of the interview setting.

The authors provide a mechanism for quantifying much of the data within the CDP. The methods employed can be fairly complicated at first, but are well documented in the manual. Scoring should become quite easy for anyone familiar with the administration of the interview. The only serious deficiencies in the documentation occur when scoring the subsections on Family History and Alcohol-Related Life Problems. In both cases, weights are assigned to various items, but no indication was given of how the weights were determined. It would seem desirable for the manual to include documentation for how scoring weights were determined or to at least reference articles in the literature where that information may be obtained.

In interpreting the results, the authors offer no information on the validity or reliability of the information obtained using the CDP. A subsection of the CDP includes the Michigan Alcoholism Screening Test (MAST). It would seem reasonable to assume that information obtained on that subsection would be comparable to a separate administration of the MAST and that research relevant to the validity and reliability of the MAST would apply as well.

Normative data for the CDP is based on a single sample of 103 outpatient "problem drinkers" at the University of New Mexico. The relatively narrow scope of the authors' sample calls into question the utility of the interview in other than outpatient settings. While the authors claim that information obtained using the CDP is "relevant to the selection, planning, and implementation of treatment," it would appear that the interviewer must rely on his or her clinical judgment or knowledge of other research in utilizing this data with groups different than the sample. The authors do provide suggestions from the research and an appendix with suggested rules for interpreting the data; however, the final analysis of the information seems too dependent on the clinical intuition or experience of the interviewer or interpreter.

Overall, the CDP is a comprehensive, structured interview such as the authors claim. It should prove useful to anyone seeking to establish a large, uniform data base of information relevant to alcoholic clients. In fact, the ease with which the CDP could be coded for entry into a computer is perhaps this instrument's greatest strength. The limitations evident within the administration, scoring, and interpretation of the CDP suggest that clinicians and researchers may be better served by an assessment tool that is easier and more efficient to administer, offers better documentation of validity and reliability, and/or is developed and tailored to meet local needs.

[1.17]
Denver Community Mental Health Questionnaire—Revised.

Purpose: Assesses client social history by means of a 79-item questionnaire.
Population: Mental health clients.
Publication Date: 1978.
Acronym: DCMHQ-R.
Scores: 13 scales covering 4 areas: Personal Distress, Alcohol and Drug Abuse, Social and Community Functioning, Client Satisfaction.
Administration: Individual.
Price Data: Not available.
Time: (20–30) minutes.
Author: James A. Ciarlo.
Publisher: James A. Ciarlo [No reply from publisher; status unknown].

Cross References: The review by R. W. Payne originally appeared in 9:310 (3 references); see also T3:677 (2 references).

Review of the Denver Community Mental Health Questionnaire—Revised, by R. W. PAYNE, Professor of Psychology, University of Victoria, Victoria, British Columbia, Canada:

The Denver Community Mental Health Questionnaire is a 79-item standardized social history interview designed to be used by "non-professional" level case workers. A modified form can be used as a self-administered questionnaire. The questions cover four general areas—personal distress, alcohol and drug abuse, social and community functioning, and client satisfaction. The questions in each area are subdivided into several scales, there being 13 scales in all. The questions proceed logically from one scale to the next, and from one area to the next.

Standardization data are based, for the most part, on a "random Denver community sample" (Scales 1–11 and 13), while standardization data for Scale 12 (Client Satisfaction) was based on a "sample of 500 Denver Health and Hospitals Mental Health program clients." The raw score for each scale can be converted to a standard score with a mean of 50 and, with some exceptions, a standard deviation of 5. The length of the scales varies considerably, ranging from only two items for the "Interpersonal Aggression - Friends" scale to nine items for the "Psychological Distress" scale. It should be noted that no items score on more than one scale, and the "scales" are merely clusters of questions dealing with the same area, and were derived from a purely logical analysis. For example, the two questions which define the "Interpersonal Aggression—Friends" scale are, "When you are with your friends how often do you argue with them?" (never, seldom, often, constantly), and "When you are with your friends how often do you physically fight?" (never, seldom, often, constantly). The total possible range of raw scores for this scale is only 0 to 6 ("never" is scored 0). Data presented in the manual suggest that the mean raw score for the standardization sample on this scale was between 0 and 1. Thus, although standard score equivalents can be obtained from the table, they are not meaningful for this scale, because the data are so extremely skewed. (The modal raw score was probably 0, so that to say of this standard score distribution that it has a mean of 50 and a standard deviation of 5 is meaningless, since the highest possible standard score is 54, and this is also probably the modal score.) It would have been much more useful to the test user if the authors had done away with the "standard score" table altogether, and merely shown the frequency of each raw score in their standardization sample.

The same general criticism applies to a lesser degree to the "standard" scores for all the other scales. All the distributions seem to be very skewed in the direction of low (i.e., "normal") scores. The main value to the user of scoring the questionnaire at all is surely to allow some comparison to be made between one's particular client and the standardization sample of Denver clients. But this sort of comparison is really not possible without the frequency distribution of all the raw scores for all the scales. This information could easily have been presented in a table of exactly the same size as the table of standard score equivalents given in the manual.

The main value of this test is as a preliminary screening device, and as a rough check on the possible improvement in social adjustment following treatment. The authors provide some evidence that four of the scales are relatively reliable, as assessed by a 2-week test-retest study. The correlation coefficients ranged from only .60 for the two-item "Interpersonal Aggression—Friends" scale to .83 for the "Interpersonal Isolation/Family" scale, a 4-item scale evaluating the extent to which the client socializes with and can depend on other members of his family.

The validity of a measure such as this obviously depends a great deal on whether the clients answer the questions truthfully, or whether they try to make themselves seem more socially acceptable. One study by Ciarlo and Reihman (1977) suggests that the correlations between clients' self-report scores and clinicians' ratings of the same variables may be very low, as only two correlation coefficients over .40 were found for these scales. Of course many of the clients for which this questionnaire is intended are alcoholics or drug abusers, and taking the client's word on his or her own consumption and social behaviour might not be wise. At the very least it would seem important to get independent confirmation of the facts from at least one other informant. This is, of course, not so much due to any shortcomings in this potentially very useful standardized interview, as it is due to the characteristics of many of the clients with which it is used.

REVIEWER'S REFERENCE

Ciarlo, J. A., & Reihman, J. The Denver Community Mental Health Questionnaire: Development of a multi-dimensional program evaluation instrument. In Coursey, R., Spector, G., Murrell, S., & Hunt, B. (Eds.), PROGRAM EVALUATION FOR MENTAL HEALTH: METHODS, STRATEGIES, AND PARTICIPANTS, (pp. 131-167). New York: Grune & Stratton, 1977.

[1.18]

Driver Risk Inventory.

Purpose: "Designed for DUI/DWI offender risk assessment."

Population: Convicted DUI and DWI offenders.

Publication Dates: 1986–1992.

Acronym: DRI.

Scores: Behaviors/characteristics relevant to DUI offenders in 5 areas: Validity, Alcohol, Drugs, Driver Risk, Stress Coping Abilities.

Administration: Individual or group.

Price Data, 1992: $5 to $6 per test; other price data available from publisher.

Time: (30–35) minutes.

Comments: Self-administered, computer-scored test.

Author: Behavior Data Systems, Ltd.

Publisher: Behavior Data Systems, Ltd.

Cross References: The review by Frank Gresham originally appeared in 12:125.

Review of the Driver Risk Inventory by FRANK GRESHAM, Professor and Director, School of Psychology Program, University of California, Riverside, Riverside, CA:

The Driver Risk Inventory (DRI) is a computer-administered, computer-scored, and computer-interpreted self-report instrument designed for use with individuals convicted of Driving While Intoxicated (DWI) or Driving Under the Influence (DUI). The DRI comprises 139 items and requires 25 minutes to complete. It is typically administered on IBM-compatible computers, but can be administered in test booklet format. Regardless of administration mode, it is computer scored and interpreted. The DRI is written on a 6th grade reading level and is available in both English and Spanish.

STANDARDIZATION SAMPLE AND NORMS. The technical manual published in 1992 by Behavior Data Systems, Ltd. is unclear as to who the DRI was standardized on, how many subjects were in the standardization sample, what states were involved in the standardization, and the demographic breakdown of the standardization sample. According to the manual, the DRI database is being continually expanded and is updated annually. This, however, is no excuse for not providing a clear description of the most currently available standardization data. In short, one does not know from reading the manual exactly upon whom the DRI was standardized.

SCALES AND SCORES. The DRI comprises five scales: (*a*) Truthfulness, which is a validity scale designed to identify self-protective, recalcitrant, and guarded individuals trying to conceal information; (*b*) Alcohol, which is a measure of alcohol proneness and alcohol-related problems; (*c*) Drugs, which is a measure of drug-abuse related problems; (*d*) Driver Risk, which is a measure of driver risk independent of that person's involvement with alcohol or drugs; and (*e*) Stress Quotient, which is a measure of the respondent's ability to cope with stress.

Scores on each scale are reported as percentile ranks and are assigned "risk levels" or "risk classification ranges." Four ranges are presented for each scale: (*a*) Low Risk, 0 to 39th percentile; (*b*) Medium Risk, 40th to 69th percentile; (*c*) Problem Risk, 70th to 89th percentile; and (*d*) Severe Problem Risk, 90th to 100th percentile. Scores on four of the scales (Alcohol, Drugs, Driver Risk, and Stress Quotient) are corrected by their correlations with the Validity Scale to yield "truth-corrected" scores.

RELIABILITY AND VALIDITY DATA. The manual provides evidence for internal consistency and interrater reliabilities. Coefficient alphas based on several studies consistently are in the .70 to .90 range with a median coefficient alpha of .81. Interrater agreement based on the correlations between DRI scales and independent DWI examiners ranged from .02 (Stress Coping Abilities) to .63 (Alcohol) with a median coefficient of .44.

Validity data are based on correlations between the DRI and various other scales and measures such as the MMPI MacAndrews Scale, number of moving violations, blood alcohol content at time of arrest, Michigan Alcohol Screening Test (MAST), Mortimer-Finkins Interview, and the

Substance Abuse Questionnaire. Some of the validity coefficients, although significant, are extremely low (e.g., .05 to .15) and achieved statistical significance because of extremely large sample sizes (Ns = 480 to 1,487).

SUMMARY. The DRI represents a convenient computerized approach to screening drivers who may be at risk for future DWI/DUI offenses. The technical manual is unclearly written, "scattered," and poorly documented. Tables of data are presented without any apparent organization and often lack clear description of the samples upon which the data are based. At present, the validity data in the manual are not convincing and users should be cautious in using the DRI to make important decisions regarding driver risk.

[1.19]
Drug Use Questionnaire.

Purpose: To assess "potential involvement with drugs."
Population: Clients of addiction treatment.
Publication Date: 1982.
Acronym: DAST-20.
Scores: Total score only.
Administration: Group.
Price Data: Available from publisher.
Foreign Language Edition: Available in French.
Time: (5–10) minutes.
Comments: Self-report inventory; manual is entitled "Directory of Client Outcome Measures for Addiction Treatment Programs"; previously entitled Drug Abuse Screening Test.
Author: Harvey A. Skinner.
Publisher: Addiction Research Foundation [Canada].
Cross References: Reviews by Philip Ash and Jeffrey S. Rain will appear in the 13th MMY.

Review of the Drug Use Questionnaire by PHILIP ASH, Director, Ash, Blackstone and Cates, Blacksburg, VA:

The Drug Use Questionnaire (DAST-20) is a 20-item yes-no response, single score inventory derived from an earlier 28-item version, the Drug Abuse Screening Test (Skinner, 1982). It should be noted, however, that although the individual copies of the inventory use the title "Drug Use Questionnaire (DAST-20)," in the manual this 20-item inventory is entitled "Drug Abuse Screening Test (DAST)," and nowhere in the nine pages of the manual is the title "Drug Use Questionnaire" used or referred to. A briefer (10-item)

version is also said to have been developed, as well as an adolescent version in which the word "work" has been replaced by "school," but no reports have been published on the psychometric properties of these scales.

Modeled after the Michigan Alcoholism Screening Test (MAST; Selzer, 1971), the DAST (and/or DAST-20) is intended to help in evaluating the seriousness of an individual's drug involvement, both for client assessment and in treatment evaluation research. Focusing on features of drug dependence such as inability to stop using drugs, withdrawal symptoms, and "other consequences relating to the use or abuse of prescribed, over-the-counter and illicit drugs" (p. 82), it asks respondents to indicate "whether they have experienced each drug-related problem in the past 12 months" (p. 82).

The manual consists mostly of summaries of research previously reported for the original 28-item DAST. It should be noted, however, the *Directory of Client Outcome Measures for Addictions Treatment Programs*, in which the manual for the DAST occupies a mere nine pages, contains a rich collection of information about a large number of substance (including alcohol) abuse measures as well as measures in other life areas. The *Directory* is well-worth perusing for its own value.

Reliability and validity data are based primarily upon studies of the original 28-item DAST, but Skinner's (1982) original report also studies the 20-item subset, and found that the two versions were "almost perfectly" (p. 83) correlated (r = .99).

Internal consistency estimates for both versions were high. Cronbach alpha estimates for the 28-item DAST were .92 for a sample including both alcohol and drug users, and .95 for the 20-item DAST. For a subsample of drug abusers, alpha = .86 for each version. The number of cases involved is not reported. In another study (Skinner & Goldberg, 1986), for a sample of 105 narcotics users, alpha = .74. No test-retest reliability estimates are reported.

No validity data are presented for the DAST-20 as such. For the original 28-item DAST, correlations of total score with frequency of use of specific drugs varied as follows: cannabis (r = .55), barbiturates (r = .47), amphetamines (r = .36), opiates other than heroin (r = .35). In a sample of narcotics users, DAST scores were related to the number of drugs currently used ($r = .29$), cannabis use ($r = .55$), and similar issues ($r = .30$ to $.38$). Correlations between .74 and .75 were found between DAST scores and DSM-II diagnosis of lifetime and current drug abuse/dependence (Gavin, Ross, & Skinner, 1989). Skinner (1982) found only modest correlations between response bias measures and DAST scores. Scores on the DAST were also found to be correlated positively with measures of impulsive and reckless behaviors ($r = .42$) and deviant attitudes ($r = .54$).

The only "norms" offered include the "average DAST [28-item] score" (p. 86) for four groups: clients with (a) alcohol problems (4.5); (b) drug and alcohol problems (15.2); (c) drug problems only (17.8); and (d) narcotics users seeking treatment (12.8). In none of the reported studies were control (nondrug-user) groups employed.

Two factor analyses yielded disparate results. One principal components analysis (Skinner, 1982) based upon a sample including both alcohol and drug abusers yielded a "strong" single underlying drug abuse factor. The second study (Skinner & Goldberg, 1986), based upon a sample of narcotics users, yielded five dimensions (factors): drug dependence, social problems, medical problems, polydrug abuse, and previous treatment.

In summary, as a quick and dirty screen of young to middle-aged adults seeking treatment for substance abuse, the Drug Use Questionnaire (DAST-20) may serve a useful purpose in identifying at least the two extremes of minimal users (whose major problem may not be substance abuse) and very heavy users. However, one must retain a measure of skepticism with respect to the stability of data such as validity coefficients when the number of items in the scale to which they are applied has been reduced by almost a third under the scale upon which they were calculated. Even the authors state that it is only highly likely the longer scale statistics apply to the DAST-20. Also, nowhere is the rationale or related data for the deletion of 8 items of the original version given. Finally, the name change from DRUG ABUSE SCREENING TEST to DRUG USE QUESTIONNAIRE on the forms given to examinees is confusing. At the minimum, an independent manual for the 20-item DRUG USE QUESTIONNAIRE would seem to be required to meet the standards for good psychometric practice. Also,

validity data and norms specific to the DAST-20 are needed.

For much more comprehensive assessment of *how* and *why* a client appears for substance abuse treatment, much more detailed and sophisticated instruments may be found, such as the Personal Experience Inventory (PEI; T4:1971; Winters and Henly, 1989), the Personal Experience Inventory for Adults (PEI-A; 1.27 this volume; Winters, 1994), the American Drug and Alcohol Survey (Oetting, Beauvais, & Edwards, 1989), and the Drug Use Screening Inventory (Tarter, 1990).

REVIEWER'S REFERENCES

Selzer, M. L. (1971). The Michigan Alcoholism Screening Test: The quest for a new diagnostic instrument. *American Journal of Psychiatry, 127,* 1653–1658.

Skinner, H. A. (1982). The American Drug Abuse Screening Test. *Addictive Behaviors, 7,* 383–371.

Skinner, H. A., & Goldberg, A. E. (1988). Evidence for a drug dependence syndrome among narcotic users. *British Journal of Addiction, 81,* 479–484.

Gavin, D. R., Ross, H. E., & Skinner, H. A. (1989). Diagnostic validity of the Drug Abuse Screening Test in assessment of DSM-III drug disorders. *British Journal of Addiction, 84,* 301–307.

Oetting, E., Beauvais, F., & (1989). The Drug and Alcohol Survey. Fort Collins, CO: Rocky Mountain Behavioral Sciences Institute.

Winters, K. C., & Henly, G. A. (1989). Personal Experience Inventory. Los Angeles: Western Psychological Services.

Tarter, R. E. (1990). Evaluation and treatment of adolescent substance abuse: A decision tree method. *American Journal of Drug and Alcohol Abuse, 16,* 1–46.

Winters, K. C. (1995). Personal Experience Inventory for Adults. Los Angeles: Western Psychological Services.

Review of the Drug Use Questionnaire by JEFFREY S. RAIN, Assistant Professor and Chairman, Industrial/Organizational Psychology Program, School of Psychology, Florida Tech, Melbourne, FL:

The Drug Use Questionnaire (entitled Drug Abuse Screening Test [DAST-20] in the manual) is a 5-minute self-report instrument purported to measure the "seriousness of drug involvement for both clinical case findings during assessment and use in treatment evaluation research" (p. 82). Items cover symptoms of drug dependence and consequences of drug use. Respondents indicate if they agree or disagree with each statement by circling "yes" or "no." The Michigan Alcoholism Screening Test (MAST; Selzer, 1971) formed the basis of the 28-item original DAST, the predecessor of the DAST-20. An adolescent version, a 10-item brief version, and a French version were developed also; however, no data were presented on which they could be reviewed. The DAST-20 is presented as one of the measures in the *Directory of Client Outcome Measures for Addictions Treatment Programs.*

Potential users of self-report measures in general, including the DAST-20, should first take into consideration those conditions under which overall validity is likely to be enhanced. Specific to alcohol and drug self-report measures, the availability of corroborating indices of drug use, the establishment of rapport with the client, the motivation of the client not to distort responses, and the length of time between current use of drugs and the assessment session each could function to reduce the usefulness of the data collected. These factors should still be considered even though research studies, in general, suggest that self-report measures can provide reliable and valid data.

Specific to the self-report issues, responses to some of the items may be dependent on the circumstances under which the DAST-20 is given and may cause a negative reaction by the client. Clients may be voluntary inpatients, court mandated participants, or individuals in crisis. Wording indicating the client's use is "abuse" (Item #3) or asking them to determine certain outcomes as being caused "because of your use of drugs" (Item #11) may provoke a reaction by the client. Clients may not be prepared to describe themselves as having "abused" drugs prior to treatment. Likewise, they may be unwilling to acknowledge the impact of their drug use/abuse on family or work before or during therapy. It should be noted that response bias analyses indicated low to moderate potential bias, though significance levels and sample sizes were not presented.

The reliability and validity data presented for the DAST-20 suggest it has the foundation to be a worthwhile screening or tracking instrument. Most of the concerns raised in reviewing the DAST-20's technical information might be answered if the *Directory of Client Outcome Measures for Addictions Treatment Programs* provided more space and thus more detailed information could have been presented. A test manual following the *Standards for Educational and Psychological Testing* (AERA, APA, & NCME, 1985) should be developed.

Reliability statistics presented were based on an earlier 28-item version of the DAST-20. Internal consistency reliabilities from the 28-item version were .86 or higher, which is very good. The only study reported that used the 20-item version yielded a coefficient alpha of .74, a substantial drop in reliability. The reliability decrease could be explained by the fact that reliability tends to de-

crease as the number of test items decrease. Extending this relationship, the adequacy of the reliability of the 10-item "brief" DAST must also be questioned.

Further, the level of reliability could be inflated by the number of "no" responses; the average score from the original sample was approximately 9.2, leaving half the items as "no." If "no" responses are interpreted as "not applicable" then the reliability may be in large part based on nonapplicability of an item. Disaggregating reliability by sample population would be instructive. The average score for individuals with only drug problems was 17.8 and may provide a better evaluation of reliability of the whole test.

As with the reliability examples above, validity findings raised further questions. The data suggested the 28-item version possessed elements of criterion-related and construct validity. Data for the DAST-20 were less specific; more of the data were based on the 28-item version. As with the reliability data, reporting significance levels and sample sizes would be helpful. Analyses where sufficient detail was presented indicate that the DAST is able to differentiate between individuals with alcohol only, drug and alcohol, and drug only problems.

A potential strong point of the DAST-20 may be its ability to measure change across time. The time frame may be varied from 6 months, 12 months, to 24 months. Used in this manner, it may provide a quick drug use symptoms and consequences screen on a case-by-case basis. In particular, test-retest reliabilities should be conducted to support this application.

Administration and scoring of the DAST-20 is very simple and straightforward. It is also very inexpensive. Comparison to norms and sample disaggregations was limited to data from three studies totaling 829 subjects.

In short, the DAST-20 has a good beginning and the association with its developmental underpinnings (i.e., MAST). However, more psychometric detail must be presented and additional studies conducted to increase its normative base before more definitive conclusions are drawn. Publication in the *Directory of Client Outcome Measures for Addictions Treatment Programs* may have limited the space to address some of the above issues with available validation studies. Depending on the veracity of the responses required, the DAST-20 should be used in conjunction with other indices and by experienced staff/professionals.

REVIEWER'S REFERENCES

Selzer, M. L. (1971). The Michigan Alcoholism Screening Test: The quest for a new diagnostic instrument. *American Journal of Psychiatry, 127,* 1653–1658.

American Educational Research Association, American Psychological Association, & National Council on Measurement in Education. (1985). *Standards for educational and psychological testing.* Washington, DC: American Psychological Association, Inc.

[1.20]
Information Test on Drugs and Drug Abuse.

Purpose: To discover what subjects know about drugs and drug abuse.
Population: Grades 9–16 and adults.
Publication Dates: 1957–1968.
Scores: Total score only.
Administration: Group.
Manual: No manual.
Price Data: Available from publisher.
Time: Administration time not reported.
Comments: For research purposes only.
Author: H. Frederick Kilander and Glenn C. Leach.
Publisher: Glenn C. Leach, Publisher.

This test has not been reviewed in *The Mental Measurements Yearbook.*

[1.21]
Information Test on Smoking and Health.

Purpose: To discover what subjects know about issues related to smoking and health.
Population: Grades 9–16 and adults.
Publication Date: 1984.
Scores: Total score only.
Administration: Group.
Manual: No manual.
Price Data: Available from publisher.
Time: Administration time not reported.
Comments: For educational or research purposes only.
Author: H. Frederick Kilander.
Publisher: Glenn C. Leach, Publisher.

This test has not been reviewed in *The Mental Measurements Yearbook.*

[1.22]
Inventory of Drinking Situations.

Purpose: "Designed to assess situations in which a client drank heavily over the past year."
Population: Ages 18 to 75.
Publication Date: 1987.
Acronym: IDS.

Scores, 8: Personal Status (Unpleasant Emotions, Physical Discomfort, Pleasant Emotions, Testing Personal Control, Urges and Temptations), Situations Involving Other People (Conflict with Others, Social Pressure to Drink, Pleasant Times with Others).
Administration: Group.
Forms, 2: IDS-100, IDS-42 (Brief Version).
Price Data, 1993: $25 per specimen set including user's guide (53 pages), 25 questionnaires, 25 answer sheets, 25 profiles; $13.50 per user's guide; $12.75 per 25 IDS-42 (Brief Version) questionnaires, 25 answer sheets, and 25 profile sheets; $14.75 per 25 IDS-100 questionnaires, 25 answer sheets, and 25 profile sheets; $140 per computer software program (50 uses); $450 per computer software program (200 uses).
Foreign Language Edition: Both forms available in French.
Time: (20–25) minutes.
Comments: IDS-42 (Brief Version) is for research use only.
Authors: Helen M. Annis, J. Martin Graham, and Christine S. Davis.
Publisher: Addiction Research Foundation [Canada].
Cross References: Reviews by Merith Cosden and Kevin L. Moreland will appear in the 13th MMY: see also T4:1265 (2 references).

Review of the Inventory of Drinking Situations by MERITH COSDEN, Professor, Department of Education, University of California, Santa Barbara, CA:

The Inventory of Drinking Situations (IDS) is a self-report instrument designed to identify situations in which respondents drank heavily over the past year. The need for this instrument stems from the literature on relapse for clients in treatment for substance abuse. This literature indicates that certain types of situations are more likely to trigger heavy drinking than others, and that these situational "triggers" vary across individuals. The IDS can be used to understand specific drinking problems and to delineate situations under which an individual is more likely to relapse.

The IDS has 100 items that describe eight situations in which drinking is likely to occur. These situations were adapted from a taxonomy of potential relapse determinants developed by Marlatt and Gordon (1985). Five situations are defined by personal states: Unpleasant Emotions, Physical Discomfort, Pleasant Emotions, Testing Personal Control, and Urges and Temptations. The other three are social situations: Conflict with Others, Social Pressure to Drink, and Pleasant Times with Others. In developing the scale the authors considered items from extant substance abuse assessment scales as well as creating their own items based on their work with clients who were alcohol dependent. Items were reviewed by clinicians in the field and pilot tested on men in an inpatient employee assistance program.

The IDS is self-administered, and comes in paper-and-pencil and computerized formats. In either format it takes approximately 20 minutes to complete. It can be administered individually or in group settings. Correlations between paper-and-pencil and computerized versions (with a 2-week interval) of the IDS are reported for 27 clients and range from .75 to .91 across subscales. The manual notes that the IDS should not be used with individuals who are under the influence of alcohol or who are experiencing alcohol withdrawal. One concern of the reviewer is that both administration formats require the client to read and respond independently. Self-administration may be contraindicated if the client is illiterate, or if heavy drinking has impaired the client's cognitive abilities. Administration of the IDS through interview format should be considered.

Each item is rated on a 1—4 scale, as respondents indicate the frequency with which they have engaged in heavy drinking over the past year in that situation as *never, rarely, frequently,* or *almost always*. Six of the scales contain 10 items, and two of the scales, Unpleasant Emotions and Conflict with Others, contain 20 items. The manual explains all scoring procedures. Subscale scores are obtained by adding the scores for items on each subscale. Problem Index scores are derived by dividing each subscale score by the maximum possible score for that subscale and multiplying by 100. A form for graphing Problem Index scores is provided.

Scores can be interpreted in several ways. Problem Index scores, which range from 0–100, provide a general assessment of the severity of one's drinking. The manual suggests that subscale scores of 67–100 reflect a history of heavy drinking and define situations that may be risky for the client in terms of relapse. The Client Profile, consisting of the eight subscale Problem Index scores, can be used to determine patterns of drinking problems, such as whether a client drinks more in the company of others, alone, or under positive or negative affective states. Finally, a client's raw scores can be compared to the standardized scores for the normative sample.

The normative sample was originally composed of 247 clients who had received treatment for alcohol problems in a Canadian clinic. As this sample was primarily male (81.8%), an additional 96 women from the same clinic were subsequently included, resulting in a total sample of 193 males and 130 females. Education level, substance abuse history, and marital status for clients in the sample are provided in the manual, but ethnicity is not noted. Differences in subscale scores were found for men and women and as a function of age. The manual presents subscale scores by gender and three age groupings, which differ slightly for men and women. For men, the age groupings are under 36, 36–55, and over 55, and for women the groupings were under 36, 36–45, and over 45. Differences in the age groupings for men and women reflect differences in subscale score patterns by gender, as well as differences in the distribution of male and female clients in the sample by age.

The manual provides internal consistency data on each of the eight subscales. Alpha levels range from .87 to .96, reflecting high internal consistency for each subscale, whereas item-total correlations within each of the subscales was somewhat lower (.39 to .82). As noted below, there are questions raised in the literature as to whether the scale represents eight or fewer distinct situations. Other types of reliability, including interrater reliability, are not discussed in the manual.

Studies of the factor structure of the IDS do not fully support the original eight-factor structure. Initially, factors were rationally derived, based on Marlatt and Gordon's (1985) taxonomy of relapse situations. A principal components analysis was conducted separately on each of the eight subscales using scores obtained from the normative sample. Six of the eight subscales were unifactorial; the subscale labeled Conflict with Others had four factorial components, whereas Pleasant Times consisted of two factors. The nature of these subfactors was not further examined. In a subsequent study (Cannon, Leeka, Patterson, & Baker,

1990) a principal components analysis was conducted on all items based on responses by 336 male inpatients in an Alcohol Dependence Treatment Program. Three components were identified in this manner, contributing to 43% of the test variance: Negative Findings, Positive Findings, and Conflict with Others. Cannon et al. report that the authors of the IDS (Annis and her associates) were able to replicate their findings with data from the normative sample when they followed the same statistical procedures. The validity of these three subscales in relation to the validity of the original eight subscales requires further study.

The manual reports on the content validity and concurrent validity of the IDS. Content validity was evaluated by asking raters to place test items into the eight categories; they were able to do so with a high degree (92%–99%) of interrater agreement. External validity has been assessed through correlations between other measures of substance abuse, levels of drinking, and IDS subscale scores. Differences in subtest scores for heavy, moderate, and light drinkers have been noted. Integral to the significance of the IDS, however, is its ability to predict relapse situations; that is, are the situations in which clients report higher levels of drinking more likely to be those in which they experience a relapse? Studies of the predictive validity of the IDS are not available.

In addition to the original IDS, there is a computerized version for the IBM. Questions are displayed on the computer screen, and clients are asked to press the number on the keyboard that most accurately describes their behavior over the past year. The program scores the IDS, displays Problem Index scores on a bar graph, and provides a list of specific situations under which the client noted heavy drinking *frequently* or *almost always*.

A shortened form of the IDS, with 42 items, was developed as a research tool. Based on the principal components analysis of the original subscales, test items with the highest item-subscale correlations were selected for the short form. Four items were selected to represent each of the six unifactorial subscales; 18 additional items were selected to represent the two multifactorial subtests, Conflict with Others and Pleasant Times with Others; 18 additional items were selected. Internal reliability of the subscales is in the .80–.92 range,

whereas correlations between the long and short form subscales range from .93 to .98. Subsequent studies (Isenhart, 1993) identified a five-factor structure for the short form of the IDS, with the five scales highly correlated with one higher-order dimension.

Although the scale specifically addresses use of alcohol, many people seeking treatment for substance abuse problems are both drug and alcohol users. Several investigators (e.g., Cannon, Rubin, Keefe, Black, Leeka, & Phillips, 1992) have used the IDS to study differences between alcohol and drug users. In doing so, Cannon et al. changed the wording of the stem in the IDS from "drank heavily" to "drank or used drugs heavily." Use of the instrument in this manner requires further psychometric study.

The IDS can provide valuable information for treatment planning for clients with drinking problems. Its strengths include its ease of administration, clinical relevance, and concurrent validity with regard to differentiating clients with moderate and heavy drinking problems. There is a need for research on the predictive validity of the instrument. Application of the IDS to populations in which both drugs and alcohol are concerns also warrants further study.

REVIEWER'S REFERENCES

Marlatt, G. A., & Gordon, J. R. (1985). Relapse prevention: Maintenance strategies in the treatment of addictive behaviors. New York: Guilford.

Cannon, D. S., Leeka, J. K., Patterson, E. T., & Baker, T. B. (1990). Principal components analysis of the Inventory of Drinking Situations: Empirical categories of drinking by alcoholics. *Addictive Behaviors, 15,* 265–269.

Cannon, D. S., Rubin, A., Keefe, C. K., Black, J. L., Leeka, J. K., & Phillips, L. A. (1992). Affective correlates of alcohol and cocaine use. *Addictive Behaviors, 17,* 517–524.

Isenhart, C. E. (1993). Psychometric evaluation of a short form of the Inventory of Drinking Situations. *Journal of Studies on Alcohol, 54,* 345–349.

Review of the Inventory of Drinking Situations by KEVIN L. MORELAND, Professor of Psychology and Chair, Fordham University, Bronx, NY:

The Inventory of Drinking Situations (IDS-100) is a 100-item questionnaire that assesses situations in which an alcohol rehabilitation client drank heavily *almost always, frequently, rarely,* or *never* during the past year. It was developed as a situation-specific measure of drinking that could be used to identify an individual client's high-risk situations for alcoholic relapse (User's Guide, p. 1). A 42-item short form of the IDS (IDS-42) is also available. The IDS-100 is recommended for clinical purposes whereas the IDS-42 may be preferable for research applications where time is at a premium. A computer-administered version of the IDS is available that shows promising congruence with the paper-and-pencil version used to develop the instrument.

The classification of drinking situations embodied in the IDS was based on the extensive efforts of Marlatt and his colleagues to determine what causes alcoholic relapse (e.g., Marlatt & Gordon, 1985). Eight expert judgment-based subscales are divided among two superordinate classes also based on expert judgment: Personal States and Situations Involving Other People. Most of the former are not "situations" in the way that term is ordinarily used to characterize the extrapersonal environment. Rather, they are subjective states such as Unpleasant Emotions (e.g., "When I was lonely"), Physical Discomfort (e.g., "When I had a headache"), Pleasant Emotions (e.g., "When I was enjoying myself"), and Testing Personal Control (e.g., "When I started to think I wasn't really hooked on alcohol"). The fourth Personal State, Urges and Temptations, includes a few subjective states (i.e., Urges like "When I remembered how good it [liquor] tasted") and a number of extrapersonal situations (i.e., Temptations like "When I passed by a bar"). Situations Involving Other People comprises subscales tapping Conflict With Others (e.g., "When someone criticized me"), Social Pressure to Drink (e.g., "When my boss offered me a drink"), and Pleasant Times with Others (e.g., "When I wanted to celebrate with a friend").

ITEM DEVELOPMENT. Suggestions for item content were drawn from a number of sources including other inventories, clinicians, persons recovering from alcoholism, and clients being treated for alcohol problems. "A draft of the resulting questionnaire was sent to five clinicians who had extensive experience working with alcoholics to solicit comments on item clarity and on item coverage .... Similar feedback was also solicited in a pilot testing ... on alcoholics" (User's Guide, p. 2). Formal psychometric considerations did not influence the final composition of the IDS-100. All of the subscales except Unpleasant Emotions and Conflict With Others comprise 10 items, the latter each comprise 20 items.

Despite the authors' extensive efforts to write good items, some potential problems are apparent.

Some items are so general that they seem only to summarize the content of the remainder of the subscale (e.g., the Social Pressure to Drink item "When I was offered a drink and felt awkward about refusing"). Other items are so specific that the situations may be irrelevant to substantial numbers of persons with alcohol problems (e.g., "When my boss offered me a drink"). Still other items appear to tap more than one construct (e.g., the Unpleasant Emotions item, "When I was troubled and I wanted to think more clearly"). That item might better exemplify the category if it ended at "troubled." Interestingly and importantly, these potentially problematic items tended not to clear the psychometric hurdles necessary for inclusion in the IDS-42.

Items for the IDS-42 were selected by examining unrotated principal components within each of the eight IDS-100 subscales. Only Conflict With Others (4) and Pleasant Times (2) yielded more than one principal component with an eigenvalue greater than one. Items for the IDS-42 are those with the highest item-component correlations unless two items were judged too similar in content, in which case one was replaced by the next highest correlating item. The IDS-42 comprises four items for each of the unifactorial subscales and three items for each component of the multifactorial subscales. Correlations between the IDS-42 subscales and their IDS-100 counterparts ranged from .93 to .98.

NORMS. Normative data for the IDS-100 are based on 323 "individuals with a wide variety of alcohol-related problems who were assessed on admission" (User's Guide, p. 8). Multivariate analyses of this sample led the authors to provide separate T-score conversions by sex or age for every subscale except Physical Discomfort. This seems ill-advised. The total normative sample is small. Subdividing it yields some tiny subsamples (e.g., 30 men over age 55). Although it is common to study demographic variables, I believe that IDS users would be better served by studies of psychological variables (e.g., sex role identity rather than gender). Perhaps Conflict With Others *is* a curvilinear function of age, younger people tending toward more interpersonal conflict in general and the interpersonal conflicts so often generated by alcoholism eventually being somewhat offset by the mellowing of middle age. The ability to assess these hypotheses is obscured by the use of different norms for different age groups. I suggest that users calculate a single set of norms from the data available in Appendix B of the User's Guide (pp. 33–41).

For interpretive purposes the authors emphasize a "Problem Index" score, which is simply the percentage of the maximum possible score. Although these scores are, no doubt, easier to discuss with clients than are T scores, no other justification is provided for their use. I recommend that they be used only to illustrate inferences that have been properly drawn from norm-referenced scores.

Psychometric Properties.

RELIABILITY. The eight IDS-100 subscales are very internally consistent. Cronbach alphas ranged from .87 (Urges and Temptations) to .96 (Unpleasant Emotions) in a very carefully described sample "of 247 clients who had voluntarily sought treatment ... [and] their major substance of abuse was ... alcohol" (User's Guide, p. 2). Not surprisingly, the IDS-42 subscales are slightly less reliable than their IDS-100 parents, with alphas ranging from .80 (physical Discomfort and Urges and Temptations) to .92 (Conflict with Others). The User's Guide provided no data concerning the stability of either form of the IDS.

VALIDITY. The issue of content coverage was dealt with in the section on item selection. Additionally, three undescribed raters were asked to sort the IDS-100 items into the eight subscales. Interrater agreement ranged from 92% to 99%.

The test authors presented evidence that all the IDS-100 scales are positively related to drinking behavior as indexed by variables such as scores on the Alcohol Dependence Scale (Skinner & Horn, 1984). However, as the authors noted, "research is needed ... to establish its relation to relapse episodes, and to document ... its utility as a treatment planning tool" (User's Guide, p. 9).

Intercorrelations among subscales were not provided in the User's Guide, but item-level factor loadings for the IDS-42 were. Details of the factor analytic method are not provided, although it was obviously exploratory and employed an oblique rotation; the sample is presumably the same one used to assess other psychometric properties of the IDS.

The factor structure did not completely conform to the a priori structure. Items from Unpleasant Emotions and Conflict With Others merged into one factor as did Pleasant Times With Others and Social Pressure to Drink. Two new dimensions emerged composed mainly of items from Conflict With Others: Social Problems at Work and Problems With Intimacy. The first order factors composed two second order factors that reflected positive (e.g., Pleasant Emotions) and negative (e.g., Physical Discomfort) motivations to drink rather than the two superordinate a priori classes of Personal States and Situations Involving Other People.

SUMMARY. The authors of the IDS are clearly sophisticated clinicians and psychometricians. The IDS appears to be the best instrument of its kind. On the other hand, the User's Guide includes some interpretive advice that is, at best, hard to defend (e.g., emphasis on the Problem Index scores) and omits some critical information (e.g., intercorrelations among the scales). I hope the authors will soon update the decade-old User's Guide both to respond to critics and to inform users about new research that will improve the use of an already useful tool.

REVIEWER'S REFERENCES

Skinner, H. A., & Horn, J. L. (1984). *Alcohol Dependence Scale (ADS): User's guide.* Toronto: Addiction Research Foundation of Ontario.
Marlatt, G. A., & Gordon, J. R. (1985). *Relapse prevention: Maintenance strategies in the treatment of addictive behaviors.* New York: Guilford.

[1.23]
The Manson Evaluation, Revised Edition.

Purpose: Identifies alcoholics and potential alcoholics.
Population: Adults.
Publication Dates: 1948–1987.
Scores, 8: Anxiety, Depressive Fluctuations, Emotional Sensitivity, Resentfulness, Incompleteness, Aloneness, Interpersonal Relations, Total.
Administration: Individual or group.
Editions, 2: Paper-and-pencil, microcomputer.
Price Data, 1993: $55 per complete kit; $29.50 per 25 test booklets/profiles ('87); $27.50 per manual ('87, 28 pages); $125 per IBM computer package including diskette (tests up to 25) and user's guide.
Time: (10–20) minutes.
Comments: Self-administered.
Authors: Morse P. Manson and George J. Huba.
Publisher: Western Psychological Services.
Cross References: Reviews by Tony Toneatto and Jalie A. Tucker originally appeared in 11:226; see also T2:1271

(2 references) and P:152 (1 reference); for a review by Dugal Campbell, see 6:137 (5 references); for reviews by Charles H. Honzik and Albert L. Hunsicker, see 4:68 (4 references).

Review of The Manson Evaluation, Revised Edition by TONY TONEATTO, Psychologist, Addiction Research Foundation, Toronto, Ontario, Canada:

The stated purposes of The Manson Evaluation (ME) are to identify individuals with personality structures common to alcoholics and those who may be prone to abusing alcohol. A third stated purpose of the test, to understand "the psychodynamic processes" in such individuals, is not addressed in the manual. The ME is deficient in several areas, particularly the conceptual basis of the test, characteristics of the samples used in its construction and validation, and in its psychometric properties.

The basic assumptions underlying the ME, that there is a personality structure common to alcoholics and alcohol-abuse prone individuals, can be seriously challenged. No work is cited to support this hypothesis. Current research suggests that the concept of an alcoholic personality is not a viable one. If such a concept is to be assessed, strong evidence for its existence needs to be well documented. Consequently, the construct validity of the ME is seriously undermined.

The authors make use of "risk group," which refers to the a priori probability of being an alcoholic (e.g., 5, 10, 20, 50%). In combination with the ME score, it yields the probability that the individual has an alcohol abuse prone personality. The authors to not discuss how one determines such a "risk" for a given individual but state that only skilled examiners can make such evaluations. If an examiner could assess such risk, what exactly would the purpose of the ME be? Furthermore, how are the probabilities that result from combining risk and ME scores to be interpreted, for example, what does a 67% chance of being alcohol prone really mean? And how is being alcohol prone different, conceptually, from being at "risk" for alcoholism? What are the social implications of designating someone who is not currently abusing alcohol as abuse prone? What is the predictive validity of such formulae?

The subject sample used in the original construction of the test is inadequately described. Mean age, sex composition, drinking history and patterns, marital status, and many other variables, are completely lacking. The sample is limited to Caucasians from one geographical area. Only alcoholics who are AA members or inpatients were studied. Are they representative of alcoholics as a whole? Of the nonalcoholics used in the construction of the test, two-thirds were individuals from families with a member in AA. Is this appropriate considering the possible risk for alcohol abuse inherent in individuals with this family background? In any case, no description of the nonalcoholics' actual drinking is presented making it impossible to evaluate their drinking. The authors also group abstainers with moderate drinkers. Might these two groups represent distinct populations?

In the original validation study, basic demographic and descriptive data are lacking (e.g., mean age, marital status, drinking history). As well, although one-third of the alcoholics were female (which does not reflect the proportion of alcohol abusers who are women), more female than male nonalcoholics were used. The authors also explicitly state that for the validation study nonalcoholics from AA circles were not included indicating that the validation of the ME used a nonalcoholic sample very different from that used in test construction (where 67% were from AA circles).

The quality of the sampling in the 1985 validation study is poor. Sampling was limited to those applying for jobs at one company. An alcoholic sample was not included, severely limiting the scope and relevance of this validation study, and necessitating the use of norms, reliability and validity information determined in 1965 in the case of alcoholics. Except for gender distribution, mean age, and education no other descriptive data are provided.

The authors do not describe how the seven subscales were derived. A perusal of the item content of the seven subscales, however, shows a poor fit with the subscale label. For example, Incompleteness (a "trait"?) consists of items that do not easily satisfy the definition of this subscale.

About 18% of the items were keyed on more than one subscale and, in one case, on three subscales. This is indicative of the lack of conceptual clarity characteristic of the ME.

In the original analyses of the test's psychometric properties, reliability was limited to a KR-

20 evaluation (r = .94) for the entire scale. The reliability data generated from the 1985 sample (which did not include an alcoholic group of subjects) are more extensive than in the original validation study but not more supportive. The KR-20 internal consistency coefficients for the subscales and full scale appear adequate although low.

The validity data presented by the authors are difficult to interpret. Although predictive validity appears to be the intention, the procedures described suggest that concurrent validity was actually assessed. Nor is it clear how significant sex differences in the full ME scores is evidence of predictive validity. The data presented for the validity of this test are not persuasive. For example, the item factor analysis yielded a general dimension of personality functioning despite the claim that the ME assesses two personality dimensions. A factor analysis of the seven trait scores yielded a two-factor solution that did reflect the two personality dimensions but only if males and females were analyzed separately. The data presented as factor loadings in Table 5 of the manual for the two-factor solution appear to be incorrect as several loadings exceed ± 1.0. It is possible that factor scores, not factor loadings, were reported. Norms based on the 1985 sample are limited to means and standard deviations for the males, females, and total sample, for the full scale and the subscales.

In summary, the conceptual, sampling, and psychometric limitations discussed in this review strongly suggest that the ME is an inadequate instrument that cannot be recommended for use either in clinical or in research contexts.

Review of The Manson Evaluation, Revised Edition by JALIE A. TUCKER, Professor of Psychology and Co-Director of Clinical Training, Auburn University, Auburn, AL:

Originally published in 1948, the 72-item Manson Evaluation was designed as a screening instrument to discriminate adult alcoholics from nonalcoholics in clinical and employment evaluations. Guided by then popular notions that alcoholism is subserved by a distinct constellation of psychopathological personality traits, the test purports to assess three personality dimensions viewed as reflecting psychoneurotic tendencies (Anxiety,

Depressive Fluctuations, and Emotional Sensitivity) and four dimensions viewed as reflecting psychopathic tendencies (Resentfulness, Incompleteness, Aloneness, and Interpersonal Relations). An indirect method of test construction guided the scale's original development. Final test items were selected from a pool of 470 general personality items that discriminated between alcoholics, who were recruited from Alcoholics Anonymous (A.A.) and institutional programs, and nonalcoholics, many of whom were family members of the alcoholic subjects. In Manson's original validation study that included 268 alcoholic and 303 nonalcoholic men and women, diagnostic accuracy was about 81% using an optimal cut point approach. Murphy (1956) subsequently replicated these findings using active alcoholics in treatment and nonalcoholics, but did not find the test effective in discriminating A.A. members who had been abstinent for 6 months or more.

The Manson Evaluation has been criticized previously on numerous grounds (see Campbell, 1965; Gibbins, Smart, & Seeley, 1959; Miller, 1976), including (*a*) the inequivalence and select nature of the alcoholic and nonalcoholic subjects included in the original validation research; (*b*) the lack of evidence supporting the seven scale dimensions, which were based on subjective/rational groupings of items; and (*c*) the use of a validation sample with a base rate of alcohol problems (50%) that greatly exceeds that found in the general population (10%).

The revised edition of the test does little to redress these concerns. The revision retains all original scale items grouped in the same seven dimensions, and the only apparent substantive change is the addition of new normative data collected from 326 job applicants who were seeking clerical, manual labor, or professional positions in a single company in Los Angeles, California. The use of subjects who were unselected along any index of psychological disturbance, including alcohol problems, would seem to have been prompted by the base rate concern noted above, but, remarkably, no data were collected on their drinking patterns or problems apart from the Manson Evaluation. Consequently, no basis exists for determining the test's ability to identify alcoholics within a nonclinical sample recruited in an employment setting, and, without such data, the claims made for the utility of the test as an employee screening device are unconscionable.

Another feature of the revised edition that also pertains to the base rate issue is the use of different norms and interpretative guidelines depending on the examiner's estimation that the test subject is a member of a population sample with a particular probability of alcoholism (5%, 10%, 25%, or 50% probability). The test manual gives rough guidelines for making this estimation, with a 5% probability viewed as applicable in personnel screening situations and a 50% probability viewed as applicable for individuals with a history of serious alcohol-related negative consequences, such as drunk driving arrests. Although these endpoints may seem self-evident, the basis for determining intermediate probabilities of risk is unclear, and the use of different probability levels has widely discrepant interpretative consequences for subjects who score in the intermediate range of the test. For example, based on assignment to the 5%, 10%, 25%, and 50% risk groups, respectively, a female's raw score of 35 (of 72 total) would yield an alcohol abuse proneness score of 27%, 44%, 70%, and 87%, respectively. Such latitude in scoring and interpretation further compounds the potential for abuse in using the test for personnel screening and for other purposes that entail substantive decisions about individuals' livelihood and well-being.

The manual for the revised edition contains new information about the test's internal consistency and factor structure derived using the employment sample, but these data do little to obviate earlier concerns about the test's subjectively determined personality dimensions. Alpha coefficients for the seven scales ranged from .44 to .75, and the factor analysis of scale scores yielded a single factor solution that was interpreted as reflecting general psychopathology. Although a two-factor solution also was presented and was interpreted as supporting the test's partition of traits into neurotic and psychopathic categories, the two factors were significantly correlated ($r = .68$), and the pattern of rotated factor loadings is unconvincing evidence for the hypothesized partition.

In reviewing the original Manson Evaluation, Miller (1976) noted the test's lack of empirical evaluation since the 1950s and observed that the scale had "fallen into disuse" (p. 651). The revised edition offers little to recommend its resurrection. The test's fundamental premise regarding a distinct alcoholic personality has been thoroughly discredited empirically in the decades since the test's initial publication, and it is disheartening that the revised edition is essentially unchanged from the original and thus is impervious to 40 years of relevant research. Great strides also have been made in the classification and measurement of alcohol-related disorders (e.g., Donovan & Marlatt, 1988; Lettieri, Nelson, & Sayers, 1985), and the revision is insensitive to this body of work as well. At best, the Manson Evaluation is of historical interest in reflecting views of alcoholism that were popular during its inception, but its contemporary use cannot be recommended. Readers interested in empirically supported, alternative procedures for the detection and evaluation of alcohol problems are referred to the comprehensive volumes on assessment edited by Donovan and Marlatt (1988) and by Lettieri et al. (1985).

REVIEWER'S REFERENCES

Murphy, D. G. (1956). The revalidation of diagnostic tests for alcohol addiction. *Journal of Consulting Psychology, 20,* 301–304.

Gibbins, R. J., Smart, R. G., & Seeley, J. R. (1959). A critique of the Manson Evaluation Test. *Quarterly Journal of Studies on Alcohol, 20,* 357–361.

Campbell, D. (1965). [Review of the Manson Evaluation.] In O. K. Buros (Ed.), *The sixth mental measurements yearbook* (pp. 285–286). Highland Park, NJ: Gryphon Press.

Miller, W. R. (1976). Alcoholism scales and objective assessment methods: A review. *Psychological Bulletin, 83,* 649–674.

Lettieri, D. J., Nelson, J. E., & Sayers, M. A. (Eds.) (1985). *Alcohol treatment assessment research instruments* (National Institute on Alcohol Abuse and Alcoholism Treatment Handbook Series #2, DHHS Publication No. ADM85-1380). Washington, DC: U.S. Government Printing Office.

Donovan, D. M., & Marlatt, G. A. (Eds.) (1988). *Assessment of addictive behaviors.* New York: Guilford Press.

[1.24]
Michigan Alcohol Screening Test.

Purpose: Designed as a screening test for assessing alcohol abuse.

Population: Adults.

Publication Dates: 1971–1980.

Acronym: MAST.

Scores: Total score only.

Administration: Group or individual.

Manual: No manual available.

Price Data, 1996: $40 per copy, which includes scoring key and permission to duplicate the test.

Foreign Language Edition: Spanish and Japanese versions available.

Time: (10) minutes.

Comments: Can be self-administered.

Author: Melvin L. Selzer.

Publisher: Melvin L. Selzer.

This test has not been reviewed in *The Mental Measurements Yearbook*.

[1.25]
The Multidimensional Addictions and Personality Profile.

Purpose: Designed as "an objective measure of substance abuse and personal adjustment problems."
Population: Individuals experiencing substance abuse and mental health disorders.
Publication Dates: 1988–1996.
Acronym: MAPP.
Scores, 15: Substance Abuse Subscales (Psychological Dependence, Abusive/Secretive/Irresponsible Use, Interference, Signs of Withdrawal, Total), Personal Adjustment Subscales (Frustration Problems, Interpersonal Problems, Self-Image Problems, Total), Defensiveness and Inconsistency Scores (Defensiveness, Inconsistency, Total); Minimizing Response Pattern Scales (Substance Abuse, Personal Adjustment, Total).
Administration: Group and individual.
Price Data, 1995: $65 per 50 answer booklets; $30 per manual ('96, 110 pages); $22 per French and Spanish translation package including written and audiotaped instructions and questions; $170 per Advanced Computer scoring package including 50 tests and a research module.
Foreign Language Edition: French and Spanish translation package available (including printed questions with audio tape).
Time: (20–25) minutes.
Comments: Previous edition entitled The COMPASS; IBM or compatible with 2 disk drives and at least 640K RAM, monitor, and printer required for computer scoring option.
Authors: John R. Craig and Phyllis Craig.
Publisher: Diagnostic Counseling Services, Inc.

This test has not been reviewed in *The Mental Measurements Yearbook*.

[1.26]
Personal Experience Inventory.

Purpose: "To identify problems associated with adolescent chemical involvement."
Population: Ages 12–18.
Publication Dates: 1988–1989.
Acronym: PEI.
Scores: 45 scores/screens: Chemical Involvement Problem Severity Section: Basic Scales (Personal Involvement with Chemicals, Effects from Drug Use, Social Benefits of Drug Use, Personal Consequences of Drug Use, Polydrug Use), Clinical Scales (Social—Recreational Drug Use, Psychological Benefits of Drug Use, Transsituational Drug Use, Preoccupation with Drugs, Loss of Control), Validity Indicators (Infrequent Responses, Defensiveness, Pattern Misfit), Drug Use Frequency/Duration/Age of Onset (Alcohol, Marijuana, LSD, Psychedelics, Cocaine, Amphetamines, Quaaludes, Barbiturates, Tranquilizers, Heroin, Opiates, Inhalants); Psychosocial Section: Personal Risk Factor Scales (Negative Self-Image, Psychological Disturbance, Social Isolation, Uncontrolled, Rejecting Convention, Deviant Behavior, Absence of Goals, Spiritual Isolation), Environmental Risk Factor Scales (Peer Chemical Environment, Sibling Chemical Use, Family Pathology, Family Estrangement), Problem Screens (Psychiatric Referral, Eating Disorder, Sexual Abuse, Physical Abuse, Family Chemical Dependency, Suicide Potential), Validity Indicators (Infrequent Responses, Defensiveness).
Administration: Group.
Parts, 2: Chemical Involvement Problem Severity Section, Psychosocial Section.
Price Data, 1993: $135 per complete kit including 5 prepaid mail-in answer booklets for computer scoring and interpretation and manual ('89, 103 pages); $47.50 per manual; $18.50 per mail-in answer booklet; $19.50 per 10 microcomputer answer booklets; $285 per 25-use IBM microcomputer disk (specify 5.25-inch or 3.5-inch); $18.50 each per FAX scoring service.
Time: (45–55) minutes.
Authors: Ken C. Winters and George A. Henly.
Publisher: Western Psychological Services.
Cross References: Reviews by Tony Toneatto and Jalie A. Tucke originally appeared in 11:284.

Review of the Personal Experience Inventory by TONY TONEATTO, *Psychologist, Addiction Research Foundation, Toronto, Ontario, Canada:*

The Personal Experience Inventory (PEI) was designed, according to the authors, to fill in the gaps in the assessment of drug use by adolescents by providing "clinicians with a comprehensive and standardized self-report inventory to assist in the identification, referral, and treatment of problems associated with teenage alcohol and drug abuse" (manual, p. 1). In doing so, the PEI goes beyond simply assessing the type and frequency of drug use but also describes the rewards, consequences, and social effects of drug use. In addition, the PEI also assesses "risk factors," both personal and environmental, that may be important in treating drug abuse (e.g., Negative Self-Image, Family Pathology, Sexual Abuse). These elements are organized into two parts, Chemical Involvement

Problem Severity (CIPS; 153 questions) and Psychosocial (147 questions). Either part can also be administered on its own. Several types of validity indicators to assess response distortion tendencies are also built into the test, which further enhances the attractiveness of this instrument.

The authors describe precisely the content and purpose for each of the scales that comprise the PEI, the population to which the test can be appropriately administered (i.e., adolescents between the ages of 12 and 18 who are believed to be experiencing some drug problem), and limitations in its use. Two sets of norms are provided, drug clinic and school, to permit an evaluation of the subjects' standings relative to other drug users and to their own high school peers. The computerized scoring and interpretation service available to PEI users is presented in sufficient detail to allow prospective users to evaluate the kind of information the PEI is capable of providing.

The construction of the PEI was first preceded by an evaluation of existing assessment tools which defined the type of instrument that was most needed. Subjects (who were largely male, white, and between 15 and 17 years of age) were recruited from several treatment centers, with 40% of the sample originating outside of Minnesota, where the test was developed. The CIPS scales were developed on a sample of 398 subjects and replicated on a second sample of 247. Similarly, the Psychosocial scales were developed on a sample of 293 and replicated on a second sample of 165. In both replication samples reliability coefficients were quite favorable (range of .81 to .97 for CIPS scales and of .74 to .90 for the Psychosocial scales).

Reliability of the PEI was assessed for internal consistency (coefficient alpha) and temporal stability (test-retest) using subjects from a variety of settings (drug clinic, juvenile offenders, school). Internal consistency coefficients were good to excellent for all samples and subgroups (N = 2,202) averaging .89 for the 10 CIPS scales, .81 for the 12 Psychosocial scales, and .68 for the 4 Response Distortion scales. Test-retest data were reported for both 1-week and 1-month intervals and for both school (N = 123) and clinic samples (N = 149). As expected, reliability (1-month interval) for the school (median .79 for CIPS scales) and clinic waiting list samples (median .84 for CIPS scales, median .72 for Psychosocial scales) was very good; longer test-retest intervals, especially if subjects received treatment, yielded lower coefficients, as might be expected. The authors caution use of the PEI following interventions for drug abuse.

Content validity appears to be quite adequate. The authors used published research findings, experts in the field, and clinicians to develop their initial 600-item pool. One item of concern, however, is use of the response anchors for many questions which are not well defined (i.e., sometimes, often, almost always).

In order to establish construct validity, the authors demonstrate that the PEI possesses: (a) convergent validity: Correlations of several PEI scales were fairly high and significant with related measures such as the Alcohol Dependence Scale, the Drug Use Frequency Checklist, and the Minnesota Multiphasic Personality Inventory (MMPI); (b) criterion validity: The PEI scale scores, especially the CIPS scales, differentiated those with and without a prior treatment history (based on a sample of 348) and those who received more intensive treatment referrals (N = 141) from less intensive referrals (outpatient, N = 72; no treatment, N = 47); and (c) discriminant validity: PEI scores differentiated clinical (drug clinic; N = 889; juvenile offenders, N = 160) and nonclinical samples (school, N = 567). Unfortunately, predictive validity was not assessed although it was identified as a focus for future research. Analyses of the internal structure of the PEI show that one factor accounted for most of the variance (70%) of the CIPS scales, not unexpectedly, as the scales comprising this part of the PEI reflected a common content area. The factor analysis of the psychosocial scales yielded a four-factor solution (psychological maladjustment, deviance, alienation, and family problems) which correlated well with other PEI scales.

In summary, the PEI is a much needed addition to the battery of adolescent drug use and abuse assessment. It is comprehensive, well grounded theoretically, and possesses good psychometric properties.

Review of the Personal Experience Inventory by JALIE A. TUCKER, Professor of Psychology and Co-Director of Clinical Training, Auburn University, Auburn, AL:

The recent proliferation of adolescent substance abuse treatment programs has not been matched by comparable advances in the development of age-appropriate assessment (or treatment) procedures. Consequently, clinical assessment procedures developed with adult substance abusers often have been used uncritically with younger clients, or adolescent-specific measures designed for use in school-based survey research have been used clinically without evaluation of their adequacy for this purpose. The Personal Experiences Inventory (PEI) was developed in response to the need for a measure of adolescent substance abuse that is sufficiently comprehensive for use in clinical situations. Designed primarily for use by an experienced clinician as part of an initial clinical evaluation of 12- to 18-year-olds suspected of substance misuse, the PEI provides a multidimensional assessment of substance use patterns and problems for up to 12 classes of abused drugs. As the authors note, it is not intended for use as a survey research instrument or for arriving at a formal diagnostic statement, but is best suited for providing a broad-spectrum assessment of adolescent substance disorders that is essential for effective disposition decisions and treatment planning.

The 300-item questionnaire assesses multiple dimensions within two major domains of substance-related dysfunction (i.e., severity of chemical involvement and associated psychosocial dysfunction). This emphasis is consistent with current views of substance abuse as multidimensional disorders that are defined both by excessive substance use and by adverse psychosocial, health, and related consequences. The chemical involvement section comprises five "basic" and five "clinical" scales that evaluate primarily the severity of substance involvement; also included are questions about the quantity and frequency of use of different drugs. The psychosocial section assesses eight personal risk factors for substance misuse (e.g., Negative Self-Image, Social Isolation) and four environmental risk factors (e.g., Peer Chemical Environment, Family Pathology) and also screens for other serious problems, including Sexual and Physical Abuse, Eating Disorders, and Suicidal Potential, that have obvious referral implications. The two major sections were developed for use either independently or conjointly, and each con-

tains several validity indicators to detect distorted or infrequent response patterns. The test is computer scored through services made available by Western Psychological Services, and a sixth grade reading level is required.

Test construction was meticulous, thorough, and attentive to research on adolescent substance abuse. Detailed description of the standardization procedures and reliability and validity studies are presented in the test manual and also are reported in journal articles (e.g., Henly & Winters, 1988; Winters & Henly, 1987). Initial item selection was derived from a review of relevant research and from several existing questionnaire measures of substance disorders. Separate standardization procedures were conducted for each of the two major test sections using 12- to 18-year-olds who were being evaluated for substance abuse treatment in Minnesota facilities (total combined N = 1,120). Although males and females with different backgrounds were included, most subjects were white males between the ages of 15 and 17. Additional normative data were collected from students in grades 7 through 12 (N = 693) and from juvenile offenders (N = 389) in different geographic areas in the U.S. and Canada.

Reliability studies showed good to excellent internal consistency as measured by alpha coefficients for the great majority of PEI scales, and these findings held across sample type, sex, age, and ethnic subgroups. Results pertaining to the temporal stability of scores across 1-week and 1-month intervals, although generally adequate, were somewhat less robust and varied by sample type. Of particular concern was the finding that subjects who underwent drug treatment during the 1-month test-retest interval showed increased reporting of substance use from the first to the second administration. The authors apparently attributed this to subjects' greater willingness to admit drug use after the treatment intervention, but the instability in responding cautions against the test's use as a measure of treatment outcome in evaluation research.

Validity studies conducted to date indicated that the PEI, and especially the chemical severity section, effectively discriminated among subjects who varied by prior treatment history, treatment referral decisions, sample type (e.g., drug clinic vs.

school), and intake diagnosis. Modest associations were obtained between subject and parent reports of some PEI scales, but the lack of significant agreement for most scales is a worrisome limitation that warrants further investigation. Also, some convergence was observed between subjects' PEI scores and scores on other measures of substance-related dysfunction (e.g., the Alcohol Dependence Scale; Horn, Skinner, Wanberg, & Foster, 1984) and psychopathology (i.e., the Minnesota Multiphasic Personality Inventory [MMPI]), but the appropriateness of using these instruments developed with adults for comparison with the PEI is questionable. Moreover, the PEI was not compared with existing measures of alcohol expectancies that have a demonstrated predictive relationship with subsequent alcohol use in adolescents (reviewed by Leigh, 1989). This oversight is worth pursuing in future research.

The results of factor analytic studies were not particularly encouraging about the internal structure of the PEI, and this comprises its major limitation. Analysis of the five basic scales of the chemical severity section yielded a single factor that accounted for over 70% of the variance and that was highly correlated with a single scale (the Personal Involvement With Chemicals scale). Analysis of the psychosocial scales yielded a four-factor solution that bore little relationship to the organizational structure of the 12 scales included in this section of the PEI. Also, the scales and factors included in the chemical severity and psychosocial sections were intercorrelated to a considerable degree, which further attests to the need to reduce scale redundancies in revisions of the PEI. Finally, research evaluating the ability of pre-treatment PEI scores to predict treatment outcome is lacking and is important for establishing the overall utility of the measure.

These unresolved validity issues notwithstanding, the PEI has much to recommend its use for the clinical purposes for which it was designed. The test fills an important gap in the assessment of adolescent substance disorders and, if used as intended as part of an overall clinical evaluation, it should assist clinicians in obtaining the comprehensive information required for effective disposition decisions and treatment development. Although modification of the complex scale structure to reduce redundancies seems indicated, the au-

thors' careful attention to the relevant research and their focus on the multidimensional nature of substance misuse in developing the PEI are commendable. If revisions of the PEI are equally attentive to empirical and conceptual considerations, the instrument should come to enjoy widespread clinical usage.

REVIEWER'S REFERENCES

Horn, J. L., Skinner, H. A., Wanberg, K., & Foster, F. M. (1984). Alcohol Dependence Scale (ADS). Toronto: Addiction Research Foundation.

Winters, K. C., & Henly, G. A. (1987). Advances in the assessment of adolescent chemical dependency: Development of a Chemical Use Problem Severity Scale. Psychology of Addictive Behaviors, 1, 146-153.

Henly, G. A., & Winters, K. C. (1988). Development of Problem Severity Scales for the assessment of adolescent alcohol and drug abuse. International Journal of the Addictions, 23, 65-85.

Leigh, B. C. (1989). In search of the seven dwarves: Issues of measurement and meaning in alcohol expectancy research. Psychological Bulletin, 105, 361-373.

[1.27]

Personal Experience Inventory for Adults.

Purpose: Designed to yield "comprehensive information about an individual's substance abuse patterns and problems."

Population: Age 19 and older.

Publication Dates: 1995–1996.

Acronym: PEI-A.

Scores, 37: Problem Severity Scales (Personal Involvement with Drugs, Physiological Dependence, Effects of Use, Social Benefits of Use, Personal Consequences of Use, Recreational Use, Transsituational Use, Psychological Benefits of Use, Preoccupation, Loss of Control, Infrequency—1, Self-Deception, Social Desirability—1, Treatment Receptiveness), Psychosocial Scales (Negative Self-Image, Psychological Disturbance, Social Isolation, Uncontrolled, Rejecting Convention, Deviant Behavior, Absence of Goals, Spiritual Isolation, Peer Drug Use, Interpersonal Pathology, Estrangement in the Home, Infrequency—2, Social Desirability—2), Problem Screens (Suicide Risk, Work Environment Risk, Past Family Pathology, Other Impulse-Related Problems, Significant Other Drug Problem, Sexual Abuse Perpetrator, Physical Abuse Perpetrator, Physical/Sexual Abuse Victim, Need for Psychiatric Referral, Miscellaneous).

Administration: Group.

Parts, 2: Problem Severity Scales, Psychosocial Scales.

Price Data, 1996: $135 per kit including 5 prepaid mail-in answer booklets and manual ('96, 100 pages); $18.50 or less per mail-in answer booklet; $275 or less per IBM microcomputer scoring disk (25 uses; 3.5-inch); $19.50 or less per 10 microcomputer answer booklets for use with microcomputer disk; $17.50 each for FAX scoring service.

Time: (45–60) minutes.

Comments: Untimed self-report inventory; computer scored only.

Author: Ken C. Winters.
Publisher: Western Psychological Services.

Review of the Personal Experience Inventory for Adults by MARK D. SHRIVER, Assistant Professor, University of Nebraska Medical Center, Omaha, NE:

The stated purpose of the Personal Experience Inventory for Adults (PEI-A) is to function as "a comprehensive, standardized self-report inventory to assist in problem identification, treatment referral, and individualized planning associated with addressing the abuse of alcohol and other drugs by adults" (p. 3). It is designed to yield "comprehensive information about an individual's substance abuse patterns and problems [and] ...also helps to identify the psycho-social difficulties of the referred individual" (p. 3). The PEI-A is developed from, and an extension of, the PEI (1989) which is a self-report measure of drug and alcohol use for adolescents ages 12 to 18 (see *Mental Measurements Yearbook* [1992] 11:284 for reviews by Tony Toneatto and Jalie A. Tucker).

The manual states that the PEI-A "was designed primarily as a clinical descriptive tool for use by addiction professionals" and that it "is intended to supplement a comprehensive assessment process" (p. 5). Specifically, the PEI-A was developed to measure the following characteristics:

1. The presence of the psychological, physiological, and behavioral signs of alcohol and other drug abuse and dependence.

2. The nature and style of drug use (e.g., consequences, personal effects, and setting).

3. The onset, duration, and frequency of use for each of the major drug categories.

4. The characteristics of psychosocial functioning, especially factors identified as precipitating or maintaining drug involvement and expected to be relevant to treatment goals.

5. The existence of behavioral or mental problems that may accompany drug use (e.g., sexual abuse or co-addiction).

6. The sources of invalid response tendencies (e.g., "faking bad," "faking good," inattention, or random responding).

The appropriate use of any measure for its intended purposes is dependent on its sample representation, reliability, and validity. This information is reviewed respective to the PEI-A's stated purposes described above.

TEST ADMINISTRATION. The manual provides easy-to-read instructions on test administration, which will assist with increasing standardization of the administration. The manual states that the reading level of the measure is approximately sixth grade (p. 7), and the test may be read to clients with lower reading abilities. No discussion is presented, however, regarding whether this type of administration occurred during norming of the test, or how this type of administration may affect the reliability or validity of the self-report measure, as the examiner is directly involved with administration, which runs counter to one of the intended goals for test development (p. 29).

The test is scored by computer, either through a mail-in service, a FAX service, or by computer disk. The mail-in service typically requires approximately 3–5 working days to return scores (p. 75). This may be too long in some clinical settings. Interpretations of each scale are provided in the computer-generated report.

TEST DEVELOPMENT. The content of the PEI-A is largely derived from the PEI. A panel of experts is reported to have examined the items on the PEI and made changes where necessary to adapt the items to an adult population. The panel of experts was composed of "Groups of researchers and drug treatment service providers" (p. 30), but no further indication is provided in the manual about who these individuals are, where they are from, and what respective experience/ expertise they have in item/test development. Item selection and scale development proceeded on a "rational basis" (p. 30). In addition to the PEI, a drug use frequency checklist adapted from adolescent and adult national survey instruments was incorporated into the drug consumption section of the PEI-A.

The initial items and scales of the PEI-A were examined with a sample of 300 drug clinic subjects (150 males, 150 females) for internal scale consistency (alpha coefficients) and interscale correlations. Correlations between Problem Severity Scales "were somewhat higher than desired for scales intended to contribute substantial unique and reliable information about the respondent, ranging from .55 to .92" (p. 33). Alpha correlations of individual scales were good, typically within the .75 to .93 range (pp. 32–33). Following examination of the correlations on this initial sample of subjects "only minor adjustments in item assignment" were made in scales (p. 33).

The content of the Problem Severity Scales is described as "multidimensional, oriented around signs and symptoms of drug abuse and dependence, and not anchored in any single theoretical model" (p. 30). Review of the items on the measure suggests that the content appears appropriate for the purposes listed above. Review of the empirical evidence for sample comparisons, reliability, and validity will help determine if items originally developed for adolescents and refined for adults based on unknown expert opinion are truly valid for adults.

The test items were not analyzed statistically for possible bias. The test was examined for differences in internal consistency across gender and race, and significant differences were not found; however, predictive validity and differential decision making across gender and race have not yet been examined. Differences in primary language of the subjects was not discussed and it is difficult to determine how language (i.e., not primarily English) might affect responses (written or oral) on the PEI-A.

SAMPLES FOR TEST VALIDATION AND NORMING. Three samples were chosen for test norming: 895 drug clinic clients from Minnesota, Illinois, Washington, California, Missouri, and Ontario, although specific numbers from each state are not provided; 410 criminal offenders, most from Minnesota; and 690 nonclinical participants, all from Minnesota. All sample subjects were volunteers. No discussion is provided in the manual regarding the possible impact on client self-report due to the sample selection process, and whether valid interpretation of the results can be made with individuals who may be tested under some type of coercion such as for court-ordered treatment. Sample demographic information is provided in the manual regarding mean age, age range, gender, minority, percent in prior treatment, marital status, employment status, and education (p. 36).

Scores from the measure are compared with the drug clinic sample in the form of T scores; however, score comparisons (T scores) are also provided at the end of the computerized report for the nonclinic sample. Given the restricted geographic sampling of the nonclinic group, it is difficult to determine if this comparison provides useful information for individuals who are not from Minnesota. It is also unclear if the nonclinic sample participated by mail as described on page 35 of the manual or through group testing as described on page 36 of the manual. Both contexts for test taking are somewhat different from the typical administration (e.g., individualized, in drug clinic) described in the manual and may limit score interpretations even further.

The drug clinic sample is described in terms of two groups: outpatient and residential treatment. Only 37.5% of the outpatient drug clinic sample is female (approximately 188). Only 36.3% of the residential drug clinic sample is female (approximately 143). Separate T scores are provided for male and female samples (p. 36). Only approximately 113 members of the outpatient drug clinic sample are of an ethnic minority status, and approximately 68 members of the residential drug clinic sample are of an ethnic minority status. Minority is not defined further (e.g., African American, Hispanic, Native American), although it is conceivable that minority status may differentially impact drug use. In addition, although the gender representation may be an accurate reflection of general population drug use, the small sample size for females limits normative comparisons. Reported drug use patterns may also differ by gender.

Information is not provided on whether the norm groups come from rural or urban settings. A rural or urban context may impact drug use (i.e., availability of drugs). Also, specific numbers are not provided relative to the geographic regions from which the drug clinic samples originate, and as indicated by the authors (p. 36), geographic region may impact reported drug use (i.e., higher cocaine use in California and Washington reported relative to Midwest states and Ontario).

In summary, caution is advised in using the PEI-A with females, minorities, and individuals from geographic regions other than those sampled. In addition, the comparison with nonclinic population may not be useful for individuals outside of Minnesota. The test norms appear to be useful for comparing Caucasian males with possible drug use history with the drug clinic sample.

RELIABILITY. Internal consistency reliabilities are provided (coefficient alpha) for the entire sample and provided for male, female, white, and minority samples (pp. 37–41). In addition, test-retest reliabilities are presented for one week and for one month using the drug clinic sample, although there was some intervening treatment between pre- and posttest scores (pp. 42–43). Only reliabilities for the drug clinic and nonclinic samples will be discussed as these represent the primary comparative groups for examinees.

Coefficient alphas are generally good for the Problem Severity Scales (median .89 range .72 to .94) and the Psychosocial Scales (median .81 range .67 to .91). The coefficient alphas are low for the Validity Scales (median .63 range .58 to .77) (p. 37). The authors claim the validity reliability estimates compare favorably with other instruments, and this may be true; however, these values are just acceptable given the use to be made of these scores.

Median test-retest reliabilities at one week (70 individual) were as follows: Problem Severity scales .71 (.60 to .88), Psychosocial scales .66 (.55 to .87), and Validity Indices .52 (.40 to .57). One-month test-retest reliabilities were lower as expected given intervening treatment (pp. 42–43). Given that some subjects were provided intervening treatment in the one-week test-retest group also, it can reasonably be said that test-retest reliability has not been adequately examined and no conclusions can be drawn regarding temporal stability of the test. This makes it less useful pre- and post-treatment as it is difficult to determine if changes in scores are due to treatment or lack of score stability. This is in conflict with the authors' conclusions, however, that scores can be compared pre- and posttreatment (p. 43).

In summary, the internal consistency estimates of the Problem Severity Scales and the Psychosocial Scales range from good to acceptable. More research is definitely needed on the stability of the test scores (test-retest) before conclusions can be drawn regarding the test's usefulness pre- and posttreatment.

VALIDITY. One potential use of this instrument is to determine appropriate treatment options for individuals. Drug clinic subjects ($N = 251$) were classified into three referral categories: no treatment, outpatient treatment, and residential treatment based on clinical staff ratings. Mean scores on the PEI-A Problem Severity Scales were examined and expected differences in scores were found for the three groups (p. 46). Future researchers, however, may want to look at the contribution the PEI-A provides above and beyond other information used in making referral decisions. In other words, are these mean score differences useful? Also, significant differences in mean scores according to sample group membership (nonclinical, drug clinic, and criminal offender) were also found (p. 46). Again, an empirical examination as to how this information contributes as part of a comprehensive assessment would be useful.

Seven of the Problem Screens were compared with staff ratings to determine sensitivity and specificity of the screens, essentially the degree of agreement regarding the existence of problems (p. 48). For the total sample, there were significant correlations ($p<.05$) for agreement between the PEI-A and staff ratings for negative ratings (i.e., individual not identified with having problem), but not for positive ratings (i.e., individual identified as having problem) (p. 49).

The Validity Indices were found to correlated as expected with Minnesota Multiphasic Personality Inventory (MMPI) Validity scales (p. 48).

To assess the construct validity of the scale, correlations with tests purported to measure similar constructs were examined. Moderate correlations were found between the Problem Severity Basic Scales scores and the Alcohol Dependence Scale (.41–.66; p. 44; ADS; Horn, Skinner, Wanberg, & Foster, 1982). In addition, correlations are also provided for Problem Severity Scale scores and the Drug Use Frequency Checklist; however, the Drug Use Frequency Checklist is actually part of the PEI-A so the usefulness of this information for construct validity is weakened. The Psychosocial Scales of the PEI-A were found to correlate significantly with MMPI scales, suggesting the psychosocial Scales are measuring psychopathology to some extent (p. 45), but there does not appear to be much differentiation between the PEI-A scales as all but Rejecting Convention and Spiritual Isolation correlate highly with each of the MMPI scales. Finally, information is provided that "select" PEI-A scales (p. 45) correlate significantly with a Significant Other Questionnaire. However, the Significant Other Questionnaire is also developed from PEI-A items, which again attenuates the meaningfulness of this relationship.

In summary, the validity evidence presented in the manual does not appear to address specifically the intended purposes/applications of the test noted above. The content looks good, but much more empirical research is needed on the validity of this instrument specifically related to the applications for which it is intended. Future research should address whether this instrument contributes significantly (above and beyond other information in a comprehensive assessment) to decision making involved in assessing and treating individuals with alcohol and drug use problems.

SUMMARY. The PEI-A may be most useful for examining alcohol and drug use in white males who are compared with a drug clinic sample. Results of this test are intended to tell the clinician whether an individual is similar to individuals in the drug clinic sample and to provide some information on the impact of drugs on the individual's life. Caution is urged in using the PEI-A with females and minorities given the small sample sizes. Geographic region and urban-rural differences may also impact reports of drug use and should be considered by the test user. In addition, this test may not be useful for individuals whose primary language is not English. The use of the nonclinic scores for comparisons is questionable for individuals outside Minnesota. Estimates of the internal consistency reliability of the scales and content appear good. Additional research on test-retest reliability is needed. More research on the validity of the PEI-A as part of a comprehensive assessment is needed. The PEI-A looks promising, but users are encouraged to heed the test author's statement that this test should only be used as part of comprehensive assessment.

REVIEWER'S REFERENCES

Horn, J. L., Skinner, H. A., Wanberg, K., & Foster, F. M. (1982). Alcohol Dependence Scale (ADS). Toronto: Addiction Research Foundation.

Toneatto, T. (1992). [Review of the Personal Experience Inventory.] In J. J. Kramer & J. C. Conoley (Eds.), *The eleventh mental measurements yearbook* (pp. 660–661). Lincoln, NE: Buros Institute of Mental Measurements.

Tucker, J. A. (1992). [Review of the Personal Experience Inventory.] In J. J. Kramer & J. C. Conoley (Eds.), *The eleventh mental measurements yearbook* (pp. 661–663). Lincoln, NE: Buros Institute of Mental Measurements.

Review of the Personal Experience Inventory for Adults by CLAUDIA R. WRIGHT, Professor of Educational Psychology, California State University, Long Beach, CA:

The Personal Experience Inventory for Adults (PEI-A) is a standardized self-report instrument for use by service providers in the substance abuse treatment field to assess patterns of abuse and related problems in adult clients (age 19 or older). The two-part, 270-item PEI-A is made up of 10 problem severity scales and 11 psychosocial scales, 5 validity indicators, and 10 problem screens; it parallels in content and form the two-part, 300-item Personal Experience Inventory (PEI; 11:284) developed for use with adolescents (age 18 or younger). A broad theoretical framework, influenced by Alcoholics Anonymous, social learning, and psychiatric models, underlies the development of both inventories. The manual presents a thorough treatment of test development, standardization, and validation procedures along with clear test administration and computer-scoring guidelines and useful strategies for score interpretation. The inventory is written at a sixth-grade reading level. No provisions are made for non-English-speaking test takers.

NORMING PROCEDURES. Norm tables were constructed separately for males and females in two standardization samples (clinical and nonclinical). Normative data were obtained primarily from Midwestern Whites, raising concerns about the generalizability of score interpretations to clients classified as nonwhite. Demographic information presented in the PEI-A manual indicates that 20% of the clinical sample ($n = 895$) was classified as minority. Clinic respondents attended outpatient and residential Alcoholics Anonymous-based programs at 12 sites (located in 3 midwestern and 2 western states and 1 Canadian province). No rationale was provided for site selection. A total of 690 Minnesota residents comprised the nonclinical sample; 11% were classified as minority. A sample of 410 criminal offenders (77% were male; 68% of the sample was nonwhite) was used to provide data for some validation analyses.

Caution is warranted in applying the PEI-A norms to members of nonwhite groups in either clinical or nonclinical settings. The test developer is to be commended for briefly acknowledging this limitation. Sampling that includes more regions, broader ethnic representation, and types of treatment program sites is essential.

RELIABILITY. For 1,995 respondents, median Cronbach alphas were (a) Problem Severity Scales = .89 (range: .81–.93); (b) Psychosocial Scales = .80 (range: .75–.88); and (c) three of the five Validity Indicators = .70 (range: .65–.73). When subsamples were broken out by gender, ethnicity (white or minority), and setting (nonclinical, drug clinic, or criminal offender), patterns of reliability estimates were comparable to those obtained with the total sample. One-week (n = 58; .42–.78, mdn = .69) and one-month (n = 49; .39–.72, mdn = .52) stability indexes for problem screens were lower than desired due to respondents' exposure to treatment programs during the test-retest intervals.

CONTENT VALIDATION. Common content validation procedures were followed. Researchers and treatment providers rated PEI items intended for inclusion in the PEI-A with respect to clinical relevance and importance to adult substance abuse. Based upon rater feedback, minor item modifications were made.

CRITERION-RELATED VALIDITY. Concurrent validity evidence for the PEI-A was provided by data comparisons examining the effects on scale scores of (a) treatment history for substance abuse among drug clinic clients (no sample size reported); (b) referral recommendation (no treatment, outpatient, or residential) (N = 251); (c) setting (nonclinical, drug clinic, or criminal offender) (N = 1,978); and (d) *DSM-III-R* (American Psychiatric Association, 1987) diagnosis of abuse or dependence upon alcohol or drugs (N = 244). The observed group differences obtained from scores on the 10 Problem Severity Scales supported the view that individuals referred to treatment settings (outpatient or residential) had greater problems with higher substance use, dependence, and related consequences of usage compared to those for whom no drug treatment was recommended. The 11 Psychosocial Scales fared less well in distinguishing among the three groups with only three scales (Negative Self-Image, Deviant Behavior, and Peer Drug Use) yielding statistically significant differences. In a separate analysis, scores obtained from a nonclinical subsample (n = 687) were significantly lower on each of the 21 scales (all p < .01) when compared with those from drug clinic (n = 887) and offender (n = 404) groups. For the *DSM-III-R* Diagnosis comparison, clients identified as dependent on alcohol or drugs had significantly higher scores on the 5 Basic Scales when compared to those classified as abusing these substances.

Although the measure is purportedly used to assist in treatment referral, no predictive validity information was presented linking referral decisions based upon standing on the PEI-A scales and outcome success.

CONSTRUCT VALIDITY. Only modest to moderate levels of construct validity evidence were presented based on correlations between PEI-A Problem Severity Basic scale scores and performance on the Alcohol Dependence Scale (ADS; Horn, Skinner, Wanberg, & Foster, 1982) and the PEI-A Drug Use Frequency Checklist. Moderate coefficients were obtained for a sample of 89 clients indicating that the 5 Basic Scale scores were somewhat related to ADS scores (.52–.63, mdn = .59) and Checklist scores (.41–.66; mdn = .55). For a sample of 213 clinic respondents, correlations among the 11 PEI-A Psychosocial Scales and 9 Minnesota Multiphasic Personality Inventory (MMPI) Scales yielded 62 out of 99 possible coefficients ranging from .20–.69, mdn = .38 (all p < .001) indicating, for the most part, only modest levels of shared variance (4% to 48% explained, mdn = 14%). Moderate coefficients (above the median) were associated with PEI-A scales that deal with personal adjustment issues (e.g., Negative Self-Image, Psychological Disturbance, Social Isolation, and Absence of Goals). PEI-A scale scores dealing with personal values and environmental influences (e.g., Rejecting Convention and Spiritual Isolation) yielded negligible correlations with the MMPI. PEI-A and MMPI validity indicators also were moderately correlated.

Inspection of intercorrelations among the 10 Problem Severity Scales revealed moderate to strong coefficients posing a multicollinearity problem. It is evident from data reported in the manual that the statistical contribution of unique variance to score interpretation associated with each of the 5 Clinical Scales adds little or no unique information (r_{xy}s ranged from .04 to .09, mdn = .05). This outcome was consistent with that reported for the same 10 scales of the PEI. The 5 Clinical Scales were retained "because users have found these scales helpful" (manual, p. 33). The retention of redundant scales requires more detailed explanation than that provided in the manual. For future research and test development purposes, targeting items from scales that contribute unique information for provider applications and removing redundant items would strengthen this section of the inventory.

Intercorrelations among the Psychosocial Scales revealed patterns of coefficients more distinctive of a multidimensional scale (as intended) with proportions of unique variance ranging from .18 to .57 (*mdn* = .29). However, lower reliability estimates and the inability of these scales to distinguish between referral groups is of concern.

SUMMARY. The Personal Experience Inventory for Adults (PEI-A) offers a beginning point to the service provider for assessment. Most PEI-A scale scores demonstrate adequate levels of reliability and distinguish between clinical and nonclinical groups. Current norms may be too restrictive for some settings. Based upon validity evidence provided, caution is warranted in all testing with use of scores from the Clinical Scales, which are redundant with the Basic Scales and with scores from the Psychosocial Scales, which have shown only low to moderate relationships with related constructs. PEI-A computer-generated recommendations for individual clients should be considered in light of these limitations and decisions made in conjunction with other measures.

REVIEWER'S REFERENCES

Horn, J. L., Skinner, H. A., Wanberg, K., & Foster, F. M. (1982). *Alcohol Dependence Scale (ADS)*. Toronto: Addiction Research Foundation.
American Psychiatric Association. (1987). *Diagnostic and statistical manual of mental disorders* (3rd ed.). Washington, DC: Author.

[1.28]
Personal Experience Screening Questionnaire.

Purpose: "Designed as a brief screening tool to aid ... in the identification of teenagers likely to need a drug abuse assessment referral."
Population: Adolescents.
Publication Date: 1991.
Acronym: PESQ.
Scores, 3: Infrequency, Defensiveness, Problem Severity.
Administration: Group.
Price Data, 1993: $70 per complete kit including 25 test forms and manual (30 pages); $29.50 per 25 test forms;

$42.50 per manual.
Time: (10) minutes.
Author: Ken C. Winters.
Publisher: Western Psychological Services.
Cross References: For reviews by Stuart N. Hart and Richard W. Johnson originally appeared in 12:286 (1 reference).

Review of the Personal Experience Screening Questionnaire by STUART N. HART, Associate Professor of Counseling and Educational Psychology, Indiana University-Purdue University at Indianapolis, Indianapolis, IN:

The primary general purpose set for the Personal Experience Screening Questionnaire (PESQ) was "to provide clinicians with a standardized self-report screening tool to assist in the identification of teenagers needing a drug abuse assessment referral" (p. 1). The author intended more specifically to provide a quick screening, standardized, adolescent-specific instrument, sensitive to alcohol and other drug abuse and to response distortion tendencies. To accomplish this the author produced the 40-item PESQ intended for youth 12 to 18 years of age and consisting of three subsections dealing with drug involvement problem severity, psychosocial problems, and personal drug history; and including items to assess faking bad and faking good response tendencies.

The manual for the PESQ is well developed and presents information in a clear and logical manner, which displays the respect of the author for the criteria of the *Standards for Educational and Psychological Testing* (AERA, APA, & NCME, 1985). The PESQ can be easily administered by a properly prepared and supervised technician or clerk and interpretations should be made or closely supervised by an appropriately trained professional. No time limit for completion of the PESQ is set but it is usually completed in approximately 10 minutes. Individual administration is preferred but group administration is indicated to be acceptable and was incorporated in addition to individual administration in the development of normative data. Required test materials include a two-sided PESQ "Auto-Score" form and a pencil. Examinees place their responses on the questionnaire/ answer sheet, and the responses transfer to the scoring section on the examinee-inaccessible inside of the form. The instructions and items of the

PESQ are at approximately the 4th grade reading level. By having an examinee read the instructions aloud the examiner can determine whether it will be necessary to read the items to the examinee.

The PESQ scores are organized to provide results for three scales labeled Problem Severity, Defensiveness, and Infrequency; and to provide information on two content areas labeled Psychosocial Indicators and Drug Use History. Part I of the PESQ contains 18 items that accumulate to give a global measure of Problem Severity indicating the extent to which the individual is psychologically and behaviorally involved with drugs. The items fall within subcategories exploring frequency of use of drugs under various conditions and behaviors associated with drug use and procurement. Part I also includes the three items of the Infrequency scale, to measure faking bad and dealing with extremely unlikely drug use behavior. All items of Part I are responded to on a 4-point scale (i.e., *never, once or twice, sometimes, often*). Part II of the instrument contains eight items that accumulate to provide information for the content area of Psychosocial Indicators covering "emotional distress, problems with thinking, and physical and sexual abuse" associated with adolescent drug use. Part II also includes the five items of the Defensiveness scale to measure faking-good response tendencies. All items of Part II require yes or no responses. Part III requests information about the respondent's Drug Use History by asking the frequency of use of various drugs during the last 12 months and provides seven response options ranging from never to over 40 times for alcoholic beverages and marijuana or hashish and once or more for a list of hard drugs; and additionally two questions arc asked about the time when the person first got high or first used drugs regularly.

Scoring the PESQ is relatively easy, requiring only that simple instructions inside the response form be followed to accumulate totals for the three scales and two content areas. To guide interpretations cutoff scores and ranges are provided for the Problem Severity scale by age and sex subgroupings. Scores above specified points are labeled "red flag" to indicate the examinee may be in need of a referral and that a "more complete and reliable drug abuse assessment" (p. 10) is advised, or "green flag" to indicate a referral is probably not

needed. The results for the Infrequency and Defensiveness scales are to be used to modify considerations of profile results, particularly for the Problem Severity scale. Scores above the red flag cutoffs for the faking-bad and faking-good scales suggest that the validity for the rest of the profile is in question and that caution is needed in interpreting results, whereas scores in the green flag range indicate "the profile is probably valid" (p. 10). Information contained in answers to specific questions on the three scales and from the two content areas provides the interpreter with opportunities to derive additional meaning. The author urges the interpreter be knowledgeable regarding drug abuse and interpretation of these tests in order to maximize the validity of the test.

The PESQ was developed through the Chemical Dependency Adolescent Assessment Project (CHDAAP), which was established in 1982 to develop "assessment tools to aid clinicians in the identification, referral, and treatment of teenagers suspected of drug abuse" (p. 11). The Problem Severity scale of the PESQ was developed by selecting unused items from the pool of items previously used to construct the Personal Involvement With Chemicals scale of the Personal Experience Inventory (PEI), a well-respected CHDAAP instrument meant for the clinical evaluation of drug abuse and treatment needs (see reviews of the PEI in *The Eleventh Mental Measurements Yearbook*; 11:284). These items were part of the set that had a high loading for a general drug abuse severity factor. The specific items selected for the Problem Severity scale of the PESQ met requirements of having Pearson product-moment correlations greater than .50 with the PEI Personal Involvement With Chemicals scale, and less than -.40 with the Marlowe-Crowne Social Desirability scale. The PESQ five faking-good Defensiveness scale items were derived from the Marlowe-Crowne Desirability Scale, whereas the three faking-bad, inattentive, or random responding Infrequency scale items and the content area items were derived from logical analyses of the PEI's psychosocial section and adapted from national survey instruments.

Reliability of the PESQ has been addressed only through internal consistency estimates for the Problem Severity scale thus far. The population sample employed for this purpose included 2,744 subjects from schools (n = 1,885), juvenile detention centers (n = 611), and drug clinics (n = 248). School and juvenile center populations completed questionnaires similar to the PESQ which included the 18 Problem Severity items whereas the drug clinic sample completed 203 items of the original PEI pool. Quite good alpha coefficients ranging from .90–.95 were produced across samples. Internal consistency measures were essentially the same regardless of the nature and length of the larger item pool within which the PESQ items were placed; and across male and female, white and non-white subjects. Test-retest reliability, stability over time, clearly needs to be addressed in future research. Although it would be expected to be adequate on the basis of the very good to good test-retest results that have been found for the similar longer scale on the PEI, this is not sufficient evidence.

The content validity of the Problem Severity scale of the PESQ is clearly tied to the content validity of the PEI, which has been judged to be "quite adequate" (Toneatto, 1992). PESQ items were selected from the item pool used to construct the PEI. A "broad spectrum approach" (p. 17) to adolescent use problem severity guided the development of this pool, which included 10 scales produced by "statistical and rational approaches" (p. 17) derived from 24 content categories identified as relevant. A Pearson product-moment correlation of .94 was found for the relationship between the PESQ Problem Severity scale and PEI personal involvement with chemicals section of its problem severity scales. The items of the Defensiveness scale (adapted from the Marlowe-Crowne Social Desirability Scale) and of the Infrequency scale resulted from a review of empirical knowledge and from consultant advice. They appear to have adequate content validity but, as with all the items of the PESQ, the user must determine their relevance for the population and setting to which they will be applied.

The construct validity of the PESQ is also closely tied to the construct validity of the PEI Personal Involvement with Chemicals scale which has been found to best tap the core of its chemical severity section (Tucker, 1992). This fact, added to knowledge of the fairly high and significant correlations between the PEI and related measures (Toneatto, 1992), the high internal consistency found for the PESQ, and the ability of the PESQ

to discriminate between those at various levels of drug abuse (see later section), indicates its construct validity is satisfactory.

Criterion validity, of greatest significance in determining the usefulness of a screening device, appears to be strong for the PESQ. The PESQ has been assessed for its criterion validity relative to distinguishing between treatment populations, current diagnoses, and counselor referrals. Individuals with drug treatment histories and with a clinical diagnosis of dependence were found to have significantly higher PESQ Problem Severity scale scores than those with no prior treatment histories and those with abuse but not dependence problems. Problem Severity scale scores for a drug clinic population were found to be significantly higher than those of juvenile offenders, which were in turn found to be significantly higher than those of a normal school population. Individuals from a school clinic sample referred by counselors for further drug abuse evaluations had significantly higher Problem Severity scale scores than those not referred for this purpose. A post hoc analysis of the relationships between the two response bias scales and the Problem Severity items produced correlations similar to those found for the response bias scales and the PEI Personal Involvement With Chemicals scale items.

The "red flag" criterion is inherently a criterion validity issue. It was developed through discriminant analysis applied to the first half of the school clinic sample in a cross validation procedure. The cut-point on the Problem Severity scale of 40T, one standard deviation below the drug clinic sample, was identified as optimal and found to correctly classify 88% of the initial school clinic sample (sensitivity .91, specificity .84) and 87% of the second half of the school clinic sample (sensitivity .88, specificity .85). This cut-point falls 1 1/2 standard deviations above the mean of the school sample and appears to be appropriate for differentiating those who do and do not need a more comprehensive drug abuse evaluation.

The PESQ, in particular its Problem Severity scale, appears to be a well-developed screening device, which should be quite useful for its intended purposes. Its psychometric properties are strong with the exception of the need to establish temporal stability and to clarify the validity and reliability of the area scores. The "red flag" cut-point provides a good guide to decisions about 12–18-year-old individuals who do and do not require more comprehensive evaluations. The practical and research application potentials of the instrument are promising.

REVIEWER'S REFERENCES

American Educational Research Association, American Psychological Association, & National Council on Measurement in Education. (1985). *Standards for educational and psychological testing*. Washington, DC: American Psychological Association.

Toneatto, T. (1992). [Review of the Personal Experience Inventory]. In J. J. Kramer & J. C. Conoley (Eds.), *The eleventh mental measurements yearbook* (pp. 660–661). Lincoln, NE; Buros Institute of Mental Measurements.

Tucker, J. A. (1992). [Review of the Personal Experience Inventory]. In J. J. Kramer & J. C. Conoley (Eds.), *The eleventh mental measurements yearbook* (pp. 661–663). Lincoln, NE; Buros Institute of Mental Measurements.

Review of the Personal Experience Screening Questionnaire by RICHARD W. JOHNSON, Adjunct Professor of Counseling Psychology and Associate Director of Counseling & Consultation Center, University of Wisconsin-Madison, Madison, WI:

The Personal Experience Screening Questionnaire (PESQ) serves as one of three instruments in a comprehensive assessment package created for adolescents suspected of drug abuse. The PESQ, a brief self-report inventory that can be completed in 10 minutes or less, should be administered first as a screening device to determine if a more thorough assessment needs to be undertaken. The other two instruments, the Personal Experiences Inventory (PEI; 11:284) and the Adolescent Diagnostic Interview (ADI; 16), are employed if scores on the PESQ suggest that alcohol or other drug abuse may be an issue.

The PESQ provides a broad range of information concerning the nature and the extent of drug use and related matters. It contains 40 items divided into five parts as follows: (*a*) a Problem Severity scale of 18 items with 4-point response options (*never, once or twice, sometimes, often*); (*b*) a Defensiveness scale of 5 items that measures "faking good"; (*c*) an Infrequency scale of 3 items that measures "faking bad" or careless or random responding; (*d*) 8 individual items that assess psychosocial concerns (emotional distress, problems with thinking, and physical and sexual abuse); and (*e*) 6 items that provide a history of drug usage.

In contrast with most drug assessment measures, the PESQ was constructed especially for adolescents. A number of the questions refer specifically to situations that involve teenagers (e.g., skipping school, making excuses to teachers or parents) but not other age groups. It differs from similar instruments by including validity scales to detect either denial or exaggeration of problems, both frequent concerns when assessing drug use by adolescents in institutional settings.

The instrument can be easily hand-scored by opening a seal on the test booklet that separates the answer sheet from a scoring guide inside the test booklet. In the course of using the PESQ with a client, we noted that one of the items on the Defensiveness scale (Item 29) was keyed in the wrong direction on the score sheet. Test users should check this item (one of only five items on the Defensiveness scale) to make sure that it is keyed correctly in their test booklet.

The PESQ has been normed on adolescents 12 to 18 years old in three settings: drug clinic assessment programs, juvenile detention centers, and public schools. The normative samples have been used to set cutoff scores ("red flags") for referral purposes. The cutoff scores vary somewhat depending on the age and sex of the respondents. However, very little information regarding the actual distribution of scores among the samples has been provided in the test manual. It would be helpful to know the means and standard deviations for all scales and the results of item analyses for the different norm groups. Additional normative data for minority groups are also needed.

The Problem Severity scale of the PESQ possesses high interitem consistency (alpha coefficients = .90 to .95) across different settings and types of clients. No attempt has been made to determine the interitem consistency of the Defensiveness or Infrequency scales because of their brevity. Information regarding the test-retest reliabilities for each scale also should be reported.

The PESQ derives much of its validity from studies conducted on the PEI. Factor analytic studies with the PEI revealed one large general factor that accounted for much of the variance in surveys of drug use among adolescents. This factor, severity of drug use, is measured by the Problem Severity scale of the PESQ. Scores on the Problem Severity scale correlate highly with the scale (Personal Involvement with Chemicals scale) on the PEI that measures this factor.

The most crucial question concerning the validity of the PESQ pertains to its effectiveness in detecting those adolescents in need of a comprehensive drug assessment program. Ideally, the instrument should identify those young people at risk for substance abuse at the same time that it rules out the dangers of addiction for others not at risk. In a cross-validation study reported in the test manual, the author successfully used the PESQ to select 88% of those students who needed additional drug assessment based on a variety of criteria (official records, collateral reports, and interview data) while eliminating 85% of those students who did not need such assessment. In other words, it proved to be both highly sensitive (few false negatives) and highly selective (few false positives). These results should be substantiated by research in other settings.

In conclusion, the PESQ presents a number of advantages as an assessment tool. It has been integrated with other drug assessment procedures as part of an ongoing research and treatment program. It is more comprehensive and less easily faked than other inventories designed specifically for adolescents such as the Adolescent Drinking Index (ADI; 17) or the Adolescent Alcohol Involvement Scale (AAIS; Mayer & Filstead, 1979). It can be conveniently administered, scored, and interpreted. Although the PESQ can benefit from further study as described above, research conducted thus far indicates that it is highly reliable and valid for the purpose for which it was designed. I recommend it as a screening instrument for assessing drug use among adolescents.

REVIEWER'S REFERENCE

Mayer, J., & Filstead, W. J. (1979). The adolescent alcohol involvement scale: An instrument for measuring adolescents' use and misuse of alcohol. *Journal of Studies on Alcohol, 40,* 291–300.

[1.29]

Phase II Profile Integrity Status Inventory and ADdendum.

Purpose: "Measures a person's status regarding honesty in the work place," the ADdendum elicits information about an examinee's use and abuse of alcohol and drugs.
Population: Job applicants and employees in staff positions.
Publication Dates: 1978–1982.
Scores, 8: Ability to Rationalize Dishonesty, How Often a Person Thinks or Plans About Doing Something Dishonest, Basic Honest Attitudes, Basic Dishonest Attitudes, Major Admissions of Dishonesty, Minor Admissions of Dishonesty, Lie, Total.
Administration: Group.
Forms, 2: Prospective Employees, Current Employees.
Price Data, 1985: $15 or less per self-score or PACE (Profile Assessment by Computer Evaluation) answer sheet for prospective employees (includes ADdendum alcohol and drug disclosure form) or for PACE answer sheets for current employees; included with each 10 answer sheets is a reusable question booklet, set of scoring templates, and test administration guide ('82, 16 pages); $3 per additional question book; $3 per additional set of templates and test administration guide; PACE allows for immediate assessment via toll-free number with printout of computer evaluation following by mail (additional $5 per answer sheet assessment charge for current employees).
Foreign Language Edition: Available in Spanish for PACE version prospective employees only.
Time: (25–30) minutes.
Author: Gregory M. Lousig-Nont.
Publisher: G. M. Lousig-Nont & Associates, distributed by R. B. Ishmael & Associates.
Cross References: Reviews by Benjamin Kleinmuntz and Kevin L. Moreland originally appeared in 10:283.

Review of the Phase II Profile Integrity Status Inventory and ADdendum by BENJAMIN KLEINMUNTZ, Professor of Psychology, University of Illinois at Chicago, Chicago, IL:

The assignment to review the Phase II Profile Integrity Status Inventory and its ADdendum, Alcohol Drug Abuse Disclosure Form brings to mind a story told by Lykken (1980) in his superb book on the uses and abuses of lie detectors. Lykken describes the case of a nun who was denied employment with B. Dalton Bookstores after having "failed" an honesty test. Sister Terressa, according to the story, had been rejected for a part-time job with the Minneapolis branch of the store because (or so she was told) she had obtained the lowest score that they had ever seen. Her subsequent testimony before The Minnesota Legislature in 1976 was responsible, in part, for the Minnesota statute that forbids the use in employment applications of polygraphs, voice stress analyzers, or any device that purports to test the honesty of current or prospective employees.

It was not the intent of this legislation to mandate that one has a statutory right to any job for which one applies and is qualified. But this law does imply that people do have a right to be "fairly considered" for employment, which means not to be rejected on the basis of irrelevant information about them. This right is reaffirmed for minority groups by the Equal Employment Opportunity Commission's (EEOC) guidelines that stipulate that psychological tests are irrelevant as preemployment screening devices if validity cannot be demonstrated.

Honesty, of course, is relevant to most jobs, especially those that place the prospective employee in a situation of trust. Therefore, a test that claims to measure and predict honesty is potentially relevant and fair. But it will only qualify as relevant and fair if honesty is indeed measured. Hence the question of fairness in the case of Sister Terressa revolves around whether or not she was fairly denied a job on the basis of a valid test that measures honesty.

The claims for the Phase II Profile's ability to detect dishonesty are no different than those made by the honesty testing industry at large. One accompanying flyer, for example, states that "It's a great feeling when you know you've hired an honest, dependable employee . . . you can have that great feeling every time with the Phase II Profile." Other claims in the brochure are that it is "developed by a professional . . . (M.A., M.S.D.D., A.C.P., C.P.P. Noted Criminologist and Polygraph Expert) . . . is psychologically validated . . . does not violate EEOC hiring standards . . . (has the approval of) . . . a Staff Psychologist with a Ph.D . . . from Brigham Young University. gives you valuable insight. (and a 'guarantee' of) . . . complete satisfaction." The skeptical prospective user can also find comfort in the testimonials from satisfied customers at TeleCheck ("the employees we have hired since using Phase II are fantastic"); Radio Shack ("I anticipate acquiring a minimum total of 10,000 each over a 12 month period"); Brown's Sporting Goods of Peoria, Illinois ("the Profile Tests. have proven to be invaluable in determining the calibre of personnel"); and from the President of Restaurant Operations, also of Peoria, Illinois in a letter which claims that since beginning to use the test "on or about November 6, 1981 . . . we were $10.00 over in our cash control . . . after having lost over $180 in cash in thirty days . . . and had improved our food cost by one full percentage point."

In the event that the prospective user is not convinced by these testimonials, he or she is offered further reassurance by the author of the Phase II. "Dishonesty is a matter of opportunity, need and attitude . . . all three must be present. Our test effectively ferrets out those whose attitude will predispose them to steal whenever the need and opportunity arise." Claims are based on two solid case histories, one of which is partially presented here. "She passed our interviewing process with flying colors. Her references were of the best. There wasn't a single hint of dishonesty in her work history of bookkeeping for our biggest competitor. That's why we were shocked when we discovered that she was pocketing checks from our customers." Guess what finally solved her "desolate" employer's problem? Of course, The Phase II Profile. The second case history is equally fatuous.

For a glimpse at the rationale and evidence for these claims, the prospective user can turn to four sources: A Test Administration guide, a Report on Statistical Validation Studies, a Report on Adverse Impact Studies, and a letter from the Law Offices of Jenner and Block, a prestigious Chicago law firm that "analyzed" one of its client's tests (Phase II) in the context of the EEOC Uniform Guidelines on Employer Selection Procedures.

The Test Administration Guide is a clearly written booklet that takes great care in instructing the user how to "count all of the marks which fall inside each of the 7 different symbols (Diamonds, Hexagons, Triangles, Squares, Tombstones [sic], Arrows, and Circles) . . . before you call the toll free number." It also instructs the user to be prepared to give the PACE OPERATOR your PACE AUTHORIZATION NUMBER, and so on. The guide also provides interpretations of specific score values within each of these categories. Thus, for example, we learn that the 10 diamonds represent the "Lie Scale" and a score of 10 represents 100% truthful responses, 9 is a 90% truthful attempt by the subject, and so on. We also learn that "The 'lie scale' is used to make sure people are not trying to phoney the test and make themselves look perfect."

The 10 hexagons "indicate how much a person thinks or plans about doing something dishonest." The 14 triangles "show a person's ability to rationalize dishonesty." The 31 squares "represent attitudes we have found statistically associated with individuals having dishonest attitudes." The 7 tombstones "represent minor admissions of dishonesty, or acts of dishonesty that happened quite some time ago." The 25 arrows "indicate actual admissions of dishonesty, or that the person would do something dishonest if given the chance." We also learn that "98 to 100% of the people who mark arrows have been involved in serious activity involving dishonesty." Finally, there are 48 circles that "represent attitudes we have found statistically are associated with basically honest individuals (71%)." Of course, no evidence supporting these interpretive claims, or how interpretations were determined, nor the score values accompanying such claims appear in the published research literature. But more importantly, nowhere do they provide evidence in the accompanying manual, "Statistical Validation Report." This is a clear violation of the EEOC Guidelines that indicate that the meaning of test scores as well as their cutting scores and how they were derived must be stipulated.

In the "Test Administration Guide," the publishers also include an example of an optional Confidential Phase II Profile Pace Computer Report addressed to the Personnel Director of the client (i.e., company). There the Personnel Director (not necessarily a psychologist nor anyone with even an elementary or a high school education) learns that the applicant took "too long" to complete the test, has a "poor attitude regarding honesty," resembles a "confirmed thief," "rationalizes (his) dishonesty," and has stolen "$5 from jobs in the last two years" as well as $25 in "merchandise from all jobs." Again, no supporting evidence is provided that these are valid or accurate statements. But no matter, because we are urged to "be sure to use both tests" to provide confirmation of the applicants' unfitness for employment. However, the authors do admit that the ADdendum, Alcohol Drug Abuse Disclosure Form "is not perfect." It is a good deal less than perfect. It is useless, as I indicate below.

The brochure called "Statistical Validation Studies" describes three studies conducted by D. L. Ennis, a Ph.D. Psychologist, who designed these statistical studies to provide evidence that the Phase II Profile Integrity Status Inventory was valid. The first study reports a .97 reliability (where "1.0 would indicate a perfect relationship") with a level of significance at greater than .001 for 60 unspeci-

fied subjects. Absolutely no validity information is provided, which possibly goes unnoticed by most prospective users (e.g., lawyers, personnel managers) because reliability and validity are commonly confused with one another. The second study used 660 unspecified subjects, half of whom "passed their preemployment polygraph" and half "failed it and admitted various activities of theft." Aside from using the highly fallible criterion of polygraph tests (see Kleinmuntz and Szucko, 1982, 1984; OTA, 1983; Szucko & Kleinmuntz, 1981), the publishers provide no validity coefficients, but do state that the "statistics indicate a very definite correlation between Phase II Profile Scores and subsequent pre-employment polygraph test results," whatever that means. The third study used research tactics similar to the previous one, except with fewer subjects (240), again unspecified, and divided these into halves consisting of those who passed and failed the polygraph exam. This time a Pearson Product Moment correlation coefficient of -.64 is reported, which would suggest a highly valid relationship—unless, of course, one examines the wording used to define the thieves and the amounts they presumably stole: They "failed" the polygraph and "admitted they had in fact lied" and also (admitted) to activities of "theft." As indicated earlier, to have "failed" a polygraph may be a badge of honesty, given that the false positive rate (innocents classified as guilty) runs as high as 55 percent in some studies (Horvath, 1977) and according to a whole host of studies (OTA, 1983), is at least a 50-50 proposition for most honest persons. But more to the point, admitting to thefts is not necessarily a confession of untruthfulness; rather, it might very well be a sign of honesty in that one is admitting to have taken something during the course of a lifetime. In addition, admitting to taking some vague amount of money is a meaningless criterion of theft. For example, Study III indicates that "only subjects whose admissions were $100 or less were used in this study." Whom does this include? It could include people who truthfully admitted to taking $1.00, $2.00, or any amount up to $99.99. How does this disqualify them for employment?

Not a shred of evidence is presented regarding the standardization, reliability, or validity of their highly touted ADdendum, Alcohol Drug

Abuse Disclosure Form. But this does not deter the distributors from interpreting the meaning of various scores and of warning employers to "exercise caution in considering this person for employment" when certain scores are achieved because "you must realize that people have a tendency to minimize their admissions." Did it occur to this test's developers that some people may actually maximize or exaggerate their transgressions, especially when socialization has been of the "straight-arrow" variety?

This issue of minimizing or maximizing admissions takes us full circle to Sister Terressa's probable admission of theft on the B. Dalton's honesty examination and her "failing" score. I want to reemphasize that such an admission—no matter what the merchandise or dollar amount—is an act of honesty, not dishonesty. Clearly, it is more likely that honest rather than dishonest people admit to having been dishonest at one time in their lives, and therefore are the ones most likely to "fail" these tests. Moreover, the logic of this and most other honesty tests seems to be that if one has thoughts about thefts; or has knowledge of people stealing from employers; or has information or a perception about the extent of theft in our society; or, worst of all, if one has a lenient attitude toward theft (drugs, alcohol, or violence), then one is dishonest. But the fallacy in this form of reasoning should be apparent. "It is not likely that most people who recommend leniency are thieves. It is not true that all those who see this as a sinful place are great sinners themselves" (Lykken, 1980, p. 201).

Having argued that the rationale, standardization, and psychometric evidence for the Phase II all leave something to be desired, I now turn to a brief review of the distributors' Adverse Impact Studies brochure and their attorneys' testimonial that "we see nothing in the Uniform Guidelines which precludes use of the Phase II Profile as a measure of employee honesty." The Adverse Impact brochure consists of thumbnail descriptions of three studies. One of these studies used 33 unspecified white and 33 equally unspecified black applicants whose mean scores were "insignificant at the .05 level indicating that the Phase II Profile is racially nondiscriminatory." The second study consisted of 40 male and 40 female job applicants—again, not described in terms of age, race,

education, socioeconomic group, and so on. The "difference in the . . . scores was found to be insignificant at the .05 level," this time demonstrating that the test "is nondiscriminatory as to sex." And the third study was conducted with "30 job applicants under age 35" (15?, 18?, 21?, 25?, 29?) and "30 job applicants over age 40" (41?, 51?, 61?, 69?) and "the significance was in favor of the protected group (40 and over)." The conclusion? The Phase II Profile does not have adverse impact on racially, sexually, and age-protected classes. Of course, this is nonsense because it is impossible to infer these conclusions from test scores alone, especially because they were obtained from nonspecified subjects who could have been successful applicants and because—and I quote from the Jenner and Block Law Offices letter—"an employer's overall employment practices" need to be assessed as well as "the employer's general position concerning equal employment opportunity, including its affirmative action plan and results achieved under the plan." Consequently, the Law firm's concluding reassurance to its client that, "we see nothing . . . which precludes use of the Phase II Profile," is wrong by its own understanding of the meaning of adverse impact as contained in the Guidelines. What is worse, this reassurance is seriously misleading as well to prospective users because the test scores and the arbitrary test score cutting points for honesty versus dishonesty were not properly validated—at least not according to any of the existing Standards for Educational and Psychological Testing (AERA, APA, & NCME, 1985).

There is also a Spanish version of The Phase II Profile Integrity Status Inventory. Absolutely no data are provided to indicate that any standardization, reliability, or validity studies were conducted for this version. It is safe to assume, therefore, that this inventory is at least as flawed psychometrically as its English counterpart. This is unfortunate because persons taking this test are protected class individuals, and thus more susceptible to being victimized by test scores that signify nothing about them.

Given the information reviewed, I conclude that the use of so-called honesty tests to make hiring or promotion decisions are on the same shaky ground as are the polygraphs against which they were validated, and are the equivalent of a random procedure. Individuals may just as well use a lottery because both methods randomly and unfairly deny persons access to certain jobs on the basis of irrelevant and flawed information. In that sense they are themselves dishonest devices. They are dishonest toward employers because they reject many potentially productive workers, hence causing greater costs than savings. And they are dishonest toward prospective employees because they constitute an unfair method of screening. Therefore, no corporate user should waste money and time denying employment on the basis of this questionable tool and no person should be denied the opportunity for a job on the basis of scores from this instrument. It is my contention that it is illegal and unethical to do so in the case of minority or protected class applicants, and it is unethical and unconscionable to do so in all other instances.

REVIEWER'S REFERENCES

Horvath, F. (1977). The effect of selected variables on interpretation of polygraph records. *Journal of Applied Psychology, 62*, 127-136.

Lykken, D. T. (1980). *A tremor in the blood: Uses and abuses of the lie detector.* New York McGraw-Hill.

Szucko, J. J., & Kleinmuntz, B. (1981). Statistical versus clinical lie detection. *American Psychologist, 36*, 488-496.

Kleinmuntz, B., & Szucko, J. J. (1982). On the fallibility of lie detection. *Law and Society Review, 17*, 85-104.

Office of Technology Assessment (OTA). (1983). *Scientific validity of polygraph testing A research review and evaluation.* Congress of the United States, Washington, DC. (OTA-TM-H-15).

Kleinmuntz, B., & Szucko, J. J. (1984). A field study of the fallibility of polygraphic lie detection. *Nature, 308*, 449-450.

Sackett, P. R., & Harris, M. M. (1984). Honesty testing for personnel selection A review and critique. *Personnel Psychology, 37*, 221-245.

American Educational Research Association, American Psychological Association, & National Council on Measurement in Education. (1985). *Standards for educational and psychological testing.* Washington, DC American Psychological Association, Inc.

Review of the Phase II Profile Integrity Status Inventory and ADdendum by KEVIN L. MORELAND, Consultant, NCS Professional Assessment Services, Minneapolis, MN:

The Phase II Profile includes three components, two of which will be reviewed here. The Integrity Status Inventory (ISI) is "a psychological paper and pencil test that . . . measures a person's status regarding honesty in the work place" (Lousig-Nont, 1985). The ADdendum is "a uniquely designed disclosure form to elicit information regarding alcohol and drug abuse" (Lousig-Nont, 1985). (The In House Security Survey, a counterpart of the ISI designed to assess the "integrity status" of current employees, will not be reviewed here.)

ITEMS AND INSTRUCTIONS. The ISI comprises 116 items in the seven content catego-

ries listed in the test description preceding this review. There are true-false, yes-no, and multiple-choice questions. The following true-false question gets at Ability to Rationalize Dishonesty "Sometimes a person may have a good reason to steal from a place where they work." The ADdendum is composed of 21 multiple-choice questions. Seven questions ask how many times the respondent has purchased, used, used at work, or sold various drugs; several similar questions ask the last time one engaged in these activities. The final seven questions ask about alcohol use. An example of the latter is "How many times have you missed work because of intoxication? Refuse [to answer], Daily, I lost count, . . . 1 or 2 times, I never have." Both of these portions of the Phase II Profile are available in Spanish as well as English.

Because the items on both portions of the Profile are "clear purpose" (cf. Sackett & Harris, 1985), the author has employed "[p]sychologically structured directions . . . worded in such a way as to lower the threshold of reluctance to admit [deviance]" (Lousig-Nont, 1985). For example, the ADdendum exhorts the respondent:

> Our computer studies have shown that over 98% of the people that say they have used Marijuana 16 to 50 times, have also purchased Marijuana. So, if you mark you have used Marijuana 16 to 50 times, and try to lie about the fact that you may also have purchased Marijuana, the questionnaire knows that there is a high probability that you are not telling the TRUTH. (Lousig-Nont, 1981).

SCORING, NORMS, AND INTERPRETATION. Complete raw scoring information for the ISI was not available to this reviewer. It is clear that the items in six of the seven content categories (the publisher reported that the Minor Admissions of Dishonesty do not correlate with polygraph results) are weighted and combined to form the Total Score, which is used in decision making. The ADdendum is scored by computing a weighted raw score for each of the items. Different weighting schemes are used for each of the three types of ADdendum items.

No norms are offered for the ISI or the ADdendum. Cutting scores of undescribed origin are offered for the ISI Total Score and each of the ADdendum items.

Interpretation of the ISI is straightforward Total Scores less than 140 are characteristic of those who admit theft, scores greater than 147 are characteristic of those who do not admit theft, and those scoring between 140 and 147 are about equally split between the two groups. Interpretation of the ADdendum is more complex. There are several rules for combining the results of the "how much" questions with the "how recent" questions in a configural manner.

RELIABILITY. One reliability study of 60 subjects yielded a 10-day test-retest reliability coefficient of .97 for the ISI Total Score (Lousig-Nont, 1982a). No reliability studies were reported for the ADdendum.

VALIDITY. Two validity studies of the ISI used theft admissions during polygraph examinations as criteria (Lousig-Nont, 1982a). In one, the standard cutting scores accurately identified 89% of two equal-sized groups ($N = 330$) of admitted thieves and those not admitting to theft. A second study of 240 subjects yielded a correlation of -.636 between ISI Total Scores and self-reported dollar amount stolen. A validity study of questionable relevance given the purpose of the ISI, involved separating 28 welders laid off in a reduction of force from 25 peers chosen for retention (McCarty & McCarty, undated). The ISI outperformed 14 measures of aptitude, health, and personality in this study. No validity data were available for the ADdendum.

ADVERSE IMPACT. Three studies employing samples of 30–40 subjects per group yielded no mean ISI Total Score differences between blacks and whites or men and women; those over the age of 40 had higher mean scores than those under 35 (Lousig-Nont, 1982b). An undated photocopied sheet, partly typed and partly handwritten, provided by the publisher reported the 80/20 test of compliance with federal guidelines comparing a sample of 45-58 black and Hispanic men and women with 623 white subjects. These data indicated compliance with federal guidelines for all the protected groups except Hispanic men. A handwritten note indicated that new data had boosted the pass rate for Hispanic males to 79% that of the white males, but no further details were offered. No adverse impact data were available for the ADdendum.

SUMMARY AND EVALUATION. Unlike the publishers of many of the "clear purpose" honesty tests based on polygraph examinations, the publishers of the Phase II Profile have clearly recognized the need to establish the credibility of their instruments within the community of psychometric scientists. Unfortunately, at this time, they have made only the barest of starts. Obviously, few reliability and validity data are available for the ISI and none for the ADdendum. The available data are reported in very cursory fashion. I have provided almost as much detail in this brief review as is available in the published studies. Finally, there is controversy over the use of polygraph results as validity criteria (cf. Sackett & Harris, 1985). In my view, these instruments should not be used to make practical hiring decisions absent local validation.

REVIEWER'S REFERENCES

Lousig-Nont, G. M. (1981). Phase II Profile ADdendum. Las Vegas, NV: Lousig-Nont & Associates.

Lousig-Nont, G. M. (1982a). *Phase II Profile statistical validation studies.* Las Vegas, NV: Lousig-Nont & Associates.

Lousig-Nont. G. M. (1982b). *Phase II Profile adverse impact studies.* Las Vegas, NV: Lousig-Nont & Associates.

Lousig-Nont, G. M. (1985). *It's a great feeling when you know you've hired an honest, dependable employee.* Las Vegas, NV: Lousig-Nont & Associates.

Sackett, P. R., & Harris, M. M. (1985). Honesty testing for personnel selection Review and critique. In H. J. Bernardin & D. A. Bownas (Eds.), *Personality assessment in organizations* (pp. 236-276). New York: Praeger.

McCarty, T., & McCarty, J. J. (undated). *Employee theft: One solution to this increasing problem.* Joliet, IL: R. B. Ishmael & Associates.

[1.30]

QUESTS: A Life-Choice Inventory.

Purpose: To assess outcomes of substance abuse prevention education.

Population: Grades 9–12.

Publication Dates: 1974–1976.

Acronym: QUESTS.

Scores, 6: Needs Recognition, Values Classification, Adaptive Autonomy, Perception of Reality, Self-Worth, Total.

Administration: Group.

Price Data: Not available.

Time: (23 30) minutes.

Comments: Scoring must be done by publisher.

Authors: Norman J. Milchus, Omar D. Numey, and David N. Rodwell.

Publisher: Person-O-Metrics, Inc. [No reply from publisher; status unknown].

This test has not been reviewed in *The Mental Measurements Yearbook.*

[1.31]

Recovery Attitude and Treatment Evaluator.

Purpose: Intended for use after diagnosis of alcohol or other drug dependency to determine the "patient's level

of resistance to treatment and other important information" to be considered in treatment planning.
Population: Adults.
Publication Dates: 1987–1996.
Acronym: RAATE–CE; RAATE–QI.
Scores: 5 dimensions: Resistance to Treatment, Resistance to Continuing Care, Acuity of Biomedical Problems, Acuity of Psychiatric/Psychological Problems, Social/Family Environmental Status.
Administration: Individual.
Forms, 3: Clinical Evaluation, Initial Questionnaire, Automated RAATE–QI.
Price Data: Available from publisher.
Time: (30–45) minutes for Clinical Evaluation; [20–30] minutes for Initial Questionnaire or Automated RAATE–QI.
Comments: Automated RAATE–QI requires minimum 386 IBM compatible with Windows 3.1 or later, 8 MB RAM, mouse, printer, and color monitor.
Authors: David Mee-Lee, Norman G. Hoffmann, and Maurice B. Smith (manual).
Publisher: New Standards, Inc.

This test has not been reviewed in *The Mental Measurements Yearbook*.

[1.32]
SAQ—Adult Probation [Substance Abuse Questionnaire].

Purpose: "Designed specifically for adult probation department and corrections use as a risk and needs assessment instrument."
Population: Adult probationers.
Publication Dates: 1989–1992.
Acronym: SAQ.
Scores: Behaviors/characteristics relevant to probation risk and needs assessment in 6 areas: Validity/Truthfulness Scale, Alcohol Scale, Drug Scale, Aggressivity Scale, Resistance Scale, Stress Coping Abilities.
Administration: Individual or group.
Price Data: $5–7 per test; other price data available from publisher.
Time: (25–0) minutes.
Comments: Self-administered, computer-scored test.
Author: Behavior Data Systems, Ltd.
Publisher: Behavior Data Systems, Ltd.
Cross References: The review by Tony Toneatto originally appeared in 12:338.

Review of the SAQ-Adult Probation [Substance Abuse Questionnaire] by TONY TONEATTO, Scientist, Addiction Research Foundation, Toronto, Ontario, Canada:

The Substance Abuse Questionnaire-Adult Probation (SAQ-AP) is a 153-item test, computer administered and scored, requiring approximately 30 minutes to complete. The SAQ-AP is designed to aid probation officers and parole staff in assessing the severity of substance abuse, violence proneness, and emotional disturbance of adult parolees. Risk levels for six scaled measures (Truthfulness, Alcohol, Drug, Aggressivity, Resistance, Stress Coping Abilities) are generated in percentile form with each scale accompanied by the appropriate, computer-generated, recommendations. The Truthfulness or Validity scale provides a measure of the validity of the client's response based on the degree of defensiveness demonstrated and is used to determine the validity of the individual's response profile.

The authors of the SAQ-AP suggest that it is suitable for use by staff who are neither clinicians nor diagnosticians but who must nevertheless identify potentially risky behavior on the part of their parolee clientele and develop appropriate courses of action. The SAQ-AP also identifies important attitudes towards, and motivation to change, risk behaviors, how the client perceives their problems, and degree of, and reasons for, involvement in the legal system. The authors also briefly describe a short form of the SAQ-AP to be used when time is at a premium or for clients who have difficulty reading. The short form consists of 64 items, requires 10 minutes to complete, but only provides scores on four scales (Truthfulness Scale, Alcohol Scale, Drug Scale, Risk Scale).

The SAQ-AP II, developed in 1993, includes two additional scales (Antisocial, Violence) and consists of 169 items. The SAQ-AP II also contains an additional 40 items measuring the degree to which various difficulties (e.g., insomnia), self-perceptions (e.g., self-control), and emotional states (e.g., tension) characterize the individual. However, at no point in the various literature describing the SAQ-AP is it explicitly stated if, and how, the responses to these items are utilized in the generation of the scaled measures. Because the SAQ-AP II is very recent and no evaluation of the psychometric properties of version II have yet been reported this review focuses on the SAQ-AP.

There is some concern about the nature of the computer-generated recommendations produced on the basis of the clients' response profiles. Such interpretive strategies are generally meaningful at an aggregate level but difficult to apply to any one individual. The recommendations provided by the SAQ-AP tend to be very brief, general, and highly restricted in the kinds of suggestions offered and typically direct the parole or probation official either to increase supervision of the parolee or to obtain treatment for the indicated problem (e.g., alcohol, violence). Although the ready availability of such recommendations may make them convenient and efficient it does raise the issue of how such advice improves upon the parole/probation official's own assessment and awareness of the parolee's history. For example, the SAQ-AP recommends that an individual who scores in the problem range on the Resistance scale be shown firm structure, clear behavioral expectations, and consequences for noncompliance. How should the parole official interpret this advice? What is firm structure? Expectations for what kind of behavior? What kinds of consequences and for which types of noncompliance? A major limitation of the SAQ-AP (and SAQ-AP II) is the difficulty in the interpretation and operationalization of what are essentially very general recommendations.

In addition, the SAQ-AP is unbalanced in its assessment because it focuses on risk assessment, deficiencies, and problems but fails to assess information that might be of greater utility in developing interventions such as the types of high-risk situations that elicit alcohol abuse or violence, client strengths and assets, or the nature of the coping skills the client does possess.

A great deal of data on the reliability of the SAQ-AP (but not for version II, which also includes the Antisocial scale and the Violence scale) is provided with a large number of subjects in various settings and geographic regions. Cronbach alphas tend to be high for all of the scales, generally greater than .80. Test-retest reliability coefficient of .71 (one-week time interval) is provided for parolee populations.

The validity of the SAQ-AP is much less established.

Considerable data on the concurrent validity of the instrument are provided but only in its association with the Minnesota Multiphasic Personality Inventory (MMPI) (except for two studies with the polygraph test and the Driver Risk Inventory). Evidence of the association between the SAQ-AP and other measures of alcohol or drug dependence, aggressivity, antisocial behavior, or social desirability is not reported. Thus, the range of alternative and valid instruments that could be used to assess the concurrent validity of the SAQ-AP is severely limited; in any case the size of the correlations with the MMPI, albeit statistically significant, tend to be rather small and do not provide strong evidence of the SAQ-AP's concurrent validity. Predictive validity data for the SAQ-AP are conspicuously lacking. Such data, critical to evaluating whether the results generated by this instrument are actually associated with outcomes, are absent. For example, do individuals who score as high risk individuals have a higher rate of recidivism? Furthermore, there is no assessment of the construct validity of the SAQ-AP. For example, do individuals who score high on the alcohol or drug scales also meet diagnostic criteria for psychoactive substance use disorder? Do those who score high on measures of antisocial or aggressive behavior meet diagnostic criteria for antisocial personality disorder? Given the wide range of constructs that appear to be assessed by this instrument it is probably inaccurate to label this instrument as a measure of substance abuse as implied by the title. Thus, the overall evidence for the validity of the SAQ-AP is very poor.

The summary of research on the SAQ-AP does not report any norms for the population for which this test is designed. Although the authors state that the percentiles generated in their computer report incorporates such information, presentation of such data in the research summary would have been useful.

One positive feature of the SAQ-AP is that the authors appear committed to exploring gender differences and to that end report several studies showing that gender differences occur in only some geographic regions. The authors also claim that the SAQ-AP, when administered in these regions, is normed differently to reflect such gender differences.

In summary, although the reliability of the SAQ-AP is generally well established, the validity of the SAQ-AP is less well established. Concurrent validity is limited primarily to the MMPI; nothing can be said of its predictive or construct validity. It bears repeating that the SAQ-AP II has yet to be submitted to the psychometric evaluation conducted on the SAQ-AP. Conceptually, the question still remains as to whether the SAQ-AP conveys any useful information additional to simply asking the client if they have an alcohol-drug problem, if they are violent, and how they cope with stress. Integrating this in the context of their history is not addressed.

[1.33]
Situational Confidence Questionnaire.
Purpose: Designed to help clients identify high-risk drinking relapse situations.
Population: Adult alcoholics.
Publication Dates: 1987–1988.
Administration: Group.
Editions, 2: Computerized, print.
Authors: Helen M. Annis and J. Martin Graham.
Publisher: Addiction Research Foundation [Canada].
  a) SITUATIONAL CONFIDENCE QUES-TIONNAIRE.
  Acronym: SCQ-39.
  Scores, 9: Unpleasant Emotions/Frustrations, Physical Discomfort, Social Problems at Work, Social Tension, Pleasant Emotions, Positive Social Situations, Urges and Temptations, Testing Personal Control, Average.
  Price Data, 1993: $14.75 per 25 questionnaires; $13.50 per user's guide ('88, 49 pages); $70 per 50 uses software edition (includes user's guide); $225 per 200 uses software edition (includes user's guide); $25 per specimen set including user's guide and 25 questionnaires.
  Time: (10–15) minutes.
  b) ALCOHOL CONFIDENCE QUESTION-NAIRE.
  Acronym: ACQ-16.
  Scores: Total score only.
  Time: Administration time not reported.
  Comments: Brief version of the Situational Confidence Questionnaire; test items listed in SCQ user's guide.
Cross References: Reviews by Merith Cosden and Cecil R. Reynolds will appear in the 13th MMY; see also T4:2467 (1 reference).

Review of the Situational Confidence Questionnaire by MERITH COSDEN, Professor, Department of Education, University of California, Santa Barbara, CA:

The Situational Confidence Questionnaire (SCQ-39) is a self-report measure of self-efficacy

for being able to control one's drinking. The scale is based on the premise that cognitive factors, including self-efficacy, play a role in relapse and relapse prevention. The SCQ was designed to determine self-efficacy for controlled drinking across potential drinking situations, and to assess domains in which clients with substance abuse problems are most likely to relapse.

The 39 items on the SCQ are linked to items on the revised Inventory of Drinking Situations (IDS) by the same authors (see Cosden, test 1.22 in this volume, for a critique). On the IDS, individuals are asked to rate the frequency with which they have engaged in heavy drinking under specific situations; on the SCQ, they are asked about their confidence in being able to resist the urge to drink heavily in these same situations.

Thus, the items and subscales used on the SCQ were derived from the items and subscales of the IDS. Initially, the IDS was composed of 100 items fit into eight subscales. Five subscales described personal states that might result in drinking (i.e., Unpleasant Emotions, Physical Discomfort, Pleasant Emotions, Testing Personal Control, and Urges and Temptations), and three subscales described social situations that could promote drinking (i.e., Conflict with Others, Social Pressure to Drink, and Pleasant Times with Others). These situations were derived from a review of literature on factors related to relapse for men with drinking problems. An early version of the SCQ had 100 items, which were matched to each of the 100 original IDS items.

The number of items on the IDS was reduced by selecting the 42 items that had the highest item-subscale correlations. These 42 items include four items in each of the six original subscales, which were found to be unifactorial, and 18 items from the original Conflict with Others and Pleasant Times with Others subscales, which were found to be multifactorial. In a subsequent confirmatory factor analysis, three items were found to be strongly related to more than one variable and dropped, resulting in the current 39 items. A second confirmatory factor analysis, based on the 39 items, resulted in a model with eight different subscales, reflecting a regrouping of items. A final, confirmatory factor analysis conducted on the new model was satisfactory, supporting the following factors: Unpleasant Emotions/Frustration, Physical Discomfort, Social Problems at Work, Social Tension, Pleasant Emotions, Positive Social Situations, Urges and Temptations, and Testing Personal Control. A series of confirmatory factor analyses conducted on the first order correlation matrix determined the best second order factor structure. Although the model for the IDS placed all subscales into two categories, the best fit for the SCQ data was a three-factor model; the first four subscales were grouped under a factor labeled Negative Affect Situations, the second two subscales were grouped under a factor called Positive Affect Situations, and the last two subscales were grouped under a factor named Urges and Testing.

The normative sample for the 42-item SCQ consisted of 424 clients in two Canadian substance abuse treatment facilities. The gender (27% female, 73% male), age (average 41 years, range from 18–76), educational history (44% completed high school), and alcohol abuse histories (average 8 years of problem drinking) were provided. Neither ethnicity nor history of abuse of other drugs were described, however.

The construct validity of the SCQ was assessed by correlating subscale scores with measures of problem drinking. In the manual, significant correlations are reported between number of drinks, number of days spent drinking, and all subscale scores. There is little differentiation between subscale scores with one exception: Only Positive Social Situations was significantly correlated with time drinking with others, indicating that clients who reported less confidence in their ability to restrain from heavy drinking in positive social situations also reported drinking more in social situations. In a study of construct validity, Miller, Ross, Emmerson, and Todt (1989) found significant differences between clients with long-term and short-term sobriety on all subscales of the SCQ except Testing Personal Control. Few studies to date have attempted to assess the predictive validity of the SCQ. Two unpublished studies by Solomon and Annis and Annis and Davis are cited in the manual. In the first study, SCQ scores obtained at intake to a substance abuse program failed to predict frequency of relapse (drinking episodes) and only weakly predicted the amount of drinking that occurred during these episodes. In

the second study, the authors reported that clients tended to have a serious relapse under the two conditions (reflected in lower subscale scores) in which they rated themselves as having the least amount of control.

The SCQ can be administered as a paper-and-pencil questionnaire or electronically using an IBM computer. It can also be administered individually or in small groups. The manual includes an estimate that it takes 10–15 minutes to complete the SCQ. Clients are asked to imagine themselves in a situation and rate their confidence in their ability to abstain from heavy drinking in that situation. Heavy drinking is not objectively defined, and is left to the client's perception. A scale ranging from 0% (not at all confident) to 100% (completely confident) is presented with each item. Subscale scores are obtained by calculating the mean confidence ratings for all items in a subscale. Clinically, subscale scores can be considered alone, or as part of a client profile. The manual also has tables that can be used to translate raw scores into standard scores for comparison with the normative sample.

The SCQ has been modified across studies to fit the needs of subgroups of substance abusers. Miller et al. (1989), for example, used the SCQ to assess the needs of clients in an abstinence-oriented program. Thus, they changed the stem to ask clients about their ability to avoid drinking altogether rather than their ability to avoid drinking heavily. In addition, they modified the rating scale to present alternatives in 10-point, rather than 20-point, increments. Despite these changes, the authors report similar subscale findings to those found on the original scales. In a further derivation from the original scale, Barber, Cooper, and Heather (1991) developed a Situational Confidence Questionnaire (Heroin) to assess the needs of heroin users. They changed the stem on the original SCQ to ask respondents about their confidence in resisting the urge to use heroin, but otherwise maintained the content and format of the questions. The impact of these changes on the reliability and validity of the scale requires further evaluation.

The authors of the SCQ have also developed a shorter form of the scale, called the Alcohol Confidence Questionnaire (ACQ). The ACQ has 16 items, 2 from each of the eight subscales. The manual presents a Cronbach alpha of .95 for the ACQ, whereas scores on the ACQ showed a correlation of .99 with scores on the SCQ. These psychometric properties of the ACQ suggest that it is a promising, if untested, measure of self-efficacy.

The authors note limitations to the SCQ, including the possibility that clients may fake responses in order to appear to be progressing in treatment. A major limitation noted by this reviewer is the lack of utility of the subscale scores. In most reported studies, problem drinking is associated with lower confidence ratings across most, or all, situations (subscales). There is little support for the use of individual subscales in determining specific relapse situations. This is not surprising, as psychometrically, the subscales have not been stable across studies. The SCQ appears most effective in providing a global measure of clients' perceptions of their ability to resist heavy drinking. Future use of the scale should focus on its utility as a global correlate and predictor of self-efficacy for drinking, or in developing more stable subscales, which can be used to predict specific relapse situations.

REVIEWER'S REFERENCES

Miller, P. J., Ross, S. M., Emmerson, R. Y., & Todt, E. H. (1989). Self-efficacy in alcoholics: Clinical validation of the Situational Confidence Questionnaire. *Addictive Behaviors, 14,* 217–224.

Barber, J. G., Cooper, B. K., & Heather, N. (1991). The Situational Confidence Questionnaire (Heroin). *The International Journal of the Addictions, 26,* 565–575.

Review of the Situational Confidence Questionnaire by CECIL R. REYNOLDS, Professor of Educational Psychology & Professor of Neuroscience, Texas A&M University, College Station, TX:

The Situational Confidence Questionnaire (SCQ) was "developed as a tool for therapists to monitor the development of a client's self-efficacy in relation to drinking situations over the course of treatment" (p. 1). It is also intended to be a measure of alcohol-related self-efficacy (not defined) for researchers interested in treatment outcomes and alcohol relapse. The original conceptualization of the instrument is modeled around the work of Albert Bandura in the area of self-efficacy. The authors believe the SCQ will be useful in repeat administrations during treatment and as an indication of treatment response. The various scores provided by the SCQ were derived through a series of factor analyses including exploratory and multiple confirmatory analyses with ad-

justments made in various criteria for defining factors until the authors arrived at the eight subscales they prefer.

The manual presents a 10-page discussion of the psychometric properties of the SCQ that include its normative and developmental samples, reliability evidence, validity evidence, scaling, and suggestions for interpretation. The recommended uses and description of the population for which the test is intended are presented appropriately in the manual although user qualifications are neglected.

The sample used for test development and norming is not of adequate size and is not sufficiently representative to substantiate the item selection, to establish appropriate norms, and to support conclusions regarding the use of the instrument for the intended purposes. The samples were, in fact, samples of convenience and although appearing to be a large $N(424)$, the age range of the sample (from 18 years to 76 years) and the presence of clear age differences in responses to the SCQ renders the samples inadequate. The test development sample and norming sample were the same. Changes in items and item selection are not discussed in the manual. It is not known if any changes in items were made based upon the responses of the sample or what item selection procedures were applied.

Items on the SCQ are rated by examinees on a 6-point scale. Reliability estimates for the subscales are provided for the entire age range. This would likely inflate the reliability of various subscales because there are clear age effects. It would be desirable for reliability coefficients to be reported separately by age level. When age effects are present and reliability coefficients in the form of Cronbach's alpha are reported across the entire age range, spurious inflation of reliability estimates occurs as item variances are increased disproportionately to total test variance. The reliability coefficients reported are incredibly high, with some subscales consisting of only three items having reliability coefficients as high as .93. Standard errors of measurement are reported in raw score format although standard scores are provided for interpretation, thus complicating considerably the application of the standard errors of measurement to the interpretation of standard score reporting of individual performance.

The authors provide a good discussion of the validity of the SCQ particularly providing evidence of concurrent validity and some limited predictive validity data. The authors overinterpret the outcome of these studies, however. When applied to prediction of alcohol use in certain situations and during treatment, no validity coefficients in excess of .24 are reported. The authors interpret Pearson correlations of this magnitude as providing strong predictions of behavior. The SCQ shows a variety of weak to moderate relationships to external variables and certainly does not possess adequate validity to substantiate interpretations of the performance of any individual patient. Although it may be useful in evaluating treatment outcomes based on large samples, clinical decisions about an individual patient clearly are not substantiated on the basis of evidence provided.

The scaling of the SCQ is inadequately described. A table of T-scores is provided and the discussion in the manual leads one to believe these are normalized T-scores. The manual refers to the percentage of individuals falling within one standard deviation of the mean when T-scores are normal yet an examination of the tables reveals the T-scores provided clearly are not normalized. This is misleading in the application and interpretation of these T-scores and needs clarification. This is largely characteristic of much of the information provided in the manual. The psychometric discussions are quite brief with particular methods mentioned but not described (with the exception of some of the factor analytic studies).

No data regarding test and item bias are provided with regard to ethnicity, gender, language, geographic region, or other factors. No item analyses for possible bias were conducted and the methods by which items were selected for inclusion for the final version of the test are not described.

Directions for administration and scoring of the SCQ are relatively straightforward and easily accomplished in the test booklets provided. This represents a plus for the SCQ. Another strength is its derivation from a clear theory for which the authors are to be lauded. From a psychometric perspective, however, the SCQ has many weaknesses, rendering it unusable except in large research projects. From a clinical perspective, it certainly should not be used in any way to make decisions about treatment compliance, intervention, or predicted outcomes for an individual patient.

[1.34]
Smoker Complaint Scale.

Purpose: Designed to measure changes in physiological/emotional/craving states as a function of smoking cessation.
Population: Persons quitting smoking.
Publication Date: 1984.
Acronym: SCS.
Scores: Total score and item scores only.
Administration: Individual or group.
Manual: No manual.
Price Data, 1989: Instrument available without charge from publisher.
Time: (1–5) minutes.
Comments: Self-administered.
Author: Nina G. Schneider.
Publisher: Nina G. Schneider.

This test has not been reviewed in *The Mental Measurements Yearbook.*

[1.35]
Substance Abuse Relapse Assessment.

Purpose: Designed to assess and monitor relapse prevention and coping skills.
Population: Adolescents and adults.
Publication Date: 1993.
Acronym: SARA.
Scores: 4 parts: Substance Abuse Behavior, Antecedents of Substance Abuse, Consequences of Substance Abuse, Responses to Slips.
Administration: Individual.
Price Data, 1996: $75 per introductory kit including 25 interview record forms, 25 each of 3 relapse prevention planning forms, and manual (31 pages) with stimulus card; $27 per 25 interview record forms; $11 per 25 relapse prevention planning forms (specify Form 1—Pretreatment, Form 2—Current, or Form 3—Relapse); $28 per manual with stimulus card.
Time: (60) minutes.
Authors: Lawrence Schonfeld, Roger Peters, and Addis Dolente.
Publisher: Psychological Assessment Resources, Inc.
Cross References: Reviews by Michael G. Kavan and Jeffrey S. Rain will appear in the 13th MMY.

Review of the Substance Abuse Relapse Assessment by MICHAEL G. KAVAN, Associate Dean for Student Affairs, Creighton University School of Medi-

cine and Associate Professor of Family Practice, Creighton University School of Medicine, Omaha, NE:

The Substance Abuse Relapse Assessment (SARA) is a structured interview designed to assist in developing relapse prevention goals and monitoring the achievement of these goals within substance abuse treatment programs. The major aim of the SARA is to identify the antecedents and consequences of pretreatment alcohol and/or drug use and to use this information to develop individualized treatment plans. The SARA is based on, and therefore, similar to, several drinking profiles (e.g., Drinking Profile [Marlatt, 1976], Comprehensive Drinker Profile [Marlatt & Miller, 1984], Gerontology Alcohol Project Drinking Profile [Dupree, Broskowski, & Schonfeld, 1984]). It consists of a manual with stimulus card, a four-part interview record form, and three relapse prevention planning forms. The interview record form consists of questions regarding substance abuse behavior, antecedents and consequences of use, and responses to slips. The relapse prevention planning forms allow the examiner to identify the client's substance abuse behavior chain, pretreatment skills used to avoid relapse, and current relapse prevention goals.

ADMINISTRATION AND SCORING. The SARA is designed to be administered individually to adolescents and adults who have a history of substance abuse, whose ability to avoid substance abuse relapse is in question, or who are involved in substance abuse treatment programs. It may be administered by any professional with appropriate training in substance abuse assessment and intervention. It is recommended that examiners should also have experience in the use of structured interviews and in the development of individualized treatment plans. Instructions for the interview record form are fairly clear and easy for examiners to follow. However, some clients may have difficulty keeping track of the multiple response options read to them for certain questions. For these questions, it may have been more useful to allow the examiner to show the client the various response options listed in the interview record form or present a stimulus card to the client. A stimulus card is used to identify client feelings associated with the relapse and to determine how confident

the client is regarding his or her ability to avoid substance use. The examiner may request additional information throughout the interview to clarify responses or information that is contradictory.

Once the interview record form is completed, the interviewer uses this information to complete the relapse prevention planning forms, which identify behavior chain(s) (i.e., antecedents, behaviors, and consequences) associated with substance use as well as various pretreatment and proactive coping skills. Those working with the client can then use this information to discuss relapse prevention issues during treatment. It is also recommended that these forms be revised as new information is disclosed by the client during the course of treatment. No other information is provided within the manual regarding the scoring of the SARA. Administration time is approximately one hour.

RELIABILITY AND VALIDITY. No data are provided within the manual regarding reliability or validity. The manual does provide a sample case illustration for "Joe," which highlights how the various components of the SARA can be used to develop a treatment plan for a client. Limited guidelines are provided regarding how to systematically apply the information from the relapse prevention planning forms to a treatment plan. Of importance to note is that no data are provided regarding the impact of such planning on outcome.

NORMS. The SARA was "field tested" with 101 inmates (63 males and 38 females; ages 17 to 47 years) in a sheriff's office substance abuse treatment program in Tampa, Florida. Limited data are provided from this field test. Information is provided on the inmates' major problem substances, major locations of use, persons with whom the inmates have used substances most frequently, and various antecedents to use for this group. The authors indicate that this preliminary study indicated that emotional and situational events were the major precipitants of alcohol and drug use. As such, it is recommended that treatment plans be designed to address various negative emotional, interpersonal conflicts, and peer pressure through skills training, behavioral rehearsal, and practice situations. Beyond these, the manual contains no other normative information.

SUMMARY. The SARA is a structured interview designed to assist in developing relapse prevention goals and monitoring the achievement of these goals within substance abuse treatment programs. The major goal of the SARA, which is to identify the antecedents and consequences of pretreatment alcohol and/or drug use and to use this information to develop individualized treatment plans, is admirable and desirable. However, the SARA provides no data regarding its ability to accomplish this feat. Likewise, no information is provided within the manual regarding the SARA's ability to influence treatment outcomes. In fact, the only data provided within the manual relate to a field test of 101 inmates in a Florida county jail. Surely, these are not the only persons with substance abuse problems that could possibly benefit from the SARA. Additional studies with more diverse groups are certainly necessary. Another problem with the SARA is that it fails to incorporate useful relapse prevention issues such as the quality of the client's social support network, the quality of the client's primary intimate relationships (Marlatt, 1985), and self-attribution for behavior change (Annis, 1991) into the interview process. In addition, the Interview Record Form is based on recall, which is subject to a variety of biases. Until these problems are addressed, the SARA is unfortunately relegated to only a somewhat useful, structured method for obtaining information about substance use and relapse; nothing more.

REVIEWER'S REFERENCES

Marlatt, G. A. (1976). The Drinking Profile: A questionnaire for the behavioral assessment of alcoholism. In. E. J. Mash & L. G. Terdal (Eds.), *Behavior therapy assessment: Diagnosis, design, and evaluation* (pp. 127–137). New York: Springer.

Dupree, L. W., Broskowski, H., & Schonfeld, L. (1984). The Gerontology Alcohol Project: A behavioral treatment program for elderly alcohol abusers. *The Gerontologist, 24*, 510–516.

Marlatt, G. A., & Miller W. R. (1984). The Comprehensive Drinker Profile. Odessa, FL: Psychological Assessment Resources, Inc.

Marlatt, G. A. (1985). Situational determinants of relapse and skill training interventions. In G. A. Marlatt & J. R. Gordon (Eds.), *Relapse prevention: Maintenance strategies in the treatment of addictive behaviors* (pp. 77–127). New York: Guilford.

Annis, H. M. (1991). A cognitive-social learning approach to relapse: Pharmacotherapy and relapse prevention counseling. *Alcohol and Alcoholism (Supplement), 1*, 527–530.

Review of the Substance Abuse Relapse Assessment by JEFFREY S. RAIN, Assistant Professor and Chairman, Industrial/Organizational Psychology Program, School of Psychology, Florida Tech, Melbourne, FL:

The Substance Abuse Relapse Assessment (SARA) was designed to assess and monitor relapse prevention and coping skills. Setting aside debates between medical, psychodynamic, and behavioral approaches to alcohol, tobacco, and other drug (ATOD) treatment and debates over abstinence versus relapse prevention, the SARA appears to be a very comprehensive, theory-driven, practical guide for identifying relapse risk potential and assisting in treatment planning. Whereas the SARA purports to excel in these areas, except for a limited field test, it lacks research studies specific to the instrument itself.

Addressing psychometric criteria first, the SARA is a very new instrument and lacks empirical evidence of support. In fact, statistical documentation is nonexistent. The only data presented in the manual are the descriptions of the original sample of 101 inmates of a law enforcement substance abuse treatment program in Florida. Data on reliability, validity, bias, administration, and other standard criteria for psychometric quality are not presented. Evaluations of the majority of the technical aspects of the SARA are thus precluded from this review.

With the psychometric deficits stated, a number of potentially very strong positives emerge on the SARA's practical and administrative side. The Professional Manual primarily consists of a description of the SARA and its administration as well as a case illustration and sample treatment plan. Instructions are comprehensive and easy to follow. Particularly helpful is the detailed sample case illustration, which provides clarification for instances where the administrator is unclear exactly how to complete the SARA.

Another positive feature of the SARA is the ability of this instrument to provide a good foundation on which to build treatment plans. Twelve-step programs, if used, also appear to integrate well with the SARA. Additionally, the SARA recognizes the reality of multiple-substance abuse and does not limit itself to a single substance. It does have the flexibility to consider a primary ATOD focus as well as secondary ATOD foci.

Whereas the time frame of the SARA is a 30-day reporting period, the authors acknowledge the changing nature of substance abuse relapse prevention. Therefore, the SARA should be considered a dynamic instrument requiring regular updating. At a minimum it is designed to be used before, during, and after treatment. Given the frequency of updating and the detail involved, the authors' stated caution for conditions potentially precluding the completion of the SARA cannot be overstated. Depending on the situation, the SARA may require multiple sessions to complete. Some of the effort may be reduced by having portions of the updating completed by clients as "homework" (p. 6). However, it should be noted that the detail of information requested places a heavy burden on both client and practitioner. Clients may not be capable of contributing fully to the SARA or be able to complete homework assignments with sufficient detail.

From a theoretical standpoint, the SARA is very well supported by a behavior-based approach. Applying functional analysis to substance abuse identifies a chain of behaviors (i.e., antecedents, behaviors, and consequences or ABCs) that have an impact on the abuse (e.g., Cummings, Gordon, & Marlatt, 1980). The functional analysis approach is a cornerstone of behavior therapy and, therefore, may not be readily adopted by all practitioners, but has been shown to be an effective treatment approach for substance abuse (e.g., Baer, Marlatt, & McMahon, 1993).

On the whole, the theoretical foundations give the SARA clear clinical application. Wholesale endorsement of the SARA must be reserved until its individual research base is more fully established. Still, the SARA is very user friendly, though administratively demanding. Data from the SARA appear to be highly generalizable to various traditional treatment programs (e.g., 12-step programs) as well as other alcohol, tobacco, and other drug (ATOD) cases. The proof of the SARA will be in the research but the theoretical base, instructions, and case illustrations are a solid beginning.

REVIEWER'S REFERENCES

Cummings, C., Gordon, J. R., & Marlatt, G. A. (1980). Relapse: Prevention and prediction. In W. R. Miller (Ed.), *The addictive behaviors* (pp. 291–321). Oxford, UK: Pergamon Press.
Baer, J. S., Marlatt, G. A., & McMahon, R. J. (Eds.) (1993). *Addictive behaviors across life span: Prevention treatment and policy issues.* Newbury Park: Sage.

[1.36]
Substance Abuse Screening Test.

Purpose: "Designed to screen-out those students who are unlikely to have a substance abuse problem."
Population: Ages 13—adult.

Publication Date: 1993.
Acronym: SAST.
Scores: Total Level of Risk.
Administration: Group.
Forms, 2: Response Form, Observation Report.
Price Data, 1996: $55 per complete kit including 50 Response Forms, 50 Observation Reports, and manual (34 pages); $22 per 50 Response Forms; $14 per 50 Observation Reports; $25 per manual.
Time: (5) minutes.
Authors: Terry Hibpshman and Sue Larson.
Publisher: Slosson Educational Publications, Inc.
Cross References: Reviews by Mary Lou Kelley and Mariela C. Shirley will appear in the 13th MMY.

Review of the Substance Abuse Screening Test by MARY LOU KELLEY, Professor of Psychology, Louisiana State University, Baton Rouge, LA:

The Substance Abuse Screening Test (SAST) was developed to aid in the screening of adolescents and young adults (ages 13–30) who are and are not at risk for substance abuse. The authors explicitly state that the measure is not intended for diagnosis or labeling and thus, provide an appropriately conservative statement of purpose and test limitations. The primary test consists of a 30-item questionnaire requiring the respondent to indicate whether or not each statement is true of their feelings or behavior. Items range in content from those that explicitly ask about alcohol or drug use to those tapping perceptions of loneliness, family conflict, and general mood states, among other characteristics assumed to be associated with substance abuse risk. The authors do not distinguish between alcohol and illicit drug use/abuse as they believe abusers represent a heterogeneous sample that is not functionally differentiated by the type of substance abused. However, most of the items that specifically tapped substance abuse asked about drinking rather than drug use. The authors purport that the items represent those that differentiate abusers from nonabusers. However, statistical data supporting this conclusion were not provided in the technical manual.

The test materials also include an Observation Report form for the evaluator to record observations in response to several open-ended questions as well as to provide general comments. The authors indicate that the Observation Report allows for the personalization of the screening but that, as with the SAST, the instrument is not to be used diagnostically.

The administration, scoring, and test interpretation procedures were described succinctly and clearly. The scoring involves simply summing the number of endorsed items. Three procedures are provided to aid in score interpretation. Raw scores can be placed in one of four risk levels, converted to standardized scores with a mean of 100 and standard deviation of 15; or entered into a Bayesian table for estimating substance abuse likelihood. All interpretation procedures are relatively easy to use although it is unclear how the authors determined the cutoff levels for the classification system.

Discussions of the psychometric characteristics of the test and the technical development of the instrument were often lacking in important details. For example, the authors identified the states from which the standardization sample came and the age range; however, there was no mention of the number of subjects, SES, gender, or racial composition of the sample, nor the number of individuals included who had a substance abuse problem. In contrast, the authors did provide data on mean test scores of substance abusers, nonabusers, and a variety of comparison groups as well as means based on respondent age, race, and gender. The authors did report significant differences between groups, which supported the validity of the instrument. The authors provided data on the item-total correlation coefficients, the magnitudes of which were acceptable. The authors concluded that test-retest reliability was not applicable because test stability was not a desired feature of the instrument because an individual's score should improve with treatment. This conclusion regarding test stability is wholly inaccurate as most tests assessing clinical symptomatology are potentially sensitive to treatment effects. Overall, the psychometric properties of the instrument are impossible to interpret given the lack of information on the standardization sample as well as the limited reliability data.

The test developers do not provide information on the relationship of the test scores to other measures of substance abuse. Also, it appeared that the authors included a sample of known substance abusers in, or about to enter, treatment. It is not clear how treatment resistant or denying substance abusers would respond to the questionnaire. It would have been useful had the authors included a lie scale as a component of the instrument to assess the influence of social desirability. It appears the measure would not be very useful in detecting substance abusers who are reticent in reporting about their patterns of use.

In summary, the Substance Abuse Screening Test is a short, easily administered and scored instrument for assessing drug and alcohol use. The test is intended for screening only and is not diagnostic. The authors reported that items differentiated abusers from nonabusers. Although the test has some positive features, I cannot recommend use of the instrument as a screening measure at this point given the limited psychometric data. Specifically, additional data are needed addressing the reliability and content validity of the instrument. Furthermore, it is unclear how substance abusers not interested in treatment would score on the instrument. It is my concern that the test would lead to excessive numbers of false negatives given the direct nature of many of the items.

Review of the Substance Abuse Screening Test by MARIELA C. SHIRLEY, Assistant Professor, Department of Psychology, University of North Carolina at Wilmington, Wilmington, NC:

The Substance Abuse Screening Test (SAST) was developed as a brief measure to identify individuals "who may be at risk of substance abuse" (manual, p. 7), and to help with referral decisions (manual, p. 1). Although it is questionable whether true risk can be determined in a format other than a longitudinal design, the SAST's goal is consistent with screening tests focused on the early identification of individuals with possible substance abuse problems who require further evaluation (Connors, 1995; Miller, Westerberg, & Waldron, 1995). This test comprises two parts: (a) a 30-item self-report response form, and (b) an optional 5-item qualitative Observation Report. The SAST can be administered either individually or in a group format by staff with little training in addictions or assessment. The Observation Report should be completed by an examiner who is familiar with the individual being screened, particularly when self-report is suspect. Potential for bias in observer reporting is not addressed.

The SAST was not intended to be a diagnostic instrument; it was designed to screen out individuals who do not have substance abuse problems. However, 12 of the 30 items significantly overlap with *DSM-IV* criteria for dependence (i.e., alcohol). In adolescents, questions on withdrawal and tolerance may not be appropriate. SAST items were developed using a rational approach based on the test developers' experience and a literature review, and the test includes items that directly and indirectly assess for substance abuse (problem areas assessed include: aggression, conduct disorder/ antisociality, parental conflicts, school problems, self-esteem, alienation, affect, attention/concentration, and mild cognitive impairment). Age of onset of use and family history of substance abuse are not assessed. An initial pool of 181 items was reduced to 30 by using the following approaches: (a) a rational approach, (b) by how well items discriminated between individuals with and without substance abuse problems based on item correlation with the total test score and diagnostic type (*r* range .49 to .77), and (c) by elimination of items considered to be redundant (where their correlation was lower than the similar retained item). A coefficient alpha of .895 was obtained as an estimate of internal consistency reliability. Principal components factor analysis was used on the final items to determine unidimensionality (manual, p. 15), with the first principal component dominating other factors in the analysis.

The standardization sample was obtained from samples in Kentucky, New York, Nebraska, and Kansas. No information is provided in the test manual regarding how the sample was obtained, its size, or characteristics (e.g., socio-demographics, sample size by age range, percentage of substance users vs. nonsubstance users, etc.). The age range selected (13–30) is arbitrary and confounds adolescents with adults. The authors indicate that the test discriminates well: (1) between individuals who have/do not have substance use problems (manual, p. 3); and (b) between substance abusers and individuals with other types of problems (e.g., psychiatric disorders, learning problems, behavior disorders, and physical disabilities). Scores were developed based on the probability that an individual will have a problem given the score and individual demographic characteristics (manual, p.

4). However, no data on sampling information are provided despite inferences that there were no differences for gender and race or for presence/ absence of a substance use problem.

According to the authors, the SAST has strong face validity. However, whether *risk* (i.e., individuals without current substance use problems who are at risk for developing problems) for the development of a substance use disorder (risk reduction screening) vs. *need* for further assessment in individuals who already have a substance abuse problem (disease detection screening) is measured (construct validity) is open to question (Cooney, Zweben, & Fleming, 1995). Overall, the test appears to assess *deviance* (where one behavioral problem area could be substance abuse). If so, the Problem Oriented Screening Instrument for Teenagers (POSIT) is a better measure that assesses multiple behavior problem areas and discriminates between adolescents in treatment and school settings (Rahdert, 1991). Concurrent or convergent validity relative to other widely used measures in the field that screen for potential substance abuse problems (e.g., Adolescent Drinking Index [12:17], Adolescent Alcohol Involvement Scale [Mayer & Filstead, 1979], Personal Experience Screening Questionnaire [Winters, 1992; 1.28 this volume], Drug Use Screening Inventory [Tarter, 1990; Tarter & Hegedus, 1991, 1991], Problem Oriented Screening Instrument for Teenagers [Rahdert, 1991], Rutgers Collegiate Substance Abuse Screening Test [Bennett et al., 1993]) or a reference test (e.g., Michigan Alcoholism Screening Test [Selzer, 1971; 1.24 this volume]) is not provided. Strong agreement between the total score and known history of substance abuse is claimed, yet poor documentation is provided. In an attempt to develop a test to assess *risk* the authors appear to confuse concurrent validity with predictive validity. In determining risk, predictive validity is more appropriate as the question would be "What is the likelihood that … will develop a substance abuse problem?" Further cautions of the impact of positive screens should be provided (i.e., on employability, insurability, scholarships, etc.).

Scoring is based on categorical yes/no responses with most substance abuse items requiring endorsement if the individual "ever or usually" had these symptoms. This may not be congruent with their "current" situation. In a review of special considerations in evaluating adolescents, Miller, Westerberg, and Waldron (1995) emphasized that although 90% of adolescents experiment with substances, many mature out after age 21. Interpretation of raw scores can be done in one of three ways: (a) risk level range, (b) standardized scores, and (c) Bayesian table of the likelihood that a problem exists.

Risk level cutoffs were based on efforts at maximizing sensitivity while minimizing specificity. A total score of 1–9 or 1–11 (for ages 13–18 and over 18 respectively) is unremarkable. Borderline risk is based on a score of 10–14 or 12–17 (for ages 13–18 and over 18 respectively). Moderate risk requires a score of 15–18 or 18–20, and high risk scores are 19–30 or 21–30 (for ages 13–18 and over 18 respectively for each of these risk ranges). Data are not provided on how cutoff scores were devised and what methods were used to link these to risk levels. At least 12 items bear some direct relationship to *DSM-IV* criteria (e.g., Item 20: "Once I start drinking it is hard for me to stop"). Presumably, one could endorse 9 of the 12 items yet be considered "unremarkable."

Standard scores use a mean of 100 (*s.d.* = 15) and are based on a sample of individuals who do not have a substance abuse problem and excludes substance abusers or individuals with other disorders. Standard scores were calibrated so that higher scores indicate lower risk and lower scores indicate higher risk (manual, p. 9). Again, there is no information on the sample used to derive these standard scores.

Finally, Bayesian tables are provided to help determine the likelihood that the SAST will accurately identify individuals with known problems using population baserates (manual, p. 25). Professionals utilizing these tables need to know the baserates of the community in which they live; this is often not the case as population estimates are usually given for much larger groupings of cities or socio-demographic categories. In addition, baserates for particular sample characteristics (e.g., blacks in rural communities, certain professions, etc.) are not always available. Even if baserate information were available, it is questionable how this would be utilized in a clinical setting or in facilitating a referral for further assessment. No test-retest or interrater reliability estimates are presented.

In summary, construct validity and other psychometric properties of the SAST are questionable. Although screening for substance use problems in adolescents is important, this measure is poorly developed, poorly documented, and offers no advantage over other screening instruments. Studies are needed to further evaluate its predictive validity.

REVIEWER'S REFERENCES

Selzer, M. L. (1971). The Michigan Alcoholism Screening Test: The quest for a new diagnostic instrument. *American Journal of Psychiatry, 127,* 1653-1658.

Mayer, J., & Filstead, W. J. (1979). The Adolescent Alcohol Involvement Scale: An instrument for measuring adolescents' use and misuse of alcohol. *Journal of Studies on Alcohol, 40,* 291-300.

Tarter, R. E. (1990). Evaluation and treatment of adolescent substance abuse: A decision tree method. *American Journal of Drug and Alcohol Abuse, 16,* 1-46.

Rahdert, E. R. (Ed.). (1991). *The Adolescent Assessment/Referral System manual.* Rockville, MD: U.S. Department of Health and Human Services.

Tarter, R. E., & Hegedus, A. M. (1991). The Drug Use Screening Inventory: Its application in the evaluation and treatment of alcohol and other drug abuse. *Alcohol Health and Research World, 15,* 65-75.

Winters, K. C. (1992). Development of an adolescent alcohol and other drug abuse screening scale: Personal Experience Screening Questionnaire. *Addictive Behaviors, 17,* 479-490.

Bennett, M. E., McCrady, B. S., Frankenstein, W., Laitman, L. A., Van Horn, D. H. A., & Keller, D. S. (1993). Identifying young adult substance abusers: The Rutgers Collegiate Substance Abuse Screening Test. *Journal of Studies on Alcohol, 54,* 522-527.

Connors, G. J. (1995). Screening for alcohol problems. In J. P. Allen & M. Columbus (Eds.), *Assessing alcohol problems: A guide for clinicians and researchers* (pp. 17-29) NIAAA Treatment Handbook Series 4 (NIH Publication No. 95-3745). Rockville, MD: National Institute on Alcohol Abuse and Alcoholism.

Cooney, N. L., Zweben, A., & Fleming, M. F. (1995). Screening for alcohol problems and at-risk drinking in health care settings. In R. K. Hester & W. R. Miller (Eds.), *Handbook of alcoholism treatment approaches: Effective alternatives* (2nd ed.; pp. 45-60). Boston, MA: Allyn & Bacon.

Miller, W. R., Westerberg, V. S., & Waldron, H. B. (1995). Evaluating alcohol problems in adults and adolescents. In R. K. Hester & W. R. Miller (Eds.), *Handbook of alcoholism treatment approaches: Effective alternatives* (2nd ed.; pp. 61-88). Boston, MA: Allyn & Bacon.

[1.37]

Substance Abuse Subtle Screening Inventory.

Purpose: To "identify chemical abusers and differentiate them from social drinkers and general psychiatric clients."

Population: Ages 12–18, adults.

Publication Dates: 1983–1990.

Acronym: SASSI.

Administration: Group.

Levels, 2: Adult, Adolescent.

Price Data, 1989: $75 per starter kit; $25 per 25 tests and profiles; $10 per scoring key; $60 per videotape summary of manual; $55 per manual ('85, 242 pages).

Time: [10–15] minutes.

Author: Glenn A. Miller.

Publisher: The SASSI Institute.

a) ADULT FORM.

Scores, 8: Obvious Attributes, Subtle Attributes, Denial, Defensive Abuser vs. Defensive Non-Abuser, Alcohol vs. Drug, Codependency, Risk Prediction Score-Alcohol, Risk Prediction Score-Drug.

b) ADOLESCENT FORM.

Scores, 8: Obvious Attributes, Subtle Attributes, Defensiveness, Defensive Abuser vs. Defensive Non-

Abuser, Correctional, Random Answering Pattern, Face Valid Alcohol, Face Valid Other Drug.
Cross References: Reviews by Barbara Kerr and Nicholas A. Vacc originally appeared in 12:381 (1 reference).

Review of the Substance Abuse Subtle Screening Inventory by BARBARA KERR, Professor of Psychology in Education, Arizona State University, Tempe, AZ:

The Substance Abuse Subtle Screening Inventory (SASSI) is an interesting attempt to deal with the tendency of substance abusers to deny or obscure their substance abuse. It is based on the assumption that self-report responses that do not include substance use in their content may serve as indicators of substance abuse. Most substance abuse screening measures have obvious items concerning the use of alcohol and drug use; substance abusers who deny their condition or for a variety of reasons wish to hide their substance abuse will usually "fake good" on these scales. Therefore, substance abuse screening inventories that do not take this response set into account are not likely to be effective. Mental health centers, university student health centers, and court-ordered substance abuse centers have a great need for this kind of scale, and have greeted the development of the SASSI with enthusiasm (Creager, 1989).

DEVELOPMENT OF THE SASSI. The SASSI is a single-page, paper-and-pencil questionnaire. On one side are 52 True-False questions that seem to be unrelated to chemical abuse. On the other side are the Risk Prediction Scales which allow clients to self-report on the 12 alcohol-related and 14 drug-related items. The test in intended to be readable at the fifth grade level and can also be administered orally. It takes from 10 to 15 minutes for clients to complete both tests. The SASSI can be hand scored in about 1 minute.

The items on the SASSI are empirically derived. Most other current substance abuse screening instruments are rationally constructed, based on theoretical formulations of the symptoms of alcoholism. This scale is composed predominantly of items from other empirically derived scales and new items. Items were borrowed from the Minnesota Multiphasic Personality Inventory (MMPI; 9:715), the Psychological Screening Inventory (PSI; 9:1015; Lanyon, 1973), the Michigan Alcoholism Screening Test (Selzer, 1971), and many other sources that promised to yield items which differentiated between abusers and nonabusers. The subtle items related to a wide variety of behaviors related to health, social interaction, emotional states, preferences, needs, interests, and values. Nonsubtle items are asked directly about substance abuse and its usual consequences.

Approximately 1,000 items were administered to close to 300 people in the course of the validation studies. Discriminant analyses were used to develop the major subscales. The subscales are as follows:

The Obvious Attributes Scale (OAT) is intended to measure the openness or the willingness of the client to admit to symptoms or problems related to substance abuse. A high score on this scale means that there are similarities between the client's personal style and the personal style of chemically dependent people.

The Subtle Attributes Scale (SAT) score is probably the most important scale, because it is very resistant to faking. It measures a personal predisposition to develop a dependency on drugs or alcohol. High scores means that the client is similar biologically or in personal style to chemically dependent people.

The Denial (DAN) scale was created to identify the client's defensiveness to test taking, but high scores can result from unconscious denial or deliberate attempts to conceal. Both high and low scores indicate problems: High scores are associated with excessive denial and low scores with feelings of worthlessness and deficiency.

The Defensive Abuser vs. Defensive Non-Abuser Scale (DEN) is used with the Denial Scale score in determining whether a person is in fact an abuser or whether their responses are those of a defensive non-abuser.

The Alcohol vs. Drug Scale (ALD) is intended to show whether the client prefers alcohol or other drugs. Although this is not a strong scale, usually a high score indicates alcohol preference and a low score indicates drug preference.

The Family vs. Controls Scale (FAM) is meant to be a preliminary measure of codependency. It is a weak scale at this point; it is meant to show how similar the test taker is to family members of alcohol and drug abusers.

The second part of the SASSI is made up of two previously developed scales, the Face Valid Alcohol scale (originally the Risk Prediction Scale for alcohol) and the Face Valid Drug Scale (originally the Risk Prediction Scale for drugs [SASSI manual, Appendix B, p. 18, Copper & Robinson, in press]).

Scoring and interpretation of the SASSI involves attention to the elevation and slope of the scales as well as using a variety of decision rules that lead to the classification of abuser or nonabuser. An example of such a rule is: If either of the following two conditions is met, classify as chemical abuser:

1. Obvious Attributes (OAT) or Subtle Attributes (SAT) *T*-score is above 70.

2. Obvious Attributes and Subtle Attributes *T* scores are both above 60.

VALIDITY. In the validation section of the manual, the author shows that the SASSI and the RPS measures each did better in identifying low defensive late stage abusers already involved in a residential detoxification program than the more defensive early stage abusers. It is important, therefore, to specify the population on which validity testing takes place. The combination of the SASSI and the RPS was most effective with all populations: The combination identified 90% of the residential detoxification sample, 80% of defensive early stage abusers in a family oriented intensive outpatient program, and 90% of nonabusers who were also codependents. The independent contribution of the SASSI was most important with individuals who were defensive early stage abusers. The subscales were shown to each contribute independently to the decision rules. The Subtle Attributes (SAT) scale did a good job of identifying defensiveness and the Denial (DEN) scale in identifying distortions. The Family (FAM) scale was not successful in identifying codependency.

A later study found the SASSI to be useful in identifying subtle substance abusers among rehabilitation clients in Texas; 87% of the cases already classified as substance abusers by the rehabilitation agency were identified by the SASSI. Also, 32.7% of clients who had not been previously identified as substance abusers by the agency, and about whom counselors were not aware, were classified as such by the SASSI (DiNitto & Schwab, 1991). A dissertation by Kilkunas (1988), using only the SASSI without the Face Valid Scales, still found reasonably good prediction, with the SASSI identifying 94% of controls, 78% of Alcoholics, 71% of Drug Addicts, and 96% of codependents (Creager, 1989).

The SASSI has high concurrent validity with the MacAndrew (1965) subscale of the MMPI (.87), although the use of some of these items and some very similar ones certainly contributes to the high concurrent validity.

RELIABILITY. The internal consistency of most of the subscales of the SASSI is quite low. Because of the discriminant analysis method of construction, each subscale except the RPSA, RPSD, and PAL5 is made up of heterogeneous items rather than items related to a unitary construct. Internal consistency analyses were performed for Detox patients, Outpatients, and Probation groups. Coefficient alpha ranges are reported as follows: OAT, .61–.73; SAT, .25–.49; DEN, .57–.68; DAN, .56–.82; ALD, .44–.49; FAM, .16–.60; RPSA, .90–.92; RPSD, .93–.96; PAL5, .78–.80.

The only study of test-retest reliability which has been performed was one in which the SASSI was used without the Face Valid Scales. Kilkunas (1988) tested 24 subjects on a 4- to 6-week interval and found moderate to good test-retest reliability. The reliability coefficients were reported as follows: OAT, .87; SAT, .91; DEN, .86; DAN, .91; ALD, .78; FAM, .76.

It was puzzling that the author, who obviously put tremendous thought and care into the validation of the SASSI, gave so little attention to reliability. Because of the inconsistent nature of responding of many substance abusers to psychological instruments, and because of the importance of decisions made based on the SASSI, more emphasis on its reliability should be given in future research. All indications so far are the instrument is a reliable one.

CLINICAL USEFULNESS. The SASSI is almost as good as its promotion claims it to be. It seems to have been responsibly developed, and it is clearly created with the practitioner in mind. Its ease of administration and scoring, its clear decision rules and suggestions for interpretation, and the informative and carefully written manual all make it very attractive to mental health providers who have difficult and important decisions to make about treatment.

The SASSI fits its population as well; it does seem to accurately identify those who are denying or obscuring their substance abuse, particularly among less advanced stage abusers. One quibble is that although it is supposed to be at the fifth grade reading level, it looks as though it actually would require a higher reading level, probably seventh or eighth grade.

There may be ethical issues which will require exploration if the SASSI becomes widespread in its use. It must never become the psychological equivalent of the Breathalyzer test; legal decisions about the label substance abuser must be made on the basis of interview material, this and other instruments, and on evidence of actual behavior.

REVIEWER'S REFERENCES

MacAndrew, C. (1965). The differentiation of male alcoholic outpatients from nonalcoholic psychiatric outpatients by means of the MMPI. *Quarterly Journal of Studies on Alcohol, 26*, 238–246.

Selzer, M. L. (1971). The Michigan Alcoholism Screening Test: The quest for a new diagnostic instrument. *American Journal of Psychiatry, 127*, 1653–1658.

Lanyon, R. I. (1973). Psychological Screening Inventory: Manual. Goshen, NY: Research Psychologists Press.

Kilkunas, W. (1988). [Title unavailable]. Unpublished doctoral dissertation. Muncie, IN: Ball State University.

Creager, C. (1989, July/August). SASSI test breaks through denial. *Professional Counselor*, p. 81–84.

DiNitto, D. M., & Schwab, A. J. (1991). *Substance abuse factors which interfere with entry or reentry into employment.* Report for Texas Rehabilitation Commission. Austin, TX: University of Texas at Austin School of Social Work.

Copper, S., & Robinson, D. A. (in press). Cross-validation of the Substance Abuse Subtle Screening Inventory on a college population. *American Journal of College Health.*

Review of the Substance Abuse Subtle Screening Inventory by NICHOLAS A. VACC, Professor and Chairperson, Department of Counselor Education, University of North Carolina at Greensboro, Greensboro, NC:

The Substance Abuse Subtle Screening Inventory (SASSI) consists of two separate questionnaires included in one response form. On one side of the response form is the SASSI, which is a one-page paper-and-pencil questionnaire containing 52 true and false questions designed to assess chemical abuse in an unobtrusive way; items appear unrelated to chemical abuse and, therefore, make them less threatening to the respondent. On the opposite side of the response form is the Risk Prediction Scales (RPS), which was designed to predict the degree of risk of abusing alcohol and other drugs. The RPS, which comes in two forms, was developed by Linda A. Morton (1978) in conjunction with the Department of Mental Health, Division of Addiction Services, State of Indiana. It consists

of 26 items designed to assess the level of substance-abuse risk (i.e., non-users minimally at risk, non-problematic users minimally at risk, non-users moderately at risk, non-problematic users moderately at risk, problematic users substantially at risk, and dysfunctional users totally at risk). Use of the RPS enhances the value of the SASSI.

The SASSI was developed to assess chemical dependency by being insulated to the respondent's level of honesty or faking. The author reports the instrument is independent of age, education, and socioeconomic status. The instrument provides information concerning five scales (i.e., Obvious Attributes [OAT], which is designed to differentiate substance abusers who have admitted problems from non-abusers; Subtle Attributes [SAT], which is intended to differentiate substance abusers from non-substance abusers regardless of the respondent's degree of honesty; Denial [DEN], which is designed to identify those substance abusers who are denying their behavior; Personal-Family [FAM], which distinguishes between substance abusers and non-abusers who live with dependency (co-dependency); and Alcohol/Drug Preference [ALD], which is designed to differentiate alcohol abusers from those with a poly-drug abuse pattern). The SASSI takes about 10–15 minutes to complete and can be scored in 5–10 minutes.

A single form of the SASSI is available for both men and women and is designed for respondents 18 years of age through adulthood. Also available is an adolescent form of the SASSI designed for use with children ages 12–18. The adolescent form, which is a more recent development by the test author, appears, like the adult form, to be nonthreatening and is designed for screening adolescents who may be chemically dependent. Other materials related to this instrument that are available through the SASSI Institute are an instructional videotape that provides information concerning the administration, scoring, development, philosophy, and validity data of the SASSI; training workshops (for a fee) that provide participants with the SASSI feedback system to include how the SASSI can be used to assist clients to establish goals and conduct therapeutic interventions; a computer-disk form of the SASSI designed for IBM-compatible computers; and a telephone consultation service provided by the staff at the SASSI Institute. A toll-free number is provided for this free consultation service concerning profile interpretation and program development using the SASSI.

In consulting practitioners, it appears that the computer-assisted scoring disk for IBM or compatible computers is the method of choice. The computer-scoring procedure is easy to learn and operate; clear instructions are available for using the SASSI computer version. The examinee answers the questions by typing the appropriate letter on the keyboard, and the next question appears automatically. After completing the assessment, examinees are asked whether they would like to review their answers. The computer-assisted scoring disk, which requires a password by the practitioner, enhances the scoring process and provides a visual display of the profile on the screen as well as a printed copy of the profile and results. Both the paper-and-pencil and computer versions of the SASSI are user friendly for respondents.

The SASSI's primary purpose as identified by the author is to serve as an objective screening tool to differentiate substance abusers from non-abusers. However, in addition to screening, the SASSI is frequently used by practitioners as a clinical instrument when counseling individuals and families. Yet, the SASSI's value within counseling programs has not been empirically documented. The manual provides a section on clinical interpretation of the SASSI for practitioners, but it also includes a disclaimer that such use has not been validated through empirical research. To be addressed are such questions as how valuable are the subscales in developing treatment plans?

The author reports through informal correspondence accompanying the reviewer's manual, that test/retest reliability was reported for 24 subjects as .87 (OAT), .91 (SAT), .86 (DEN), .78 (ALD), and .76 (FAM) for the adult form. Overall reliability averages appear to be acceptable (G. Miller, personal communication, August 1990). Considerable validity testing is provided in the manual. Unfortunately, adequate description concerning representativeness of the populations involved in the reported validity data is not provided. Notably absent is empirical information concerning the chronological age, social economic status, and ethnic background of the samples. Also,

woefully inadequate are some of the cell-sizes of the subsamples reported for the validity and normative information provided. For example, the intensive outpatient program samples of family chemical abusers had Ns as small as 3 for the male subgroup, 11 for the female subgroup, and 7 for the male family non-chemical abusers subgroup.

The SASSI manual is somewhat confusing and difficult to use. Practitioners have recommended that it is advisable to take the SASSI training workshop with a representative in order to properly understand how to score and interpret the instruments to achieve maximum benefit. This recommendation applies to both the paper-and-pencil and computer version printouts (C. Woods, personal communication, May 2, 1992). In summary, considering the reasonable cost of approximately $2 a test, the computer version of the SASSI is the instrument of choice as a quick screening instrument in the area of substance abuse. Because it is widely used by individuals involved with the substance-abuse field, including Alcohol Safety Action Programs, the SASSI psychometric properties should meet or exceed professional norms. The information reported in the manual is less than reassuring that this has been achieved. Although the manual appears comprehensive and thorough on quick inspection, it is poorly developed; it does not provide adequate information and the reader has to "dig" in an attempt to judge the value of the instrument. The author should consider developing a technical manual addressing the *Standards for Educational and Psychological Testing* (AERA, APA, & NCME, 1985) and a separate test user's manual written for the practitioner.

Such information as sample descriptions to include ethnic background, chronological age, socio-economic status, and/or educational level, and a reported reading level index of the two forms would be helpful additions to the manual. Also, the small number of cases used in the development of some of the scales, and the absence of current samples (some samples are pre-1977) are of concern. A more current data base for normative analysis is needed. For an instrument that is often used, additional data need to be systematically collected for the purpose of addressing psychometric issues.

The cost, short testing time, and ease of use by test takers are compelling reasons for the instrument's use. I would use the computer-assisted version and the paper-and-pencil version of the SASSI, but the former version would be my first choice. Additionally, I would suggest prospective users attend a SASSI Institute workshop to better prepare themselves for using the instruments.

REVIEWER'S REFERENCE

American Educational Research Association, American Psychological Association, & National Council on Measurement in Education. (1985). *Standards for educational and psychological testing.* Washington, DC: American Psychological Association, Inc.

[1.38]

Substance Use Disorder Diagnosis Schedule.

Purpose: Designed to elicit information related to the diagnosis of substance use disorders.
Population: Suspected alcohol or drug abusers.
Publication Date: 1989.
Acronym: SUDDS.
Scores: Scores for 12 substances (Alcohol, Marijuana, Cocaine, Sedatives, Tranquilizers, Stimulants, Heroin, Other Opioids, Hallucinogens, PCP, Inhalants, Other/Mixed); ratings for Stress; and a Depression Screen.
Administration: Individual.
Price Data: Available from publisher.
Time: (30–45) minutes.
Comments: Structured diagnostic interview; also available as a computer-administered interview.
Authors: Patricia Ann Harrison and Norman G. Hoffmann.
Publisher: New Standards, Inc.
Cross References: Reviews by Andres Barona and Steven I. Pfeiffer will appear in the 13th MMY.

Review of the Substance Use Disorder Diagnosis Schedule by ANDRÉS BARONA, Professor of Educational Psychology and School Psychology Training Director, Arizona State University, Tempe, AZ:

The Substance Use Disorder Diagnosis Schedule (SUDDS) is a structured diagnostic interview used to obtain information about specific events and behaviors useful for corroborating *DSM-III* and *DSM-III-R* diagnoses of alcohol and/or other drug dependencies. Development of the SUDDS was based on a perceived need for a structured diagnostic interview for the specific purpose of detecting substance use disorder. The 1989 version of the SUDDS represents changes and revisions of the Diagnostic Interview Schedule (DIS; Robins, Helzer, Ratcliff, & Seyfried, 1982) and the Substance Abuse Modified Diagnostic Interview (SAMDIS; Hoffman & Harrison, 1984).

The SUDDS consists of 99 items that address general background information; exposure to life events that may lead to stress or depression; and use of coffee, tobacco, alcohol, and other drugs. A "fixed-phrasing" format is used in which the examiner first elicits affirmation (yes/no) or occurrence responses on the alcohol section without probing positive responses. A follow-up of positive responses occurs at the end of the alcohol section. This two-stage process also is used to inquire about other substance use. In instances of multiple substance use, initial administration of the SUDDS is aimed at determining if a lifetime pattern of substance-use disorder can be established. Positive responses are further queried in a second administration to determine if the behavior(s) have occurred within the past year. In most instances a trained interviewer can administer the SUDDS in approximately 30 minutes. However, a history of multiple drug use will significantly increase administration time.

Information obtained from the interview is coded onto one of two diagnostic checklists (*DSM-III; DSM-III-R*) designed to assist in determining if the respondent meets the respective *DSM* criteria for substance use disorder. Positive substance use and symptomology are coded as current (i.e., occurring within the past year) or lifetime (i.e., occurring prior to the past year). The *DSM-III-R* checklist additionally provides guidelines to classify positive responses into *DSM* symptom categories and facilitate diagnoses.

A computer-assisted version of the SUDDS also is available to facilitate ease of administration for some clients and available evidence suggests that interviewer-administered and computer-administered versions are equally effective (Davis, Hoffman, Morse, & Luehr, 1992).

ADVANTAGES. The SUDDS provides clinicians an efficient way to obtain sufficient/comprehensive information to make diagnoses regarding substance use disorder according to *DSM-III* and *DSM-III-R* criteria. Use of the more fully developed *DSM-III-R* Diagnostic checklist, which includes a listing of *DSM-III-R* psychoactive Substance Use Disorder Diagnoses Codes, allows for quick reference and diagnosis. The structured format eliciting information about numerous observable events and behaviors related to substance use permits the clinician to defend objectively the diagnosis and to verify when necessary the veracity of responses by interviews with family members and other collateral sources.

WEAKNESSES. Given its length (many of the 99 items have multiple subsections), the detailed nature of the questions, and the authors' description of the instrument, the SUDDS seems most useful as a confirmatory measure. In spite of its reported quick and easy administration, it may be limited in its usefulness as a screening instrument or with populations in which drug use has not been a priori established. Although adequate for providing useful information for diagnosing substance use disorder, the SUDDS provides limited information to help clinicians determine if other diagnoses are warranted. Similarly, behaviors useful for developing treatment regimens are not included in the interview. The fixed-phrasing format limits clinical interaction and may require additional meetings to obtain information useful in developing therapeutic interventions. In addition, although the authors clearly do not consider the SUDDS to be a psychometric instrument but rather a diagnostic aid, it is questionable whether most interviewers will use it in this manner. Finally, the SUDDS-IV, which covers the key content of the *DSM-IV*, either is already available or in final stages of development. This newer version is designed to provide "clear documentation of specific events and behaviors which can be used to support a diagnosis or demonstrate that the individual denies the occurrence of events frequently associated with abuse or dependence" (N. G. Hoffman, personal communication, February 21, 1996). Although field trials have not been completed and normative data is not yet available, it is likely that the more current SUDDS-IV will have greater clinical utility.

SUMMARY. The SUDDS is a structured fixed-format interview designed to obtain data about specific events and behaviors indicative of a *DSM-III* or *DSM-III-R* diagnosis of substance use disorder. As a clinical measure, it appears useful for corroborating and formulating specific diagnoses involving substance use disorders. The SUDDS is likely to provide clinicians with sufficient documentation to satisfy the requirements of various agencies (e.g., mental health facilities, insurance companies), as well as to defend a diagnosis made on the basis of *DSM-III* or *DSM-III-R*

descriptors. Moreover, it provides an opportunity for clinicians to verify the veracity of data critical to accept or rule out a specific diagnosis.

Psychometric data involving the SUDDS are not available. Normative and additional research data involving the SUDDS and its newer version, the SUDDS-IV, would be useful in better determining the psychometric utility of the instrument. However, as an interview technique, the measure is useful in systematically collecting information related to substance use and is likely to be useful with populations where the incidence of abuse is relatively high.

REVIEWER'S REFERENCES

Robins, L. N., Helzer, J. E., Ratcliff, K. S., & Seyfried, W. (1982). Validity of the Diagnostic Interview Schedule, Version II: DSM-III diagnoses. *Psychological Medicine, 12,* 855–870.

Hoffmann, N. G., & Harrison, P. A. (1984). Substance Abuse Modified Diagnostic Interview Schedule (SAMDIS). *Psychological Documents, 14,* 10.

Davis, L. J., Jr., Hoffmann, N. G., Morse, R. M., & Luehr, J. G. (1992). Substance Use Disorder Diagnostic Schedule (SUDDS): The equivalence and validity of a computer-administered and an interview-administered format. *Alcoholism Clinical and Experimental Research, 16*(2), 250–254.

Review of the Substance Use Disorder Diagnosis Schedule by STEVEN I. PFEIFFER, Visiting Professor of Clinical Psychology, Drexel University, Philadelphia, PA:

The Substance Use Disorder Diagnosis Schedule (SUDDS) is a structured interview for documenting the diagnosis for alcohol and other drug dependencies. The instrument was developed from an earlier version called the Substance Abuse Modified Diagnostic Interview Schedule (SAMDIS) (Hoffman & Harrison, 1984).

The interview consists of a wide range of questions within seven areas: general demographic data, psychosocial stressors, a brief screen for depression, coffee consumption and smoking habits, and alcohol and drug use. Administration time can be as brief as 30 minutes with a client with minimal alcohol use to as long as 60 minutes for a client with extensive and longstanding drug involvement.

The manual states that the SUDDS is designed to assist in the diagnosis of substance use disorders. It is not recommended as a screening device, but rather is described as an in-depth inquiry with individuals already identified as likely alcohol and drug users.

The authors are to be commended for their thoughtful attention to providing detailed and clear instructions that facilitate administration and ensure a standardized interview process. The manual also provides helpful guidelines that assist in establishing *DSM-III-R* diagnoses—a useful feature of the test.

As mentioned earlier, the manual describes the test as a revision of the SAMDIS, which was based on *DSM-III* diagnostic criteria and "other widely used criteria sets" (p. 11). However, no information is provided on the procedures followed in the development of the SUDDS, including no description of how items were selected, which "widely used (diagnostic) criteria sets" (p. 11) were used, or if a pilot phase occurred.

Face validity appears acceptable, and item coverage is extensive. Nevertheless, the manual provides no evidence that any research was conducted to determine representative content coverage or construct validity. For example, no panel of experts was invited to validate the content of the SUDDS, no inter-item correlation or factor analyses were performed, and no studies were undertaken comparing the SUDDS with other substance use instruments.

Equally surprising and disappointing is the fact that the authors provide no evidence of reliability. It is critical for a clinical tool to be sufficiently reliable for use in individual decision making; the SUDDS, unfortunately, does not furnish any information on interrater, test-retest, or internal consistency. Relatedly, no effort was made to evaluate item or test bias. This is a particularly telling weakness in that one might expect interview questions on a substance use scale potentially to be influenced by culture, gender, ethnicity, SES, and geographic region.

Although the manual offers guidelines for making a *DSM-III-R* diagnosis, there are no standardization data or norms. The test user is not provided cut scores or thresholds for making a diagnosis, apparently because the authors did not undertake any validation studies before publishing the SUDDS. It is unknown, for example, what the sensitivity or specificity of the SUDDS might be for different groups of high-risk substance using populations.

The SUDDS is a structured interview for documenting suspected alcohol and drug dependency. The test has acceptable face validity and extensive item coverage, including questions on psychosocial stressors and depressive symptoms associated with substance abuse. Unfortunately, the test falls far short in omitting information on test development, norming, reliability, and validity. The manual does not provide cut scores to aid in interpreting test results, and until these weaknesses are addressed in a revised manual, the SUDDS should only be used as a research tool or in clinical practice to help formulate hypotheses but not make differential diagnoses.

REVIEWER'S REFERENCE

Hoffman, N. G., & Harrison, P. A. (1984). Substance Abuse Modified Diagnostic Interview Schedule (SAMDIS). *Psychological Documents, 14,* 10.

[1.39]

The Western Personality Inventory.

Purpose: Identifies alcoholics and potential alcoholics and measures extent of alcohol addiction.

Population: Adults.

Publication Dates: 1963–1988.

Acronym: WPI.

Scores, 14: Anxiety, Depressive Fluctuations, Emotional Sensitivity, Resentfulness, Incompleteness, Aloneness, Interpersonal Relations, Total, Regularity of Drinking, Preference for Drinking over Other Activities, Lack of Controlled Drinking, Rationalization of Drinking, Excessive Emotionality, Total.

Administration: Individual or group.

Manual: No manual; use manuals for The Manson Evaluation and The Alcadd Test.

Price Data, 1993: $90 per complete kit including 5 AutoScore test forms, 2 prepaid mail-in answer sheets for computer scoring and interpretation, Manson Evaluation Manual, and Alcadd Manual; $27.50 per Manson Evaluation Manual or Alcadd Manual; $9.50 per mail-in answer sheet; $125 per 25-use IBM microcomputer disk (specify 5.25 inch or 3.5 inch).

Time: Administration time not reported.

Comments: Combination of The Manson Evaluation (T4:1533) and The Alcadd Test (T4:143).

Author: Morse P. Manson.

Publisher: Western Psychological Services.

This test has not been reviewed in *The Mental Measurements Yearbook.*

2

TESTS WITH SECONDARY FOCUS
ON ASSESSING SUBSTANCE ABUSE

[2.1]

Adult Neuropsychological Questionnaire.

Purpose: To screen for brain dysfunction.

Population: Adults.

Publication Date: 1978.

Acronym: ANQ.

Scores: 8 content areas: General Health, Substance Abuse, Psychiatric Problems, General Neurological, Right Hemisphere, Left Hemisphere, Subcortical/Cerebellar/Spinal, Sensory/Perceptual.

Administration: Individual.

Price Data, 1995: $30 per complete kit including manual (11 pages) and 50 questionnaires.

Time: (5–10) minutes.

Comments: Can be used as adjunct to general intake interview; may be self-administered.

Author: Fernando Melendez.

Publisher: Psychological Assessment Resources, Inc.

Cross References: Reviews by Robert A. Bornstein and Julian Fabry originally appeared in 12:19.

Review of the Adult Neuropsychological Questionnaire by ROBERT A. BORNSTEIN, Professor and Associate Chairman, Department of Psychiatry, The Ohio State University, Columbus, OH:

The Adult Neuropsychological Questionnaire consists of 54 items designed to be administered as a semistructured interview. It can also be self-administered. The purpose of the questionnaire is to "inquire about complaints, symptoms, and signs that may suggest underlying brain dysfunction or other organic conditions" (manual, p. 1). It was developed initially as an aid for students who were not well versed in signs and symptoms associated with neurologic conditions. A well-organized neuropsychologically oriented inquiry of history and symptoms would be of considerable value

primarily to students or general clinicians. The test manual is essentially an interpretive guide that contains a rationale for the items that have been included. The authors suggest that formal assessment will often confirm or clarify the symptoms endorsed, although no data are presented to support this assertion. Similarly, no reliability or validity data of any kind are presented. The purported relationship between formal assessment and symptom endorsement as relevant for forensic work is fully unsubstantiated. Similarly, there is no support that this questionnaire has any value as a "reliable monitor in following the course of recovery (or decline) over a period of time" (manual, p. 1). The final paragraph of the manual introduction regards this questionnaire as "an assessment procedure," however, there are not even the most rudimentary evaluative data to support this assertion.

Apart from the lack of any supportive psychometric data, the inherent organization and content of the questionnaire leaves much to be desired. The items consist of a melange of questions directed at specific symptoms, personal medical history, and family medical history. Several of the questions are not directed at neurological or neuropsychological questions or conditions. These items, such as Number 5 related to tobacco consumption, are acknowledged to have no neuropsychological correlates, but are included to be used in subsequent medical referrals. It is unclear why questions about the identity and address of the patient's physician, or the date of the last physical examination (Items 38 and 39) should be part of the body of the questionnaire.

The ordering of questions is poorly organized with a random array of questions. This is particularly problematic because the presumed goal of this questionnaire is to help non-neuropsychologists conduct an organized neuropsychological inquiry. It would be of greater value if items were organized in coherent units related to current symptoms, personal history, and family history.

In addition to the poor organization, the content and wording of the questions are inconsistent, and in some cases ambiguous. For example, Item 9 inquires directly about changes in vision, and Item 32 inquires about changes in sense of smell. However, changes in hearing are addressed only indirectly by Item 17, "sometimes when people talk to you, do they seem to mumble?" Although several questions are devoted to possible symptoms of dizziness or loss of balance, there is no direct inquiry about changes in temperament, or problems with attention and concentration, both of which are common symptoms in neurologic populations. There is direct inquiry about relatively rare conditions such as syphilis (Item 46), but there is no direct inquiry regarding whether the patient has ever had a seizure. This is only indirectly, and poorly, addressed by Item 21 which inquires about family history of epilepsy.

The questionnaire also includes items which are very common in the general population, and almost certain to have no discriminative validity. The rationale offered for inclusion of these items (e.g., 19) is that failure to endorse the item represents a form of denial, lack of understanding, or lack of insight. There is no justification offered for this assertion. Many of the item interpretations and explanations offered in the manual are poorly justified, fail to recognize more common neurologic or psychiatric explanations, and dangerously oversimplify the questions under review, particularly in view of the intended audience for this questionnaire.

The dangerous and flawed interpretation of some items is exemplified by the major question categories that are included on the last page of the manual. Without any proper caution in the manual, these question groups could be viewed by the unsophisticated user as quasi-assessment indexes, indicative of specific disorders. The assignment of items to the "right hemisphere" and "left hemisphere" question groups amply demonstrate the problem. There are four "right hemisphere" questions; the first of which (change in sense of direction) may have some validity in relation to right hemisphere function. The other three items (change in memory, experience of déjà-vu, and change in handwriting) have no clear association with right hemisphere function. Although memory function clearly can be affected with right hemisphere function, patients are unlikely to complain spontaneously of the kind of memory deficit typically associated with right hemisphere disorders. Similarly, because memory complaints are so ubiquitous, this item could easily be included in the question categories related to psychiatric problems, general neurologic problems, and subcortical dysfunction.

The "left hemisphere" question group, which consists of five items, suffers from similar flaws. Although some of the items (e.g., 11) may bear some relation to left hemisphere symptoms, other items are not clearly related. For example, Item 18 (slurring your words) suggests dysarthria, which has no necessary association with left hemisphere function. The memory item is equally inappropriate for the left hemisphere question group for the same reasons as indicated above.

Finally, Item 24, related to temporary blindness in one or both eyes, although correctly attributed to cerebrovascular phenomena, has no association with the left hemisphere. Virtually, all of the eight symptom groupings suffer from similar flawed associations and attributions.

In summary, this questionnaire is designed to help students and non-neuropsychologists inquire about symptoms, history, or other complaints that may be associated with neuropsychological disorders. The questionnaire is poorly organized, ambiguous and inconsistent in its inquiry, and severely overinterpretive about the significance and possible attribution of specific symptoms. On the other hand, some important areas of inquiry are entirely omitted. This is a particular problem for a questionnaire intended for unsophisticated users. Furthermore, the implication that this questionnaire represents some form of quasi assessment, as suggested by the question groupings, is likely to lead to grossly incorrect interpretations. Although a well-organized inquiry of history and symptoms would be of significant value for the audience intended, this questionnaire falls seriously short of the mark. It is not recommended for use.

Review of the Adult Neuropsychological Questionnaire by JULIAN FABRY, Counseling Psychologist, Omaha Psychiatric Institute, Omaha, NE:

The Adult Neuropsychological Questionnaire is a self-report approach to evaluating an adult's neuropsychological "complaints, symptoms, or signs" (manual, p. 1) which "suggest organic brain dysfunction." The author developed this appraisal because of the apparent gap between social and psychological information and as a means to make appropriate medical referrals.

The Adult Neuropsychological Questionnaire can be used as an adjunct to a general intake interview, to make medical referrals, and to monitor recovery or deterioration of individuals as well as organize information about them. The questionnaire can be self-administered or a practitioner can ask questions focusing on the frequency, intensity, and duration of the occurrence of a particular symptom. It has been advocated that the person who uses this questionnaire be a practitioner with some fund of basic neuropsychological information.

In addition to a revised manual, the questionnaire itself consists of a booklet that can be used by the practitioner or examinee during the course of the interview or evaluation. The questionnaire consists of 54 items and they are arranged so that an appropriate response can be made (either yes/no or descriptive). The items cover a broad spectrum of information ranging from eating habits to sleep patterns, from alcohol consumption to types of headaches, losses, and changes in physical or mental functioning. It appears the author has rationally grouped the questions according to the following categories: General Health; Substance Abuse; Psychiatric Problems; General Neurological; Right Hemisphere; Left Hemisphere; Subcortical, Cerebellar, Spinal; and Sensory, Perceptual.

The manual contains no technical information regarding reliability and validity. A review of the literature did not provide any information regarding current use of the instrument.

The questionnaire would, therefore, have obvious limited use with no empirical support for differentiating subjects into pathological groups. It seems to be an instrument that is helpful in organizing clinically obtained information for the purpose of making medical referrals.

The most immediate needs are norms based on whether the instrument is used as one that is self-administered or rated by a practitioner. The hit rates for various pathological groups utilizing the preceding rationally derived categories would also extend the usefulness and predictive validity of this instrument.

This questionnaire could also benefit from being computerized to assist in organizing the information obtained for either the researcher or the practitioner. At present it remains a clinical aid that needs empirical validation.

[2.2]
Adult Personal Adjustment and Role Skills.

Purpose: Used to evaluate the community adjustment of adults.
Population: Adults.
Publication Date: 1981.
Acronym: PARS.
Scores, 8: Close Relations, Alienation—Depression, Anxiety, Confusion, Alcohol—Drug Use, House Activity, Child Relations, Employment.
Administration: Group.
Price Data, 1993: $13 per sampler set including manual (22 pages), answer sheet, and profile; $11 per 25 scales; $12 per manual.
Time: (20–30) minutes.
Author: Robert B. Ellsworth.
Publisher: Consulting Psychologists Press, Inc.

This test has not been reviewed in *The Mental Measurements Yearbook.*

[2.3]
The Anomalous Sentences Repetition Test.

Purpose: Constructed to differentiate between dementia and depression.
Population: Ages 55 and over.
Publication Date: 1988.
Acronym: ASRT.
Scores: Total error score only.
Administration: Individual.
Price Data, 1992: £40.25 per complete kit including 25 record forms and manual (24 pages); £23 per 25 record forms.

Time: (5) minutes.
Author: David J. Weeks.
Publisher: NFER-Nelson Publishing Co., Ltd. [England].
Cross References: Reviews by Michael G. Kavan and Charles A. Peterson originally appeared in 12:29.

Review of the Anomalous Sentences Repetition Test by MICHAEL G. KAVAN, Director of Behavioral Sciences and Associate Professor of Family Practice, Creighton University School of Medicine, Omaha, NE:

The Anomalous Sentences Repetition Test (ASRT) is composed of four parallel six-item tests. Its major purpose is to assist in the discrimination between early dementing illnesses and major depressive disorders in persons over the age of 55 years. However, the author claims that it may also be used to discriminate typical alcoholic Korsakoff psychosis patients from patients with Alzheimer-type dementia, assess cognitive and language abilities in younger patients where it is necessary to distinguish between a functional disorder and neuropsychological impairment, and determine the level of impairment in patients with known deficits in the above areas. Test development is based on the supposition that repetition of some sentences that are syntactically complex, meaningless, or very long discriminate between patients with cerebral damage and normals (Newcombe & Marshall, 1967).

ADMINISTRATION AND SCORING. The ASRT may be administered to individual patients by a variety of educational and health care specialists including general practitioners, educational and clinical psychologists, speech therapists, occupational specialists, teachers, and nurses. No mention is made within the manual of any specialized training required in order to administer the ASRT. The author recommends that for diagnostic purposes the ASRT be used in conjunction with a concurrent assessment of the patient's mental status. In addition, it is recommended that the tester postpone testing if noticeable signs of oversedation or untoward medication side effects are present and/or if a moderate to severe hearing impairment is present and not alleviated by hearing aids. After accounting for these factors, the tester completes a Record Form that includes current personal information regarding the patient and testing condi-

tions. The patient is then read each of six anomalous (i.e., meaningless) sentences, one at a time, and asked to repeat these word-for-word. Apparently, the tester copies these verbatim into a space provided after each sentence. Test administration conveniently takes less than 5 minutes. An error score is obtained for each sentence and then summed for a Total Error Score. These are then converted to an age-transformed score due to findings suggesting significant increases in errors with age in the dementia group, but not with the major depression group. Errors may be classified according to errors of omission, transposition, phonetic confusion, addition, substitution, and tense error. Cutoff scores for determining probable dementia or organic impairment were determined by finding the midpoint between the mean scores of elderly patients with dementia and those with depression within each of four age groups (i.e., 55–70, 71–75, 76–80, over 81 [*sic*]). According to the author, use of recommended cutoff scores within the standardization study resulted in sensitivity of 81% (i.e., 19% of patients with dementia will be missed) and specificity of 85% (i.e., 15% of patients will be mistakenly classified as such). The predictive value is 84%.

RELIABILITY. The manual provides information on two reliability studies. Ten-week test-retest reliability for 98 community-dwelling elderly (mean age = 72.9 years) was .84, whereas 23-week test-retest data on 51 "control subjects" (mean age = 51.2 years) was .86. However, no other information is provided within the manual about this sample. Weeks (1986) describes this latter group as a "pool of community volunteers" (6 males; 45 females). Alternate-form reliability for these two groups was found to range from .79 to .91 and .81 to .90, respectively. Although no other reliability information is supplied within the manual, Weeks gives a Spearman-Brown reliability coefficient for the 51 control subjects as .859.

VALIDITY. The manual provides data from the standardization study supporting the ability of the ASRT to discriminate between normal subjects, patients with depression, and patients with dementia. The difference in the number of total errors on the ASRT between the groups with depression and dementia was significant. However, Rai, Stewart, and Scott (1990) used the

ASRT in a sample of 16 patients with a diagnosis of dementia of the Alzheimer's type, 18 patients with depression, and 16 normal elderly persons and found no difference in the age-adjusted ASRT scores between the three groups. From these results, Rai et al. concluded that the ASRT is not a useful measure for providing evidence for the existence of cognitive impairment nor for differentiating between dementing and nondementing illness. The manual also provides concurrent validity data regarding the relationship between the ASRT and a battery of psychometric tests administered to varying groups of clinical patients and to a group of elderly community controls. Although most correlations are in the expected direction, some results show inconsistencies. The manual also cites a study conducted by Weeks (1986) in which 45 patients with diagnoses including Alzheimer-type dementia, Korsakoff's psychosis, psychotic depression, cerebro-vascular accident, schizophrenia, anoxic brain damage, closed head injury, cerebral tumor, syphilis, hypomania, and cerebral encephalitis received neuropsychological testing and computerized axial tomography (CAT) to determine the degree of cortical atrophy and cerebral ventricular enlargement. Pearson product-moment correlations were significant between the number of errors on the ASRT and the degree of cortical atrophy (.433) and degree of ventricular enlargement (.47). However, the manual gives no breakdown of correlations between these various diagnoses and CAT findings. Kopelman (1986) is cited within the manual as supporting the ability of anomalous sentences to discriminate between patients with depression, Korsakoff amnesia, and Alzheimer-type dementia; however, these sentences were selected from a list employed by Newcombe and Marshall (1967) as opposed to the ASRT. No other validity data are cited within the manual.

NORMS. Normative data consisting of means and standard deviations are provided for normal elderly living in the community (n = 98), elderly patients with depression (n = 100), and elderly patients with dementia (n = 100). A table presenting means, standard deviations, and standard errors from "all studies to date" (p. 8) is also supplied within the manual. Data are given on younger normal community controls and depressed patients, neurotic depressed patients, psychotic depressed patients, recovered younger depressives, younger neurologically impaired patients, and chronic alcoholic patients (range of n = 35–164). The manual includes limited information on several of these groups.

SUMMARY. The ASRT is a brief, easy-to-use, clinician-administered instrument designed to discriminate between early dementing illnesses and major depressive disorders in persons 55 and older. The author reports that it may also be used to differentiate alcoholic Korsakoff psychosis patients from patients with Alzheimer-type dementia, test cognitive and language abilities in younger patients where one must distinguish between a functional disorder and a neuropsychological impairment, and determine the level of such impairment. At present, conflicting research exists regarding the ability of the ASRT to discriminate between depressed, demented, and normal groups. In addition, limited evidence is presented to support other claims. Because of this, the ASRT should be used cautiously in clinical settings until further research can be completed on these issues. Because of the risk for false positives and missed cases with many brief screening measures, instruments such as the ASRT should not be used by themselves to determine a diagnosis of dementia. Instead, clinicians should remember that a thorough clinical evaluation including history from the patient and significant others, laboratory testing, physical examination, and functional assessment is the most important component of any initial evaluation for dementia (National Institutes of Health, 1987).

REVIEWER'S REFERENCES

Newcombe, F., & Marshall, J. C. (1967). Immediate recall of "sentences" by subjects with unilateral cerebral lesions. *Neuropsychologia, 5*, 329–334.

Kopelman, M. D. (1986). Recall of anomalous sentences in dementia and amnesia. *Brain and Language, 29*, 154–170.

Weeks, D. J. (1986). The Anomalous Sentences Repetition Test: Replication and validation study. *Journal of Clinical Psychology, 42*, 635–638.

National Institutes of Health Consensus Conference. (1987). Differential diagnosis of dementing diseases. *Journal of the American Medical Association, 258*, 3411–3416.

Rai, G. S., Stewart, K., & Scott, L. C. (1990). Assessment of Anomalous Sentences Repetition Test. *Journal of Neurology, Neurosurgery and Psychiatry, 53*, 611–612.

Review of the Anomalous Sentences Repetition Test by CHARLES A. PETERSON, Director of Training in Psychology, VA Minneapolis Medical Center, and Associate Clinical Professor of Psychology at the University of Minnesota, Minneapolis, MN:

INTRODUCTION. Imagine reading an entry in the *Mental Measurements Yearbook* that began like this: "This test, which the guitar baked on lampshade, excitedly luncheon meat a tubular sparrow." What would be the differential diagnosis? (*a*) Printer's error; (*b*) demented reviewer; (*c*) lapse in editorial judgment; (*d*) clever way to introduce a test that uses anomalous sentences to assist in the "discrimination between early dementing illness and major depressive disorders in patients over the age of 55" (manual, p. 1). The answer, most certainly, is (*d*). Despite the clinically familiar difficulty in diagnostically differentiating early dementia from depression, the Anomalous Sentences Repetition Test (hereafter ASRT) is touted as a "simple, brief," "clinical tool" or "psychometric aid" that may efficiently address Lezak's (1983) "knottiest problem." This test presumably draws on two unquestionable glittering generalities, that neuropsychiatric illness alters and impairs cognition, and that meaningless, confusing, complex, or bizarre stimuli present a greater challenge to efficient and adaptive cognition.

TEST DESCRIPTION. The anomalous (which most dictionaries equate with irregular and abnormal) sentences (6 to 10 words each) were constructed according to carefully balanced norms (e.g., concreteness, pleasantness, familiarity, etc.) on word usage. The six sentences in each of four parallel forms were subjected to varying degrees of semantic (meaning) and syntactic (structure) degradation, and are likely to be experienced by the test subject as peculiar.

ADMINISTRATION. The test manual offers reasonable guidance and caution: When used to discriminate dementia from depression, the ASRT should not be used with subjects younger than age 55. The ASRT should always be used in conjunction with a concurrent assessment of the patient's mental status, including a quantitative evaluation of depression. Testing should be postponed if there is obvious sedation or side-effects from high doses of psychotropic medications. Hearing must be adequate; alleviation of impairment by hearing aid is acceptable. The patient is instructed to repeat carefully enunciated sentences immediately after the examiner, who then records the patient's responses. Two practice sentences are first completed and followed by examiner clarification of "gross misunderstandings" of the task's demands (the author underappreciates such ques-

tions for their contribution to the diagnostic process).

SCORING. The patient's verbatim repetitions of six sentences are recorded and subsequently marked and summed for a total error score. The scoring categories are familiar to anyone who has done a language examination: errors of omission, transposition, phonetic confusion, addition, substitution, and tense change. Errors of addition and substitution are further classified as intralist intrusions, extralist intrusions, or semantic confusion. No differential diagnostic implications are noted for different errors. The total error score can then be converted into an age-transformed score, with a familiar mean of 100 and a standard deviation of 15.

STANDARDIZATION. Three roughly equivalent (by sex, age, social class, education, and IQ) groups (approximately 100 in each) of subjects were compared: (*a*) The "normal subjects" were drawn from a cross section of community-dwelling elderly. There is no indication of whether these subjects were screened and excluded for psychopathology or other medical conditions (e.g., hypertension, diabetes, coronary heart disease) that might affect mentation; therefore, these subjects might more safely be considered "not obviously patients" than normals. (*b*) "Depressed patients" were diagnosed per DSM-III, RDC, and scores on quantitative measures of depression, including the Hamilton (questionable with the elderly) and the Geriatric Depression Scale(s). (*c*) "Demented patients" were diagnosed per DSM-III and at least three occurrences within 6 months of at least 5 out of 10 checklist symptoms (e.g., disorientation, memory loss, nocturnal wandering, etc.). There is no information on the stage of the dementia. Depressed and demented patients had been followed for at least 18 months to establish the diagnosis with reasonable certainty. These subjects were also compared on a variety of concurrent measures (e.g., naming, verbal fluency, reading, etc.).

ASRT scores were able to statistically differentiate demented from depressed patients and normal subjects with good sensitivity (81%) and specificity (85%). Cutoffs were established for different ages: For example, more than 17 errors in a 55–70-year-old patient would suggest dementia, whereas more than 27 errors would be required to suggest dementia in a patient over age 81. Additional studies/data suggest that the ASRT may be sensitive to the progressive deterioration associated with dementia, and may be reasonably free of confounding influences such as amount of psychotropic medication, number and recency of previous ECT treatments, and association with some minor neurotic symptoms. The four parallel forms show psychometrically adequate equivalence and test-retest coefficients (median correlation .85).

SUGGESTIONS. (*a*) The manual should specify—and limit!—who should use this test: Visiting nurses and doctoral level clinical neuropsychologists will not use this test in an equivalent manner. There simply is no substitute for a consultation with a good neuropsychologist. (*b*) The manual should not hint that scoring this test is an easy task. No scoring examples were provided; the ASRT novice would benefit from being able to compare their fledgling efforts with clear criteria. No report of interrater reliability was offered. As scoring reliability goes, so goes validity. (*c*) The test-retest and parallel form equivalence studies should be broadened to include clinical subjects, not just "normal control subjects," who might be expected to inflate the test-retest coefficients, as opposed to more erratically performing demented subjects. (*d*) The manual should stress that the ASRT be used as part of a battery of neuropsychological tests. No matter how promising the ASRT might be, one caution looms large: Just as one swallow does not make a summer, an impairment in language repetition does not make a dementia. (*e*) Given the impact of local/ward base rates on cutting scores (Meehl & Rosen, 1955), it is psychometrically irresponsible for the manual to propose one score to differentiate dementia from pseudodementia. (*f*) Finally, further research will answer the crucial question of degree of association between the ASRT and measures of depression and attention concentration (e.g., the author states that the ASRT is "relatively unaffected by poor concentration" [p. 1] but later reports a correlation of .52 between the ASRT and a measure of short-term concentration [p. 16]).

SUMMARY. The ASRT is a plausible and carefully constructed psychometric incarnation of a reasonable idea. Although unlikely to replace the more routinely used instruments in clinical neuropsychology, the few, imperfect studies in this corner of "soft psychology" (where plausibility rivals falsifiability [Meehl, 1978]), suggest that the ASRT may prove useful to neuropsychologists in both clinical and research settings. However, the promising beginnings must now be subjected to tighter research design and anonymous repetition by labs other than that of the test's author.

REVIEWER'S REFERENCES

Meehl, P. E., & Rosen, A. (1955). Antecedent probability and the efficiency of psychometric signs, patterns, or cutting scores. *Psychological Bulletin, 52,* 194–216.

Meehl, P. E. (1978). Theoretical risks and tabular asterisks: Sir Karl, Sir Ronald, and the slow progress of soft psychology. *Journal of Consulting and Clinical Psychology, 46,* 806–834.

Lezak, M. D. (1983). *Neuropsychological assessment* (2nd ed.). New York: Oxford University Press.

[2.4]
Children's Apperceptive Story-Telling Test.

Purpose: "Identification of social, emotional, and/or behavioral problems in children."
Population: Ages 6–13.
Publication Date: 1989.
Acronym: CAST.
Scores: 19 scores and 9 indicators: Adaptive Thematic (Instrumentality, Interpersonal Cooperation, Affiliation, Positive Affect), Nonadaptive Thematic (Inadequacy, Alienation, Interpersonal Conflict, Limits, Negative Affect), Adaptive Problem-Solving (Positive Preoperational, Positive Operational), Nonadaptive Problem-Solving (Refusal, Unresolved, Negative Preoperational, Negative Operational), Factor Profile (Adaptive, Nonadaptive, Immature, Uninvested), Thematic Indicators (Sexual Abuse, Substance Abuse, Divorce, Hypothetical Thought, Emotionality, Self-Validation), Life Tasks (Family, Peer, School).
Administration: Individual.
Price Data, 1994: $109 per complete kit including 31 picture cards; 50 record/scoring forms, and manual ('89, 290 pages); $49 per set of 31 picture cards; $29 per 50 record/scoring forms; $34 per manual.
Time: (20–40) minutes.
Comments: Orally administered.
Author: Mary F. Schneider.
Publisher: PRO-ED, Inc.
Cross References: Reviews by Edward Aronow and Martin J. Wiese originally appeared in 12:73.

Review of the Children's Apperceptive Story-Telling Test by EDWARD ARONOW, Associate Professor of Psychology, Montclair State College, Upper Montclair, NJ:

Dr. Mary F. Schneider has done yeoman's service in developing a psychometrically sound apperceptive test, the Children's Apperceptive Story-Telling Test (CAST), that is appropriate for use in clinical and school settings, with multi-ethnic characters appearing in the cards. The stimuli are in color and are quite contemporary, giving this test advantages over its chief competitor, the Children's Apperception Test (CAT; T4:444).

The test manual is well organized and well written. There is a good historical overview of the use of apperceptive techniques in assessment. As Dr. Schneider notes, the main projective instruments that have historically been used in psychological testing involve inkblots, stories, and picture drawings. The original and continued popular Thematic Apperception Test (TAT; T4:2824) designed by Henry Murray at the Harvard Psychological Clinic has pictures that are black and white, somewhat out of date, and strongly suggestive of emotional themes that make it difficult to judge whether the story originates from the stimulus or from personality aspects of the subject. The same is true of the CAT. In addition, the psychometric basis of the TAT and the CAT is deficient.

The design of the CAST takes into account research that has been done previously on apperceptive techniques. For example, the cards emphasize moderate ambiguity because this has been shown to give the best results. The somber tone of the TAT is avoided. Further, the cards are in color because color has been shown to add to the productivity of subjects with attention deficit disorder.

Some test users may be disappointed by the Adlerian theoretical substructure for this test. Adlerian psychologists, educators, and mental health practitioners are certainly in a distinct minority. However, it could also be noted that Adlerian theory has a strong commonsense orientation and also strongly emphasizes social aspects of functioning, which is quite relevant to apperceptive techniques.

The author indicates the CAST has four principal uses: identification of social, emotional, and/or behavioral problems in children; intervention planning; documentation of therapeutic change; and research. The test consists of 17 cards that are administered to all subjects. Three cards are given to everyone; 14 cards have male and female versions. The test is designed for subjects ages 6 to 13. Evaluation is carried out in terms of the main

Adlerian spheres of interaction (i.e., the family, peers, and the school). The instructions used with the test are very precise, including follow-up ("prompt") questions. Responses to the cards are then scored according to thematic scales, problem-solving scales, and thematic indicators.

The thematic scales are as follows: Instrumentality, Interpersonal Cooperation, Affiliation, Positive Affect, Inadequacy, Alienation, Interpersonal Conflict, Limits, and Negative Affect. The problem-solving scales are as follows: Positive Preoperational problem solving, Positive Operational problem solving, Refusal, Unresolved, Negative Preoperational problem solving, and Negative Operational problem solving. The thematic indicators are as follows: Sexual Abuse, Substance Abuse, Divorce, Hypothetical Thought, Emotionality, and Self Validation.

All of these scales and thematic indicators are well defined, and extensive scoring examples are provided. The raw scores for the thematic scales and the problem-solving scales are converted into T-Scores that are depicted in graphic form on the CAST profile. Scores for four factors are also obtained; the Adaptive factor, the Non-adaptive factor, the Immature factor, and the Uninvested factor. Confidence bands are also provided for the various scales and factors based on the imperfect reliability of the instrument.

The author reports data pertaining to the reliability of the instrument in terms of interrater, test-retest, split half, and coefficient alpha. Interrater reliability appears quite good. Test-retest coefficients are also on the high side, although the applicability of test-retest reliability to psychological tests in general and projective techniques in particular is questionable. Internal consistency reliability is also quite good. The coefficients reported certainly compare quite favorably with reliability coefficients of other projective techniques and other apperceptive techniques in particular.

Data are also reported pertaining to the validity of the instrument. This is reported as it should be in terms of content validity, construct validity, and criterion-related validity. Data are presented that are supportive in all respects.

The standardization sample for the CAST consisted of 876 children residing in 16 states. The standardization sample was selected to be representative of the U.S. population as described in the 1980 U.S. Census reports in terms of age, gender, race, parent education, geographic location, and community size. The sample was drawn from four geographic regions defined by the 1980 Census: the Northeast, the North Central, the South, and the West. The students in the standardization sample attended both public and private schools. In addition to these 876 typical children, 322 behavior-disordered students were tested.

In short, the CAST represents the most serious and psychometrically sound effort thus far to develop an apperceptive story-telling technique for use with children. The fly in the ointment, of course, is the time requirement of the test. As reported by the author, administration takes 20 to 40 minutes, scoring takes approximately 30 minutes, and 20 to 30 minutes are required for interpretation. Many clinical, consulting, or school psychologists may be unwilling to invest such time in an apperceptive technique. This might result in the apperceptive technique taking up more of the examiner's time than the typical intelligence test. Objective tests likewise provide psychometric soundness, but require very little in terms of time from the examiner. Dr. Schneider recommends tape recording test productions and transcribing them afterwards, which would further add to the time demands of this instrument.

Nonetheless, the CAST is strongly recommended for use in preference to the CAT because of the greater neutrality of the stimuli presented, the modernity of the pictures, the use of color, and the use of White, African-American, Hispanic, and Asian children in the test stimuli. However, it seems likely that such use of the technique will be in the idiographic rather than the nomothetic manner, as has traditionally been the case, with examiners relying on clinical sense rather than scores for interpretation. The author herself obliquely suggests at one point that the technique can be used in this way. For research purposes, of course, the CAST represents a psychometrically sound apperceptive technique unparalleled by other approaches.

Review of the Children's Apperceptive Story-Telling Test by MARTIN J. WIESE, Licensed Psychologist, Educational Service Unit No. 6, Milford, NE:

The Children's Apperceptive Story-Telling Test (CAST) was developed for use in schools and clinical settings with children ranging in age from 6 to 13 years. Designed to assess social, emotional, and behavioral concerns and provide information regarding the child's functioning in the family, with peers, and at school, the CAST may be used as a formal diagnostic instrument or informally during an interview with the child.

As with other instruments of its type (e.g., Thematic Apperception Test [T4:2824], Children's Apperception Test [T4:444], and Tell-Me-A-Story [T4:2716], the respondent is asked to generate stories freely for each of the 17 picture cards presented. Unlike the aforementioned tests, interpretation of the CAST is based upon the Individual Psychology principle of Alfred Adler.

Proponents of Adler's Individual Psychology view individuals as social beings with goal-directed drives to "belong." As a result, each person is directed toward goals that are in accord with his or her social interests or life style. In other words, the total person and that person's behavior are considered within the broader context of the social milieu.

This conceptualization of human functioning also views cognition as primary; feelings and actions are subservient to thoughts. In theory, the developing child's experiences, social interactions, and observations of others come to fit into a consistent, coherent thought pattern and eventually create a relatively stable scheme of apperceptions within the child.

The CAST reflects the sociological components of Adlerian psychology by eliciting apperceptive material associated with several major life-task contexts (family, peers, and school). The apperceptive stimulus materials of the CAST serve as a screen on which the child projects his or her own ideas. Themes of social interest or belonging are deduced by the stories elicited from children. The thematic material may then be classified as adaptive (positive) or nonadaptive (negative) in nature and broken down into nine Thematic scales. Similarly, the child's problem-solving style may be classified as adaptive or nonadaptive on six Problem-Solving scales.

In addition to the Thematic scales and Problem-Solving scales, the CAST also allows the evaluator to determine the frequency with which the child's stories contain thematic indicators such as sexual abuse, substance abuse, divorce, hypothetical thought (the child's ability to generate alternative stories or endings), emotionality, and self-validation (events described in the child's story actually happened).

The set of 31 stimulus cards consists of 3 cards that are administered to both boys and girls. The remaining 14 pairs of cards are designed with separate male and female versions and only one card from each pair is administered depending on the child's gender. The cards themselves are color drawings that reflect contemporary figures in contexts of modern problems. Test administration time is estimated to be 20 to 40 minutes and the test author states that scoring will require 30 minutes, with an additional 20–30 minutes for interpretation.

Tape recording of the respondent's stories is encouraged and was the method used during standardization. It is recommended that scoring of the child's responses not be attempted during the test administration session due to the complexity of the scoring criteria. The manual contains standardized directions and includes a series of five prompt questions to be asked by the examiner following presentation of each card.

Scoring is based on the words, phrases, and sentences used by the child to reflect particular themes, which are representative of the child's values, feelings, and beliefs. After scoring the Thematic Scales, Thematic Indicators, and Problem-Solving Scales, three Life Tasks (family, peer, and school) for each story are identified and are recorded on the optional Life Task Sociogram.

The manual authors provide tables to convert raw scores from each scale to T-Scores and four factor scores (Adaptive, Nonadaptive, Immature, and Uninvested). Confidence intervals for each of the scale scores can be calculated and plotted on a profile sheet. The examiner may analyze the obtained scores through quantitative analysis, utilizing the psychometric properties of the test, and through qualitative analysis of the child's responses, the Thematic Indicators, and behavioral observations. The manual contains numerous helpful scoring examples, appendices

with common scoring terms and problem-solving examples, and an extensive case study to assist the examiner in mastering scoring procedures and interpretation.

The manual authors also provide detailed information regarding development and standardization. Standardized on a nationally representative sample of 876 school children residing in 16 states, the norm group sample was constructed to reflect the demographic characteristics of the U.S. population as described in the 1980 Census. About 7% of the sample consisted of children receiving special education services due to learning difficulties in the regular classroom setting. In addition to the standardization sample, a comparison group of 322 behavior-disordered students was tested to establish validity.

The author made a considerable effort to describe psychometric properties of the instrument and demonstrate its stability and validity. A discriminant function analysis between the scores of the behavior-disordered sample and the scores of 322 subjects randomly selected from the standardization sample provides evidence of construct validity. The analysis correctly classified 73% of the behavior-disordered sample and 80% of the standardization sample and demonstrated that the CAST discriminated between the two groups. Similarly, independent t-tests also showed significant differences between the two groups on 13 of the 15 scales.

The content validity and criterion-related validity of the CAST are also adequately addressed in the manual. Content validity was established by having practicing psychologists rate each stimulus card for the ability to elicit thematic content related to each of the scales. Criterion-related validity was established by correlating the scores from the CAST with the adaptive and clinical scales of the Roberts Apperception Test for Children (RATC). The resulting correlation between the CAST scores and the RATC scores indicated moderate relationships (most correlation coefficients ranged from .65 to .55) and provided sufficient evidence for the concurrent validity of the CAST.

Test reliability was assessed with interrater reliability, test-retest, split-half, and coefficient alpha. Interrater reliability was quite high with the medians of reliability coefficients for all 15 scales in the .90 range. An examination of test-retest reliability found the four factor scores, with a median reliability coefficient of .90, as more reliable than individual scale scores. Coefficient alpha, a measure of the internal consistency of a test, was calculated for three age levels, 6 to 8, 9 to 11, and 12 to 13 years. With the exception of the Immature Factor score at the 12–13 age level, coefficient alpha ranged from .90 to .93 for the four factors, indicating good internal consistency.

In summary, the CAST successfully meets its objective to be a valid, reliable, theory-based, objectively scored apperceptive instrument, supported by a nationally standardized representative sample of children, ages 6 through 13. The CAST has demonstrated good validity and reliability with school-aged behavior-disordered children and appears to be an adequate diagnostic instrument designed to assess a wide range of social, emotional, and behavioral adjustment issues. Hypotheses generated by the CAST Profile may also be useful to the examiner in developing therapeutic interventions relevant to the child's family life, peer relations, and school environment.

[2.5]
Clyde Mood Scale.

Purpose: To measure human emotions and behavior, which are influenced by stress or drugs.
Population: Normals and schizophrenics.
Publication Dates: 1963–1983.
Acronym: CMS.
Scores, 6: Friendly, Aggressive, Clear Thinking, Sleepy, Depressed, Jittery.
Administration: Individual.
Price Data: Not available.
Time: (5–15) minutes.
Author: Dean J. Clyde.
Publisher: Clyde Computing Service [No reply from publisher; status unknown].
Cross References: The review by Cynthia M. Sheehan originally appeared in 9:238; for a review by David T. Lykken of the original edition, see 7:55.

Review of the Clyde Mood Scale by CYNTHIA M. SHEEHAN, Director of Research, Department of Clinical Services, St. Mary's Child Care Agency, Syosset, NY:

The Clyde Mood Scale (CMS) is a revised version of a checklist of 48 adjectives "designed to measure human emotions and behavior which are influenced by certain conditions (such as stress) or by drugs (such as antidepressants). Each of the adjectives (e.g., "grouchy," "reckless") is rated on a 4-point scale anchored by "extremely" and "not at all." The scale is designed to provide the user with six factor scores labeled: Friendly, Aggressive, Clear-Thinking, Sleepy, Depressed, and Jittery.

From the information provided in the manual, it is not entirely clear what the nature and extent of the revisions are since the last edition. It is stated that the factors entitled "Depressed" and "Jittery" were previously described as "Unhappy" and "Dizzy," respectively. From this reviewer's examination of early research findings, it appears also that a previous format utilizing a deck of 52 IBM cards has been discarded, although this is not stated in the manual.

The scale lends itself to self-ratings or ratings by a variety of different personnel. The manual does, however, warn that proper interpretation of the scale requires knowing the "type of person" who made the rating because, for example, "schizophrenic patients often rate themselves as being very clear thinking, but . . .doctors and nurses do not agree." It seems only reasonable to this reviewer that such judgements required of a seriously disturbed or psychotic population would have serious consequences for the psychometric properties of the scale.

The manual describes a statistical comparison in which groups of items for both 500 self-rated and 500 other-rated checklists were subjected to separate factor analyses. The six largest factors appeared to be almost identical for the two groups; thus only one scoring key is provided, which is to be used for both self-ratings and ratings by others.

Although a variety of personnel qualified by "reasonable intelligence and familiarity with the instructions," (e.g., secretaries, nurses, research assistants, psychologists, and psychiatrists) are stated to have successfully administered the scale, the manual provides only a scant amount of evidence in support of this assertion. Correlation coefficients range from .32 to .91 between pairs of same-skill raters (i.e., 2 doctors, 2 nurses). Since the simplicity of the scale does lead one to believe that it may be appropriately used by a variety of personnel, it would be helpful to see data on interscorer agreement across skill levels (i.e., secretary/psychologist).

The scoring of the scale is best accomplished through computer scoring offered by the publisher. Steps for calculating the scores are provided, but they appear to be time consuming and cumbersome because of a complex weighting system.

Means and standard deviations are provided for the six factors for a variety of groups ($N = 100$ to 446) described only as "newly-admitted schizophrenics," "normal males," etc. It is to the credit of the scale's author that the manual cautions that the user's norm group will probably differ from those reported. The norms provided are to give "a rough idea of how normals mark the items" with "some schizophrenics shown for comparison." Local norms can and probably should be established. It would be a grievous error to assume that the reported norms are to be generalized to user-specific populations.

With the intended limited use of the scale, the validity data appropriately focus on how well this scale differentiates stressed or drugged groups from control or placebo groups. The difficulty is that the data reported in the manual reflect only one specific study in which the effects of phenothiazines on schizophrenics was evaluated. Doctors, nurses, and patients using the CMS misclassified cases at a rate of 20%–27%, depending on rater classification. Despite the author's statement that "hundreds of scientific articles have reported on the use of the Clyde Mood Scale in research," the only additional data reported in support of the scale's validity consists of references on 19 research studies related to 14 drugs or conditions, such as "antianxiety drugs" or "sleep." The reader is required to search out and evaluate the study or studies relevant to the particular drug or condition of interest. Given the data provided, the manual's statement that the reader may conclude from the information reported above that "the Clyde Mood Scale is a valid measure in a wide variety of situations" is unsupported. It is likely the CMS differentiates certain types of stresses or drug groups better than others but data addressing this issue are not discussed in the manual. Even after a search of the literature for relevant information, this reviewer remains unconvinced of the scale's validity. A summation of the data for the most common uses of the scale would be a welcome addition to the manual, as would some convergent or discriminant validity information in relation to other behavior rating scales.

The only reliability data reported is the aforementioned correlation between same skill-level raters. The limited sample size and lack of descriptive data, such as drug or condition rated, make these data unsuitable for evaluating scale use for a particular experimental interest or the uses of the scale in general.

The explicitly stated purpose of the CMS is to provide a quantifiable description of various emotions and behaviors. There is no assumption of the scale's relation to particular personality constructs, and so clinical significance of the scores is appropriately limited by the author to the circumstances surrounding the rating.

Ease of administration makes this an attractive instrument for quantifying behaviors within the context of a controlled research setting. In order to feel confident in using this instrument, however, the investigator must be willing to be active in establishing local group norms, investigating or establishing validity and reliability standards for use with the condition or drug of interest, and assessing the impact of the rater (self/other) on any clinical interpretation to be made from the scale. Those willing to expend the energy may find the CMS an aid to their research. Those unwilling to address these issues should not consider using the CMS.

[2.6]
College Adjustment Scales.

Purpose: Identifies developmental and psychological problems experienced by college students.
Population: College and university students.
Publication Date: 1991.
Acronym: CAS.
Scores, 9: Anxiety, Depression, Suicidal Ideation, Substance Abuse, Self-Esteem Problems, Interpersonal Problems, Family Problems, Academic Problems, Career Problems.
Administration: Individual or group.
Price Data, 1994: $57 per complete kit including manual (25 pages), 25 reusable item booklets, and 25 answer sheets; $20 per 25 reusable item booklets; $20 per 25 answer sheets; $20 per manual.
Time: (15–20) minutes.
Authors: William D. Anton and James R. Reed.
Publisher: Psychological Assessment Resources, Inc.
Cross References: Reviews by William E. Martin, Jr. and Edward R. Starr will appear in the 13th MMY; aee also T4:544 (1 reference).

Review of the College Adjustment Scales by WILLIAM E. MARTIN, JR., Professor of Educational Psychology, Northern Arizona University, Flagstaff, AZ:

According to Anton and Reed, the College Adjustment Scales (CAS) were developed "to provide a rapid method of screening college counseling clients for common developmental and psychological problems" (manual, p. 1). The CAS is a 108-item self-report measure with the following nine scales (12 items per scale): Anxiety, Depression, Suicidal Ideation, Substance Abuse, Self-Esteem Problems, Interpersonal Problems, Family Problems, Academic Problems, and Career Problems. Test takers are asked to respond to each item, based on its accuracy, using a 4-point scale ranging from *Not At All True* to *Very True*. The entire process for completing, scoring, and profiling the CAS is estimated by the test authors to take a maximum of 24 minutes.

DEVELOPMENT OF THE SCALES. The initial CAS scales were derived from problems encountered in the college population. Specifically, approximately 2,000 students presenting at a college counseling center for services completed an intake problems checklist. Based on their responses, two principal components factor analyses were conducted resulting in a 9-factor and a 7-factor solution. Information for which solution was retained was not provided.

The derived factors, along with additional adjustment problem areas, were used in a survey of assessment needs completed by 73 professionals from nine counseling centers. The survey findings of professionals, paired with the analyses of problems associated with students seeking services, resulted in the nine scales of the CAS. Next, a literature review was conducted to identify behavioral expressions for each of the scales. This resulted in an item pool of 181 items. These items were subsequently reviewed for bias by an expert panel; 14 items, which were determined to be biased, were rewritten. The internal consistency of items for each scale was derived from a study of 224 college students enrolled at four universities located in the Southeastern United States. Items were retained in the item pool based on three criteria (see manual) resulting in a final pool of 108 items. Final internal consistency reliability coefficients for the nine scales ranged from .80 to .92 with an average of .86.

VALIDITY OF THE SCALES. The reported test validity is based upon one group differences study and four convergent and discriminant validity studies that were conducted at several universities throughout the United States. In the first study, CAS scores were compared between a group receiving university counseling services and student not receiving services. The recipient group evidenced significantly higher scores on the CAS when compared to the nonrecipient group with Anxiety and Suicidal Ideation reflecting the most characteristic dimensions of the recipient group.

Independent samples from 33 university counseling centers were used to measure the convergent and discriminant validity of the CAS. The CAS subscales were correlated with subscales of several frequently used standardized tests measuring psychological constructs including anxiety, depression, hopelessness, personality, interpersonal problems, substance abuse, self-esteem, family adaptability, and career development. The procedure design was primarily multitrait-monomethod (self-report instruments). The findings reflected high correlations among scales measuring similar constructs (convergent validity) and low correlations among dissimilar constructs (discriminant validity). For example, the NEO Personality Inventory (NEO-PI) Neurotocism scales were correlated with the CAS subscales in three studies. On two similar subscales across the studies, correlations were high moderate or high. The correlations for Anxiety were .78, .71, and .80 and for Depression they were .64, .69, and .74. For dissimilar measures, low correlations, as illustrated by comparisons of the Openness subscale on the NEO-PI and all of the CAS subscales, were obtained throughout the three studies.

ADMINISTRATION, SCORING, AND INTERPRETATION. Standardized instructions for administration are provided in the CAS manual. The test-taking materials include a four-page item booklet written at a fifth grade reading level. Additionally, there is an answer sheet printed on carbonless white paper with the CAS Profile sheet on the reverse side that lists raw scores, percentiles, and *T* scores.

Ninety percent of the normative sample (N = 1,146) consisted of college and university students aged 17–30. The students were reasonably equally proportioned from first year through seniors. However, only 2% of the total sample were graduate students. The sample reflected national college enrollment proportions according to gender and ethnicity. The majority (54%) of the sample were raised in the Southeast compared to other regions of the United States: Northeast (13%), Midwest (10%), West (13%), and outside the United States (5%). Information was not available for the remainder of the sample.

Percentile scores and normalized T scores derived for each scale from the raw score frequency distributions of the standardization sample are used for interpretation of the results. As the authors found weak associations among gender and ethnic group and the CAS scores, no normative data are provided based on these variables. The authors suggest that when a student scores at or above a T score of 60 on any scale, further evaluation, and possibly intervention, are warranted in the area of adjustment difficulty. In addition to normative comparisons, brief descriptive guidelines are provided for interpretation of each scale. Three case illustrations are presented in the manual.

SUMMARY. The CAS is a useful screening tool for college and university counseling professionals to identify possible adjustment difficulties among students. It must be emphasized, however, that it is a screening tool. With only 12 items per major adjustment difficulty (e.g., suicidal ideation, career problems), there is room for diagnostic errors.

The methodology to develop the scales was reasonably sound and there is evidence for the validity of the scales. However, more validity studies are needed, especially concurrent validity studies related to profile interpretations examining the relationship between the CAS and other major psychological disturbance assessment instruments (e.g., Minnesota Multiphasic Personality Inventory—2 [MMPI–2; T4:1645]; and Millon Clinical Multiaxial Inventory [MCMI–III]). Additionally, both the descriptive guidelines for each scale and the number of case illustrations could be expanded.

Normative data are not available for students from various ethnic groups. Given specific reported college adjustment difficulties related to ethnocultural factors (Negy & Woods, 1992; Solberg, Ritsma, Davis, Tata, & Jolly, 1994), it may be valuable to generate percentile scores and T scores by ethnic group.

REVIEWER'S REFERENCES

Negy, C. R., & Woods, D. J. (1992). Mexican Americans' performance on the Psychological Screening Inventory as a function of acculturation level. *Journal of Clinical Psychology, 48*, 315–319.

Solberg, V. S., Ritsma, S., Davis, B. J., Tata, S. P., & Jolly, A. (1994). Asian-American students' severity of problems and willingness to seek help from university counseling centers: Role of previous counseling experience, gender, and ethnicity. *Journal of Counseling Psychology, 41*, 275–279.

Review of the College Adjustment Scales by EDWARD R. STARR, Assistant Professor of Counseling Psychology, State University of New York at Buffalo, Buffalo, NY:

The College Adjustment Scales (CAS) is a 108-item inventory designed as a quick and economical screening device for clinicians providing counseling services to college and university students. The authors attempt to provide clinicians with data regarding the most common developmental and psychological problems in this population. The inventory comprises nine subscales: Anxiety, Depression, Suicidal Ideation, Substance Abuse, Self-Esteem Problems, Interpersonal Problems, Family Problems, Academic Problems, and Career Problems. Subscales reflect many of the problems most frequently raised by college and university students, thus increasing its clinical relevance and utility. Notably absent among the subscales, though, is one related specifically to eating disorders.

The manual contains a brief and general introduction to the CAS and discusses the test materials, their use, administration, and scoring. The materials themselves are convenient, economical, and straightforward, requiring of respondents only a fifth grade reading level and a pen or pencil. The four-page item booklet is reusable, with responses recorded by students on a separate answer sheet. Raw data can be hand scored and plotted into a profile in less than 5 minutes. The profile form provides percentile scores, relative to the standardization sample, and T-score conversions. The CAS can be administered and scored by individuals without formal training in psychology. Training in its use and interpretation, however, requires graduate level training in an appropriate subdiscipline in psychology.

STANDARDIZATION. The CAS was standardized on 1,146 college and university students, ages 17 to 65 (although less than 10% of the sample is older than 30 years) from throughout the U.S. The sample is well represented with respect to geographic region and gender. However, with regard to race, although the sample closely reflected racial patterns in college enrollment nationally, due to the extraordinarily low college enrollments of certain minorities in the U.S. (e.g., Pacific Islanders and Native Americans) some oversampling of minority groups may have been more appropriate. Normative data for each subscale are provided in the manual.

RELIABILITY. Only measures of internal consistency are reported in the CAS manual. Reliability coefficients range between .80 and .92, with a mean of .86. Reliability estimates based on alternative forms of the CAS or test-retest procedures are not available. Interrater reliability is also not available, although it would be expected to be fairly high due to the minimal likelihood of inconsistencies among different raters on this type of instrument.

VALIDITY. Five validation studies of the CAS are reported in the manual. The first study compared the standardization sample to 198 students reporting current involvement in counseling for personal, academic, or career concerns. Significant differences on the subscales were obtained using multivariate ANOVA and discriminant function analysis. The remaining four studies compared specific CAS subscale results, using moderately sized samples of college students either requesting or receiving services from a college or university counseling center, to a variety of other well-established measures of the relevant constructs (e.g., the State-Trait Anxiety Inventory, Beck Depression Inventory, Beck Hopelessness Scale, NEO-Personality Inventory, Michigan Alcoholism Screening Test, Drug Abuse Screening Test, Multidimensional Self-Esteem Inventory, Family Adaptability and Cohesion Evaluation Scales III, Career Decision Scale, and the Self-Expression Inventory). Results in each study, based on correlational analysis, are consistent with predictions, with subscales having sufficient discriminant and predictive validity.

SUMMARY. There is a clear need for screening devices for this population and very little attention has been given to the development of reliable and valid instruments. In spite of some of its limitations, the CAS is certainly a solid step in the right direction. Further research should help establish its utility.

Until further data can be generated regarding its use in cross-cultural contexts, the CAS should probably be used with some caution. Although the manual authors state the available research and normative data indicate the CAS is unbiased with respect to gender and ethnic group membership, the data provided are not particularly compelling. The CAS assumes concept equivalence in cross-cultural contexts, which may cause some problems in interpreting the meaning of results. For example, the construct self-esteem, as reflected in CAS is one that is limited to Euro-American notions of self that give primacy to the individual, without concern for a more collective sense of identity as is typical, for instance, of Native American communities.

Given the CAS was developed and standardized exclusively on a college population, its use in other clinical settings cannot be recommended. Although it is not intended for use as a diagnostic aid, the CAS may be most effectively used adjunctively as part of a battery of assessment measures to rule out potential comorbidity.

The authors aptly note that because only about 10% of the standardization sample were over age 30, the CAS should be used cautiously with older students. When using the CAS to screen for eating disorders, one should analyze results at the item level to obtain specific data. This should be augmented with other methods of evaluation. Given the incidence, prevalence, and significance of eating disorders, particularly among women college students, a separate subscale would have been justified.

A major strength of the CAS is that it was developed for use in either individual or group settings. With the current proliferation of prevention programs, personal development workshops, and training groups open to the general student population on most campuses, it may be particularly well suited for use in identifying at-risk students attending these group experiences for counseling referrals. Overall, the CAS is a promising screening device in an area of indicated need. Its real utility awaits further research and clinical application.

[2.7]

Coolidge Axis II Inventory.

Purpose: Designed as a measure of personality disorders.
Population: Ages 15 and older.
Publication Date: 1993.
Acronym: CATI.
Scores, 41: 13 Personality Disorder Scales (Antisocial, Avoidant, Borderline, Dependent, Histrionic, Narcissistic, Obsessive Compulsive, Paranoid, Passive Aggressive, Schizotypal, Schizoid, Sadistic, Self-Defeating); 4 Validity Scales (Random Responding, Tendency to Look Good or Bad, Tendency to Deny Blatant Pathology, Answer Choice Frequency); 7 Axis I Scales (Anxiety, Depression, Post-traumatic Stress Disorder, Schizophrenia, Psychotic Thinking, Social Phobia, Withdrawal); 4 Neuropsychological Dysfunction Scale and Subscales (Neuropsychological Dysfunction, Memory and Concentration, Language Dysfunction, Somatic); 3 Hostility Scales (Anger, Dangerousness, Impulsiveness); 4 other clinical scales (Indecisiveness [Executive Functions], Emotional Lability, Apathy, Adjustment); Normal Clinical Scale (Introversion-Extraversion); 5 Non-normative scales (Drug and Alcohol, Sexuality, Depersonalization, Frustration Tolerance, Eccentricity).
Administration: Group.
Forms, 2: Self-report, Significant Other.
Price Data, 1996: $10 per evaluation kit including demo disk, manual on disk, 2 test booklets, and limited-use scoring software; $199 per complete kit including computer scoring software (unlimited use), manual ('93, 41 pages), and 25 test booklets; $349 per multi-user kit (same as complete kit, for use by 2 or more clinicians at the same address); $20 per 25 test booklets; $7.50 per manual.
Time: (30–45) minutes.
Comments: Computer scoring program requires DOS version 3.1 or higher and at least 640K RAM.
Author: Frederick L. Coolidge.
Publisher: The CATI Corporation.

This test has not been reviewed in *The Mental Measurements Yearbook.*

[2.8]

Composite International Diagnostic Interview.

Purpose: "For use in epidemiological studies of mental disorders."
Population: Adults.
Publication Date: 1993.
Acronym: CIDI.
Scores, 18: Demographics, Tobacco Use Disorder, Somatoform Disorders, Panic Disorder, Generalized Anxiety, Phobic Disorders, Major Depressive Episode and Dysthymia, Manic Episode, Schizophrenic and Schizophreniform Disorders, Eating Disorders, Alcohol Abuse and Dependence, Obsessive Compulsive Disorder, Drug Abuse and Dependence, Organic Brain Syndrome, Psychosexual Dysfunctions, Comments by the Respondent and the Interviewer, Interviewer Observations, Interviewer Rating.
Administration: Individual.
Price Data: Available from publisher.
Time: (75–95) minutes.
Author: World Health Organization.
Publisher: American Psychiatric Press, Inc.
Cross References: Reviews by Mary Mathai Chittooran and Janice G. Williams will appear in the 13th MMY.

Review of the Composite International Diagnostic Interview by MARY MATHAI CHITTOORAN, UC Foundation Assistant Professor of School Psychology and Special Education, The University of Tennessee at Chattanooga, Chattanooga, TN:

The Composite International Diagnostic Interview (CIDI), Version 1.1 is a comprehensive, standardized, and structured interview for the assessment of mental disorders in adults. Appropriate for use in a variety of cultures with respondents of diverse educational backgrounds, the core version of the CIDI is currently available in 16 languages. Although the CIDI was designed to be used in epidemiological studies of mental disorders, it is finding increased acceptance in clinical and research circles.

The CIDI had its inception in 1980, when questions from the National Institute of Mental Health Diagnostic Interview Schedule (NIMH-DIS) and the ninth edition of the Present State Examination (PSE-9) were combined to form a draft version. Since then, items have been modified, added, and structured to correspond to the criteria for mental disorders outlined in two major diagnostic systems—the *International Classification of Diseases* (*ICD-10*) and the American Psychiatric Association's *Diagnostic and Statistical Manual—Third Edition, Revised* (*DSM-III-R*). According to the authors of the manual, feasibility and cross-cultural acceptability were established in field trials conducted in sites around the world and the CIDI was determined to have "excellent interrater reliability (kappa >.90 in almost all diagnostic categories) and good test-retest reliability" (p. 10). Subsequent field trials confirmed previous findings and suggested a high degree of diagnostic concordance between CIDI and clinical *ICD-10* and *DSM-III-R* diagnoses.

Test materials consist of a Researcher's Manual, an Interviewer's Manual, a 105-page Interview protocol, a Computer Manual, and an IBM-compatible computer diskette that includes data cleaning and entry programs as well as scoring programs for both *ICD-10* and *DSM-III-R* diagnoses. A computer-administered version of the CIDI, the CIDI-Auto, is also available and an abbreviated version, the CIDI-Quick, is under development.

The CIDI may be administered by both clinicians and nonclinicians and all interviewers undergo rigorous training sessions offered by a CIDI training center. Interview questions are standardized and are designed to elicit descriptive information about the frequency, severity, onset, and recency of symptoms. The interviewer is responsible for gathering the information, coding it appropriately, and submitting it to the editor for data cleaning, computer entry, and scoring. A positive diagnosis is made when (a) *all* criteria for a disorder are met *AND* when (b) all *positive* criteria—as distinguished from exclusionary criteria—for that disorder are met.

COMMENTARY. The CIDI has a number of excellent features. It is the result of a large-scale collaborative project that was developed over a 13-year period, with an impressive number of field trials in international settings. Content validity appears to be adequate as interview questions were constructed upon the recommendations of an international panel of experts who also judged its cross-cultural acceptability. Interrater reliability ranges from good to excellent. Test materials are sturdy, attractive, and of good quality. The CIDI offers a highly structured format with explicit directions to interviewers, which combined with the training program (arguably one of the CIDI's greatest strengths), adds to ease of administration and minimizes a significant source of potential error. Additionally, computer-generated diagnoses may obviate concerns about human error in data entry and scoring.

The CIDI is subject to the limitations of all interviews in that its results are dependent on the skills of the interviewer but this may be especially problematic if the interviewer is a nonclinician. Respondents may display behaviors that escape the nonclinician but that could be critical to an accurate diagnosis, and decision-making, particularly with borderline cases, is often heavily influenced by clinical experience. Similarly, the generation of computer diagnoses, although advantageous in many ways (Wittchen, 1993), disregards the value of human experience in decision making.

Although the CIDI does address the use of self-descriptive phrases such as "excessive," "sickly," or "a lot of trouble," other phrases like "worried a lot" are left vague and undefined. Also of concern is the fact that the interviewer is asked to comment on respondent behaviors such as the existence of neologisms, and to determine whether the respondent is "essentially normal, a little abnormal, or very abnormal" (p. 86). These are tasks that may well be beyond the capabilities of a nonclinician and although the authors recognize the need for special training in this area, there are no formal guidelines available. There is also the danger, inherent in all interviews, that questions in sensitive areas (e.g., those dealing with sexuality or drug use) may be refused or not answered truthfully. The accuracy of the CIDI's computer diagnoses cannot be evaluated in the absence of critical materials such as the computer manual and the computer programs, which were repeatedly requested from, but not provided by, the publisher.

Although the authors of the CIDI manual address the cultural acceptability of certain items, there are still a number of questions that may pose problems in certain cultures, for example, items in which a nonnative speaker of English is asked to repeat a Western colloquialism, "No, if's and's or but's" (pp. 77–78) or to remember three objects, among them a penny. Respondents in foreign countries may not recognize drugs by their formal names and so may provide inaccurate information about drug use. Yet another item uses a cutoff of 140 pounds for men and 125 pounds for women as one of the preliminary criteria in determining the existence of an eating disorder; although this weight might be significant in the Western world, a slight build is the norm in many countries. The inclusion of such items is puzzling, given that the CIDI is specifically intended to be used with a cross-cultural population.

One of the greatest drawbacks of the CIDI is the lack of technical information offered to potential users. The Researcher's manual contains vague descriptions about the composition of samples used in field studies and only very sketchy information about the outcome of such studies. Limited data about the CIDI's reliability and validity are provided and the vagueness of terms such as "almost all diagnostic categories" and "good" reliability is misleading. Further, because the diagnostic utility of some of these mental disorders is still open to question, the validity of tests based on these classifications may be correspondingly poor. Additional information is also needed about criterion-related validity and the congruence between English-language versions and other versions. The advent of *DSM-IV* in 1994 also renders sections of the CIDI obsolete, at least until further revisions are undertaken.

An independent review of 53 studies abstracted in PSYCLIT (e.g., Wittchen, 1994) indicated that the CIDI is used most often to diagnose depression and alcohol and drug-related disorders, and that test-retest and interrater reliability range from moderate to good. A limited number of studies (e.g., Lyketsos, Aritzi, & Lyketsos, 1994) provide support for the inclusion of the CIDI in clinical decision making.

The CIDI, Version 1.1 is an ambitious attempt to develop a structured interview with cross-cultural acceptability that can be used for the diagnosis of mental disorders in adults. It is suggested that the CIDI be used primarily as a measure for epidemiological research, and that its use in clinical settings be limited, at least until the authors are able to provide additional technical information as well as support for its use in clinical settings. The CIDI's sister measure, the Schedules for Clinical Assessment in Neuropsychiatry, also developed by the WHO, may serve as an alternative measure in clinical settings (Janca, Ustun, & Sartorious, 1994). The CIDI may also be profitably used in a comprehensive battery that includes a complete history, norm-referenced measures of social-emotional functioning, behavioral observations, and clinical decision making.

REVIEWER'S REFERENCES

Wittchen, H. U. (1993). Computer scoring of CIDI diagnoses: Special Issue: The WHO Composite Diagnostic Interview. *International Journal of Methods in Psychiatric Research, 3*(2), 101–107.

Janca, A., Ustun, T. B., & Sartorious, N. (1994). New versions of World Health Organization instruments for the assessment of mental disorders. *Acta Psychiatrica Scandinavica, 90*(2), 73–83.

Lyketsos, C. G., Aritzi, S., & Lyketsos, G. C. (1994). Effectiveness of office-based psychiatric practice using a structured diagnostic interview to guide treatment. *Journal of Nervous and Mental Disease, 182*(12), 720–723.

Wittchen, H. U. (1994). Reliability and validity studies of the WHO-Composite International Diagnostic Interview (CIDI): A critical review. *Journal of Psychiatric Research, 28*(1), 57–84.

Review of the Composite International Diagnostic Interview by JANICE G. WILLIAMS, Associate Professor of Psychology, Clemson University, Clemson, SC:

The Composite International Diagnostic Interview (CIDI) is a comprehensive structured interview for making psychiatric diagnoses consistent with the *Diagnostic and Statistical Manual—Third Edition, Revised (DSM-III-R)* and the *International Classification of Disease (ICD-10)*. The instrument was developed from other structured interviews, including the Diagnostic Interview Schedule, the Present State Examination, and a structured interview based on the *ICD-10* diagnostic criteria. The CIDI is intended for epidemiological research on psychiatric diagnoses, but the manual author indicates that it can be used for other clinical and research purposes, as well. The instrument can be administered by trained interviewers with no other clinical background. Training for administering the interview is a 5-day process.

Development of the CIDI was a joint project of the World Health Organization and the National Institutes for Health. A unique feature of the CIDI is its availability in 16 languages. Development included field trials to examine reliability and validity of the instrument in different countries. The CIDI has undergone a number or revisions that have addressed its comprehensiveness, its length, and its adequacy of measurement of substance abuse and dependence. Additionally, the CIDI should be undergoing current revision to incorporate changes from *DSM-III-R* to *DSM-IV*.

RELIABILITY AND VALIDITY. References cited in the CIDI indicate adequate reliabilities for most CIDI sections. Both test-retest and interrater reliabilities have been examined. A lack of test-retest reliability has been noted for CIDI time-related items, such as age at onset of symptoms. This lack of reliability might be expected, as interviews are based solely on patient recall. However, these items have been revised since those findings.

The CIDI was constructed for content validity. Items are based on the diagnostic criteria for the *DSM-III-R* and the *ICD-10*. A major shortcoming of the CIDI Researcher's Manual is failure to provide a summary of the available information on reliability and validity. References to published works are provided, but many of the journals in which they are published will not be found in the typical library. Psychometric properties of the scales are difficult to determine because of the frequency with which the sections have been revised. Currently, a new version of the CIDI should be in preparation in response to the publication of *DSM-IV*.

The most appropriate use of the CIDI is for research. Certainly the instrument would be valuable for epidemiological research on mental disorders, as well as for research on correlates of such diagnoses. Development of the instrument in 16 languages makes it a potentially pivotal instrument for advancing cross-cultural research on mental disorders. As more information is accumulated on the reliability and validity of the CIDI in the diverse languages, it may become a standard measure for study of cross-cultural issues in psychiatric diagnosis.

Currently, the CIDI should be used with some caution. At best, the CIDI can be only as useful as the classification systems on which it is based. As controversies, criticisms, and revisions of these systems continue, the same issues and arguments will apply to the CIDI. One limitation of the CIDI is its reliance on patient self-report. Although the manual states that the CIDI could be used for clinical diagnosis, it seems inappropriate to base diagnosis on an interview by an individual without a clinical background. However, the CIDI would serve as a useful adjunct to other sources of diagnostic information.

SUMMARY. The CIDI is a comprehensive interview for making diagnoses based on the *DSM-III-R* and *ICD-10*. Reliability and validity appear adequate for research purposes, although the manual does not provide enough information about psychometric properties of the scales. The CIDI has been developed in 16 languages, making it a potentially useful instrument for cross-cultural research on mental disorders.

[2.9]
Comprehensive Assessment of Symptoms and History.

Purpose: "Designed as a structured interview and recording instrument for documenting the signs, symptoms, and history of subjects evaluated in research studies of the major psychoses and affective disorders."

Population: Psychiatric patients.
Publication Date: 1987.
Acronym: CASH.
Scores: Interview divided into 3 major sections: Present State (Sociodemographic Data, Evaluation of Current Condition, Psychotic Syndrome, Manic Syndrome, Major Depressive Syndrome, Treatment, Cognitive Assessment, Global Assessment Scale, Diagnosis for Current Episode), Past History (History of Onset and Hospitalization, Past Symptoms of Psychosis, Characterization of Course, Past Symptoms of Affective Disorder), Lifetime History (History of Somatic Therapy, Alcoholism, Drug Use and Abuse and Dependence, Modified Premorbid Adjustment Scale, Premorbid or Intermorbid Personality, Functioning During Past Five Years, Global Assessment Scale, Diagnosis for Lifetime).
Administration: Individual.
Price Data: Available from publisher.
Time: [60–180] minutes.
Comments: The CASH is one component of a modular assessment battery available from the publisher.
Author: Nancy C. Andreasen.
Publisher: Nancy C. Andreasen.
Cross References: Reviews by Patricia A. Bachelor and Barbara J. Kaplan originally appeared in 12:88 (12 references).

Review of the Comprehensive Assessment of Symptoms and History by PATRICIA A. BACHELOR, Professor of Psychology, California State University, Long Beach, CA:

The Comprehensive Assessment of Symptoms and History (CASH) is a structured interview and data-capturing instrument of research subjects' signs, symptoms, and history of major affective disorders and psychoses. The extensive scope of descriptions included in this instrument enables researchers to examine the social, biological, cognitive, and psychological correlates of behavior and use a variety of criteria to determine diagnoses. Approximately 1,000 questions spanning 150 pages may be used to probe subjects about a current relevant illness, focusing on detailed descriptions of the course of illness. Data can also be obtained from past records and/or other sources. The examiner should have experience with psychiatric patients and should practice using the CASH. Training manuals and tapes are available upon request.

The CASH interview consists of three sections: Present State (sociodemographic data is included), Past History, and Lifetime History. Content assessed within the Present State section includes positive and negative psychotic symptoms, laterality, cognitive functioning, depressive symptoms, and mania. The overall severity of symptoms is given a global rating as well. Within the Past History section, previous episodes of affective and psychotic disorders, and any interrelationships, are explored in an attempt to characterize the course of illness over time. Additional information useful in describing a patient such as other disorders, history of treatment, premorbid functioning, and psychosocial functioning are recorded within the Lifetime History section.

Each section of the CASH is introduced with a clear presentation of the purpose of the section. Items are often defined and probes suggested. Most items are scored on a 6-point Likert-type scale with well-defined anchor points. For the most part, inquiry and interview items are grouped together as are observationally based items.

No technical manual accompanied the CASH test booklet. The test booklet did not contain any information on reliability, validity, or test development, nor did it contain normative data. This is out of compliance with the *Standards for Educational and Psychological Testing* (AERA, APA, & NCME, 1985). Upon requesting materials which would describe the psychometric properties of the CASH, I was sent two reprints. The data in one of those articles provided the quantitative information used in this review.

RELIABILITY. Prospective subjects for the reliability study were patients who had consecutive acute-care admissions to the University of Iowa (Iowa City) Psychiatric Hospital. Subjects were selected if mood or psychotic symptoms were the presenting problem. Thirty subjects so identified participated in the study. Diagnostic categories of the subjects were presented but no other descriptive or demographic information was provided. The opportunistic character of the sample calls into question examinee comparability and external validity interpretation.

A crossover design was used to estimate the reliability of the CASH. Subjects were first interviewed by two raters, one conducted the CASH and the other rater observed and clarified questions at the conclusion of the interview. The following day, within 24 hours, another interview with the CASH was conducted by a third rater. All raters had access to patients' medical records and scored the CASH independently. Eight raters, each with at least one year of experience with the CASH, participated in the study. Thus, the assessment of interrater reliability is embedded within an assessment of test-retest reliability. Given this design, the estimates of test-retest and interrater reliability as measured by intraclass r coefficients on several summary ratings were of adequate magnitude to warrant claims of consistency of measurement. Half of the test-retest intraclass correlations were greater than or equal to .65 and 75% of the intraclass correlations assessing interrater reliability were equal to or greater than .65.

VALIDITY. Validity studies are ongoing. It is hoped that evidence supportive of the claims of accurate symptom reporting will be forthcoming. Two preliminary studies were mentioned in Andreasen, Flaum, & Arndt (1992) but unfortunately were not referenced. Vague statements about these studies failed to reveal which type of validity was assessed or to provide any description of subjects. Intraclass correlations were reported but the lack of supporting detail about the validity study and the data derived from it calls into question the legitimacy of the conclusion of validity. Particularly problematic was that one study used a "consensus" CASH to serve as a criterion. This reviewer would suggest that an independent assessment, such as expert ratings, would be preferable psychometrically.

SUMMARY. The CASH is an individually administered structured interview that is extensive in its coverage of signs, symptoms, and history of research subjects' psychoses and affective disorders. Over 1,000 questions are contained in the test booklet which is divided into the Present State, Past History, and Lifetime History sections. Each section of the CASH contains introductory comments, instructions for administration, suggested probes, and anchor points. No technical manual was provided. The information on the psychometric properties and standardization sample was reported in a single research article. Claims of validity are premature but there is modest support for assertions of interrater and test-retest reliability of selected summary ratings. The author should prepare a technical manual containing a complete presentation of psychometric and normative data to accompany the CASH which conforms to the

Standards for Educational and Psychological Testing (AERA, APA, & NCME, 1985). Consequently, in its current state, the CASH should be considered experimental and its use be limited to a data collection instrument in research settings.

REVIEWER'S REFERENCES

American Educational Research Association, American Psychological Association, & National Council on Measurement in Education. (1985). *Standards for educational and psychological testing.* Washington, DC: American Psychological Association, Inc.

Andreasen, N. C., Flaum, M., & Arndt, S. (1992). The comprehensive assessment of symptoms and history (CASH). *Archives of General Psychiatry, 49,* 615–623.

Review of the Comprehensive Assessment of Symptoms and History by BARBARA J. KAPLAN, Psychologist, Western New York Institute for the Psychotherapies, Orchard Park, NY:

The Comprehensive Assessment of Symptoms and History (CASH) is one of a group of interview schedules produced by the Mental Health Clinical Research Center, this one originating with the group at the University of Iowa College of Medicine. The interviews are those used in ongoing studies of individuals with schizophrenia and affective disorders, and the CASH appears likely to replace such instruments as Spitzer, Endicott, and Robin's (1978) Schedule of Affective Disorders and Schizophrenia—Lifetime Version (SADS-L). What the CASH adds to many other instruments is some systematic information on the somatic, social, and cognitive domains. This knowledge may serve as a valuable supplement to the symptoms and course of the illness as they are usually assessed.

The CASH itself includes sections to record information on the present episode and past history of the current disorder. Data are also included on the lifetime course of illness and the history of treatment with psychopharmacological substances, drug use and abuse adjustment, and personality dysfunction.

The psychometric properties of the instrument have been largely overlooked. Training manuals and tapes are available "on request," and these materials allow interviewers to learn how to negotiate the lengthy interview format. The instrument, however, is not one that can be used reliably with these materials alone. To begin with, the CASH does not include within it the basis for screening for the disorders it assesses. This work must be done prior to using the CASH. In addition, because this interview has been developed as part of the research protocol with patients already identified with schizophrenia or affective disorders, no information is available on the extent to which the interview itself discriminates these disorders from other overlapping diagnoses that reflect less serious psychopathology. In short, the CASH cannot and should not be used to make these diagnoses.

The CASH is an interview that runs about 150 pages and depending on the complexity of the syndrome and its history, might take several hours to administer. It allows the interviewer to code the presence and duration of symptoms as well as the severity of stressors that may have led to the onset of an episode.

The test itself provides no information as to the number of people on whom it has been standardized, selection of the research participants already used, or the reliability of the diagnoses generated compared to other diagnostic instruments available. The authors do indicate that users of the CASH can make diagnoses consistent with other diagnostic schemes such as the *DSM-III-R* (American Psychiatric Association, 1987). The principal author of the CASH, Nancy Andreasen, was part of the *DSM-IV* (American Psychiatric Association, 1994) Task Force so one can expect the CASH to be consistent with more recent diagnostic standards. Because of the current practice of updating diagnostic standards, this flexibility is a strength of the interview, but it also suggests that those using the CASH must possess considerable expertise in working with severely affected psychiatric populations. What the CASH does very well is to provide a *comprehensive* survey of symptoms and correlates of the disorders it assesses. Because of this strength, it can be a valuable part of the diagnostic workup or research protocol.

This is not an instrument to be used by clinicians or researchers who are still in training. Its reliability appears to depend on considerable preexisting knowledge of the disorders and the population they affect. The CASH may prove a valuable tool in expanding our knowledge of the linkages between psychopathology and the realms of social, cognitive, and biological functioning. The instrument is not appropriate, however, for most clinical settings.

REVIEWER'S REFERENCES

Spitzer, R. L., Endicott, J., & Robins, E. (1978). Schedule of Affective Disorders and Schizophrenia—Lifetime Version (SADS-L). New York: Biometrics Research, New York State Psychiatric Institute.

American Psychiatric Association. (1987). *Diagnostic and statistical manual of mental disorders, third edition—revised* (DSM-III-R). Washington, DC: American Psychiatric Association.

American Psychiatric Association. (1994). *Diagnostic and statistical manual of mental disorders, fourth edition* (DSM-IV). Washington, DC: American Psychiatric Association.

[2.10]
Diagnostic Guide to DSM III.

Purpose: Checklist for "clinician generated diagnoses" according to DSM III (does not include child, sexual, or adjustment disorders).
Population: Adults.
Publication Date: 1983.
Scores: 8 axis I scores (Organic Disorders, Substance Abuse, Psychosis, Paranoid, Affective, Anxiety, Somatoform, Dissociative), 1 axis II score (Personality Disorder), and 3 ratings (Presence of Medical History, Severity of Psychosocial Stressor, Highest Level of Adaptive Functioning Last Year).
Administration: Individual.
Price Data: Not available.
Time: 10(20) minutes.
Authors: Joel Butler, Frank Lawlis, and Myrna Niccolette.
Publisher: The Wilmington Press [No reply from publisher; status unknown].

This test has not been reviewed in *The Mental Measurements Yearbook.*

[2.11]
Employee Assistance Program Inventory.

Purpose: "Designed as an intake or screening tool for professionals in Employee Assistance Programs (EAP's)."
Population: Adults seeking vocational counseling.
Publication Date: 1994.
Acronym: EAPI.
Scores: 10 scales: Anxiety, Depression, Self-Esteem Problems, Marital Problems, Family Problems, External Stressors, Interpersonal Conflict, Work Adjustment, Problem Minimization, Effects of Substance Abuse.
Administration: Group.
Price Data, 1996: $72 per introductory kit including manual (44 pages), 25 reusable item booklets, and 25 answer sheet/profiles; $27 per 25 item booklets; $27 per 25 answer sheet/profiles; $25 per manual.
Time: (20) minutes.
Authors: William D. Anton and James R. Reed.
Publisher: Psychological Assessment Resources, Inc.

This test has not been reviewed in *The Mental Measurements Yearbook.*

[2.12]
Employee Reliability Inventory.

Purpose: Designed to be used as a preemployment instrument assessing a number of different dimensions of reliable and productive work behavior.
Population: Prospective employees.
Publication Dates: 1986–1993.
Acronym: ERI.
Scores, 7: Freedom from Disruptive Alcohol and Substance Use, Emotional Maturity, Conscientiousness, Trustworthiness, Long Term Job Commitment, Safe Job Performance, Courtesy.
Administration: Group.
Price Data, 1992: $14 or less (volume discounts available) per questionnaire including User's Manual ('93, 52 pages), Addendum for Courtesy Scale ('93, 7 pages), all documentation, training, toll-free (or in-house computer) scoring, technical support, and consultation; $55 per Americans With Disabilities Act Kit including User's Manual Addendum ('92, 19 pages), Audio version, Braille version, and Large Print version.
Special Editions: Braille, Large Print, and Audio versions available.
Time: (12–15) minutes.
Author: Gerald L. Borofsky.
Publisher: Bay State Psychological Associates, Inc.; distributed by Wonderlic Personnel Test, Inc.
Cross References: See T4:899 (2 references); the reviews by Robert M. Guion and Lawrence M. Rudner originally appeared in 12:137 (3 references).

Review of the Employee Reliability Inventory by ROBERT M. GUION, Distinguished University Professor Emeritus, Bowling Green State University, Bowling Green, OH:

Unreliable employees, unlike unreliable tests, are not necessarily undependable. Only dependable unwanted behavior is predictable. Reliability testing differs from integrity testing. The Employee Reliability Inventory (ERI) has a broader concept of unreliability. Integrity (Trustworthiness) is only one of its seven scales.

ERI development began with a pool of more than 500 items, each judged relevant to the general idea of reliable (or unreliable) behavior. Item responses of one group of people, some hospitalized for alcohol or drug treatment and some found guilty of theft, were compared to those of another group with no such history. Stepwise discriminant function analysis eliminated all but 81 items. Why so many? Perhaps because criteria were stringent, or because surviving items capitalized on chance.

In any case, the survivors formed a single scale, labeled R.

Eventually, the R scale was replaced by six scales, and a seventh—Courtesy—was added later. All are based on discriminant functions analysis of the same 81 true-false items, differing only in the groups distinguished. Scores, based on the discriminant equations, are reported as "zone scores." Four zones are apparently equal intervals on the basic score distribution; each zone has been divided into two intervals, so scores are reported in eight score categories. Normative data for each scale consist of the percentage of more than 43,000 job applicants (60,000 for the Courtesy scale) whose scores fall in each category. With so much data, different norms could be provided for various subgroups (based on ethnicity, sex, age, etc.). It would be useful to know if score distributions differ appreciably from one such group to another.

Test-retest reliability estimates for the six older scales range from .79 to .97 with intervals of 5 to 9 days. The Courtesy scale has a lower testretest coefficient, .68, with 7- to 21-day intervals. These are based on small samples and brief time intervals; I would prefer stronger evidence of score stability. Internal consistencies, estimated by three LISREL indices, are acceptable, but the scales are far from unidimensional. An undated factor analytic report provided by the author shows three or four factors for most scales.

Original validity evidence was based on group comparisons of sometimes rather extreme groups. For each scale, two groups (reliable and unreliable) were identified and discriminant functions computed. The equations were then applied to cross validation groups; validity is the percentage of correct classifications in the cross validation groups. Specifically:

A, Freedom from Disruptive Alcohol and Substance use: 53 (29) people being admitted to hospital treatment for alcohol or substance use, versus 58 (15) people with security clearance; 84% correct classifications. [Numbers in parentheses are those in cross-validation samples and are the ones used in computing percentages of correct classifications.]

E, Emotional maturity: 35 (14) people being admitted to a private hospital (no Axis I disorders) because of inability "to perform effectively on the job and in their personal lives due to the presence

of maladaptive personality traits" (manual, p. 26), versus 56 (17) job applicants with Top Secret security clearances; 84% correct classifications.

F, Conscientiousness: 10 (9) people fired within 30 days, versus 77 (93) who stayed more than 30 days; 84% correct classifications.

H, Trustworthiness: 19 (10) people found guilty of theft, versus 54 (19) job applicants with Top Secret security clearances; 90% correct classifications.

Q, Long Term Job Commitment: 22 (17) people who quit (not fired) within 30 days, versus 104 (66) who did not; 76% correct classifications.

S, Safe Job Performance: 14 (5) people who had a significant on-the-job accident in the first 4 months of employment, versus 45 (21) who did not; 85% correct classifications.

C, Courtesy: 81 (14) hotel employees in 32 departments rated as *best* in each department on an 8-point definition of courtesy, versus 31 (2) rated *poorest* in each department; 75% correct classifications.

In short, validations were marred by small primary samples, use of extreme groups, and *very* small cross validation samples. Equally troublesome is that some comparison groups do not seem to fit the scale labels. Is 30 days without quitting an acceptable sign of *long term* commitment? Is getting fired within 30 days a sign of deficiency in conscientiousness, or is it a sign of incompetence?

Necessary information is often missing. Procedures for rating and grouping some hotel employees were not described at all. From information available, we can surmise that many hotel employees were excluded from the study because we can assume that most departments had numerous employees between the best and the poorest; we can surmise, but we are not told.

More seriously, procedures and decision rules for classifying cross validation scores are not reported. Again, consider the C scale. Cross validation was based on 16 people; 14 good guys (87.5%) and only two identified as "less courteous." Classifying everyone as a good guy (100%) would have been as close to the mark as the classifications based on scale scores (75%), yet the conclusion reported is that the scale is "effective in differentiating individuals who performed on the job in a courteous manner, from those who did not" (p. 2).

Further validity evidence continues to accumulate. Borofsky (1992) used 13 items in a self-report questionnaire as criteria and six groups of people varying in expected likelihood of reliable or unreliable behavior (e.g., patients in hospitals, general job applicants, job applicants with Top Secret security clearances). The validation design is clever but not satisfying. It consisted of one-way analyses of variance testing for significantly different group means but with no measure of effect size.

Borofsky and Wagner (1993) reported a significant chi square, finding that significantly more people were employed more than 30 days when the ERI was used than when it was not. When I recomputed chi square with complete data (including those terminated), the significance evaporated.

There are other disappointments. I would have liked a more integrated discussion of validity than the discrete treatments of content, construct, and criterion-related evidence. Adverse impact ratios mean little without specifying selection ratios. A training program for users is available but not evaluated. Several ERI versions motivated by the Americans with Disabilities Act (ADA) have been created (audiotape, Braille, large print, and even a piece of paper with a large T and a large F on it to be pointed at by people who have trouble expressing themselves verbally), but the problem of interpreting nonstandard scores is ignored. To be fair, these disappointments are nearly universal; the ADA accommodation problem seems especially intractable. Others, however, are avoidable. For example, considering reliability and low scale intercorrelations, discriminant validity could be argued; a counter consideration would argue that the different scales have similar correlates. Together, these considerations could lead to useful suggestions for validity-relevant research.

Perhaps some of these disappointments stem from the fact that the user's manual is not intended to be a technical manual. Such a manual is badly needed. It is hard, however, to decide whether the disappointments stem from sparing nontechnical readers or from psychometric naiveté.

I do not want to seem too negative. The author and his colleagues have recognized a number of problems in the potential misuse of the inventory and have spoken against them clearly. They have also been more positive than most in

providing helpful features like user training, an interview, and the ADA kit. But these features remain unevaluated.

In general, the ERI is not technically well supported. There is indeed evidence of validity, but it is not compelling evidence. But is must also be said that none of the evidence argues against its use. The evidence is weak, but it is not negative. It can be used, but users need healthy skepticism leading them to search for information supporting the inferences they draw.

REVIEWER'S REFERENCES

Borofsky, G. L. (1992). Assessing the likelihood of reliable workplace behavior: Further contributions to the validation of the Employee Reliability Inventory. *Psychological Reports, 70*, 563–592.
Borofsky, G. L., & Wagner, J. (1993). Termination for cause and job tenure: The contribution of a pre-employment screening inventory. *Psychological Reports, 72*, 591–599.

Review of the Employee Reliability Inventory by LAWRENCE M. RUDNER, Director ERIC Clearinghouse on Assessment and Evaluation, The Catholic University of America, Washington, DC:

The Employee Reliability Inventory (ERI) is a well-documented and well-supported instrument that can be used to help employers screen job candidates as part of a company's pre-employment selection program. The ERI is a self-administered, true-false type questionnaire consisting of 81 statements written at the sixth-grade reading level. The results provide estimates of the likelihood the candidate would work reliably and productively with regard to six behavioral-psychological traits: (A) Freedom from Disruptive Alcohol and Substance Use, (E) Emotional Maturity, (F) Conscientiousness, (H) Trustworthiness, (Q) Long Term Job Commitment, and (S) Safe Job Performance. Properly used, the instrument appears to be well suited for companies concerned with production deviance, property deviance, and unplanned turnover.

The user's manual, training materials, and the documentation in support of the validity of the ERI left this reviewer impressed by the company's integrity and commitment to assuring appropriate and fair test use. For example, the company clearly recommends the ERI results should be used as part of a larger screening program. Potential problems identified by the ERI should be followed up with interviews and other verification activities aimed at developing information that will either clarify, confirm, or question the ERI results. They provide a manual complete with sample questions to help guide the interviewer. They repeatedly emphasize that employment decisions should be based on all information collected during the selection process. They also repeatedly emphasize the ERI should not be used with employees after they have been hired. The ERI was not developed for that purpose and there is no evidence that the ERI is valid for that purpose.

Users are provided with clear, explicit instructions on how to administer the ERI, how to use it as part of a screening program, how to safeguard the rights of test takers, and limitations to the use of the ERI. The publishers have an ERI Americans with Disabilities Act (ADA) kit to assist in assessing individuals with impaired sensory, manual, or speaking skills. Several pages are devoted to principles of test use. Several pages are devoted to reviewing the test results in the context of an overall employee selection program. The documentation clearly states how the test was developed. An ongoing research program provides insight into the field use of the ERI.

TEST DEVELOPMENT. The 81 items in the ERI were selected from an initial pool of 500 items based on discriminant function analysis. The items selected were those that best separated (*a*) a group of people with impaired on-the-job performance due to a pattern of substance use and a control group of people with no history of impaired on-the-job performance and (*b*) a group of people who have been found guilty of theft offenses and the control group. Sample sizes were relatively small—a total of 117 individuals. Nevertheless, a cross validation with a different sample correctly classified 90% of the cases.

The original ERI produced a single scale. The current ERI uses the same items but provides six scale scores that were also derived from discriminant function analysis. For each scale, groups were obtained with clearly defined reliable and unreliable behavior—individuals who had just been found guilty of theft offenses versus individuals with top security clearance, individuals who have been fired within 30 days of hire versus those who neither quit nor were fired within 30 days of hire, etc. Again, the sample sizes were low—the unreliable groups had between 10 and 53 subjects.

VALIDITY. Evidence contained in the user's manual and several journal articles attests to the validity of the instrument. The evidence in support of the validity of the ERI in the user's manual is based on accuracy of classifications for the scale development samples and for new cross-validation samples. The percent of correct classifications was typically high, in the 80–90% range. Unfortunately the samples were again quite small (as low as 5 in one group), and the nature of classification errors was not specified.

Stronger evidence of validity is emerging from a series of studies using the ERI. In the largest study, Borofsky (1992a) categorized six groups of people into one continuum of a low to high likelihood of behaving in a reliable fashion. Group sizes ranged from 104 to 3,863. The mean scores on each of the scales progressed as expected. Other studies have demonstrated the effectiveness of the ERI in particular locations. In one study, Borofsky and Smith (1993) noted a sharp decline in the number of employees who had accidents, hours lost due to accidents, unauthorized absences, and disciplinary actions after one company began using the ERI as part of its employee selection process. In another study (Borofsky & Wagner, 1993), 5.3% of the 247 employees hired using the ERI were fired for cause within 30 days of hire compared to 8.2% of the 190 employees hired without the ERI. These later two results are very impressive.

RELIABILITY. The test-retest reliability reported in the manual is quite high—ranging from .78 on the Q scale to .97 on the H scale. However, only 24 people were included in that sample and there is no information regarding their representativeness. More compelling evidence the scales provide consistent results can be found in the appendix to a prepublication manuscript by the test's author (Borofsky, 1992b). The goodness of fit statistics for the scales' ranges were typically in the .88 to .94 range based on a sample of 43,762 examinees.

ADVERSE IMPACT. Adverse impact should always be a concern in employment selection. Based on a sample of 1,350 examinees, there was no adverse impact for any scale, by race, gender, or age based on the four-fifths rule of thumb contained in the *Uniform Guidelines* (Bureau of National Affairs, 1979). Unfortunately, again, there is no information in the manual with regard to how this sample was obtained.

FAKING GOOD. The questions on the ERI appear to be the type of questions that would be susceptible to response distortion—examinees responding according to what they think would make them look better rather than providing an accurate self-description. There are several arguments that this is not a significant factor on the ERI. First, the items selected for the ERI from the larger item pool were the ones that best differentiated reliable and unreliable workers. These are the items that work best. Second, corrections for response distortion are built into the scaling. Third, the correlations between each of the ERI Scale scores with the 16PF Motivational Distortion Scale and the MMPI Lie Scale are extremely low (<.10).

SCALES. Scores are reported in terms of four zones numbered 1 to 4 and two subzones, numbered A and B. Thus, each scale is divided into eight intervals. The use of intervals is a commendable approach. This, in effect, accounts for some of the error associated with any score and it encourages better test use. Data, based on 43,000 examinees, identifying the percent of all examinees falling within each zone for each scale are provided in the manual.

SCORING. The scale scores on the ERI are based on a proprietary discriminant function. Several options are available to the test administrator for obtaining the zone scores for each scale. The answer sheets can be scored in house using a special scoring template. The item scores are then phoned into the publisher. The publishers enter user data into their computer and provide users with the results immediately. Another option is to score the results entirely in house using IBM-PC software provided by the publisher. A third option is to mail the raw answer sheets to the publisher. Upon arrival the results are scored and phoned to the user. A fourth option, to be used on a limited basis, is to fax answer sheets to the publisher.

SUMMARY. The ERI has the potential to greatly improve hiring decisions when employers are concerned with employee reliability and ongoing productivity. Preliminary field-based results have been quite promising. In the few documented situations, turnover rate, hours lost due to accidents, unauthorized absences, and the number of disciplinary actions have gone down dramatically. The publisher appears to be committed to appropriate test use and offers a great deal of written and telephone support. Because the test was developed and validated on small samples, this reviewer strongly suggests that local validity studies be conducted wherever the test is adopted.

REVIEWER'S REFERENCES

Bureau of National Affairs, Inc. (1979). *Uniform guidelines on employee selection procedures*. Washington, DC: BNA Education Systems.

Borofsky, G. L. (1992a). Assessing the likelihood of reliable workplace behavior: Further contributions to the validation of the Employee Reliability Inventory. *Psychological Reports, 70*, 563–592.

Borofsky, G. L. (1992b). *Assessing the likelihood of reliable workplace behavior*. Unpublished manuscript.

Borofsky, G. L., & Smith, M. (1993). Reductions in turnover, accidents, and absenteeism: The contribution of a preemployment screening inventory. *Journal of Clinical Psychology, 49*, 109–116.

Borofsky, G. L., & Wagner, J. (1993). Termination for cause and job tenure: The contribution of a pre-employment screening inventory. *Psychological Reports, 72*, 591–599.

[2.13]
Family Apperception Test.

Purpose: Designed to assess family system variables.

Population: Ages 6 and over.

Publication Dates: 1985–1991.

Acronym: FAT.

Scores: 35 to 40: Obvious Conflict (Family Conflict*, Marital Conflict*, Other Conflict, Absence of Conflict), Conflict Resolution (Positive Resolution, Negative or No Resolution*), Limit Setting (Appropriate/Compliance, Appropriate/Noncompliance*, Inappropriate/Compliance*, Inappropriate/Noncompliance*), Quality of Relationships (Mother=Ally, Father=Ally, Sibling=Ally, Spouse=Ally, Other=Ally, Mother=Stressor*, Father=Stressor*, Sibling=Stressor*, Spouse=Stressor*, Other=Stressor), Boundaries (Enmeshment*, Disengagement*, Mother/Child Coalition*, Father/Child Coalition*, Other Adult/Child Coalition*, Open System, Closed System*), Dysfunctional Circularity*, Abusive Remarks (Physical Abuse*, Sexual Abuse*, Neglect/Abandonment*, Substance Abuse*), Unusual Responses*, Refusals, Total Dysfunctional Index (total of scores with *) plus 5 optional Emotional Tone scores: Sadness/Depression, Anger/Hostility, Worry/Anxiety, Happiness/Satisfaction, Other.

Administration: Individual.

Price Data, 1995: $125 per complete kit including set of test pictures, 100 scoring sheets, and manual ('91, 36 pages); $62.50 per set of test pictures; $19.50 per 100 scoring sheets; $45 per manual.

Time: (30–35) minutes.

Comments: Projective test.

Authors: Alexander Julian III, Wayne M. Sotile, Susan E. Henry, and Mary O. Sotile.

Publisher: Western Psychological Services.

Cross References: Reviews by Mark J. Benson and Merith Cosden originally appeared in 12:150.

Review of the Family Apperception Test by MARK J. BENSON, Associate Professor of Family and Child Development, Virginia Polytechnic Institute and State University, Blacksburg, VA:

The Family Apperception Test (FAT) is a projective storytelling measure modeled after the Thematic Apperception Test (TAT; Murray, 1943; T4:2824). Like the TAT, the FAT consists of series of stimulus cards about which the respondent tells a story including the feelings and thoughts of the characters. The FAT joins a number of apperception tests that emulate the TAT including the Children's Apperception Test (T4:444) and the Senior Apperception Test (T4:2429; Bellak, 1986), the Roberts Apperception Test (McArthur & Roberts, 1982; T4:2285), and the Michigan Picture Test—Revised (Hutt, 1980).

The FAT is a sound measure according to three basic criteria for evaluating storytelling projectives. These three criteria include the strength of the theoretical rationale, the evocativeness of the stimulus cards, and the reliability and validity of the coding schemes.

Several family system perspectives provide the theoretical basis for the test. Although the theoretical scope could be wider, the theories cited include the major family system thinkers such as Bowen, Minuchin, Haley, and several contemporary strategic theorists. These theoretical perspectives provide the basis for several scoring categories including boundaries, limit setting, and dysfunctional circularity. The attention to the theoretical underpinnings and the use of theory in developing some of the scoring categories are important strengths of the FAT.

Despite the attention to theory, the authors fail to link theory with the purpose of the test. The purpose of the FAT is to "bridge the historical gap between individual and family assessment" (p. 1). Actually, the FAT can assess only individual perceptions about family contexts. The manual authors further claim the FAT "allows family systems hypotheses to be systematically generated from the assessment of a single family member" (p. 7). This assertion is also unjustified. Like other storytelling projectives, the FAT ultimately provides only data at the individual level. The manual should include statements indicating the FAT accesses a sample of perceptual and verbal data from an individual.

The quality of the verbal data generated by the FAT lies in the capacity of the stimulus cards to evoke a variety of family projections. Although other storytelling projectives can generate family data, the FAT is unique in eliciting family perceptions for most of the 21 pictures. Moreover, the responses to the FAT stimulus cards are fairly diverse across examinees. Most of the FAT cards, however, are less ambiguous than the typical TAT card. Because of the limited ambiguity, some cards tend to elicit descriptions rather than stories.

Stimulus cards 5, 7, 11, and 12 are more ambiguous than the others. A study reported in the manual indicates these four cards discriminated effectively between clinical and nonclinical children on scores in the conflict category (Table 6, $N = 44$). A follow-up study reported in the manual indicated these four pictures were nearly as effective as the entire set of 21 pictures in discriminating between clinical and nonclinical children (Tables 8 and 9, $N = 56$). Clinicians may find this FAT Short Form of four cards to be a valuable supplement to data derived from other measures such as the TAT.

The codings within the FAT categories provide the basis for evaluating its reliability and validity. The reliability and validity data derive from five masters theses conducted at Wake Forest University in 1987 and 1988. These five studies were based on a sample of 187 children aged 6 to 15. Each of the studies uses a subsample ranging from 44 to 83 of the children. The basis for selection of subsamples is omitted from the manual.

Two subsamples reported in the manual ($N = 44$ and $N = 83$) provide data on interjudge agreement across the coding categories. The degree of agreement is good for several categories including obvious conflict, conflict resolution, open versus closed system, and quality of relationship. There is low interjudge agreement, however, for the remaining categories. Clarification of the rating criteria or development of additional categories could increase the number of reliable scoring categories. In addition, evaluating the test-retest reliability and the split-half reliability of the measure would help to strengthen confidence in the use of the quantitative ratings.

Validity data based on two subsamples ($N = 44$ and $N = 56$) drawn from the primary sample (N

= 187) are reported. The findings indicate that many of the scoring categories discriminated between clinical and nonclinical children. Several scoring categories that would be expected to differentiate between clinical and nonclinical respondents, however, failed to show significant differences.

Because only some of the FAT scoring categories meet acceptable standards for reliability and validity, further development of scoring categories is needed. Expanding the theoretical base to include more family system theories would generate additional constructs for scoring. The broad field of family systems theories offers an ample supply of constructs for conceptualizing additional scoring categories with sufficient interjudge agreement. Additional reliable codings would increase the interpretive value of individual FAT protocols.

Although norms for the FAT are absent, this is a problem shared by other storytelling projectives as well. Clinicians are most likely to use such story projectives for hypothesis generation. In fact, the use of these measures for differential diagnosis is discouraged (Ryan, 1984).

In summary, the FAT is a valuable addition to the field of story projectives tests. The use of some family systems theories in developing the scoring is a particular strength of the test. Broadening the theoretical base to include other family systems theories holds the potential for increasing the number of reliable and valid scoring categories. The evidence in support of the validity of the Short Form FAT suggests these four stimulus cards may be particularly valuable to clinicians seeking to supplement TAT assessment with family stimulus cards.

REVIEWER'S REFERENCES

Murray, H. A. (1943). *Thematic Apperception Test manual*. Cambridge: Harvard University.
Hutt, M. L. (1980). The Michigan Picture Test—Revised. New York: Grune & Stratton.
McArthur, D. S., & Roberts, G. E. (1982). Roberts Apperception Test For Children. Los Angeles: Western Psychological Services.
Ryan, R. M. (1984). Thematic Apperception Test. In D. J. Keyser & R. C. Sweetland (Eds.), *Test critiques compendium: Reviews of major tests from the Test Critiques Series* (pp. 517–532). Kansas City, MO: Test Corporation of America.
Bellak, L. (1986). *The T.A.T., C.A.T. and S.A.T. in clinical use* (4th ed.). Orlando, FL: Grune & Stratton.

Review of the Family Apperception Test by MERITH COSDEN, Associate Professor of Counseling/Clinical/School Psychology, Department of Education, University of California, Santa Barbara, CA:

The Family Apperception Test (FAT) is a relatively new addition to the domain of picture apperception tests. This review will address the design and psychometric properties of the test and its relationship to other commonly used picture apperception tests such as the Thematic Apperception Test (TAT; T4:2824) and the Children's Apperception Test (CAT; T4:444).

The manual authors do not indicate how the cards to be used in the test were selected. That is, the process by which important family events were sampled and then depicted through drawings is not described.

The scoring categories were developed to reflect family interaction issues related to different models of family therapy systems. Thus, cards are scored for the presence of family or marital conflict, quality of relationships with family members, and boundaries, among other things. Although the manual authors provide examples of the types of responses that would receive each score, they do not provide nonexamples, nor describe how to decide between scoring categories.

Normative data are not presented. The authors state that normative data were being collected at the time the manual was published. It would have been advisable for the authors to wait to publish the test until after these norms were developed, as interpretation of test results is impeded by their absence.

General guidelines for interpretation of scoring patterns are provided. Results also may be interpreted on the basis of one's clinical judgment. Several case studies are provided using these approaches. No data are presented to validate these procedures, however. It is not evident whether basing one's interpretation of test results on the quantitative scoring criteria is any more effective than basing the interpretation on clinical judgment. It is also not clear how the information obtained through use of this test is significantly different from that obtained through other aspects of a clinical assessment. There are no data to support use of this instrument over a strong clinical interview or other type of projective device.

Currently, there are no published studies on the reliability or validity of the FAT. One needs to rely on the manual for this information. The supportive data provided in the manual are based on five unpublished masters theses.

Interrater reliability was assessed in two of these studies. Reliability coefficients are provided through kappas. Although this is an appropriate statistical measure, it may be difficult for some readers to interpret the outcomes. For example, although the authors state the kappas are very strong, the kappa values themselves are not compelling, ranging, for the most part, from fair to moderate. Only scores of conflict and conflict resolution reflect superior levels of interrater agreement. Other measures of test reliability, such as the internal consistency of the test items, and the stability of test scores over time, are not available.

The validity of the FAT was assessed in three studies. In each of these studies the author addressed the ability of the test to distinguish between students served through a clinic and those without known clinical problems. In the first of these (Lundquist, 1987, as cited in the 1988 FAT test manual) only scores for conflict differentiated between clinic and nonclinic child samples. Further, differences in conflict scores were obtained on only four out of the full set of cards.

In a second study (Buchanon, 1987, as cited in the 1988 FAT test manual) 11 out of 34 minor scoring categories were reported as significantly different between a clinic and a nonclinic sample of children. Although a MANOVA was conducted to control for experiment-wise error rates, the MANOVA itself is not reported. It is unclear, also, whether the reported differences were obtained on all or just some of the cards.

In the final study (Eaton, 1988, as cited in the 1988 FAT test manual) 30 scoring categories (some were combined from the prior studies) and a total dysfunction score were compared across clinic and nonclinic samples. Subjects ranged in age from 8 to 16. Between-group differences were obtained on 19 of the scoring categories, indicating the clinic sample reported more conflictual relationships than the control sample.

Thus, the only validity studies on the FAT assess its ability to differentiate clinic from nonclinic samples of children. There are no data to support its use for assessment of patterns of family dysfunction. This is a major limitation. Further, only some of the scores, and only some of the cards, have been found to differentiate clinic from nonclinic samples. These problems should have been addressed during the development of the scoring system, with a final scoring system reflecting only those items that successfully differentiate clients and reflect their specific needs. Finally, it should be noted that all of the reliability and validity studies were conducted with children. Although the authors suggest the test can be used with children and adults, the validity of the test for assessing adults' problems was not reported.

The authors, in developing this test, designed both a scoring system and a set of cards. They do not make a strong argument as to why their cards are preferable to those used in the TAT or CAT. The authors state the FAT cards draw for material related to family issues, but so do many of the cards on the older picture apperception tests. The questions asked during administration of the FAT are similar to those asked during administration of the other picture apperception tests. I wonder if the FAT scoring system could be used with either the TAT or CAT cards. These have a history of clinical use.

There are also some conceptual problems related to the use of this projective instrument as an assessment tool within a family systems approach to treatment. First, the test is not based on any one systems theory. Second, and more important, the test is both administered and scored individually, with little consideration for how that information could or should be used with the family. There is no discussion of how to use the test with multiple family members, or even whether multiple family members should respond to the same cards or share their responses.

In sum, neither the utility of the FAT nor its advantage over other clinical devices appear compelling. The test does not have strong psychometric properties. Although interrater reliability of parts of the coding system is adequate, other types of reliability are not assessed, and studies on the validity of the test provide limited support. The manual lacks detail in areas of scoring and interpretation. This is particularly problematic as there are no other published studies on the test instrument. It is not apparent how the information obtained through the FAT differs from that which could be obtained through clinical interviews. Finally, there is also an underlying conceptual problem with using the FAT in its designated manner for assisting in family systems approaches to therapy. There is a need for better conceptualization of how to collect and use projective information so that it will be useful to those working within family systems approaches.

[2.14]
Fast Health Knowledge Test, 1986 Revision.

Purpose: "To measure discrimination and judgment in matters of health."
Population: High school and college.
Publication Date: 1986.
Scores, 11: Personal Health, Exercise—Relaxation—Sleep, Nutrition, Consumer Health, Contemporary Health Problems, Substance of Abuse, Safety and First Aid, Disease Control, Mental Health, Family Life and Sex Education, Total.
Administration: Group.
Price Data, 1986: $60 per 50 copies (administrative materials included with each order).
Time: 40(50) minutes.
Author: Charles G. Fast.
Publisher: Charles G. Fast.
Cross References: The review by Linda K. Bunker originally appeared in 10:113.

Review of the Fast Health Knowledge Test, 1986 Revision, by LINDA K. BUNKER, Professor of Education, and Associate Dean for Academic and Student Affairs, Curry School of Education, University of Virginia, Charlottesville, VA:

The Fast Health Knowledge Test (FAST; previously called the Fast-Tyson Health Knowledge Test) is a norm-referenced knowledge test designed to evaluate 10 curricular areas Personal Health; Exercise, Relaxation and Sleep; Nutrition; Consumer Health; Contemporary Health Problems; Substances of Abuse; Safety and First Aid; Disease Control; Mental Health; and Family Life and Sex. It uses a multiple-choice format that can be administered either individually or in a group setting. The authors suggest the test can be used with high school and college students.

The FAST test is purported to "measure discrimination and judgment in matters of health." However, it actually measures knowledge of diseases and health risks, with no evidence the items measure "judgment," or even attitudes or beliefs about health.

The 100 items have been typed and reproduced (not formally type-set or published). Tests may be purchased only in multiples of 50, ranging in price from $60 for 50 copies to $90 per 100 if over 500.

The total kit contains the 1986 Form C version of the test, scoring sheets, a two-page set of instructions, and a list of references in which the FAST has been cited. There are also two unpublished papers by the authors that provide limited additional data.

TEST ITEMS. The test items are comprehensive in breadth and related to major topics of health and illness. Most items are worded clearly and unambiguously.

Two areas of important health information are not represented, or are covered in a very limited fashion accidents/suicide and smoking habits. Given the prevalence of teenage suicides, and the importance of promoting coping behaviors in teenagers, it would seem appropriate to address some questions to this area. Similarly, the fact that smoking habits, the major preventable cause of heart disease, may become established during these teenage years, would seem to suggest that it would be an important topic. There are also many other forms of substance abuse (e.g., anabolic steroids) that are not addressed in this test. In addition, several other important topics have been omitted including AIDS and compulsive eating behaviors (e.g., anorexia and bulemia; though item 35 uses these terms).

From the information provided by the authors, it appears that all items were developed prior to 1974. This may account for some of the questionable items. For example, item 57 asks about the type of dependence formed as a result of cocaine utilization (physical vs. psychological). This concept has evolved as understanding of addictive behavior and pharmacology has improved, with experts now suggesting that the distinction is somewhat arbitrary. In fact, many now believe that cocaine produces physical dependence, while the correct answer is keyed to psychological dependence.

Other examples of questionable items include item 24, which uses the phrase "oxygen debt." This term has generally been avoided in physiological research since the early 1970s, and therefore leaves the correct response ambiguous. Item 66 illustrates a problem in "foil" design as can be seen in 66C. Most students will see through any item with opposite elements (e.g., alcoholism and excellent nutrition). In addition, statistics now show that alcoholism is the number one cause of fatal automobile accidents. Therefore none of the answers appear to be correct for item 66.

PSYCHOMETRIC PROPERTIES. The author reports that norms for this test were derived from a sample of 25,000 college freshmen and 3,000 high school seniors representing a population of 140,000 and 14,000 students respectively. Given the wide band of developmental and cognitive levels of high school through college-aged students (ages 14-22), the sample provides a very limited basis (grades 12 and 13 only) from which to suggest norms are appropriate for all grade levels in high school and college (grades 8-16).

The normative data were collected from 12 states, most east of the Mississippi River. This seems to limit the generalizability of the norms.

Another questionable characteristic of the norms is their age. They were collected between 1964 and 1974. It would seem obvious to ask if the average knowledge level of students, and the relevant issues in personal health have changed over the past 15 years. It was also unclear as to whether subjects had any health background or previous coursework before completing the questionnaire. Unfortunately, the authors do not address this problem.

There is no information provided about item analyses for this multiple-choice test. It would be very helpful for the authors to provide such data in order to enhance the usefulness of the test, or provide for its modification.

The authors provide an unpublished paper entitled "A Value Added Program that Strives for Excellence Competency Data on the Health Knowledge of Students Enrolled in PE 100, Health and Physical Fitness Concepts at Northeast Missouri State University, Kirksville, Missouri, Spring, 1986." This paper provides a model for the use of the test as a pretest to facilitate the design of a health-related course for college freshmen. In addition it provides some global data of the knowledge level of college students at one university.

TEST ADMINISTRATION RESTRICTIONS. Individuals wishing to administer this test must "indicate in writing that the test will be used only for diagnostic purposes that result in guided learning in the major health areas, and *shall never* be used to evaluate students or programs against raw score norms or to judge their competency for grades, diplomas, degrees, programs, licenses or entrance requirements." The rationale is that the authors cannot guarantee the validity and reliability if the "confidentiality of the test is not retained." It is unclear why such a promise should be required, rather than merely warning users of the test's limitation, which is true of any norm-referenced test if it is not properly used.

SUMMARY. In summary, the concept for this test is a good one, and may have been a reasonable inventory in the mid-70s. However, some of the items appear to be incorrect, issues out of date, and several important areas are not covered at all. I would therefore not recommend that it be used to assess student knowledge of important health issues in the 80s or 90s.

As is the case with many "health" inventories, this test focuses on diseases and health problems rather than health enhancement. It would seem that most educational programs for high school and college students should focus on the concepts of health promotion and personal responsibility.

[This reviewer wishes to acknowledge the assistance of Ruth Saunders, Assistant Professor of Health Promotion at the University of South Carolina.]

[2.15]
Health and Daily Living.

Purpose: "To examine the influence of extratreatment factors on treatment outcome as well as to explore the social resources and coping processes people use to prevent and adapt to stressful life circumstances."
Publication Dates: 1984–1990.
Acronym: HDL.
Administration: Group.
Forms, 2: Youth Form, Adult Form B.
Price Data, 1993: $12 per test.
Time: (30–45) minutes.
Comments: May be administered as an interview or as a questionnaire.
Authors: Rudolf H. Moos, Ruth C. Cronkite, Andrew G. Billings, and John W. Finney.
Publisher: Center for Health Care Evaluation.
  a) YOUTH FORM.
  Population: Students ages 12–18.
  Scores: 9 indices: Health-Related (Self-Confidence, Positive Mood, Distressed Mood, Physical Symptoms, Medical Conditions, Health-Risk Behaviors), Social Functioning (Family Activities, Activities with Friends, Social Integration in School).

b) ADULT FORM B.

Population: Adults.

Scores: 47 indices: Health-Related Functioning (Self-Confidence, Physical Symptoms, Medical Conditions, Global Depression, Depressive Mood and Ideation, Endogenous Depression, Depressive Features, Depressed Mood/Past 12 Months, Alcohol Consumption—Quantity, Alcohol Consumption—Quantity/Frequency, Drinking Problems, Smoking Symptoms, Medication Use), Social Functioning and Resources (Social Activities with Friends, Network Contacts, Number of Close Relationships, Quality of Significant Relationship), Family Functioning and Home Environment (Family Social Activities, Family Task Sharing, Tasks Performed by Self, Tasks Performed by Partner, Family Arguments, Negative Home Environment), Children's Health and Functioning (Children's Physical Health Problems, Children's Psychological Health Problems, Children's Total Health Problems, Children's Behavioral Problems, Children's Health-Risk Behaviors), Life Change Events (Negative Life Change Events, Exit Events, Positive Life Change Events), Coping Responses (Active Cognitive Coping, Active Behavioral Coping, Avoidance Coping, Logical Analysis, Information Seeking, Problem Solving, Affective Regulation, Emotional Discharge, Help-Seeking/Mental Health Professional, Help-Seeking/Non-Mental Health Professional), Family Level Composite (Quality of Conjugal Relationship, Family Social Activites, Family Agreement on Task Sharing, Family Agreement on Household Tasks, Family Arguments, Negative Home Environment).

Cross References: Reviews by Arthur M. Nezu and Steven P. Schinke originally appeared in 10:137 (8 references).

Review of the Health and Daily Living Form by ARTHUR M. NEZU, Chief, Division of Psychology, Beth Israel Medical Center, New York, NY:

The Health and Daily Living (HDL) Form was designed as a structured procedure to assess various indices of health-related and social functioning, life stressors and strains, and coping responses and social resources. It also includes items covering certain sociodemographic factors. The HDL can be used either in an interview format or as a self-report questionnaire.

In the current HDL manual (1986), the actual forms are included in the appendices—HDL Adult Forms A and B and the Youth Form. Adult Form B is a revision of Form A of the HDL.

Form A was originally developed for use in research concerning treatment outcome among alcoholic patients and their families. Form B has been used in longitudinal studies of the outcome of treatment among a depressed patient population and their families. The authors recommend that Form B be used by investigators. The Youth Form is described as suitable for administration to adolescents between the ages of 12 and 18 who are in junior or senior high school.

The HDL appears to have been developed primarily as a research tool to examine the influence of "extratreatment factors on treatment outcome," as well as to evaluate the social resources and coping processes people use in reaction to stressful life circumstances. This work has been conducted within a theoretical framework that specifies the interrelations among the personal and environmental determinants of life stressors and the coping and social resources that moderate the negative effects of such stress on emotional and behavioral adaptation.

The major strength of the HDL lies in its extensive research use by test developers, Moos and his colleagues. In addition to providing norms for the depressed patient population ($N = 424$), means and standard deviations for the HDL indices of a demographically matched community control group ($N = 424$) are also included. Test users can then use the large community sample as potential norms against which to compare their own obtained scores. The depressed patient group can also be used as norms for depression comparisons. Unfortunately, little information beyond the sampling procedure is provided within the manual that describes either sample (e.g., lacking are age, socioeconomic status, religious affiliations, etc.). Whereas references are listed that provide additional information about these samples, specific demographic data should be included in the test manual itself to aid the test user. The authors should remedy this limitation in future revisions of the manual.

With regard to reliability data, internal consistency estimates (alphas) for several of the indices by sample indicate the HDL items have moderate to high levels of internal consistency. However, additional reliability estimates are lacking (e.g., test-retest, item-index correlations). Of major importance is the lack of test-retest coefficients. As such, the stability over time of HDL indices remains unknown. Therefore, if test users wish to use the HDL for either clinical or research purposes, interpretation beyond the particular testing point in time is questionable. It should be pointed out that some of the indices should not be expected to have high levels of test-retest reliability. For example, the amount of experienced negative life events may be quite different between two testing periods over 3 months apart. However, total lack of this information limits the generalizability of test interpretations.

A major limitation of the present manual is the lack of any validity data. Several of the indices have counterparts in the assessment literature that could be compared to assess convergent and discriminant validity. For example, one series of HDL indices involves depressive symptoms. It would be important to know the correlation between these indices and other self-report measures of depression, such as the Beck Depression Inventory (Beck, Ward, Mendelson, Mock, & Erbaugh, 1961). Comparison to the Hamilton Rating Scale for Depression (Hamilton, 1960), a clinical rating scale of patients' depressive symptomatology, could provide information about the criterion validity of these HDL indices.

Several inventories assessing stressful life events also exist (e.g., Life Experiences Survey; Sarason, Johnson, & Siegel, 1978). Again, comparison with these questionnaires could yield important information concerning various HDL psychometric properties. The total lack of validity data severely limits the use of the HDL by the average test user. Further, the use of predetermined weights concerning HDL scoring criterion for the impact of life events is highly questionable (cf. Sarason et al., 1978). Briefly, the variability among individuals experiencing similar life events is rather large. For example, one individual, for a variety of reasons (which may involve variability in coping and social resources), may be less affected by a divorce than another person. To use predetermined weights in scoring ignores this issue.

Normative and psychometric data for the Youth Form are more scanty. Only data for nine indices are included. Test users wishing to use the Youth Form should do so with great caution in interpreting their obtained results.

To summarize, the HDL was developed within the context of a sound conceptual frame-work concerning the interrelations among stressful life events, coping and social resources, and behavioral and emotional adaptational outcomes. However, limited normative data, and the lack of extensive psychometric data concerning reliability, and especially validity, severely limits its use by the general test consumer. Usage should probably be limited to preliminary types of research investigating various aspects of the authors' conceptual framework. Yet, such investigators may be advised to seek other measurement tools, such as those cited above, that have demonstrated psychometric properties. To use the HDL for the clinical assessment of a particular individual or group is highly risky.

REVIEWER'S REFERENCES

Hamilton, M. (1960). A rating scale for depression. *Journal of Neurology, Neurosurgery, and Psychiatry, 12,* 56-62.
Beck, A. T., Ward, C. H., Mendelson, M., Mock, J., & Erbaugh, J. (1961). An inventory for measuring depression. *Archives of General Psychiatry, 4,* 561-571.
Sarason, I. G., Johnson, J. H., & Siegel, J. M. (1978). Assessing the impact of life changes: Development of the Life Experiences Survey. *Journal of Consulting and Clinical Psychology, 46,* 932-946.

Review of Health and Daily Living by STEVEN P. SCHINKE, *Professor, School of Social Work, Columbia University, New York, NY:*

STRENGTHS. The Health and Daily Living (HDL) Form is a carefully researched assessment tool. The HDL in its three versions (Adult Form A, Adult Form B, and Youth Form) is suitable for administration as an interview or as a questionnaire. This versatility is a source of considerable strength for the HDL. Besides administration versatility, the HDL has been used to a rich experience of empirical research in the target areas. A great deal of this research, including applications of the HDL, has yielded published papers and other scholarly materials that are retrievable and available in the peer-reviewed literature. As such investigators and clinicians who use the HDL have access to a large body of previous research and normative comparison data.

WEAKNESSES. The HDL is not a short instrument. Form B for Adults, as an illustration, comprises 16 pages of tightly spaced questions. Although the forms contain skip items, most respondents will find themselves faced with a large number of questions about many facets of daily living, mental health, substance use, family members, and personal habits. The HDL form for adults, therefore, gathers its data at a considerable price in administration time, effort, and concentration on the part of the respondent.

The Youth Form of the HDL, however, is surprisingly short. This form occupies only four pages. The form does not include basic demographic questions essential to studying ethnic-racial correlates, family variables, or related factors that adolescent researchers may regard as important. What is more, some questions on the Youth Form do not appear easily interpreted by young persons of less than average intelligence. Illustrative are items concerning asthma, allergies, and weight gain and loss.

Perhaps more serious is the apparent middle-class bias of the Youth Form. Many items on this form assume that youth respondents are actively attending school. Fewer, though no less important items, ask respondents about extracurricular activities associated with middle-class culture. Further, several items require respondents to report on such feelings as their maturity, dependability, confidence, and intelligence. The careful crafting of the adult versions of the HDL, thus, is not paralleled in the youth version.

RELIABILITY, VALIDITY, NORMATIVE DATA. Psychometric parameters for the HDL are evident throughout the manual. Most in abundance are scoring keys and composite indices for the scales. Validity estimates of the HDL, especially for Adult Form B, are based on appropriate comparative samples and appear solid. Most alpha coefficients of internal consistency also seem within acceptable range.

Youth Form psychometrics reflect the authors' research with 70 children of depressed parents and 77 children of "normal" community residents. These parameters on validity and internal consistency appear in the range of acceptable scores, though not grounded on as rich a data base as scores for adult versions.

SUMMARY. Health and Daily Living Forms for Adult A and Adult B versions offer useful clinical and research tools. Albeit somewhat lengthy for administrative purposes, the forms have strong credentials in prior research and in their psychometric properties. Youth forms of the HDL are not as detailed and contain items that appear biased toward verbal, middle-class samples. Despite their minor flaws, all three forms of the HDL should provide valuable data for clinicians and researchers that may not be otherwise available from instruments less well tailored to the HDL's target mental health areas.

[2.16]
Hilson Adolescent Profile.

Purpose: "Designed as a screening tool to assess the presence and extent of adolescent behavior patterns and problems."
Population: Ages 10 to 19.
Publication Dates: 1984–1987.
Acronym: HAP.
Scores, 16: Guarded Responses, Alcohol Use, Drug Use, Educational Adjustment Difficulties, Law Violations, Frustration Tolerance, Antisocial/Risk-Taking, Rigidity/Obsessiveness, Interpersonal/Assertiveness Difficulties, Homelife Conflicts, Social/Sexual Adjustment, Health Concerns, Anxiety/Phobic Avoidance, Depression/Suicide Potential, Suspicious Temperament, Unusual Responses.
Administration: Group.
Price Data, 1994: $60 per starter kit including manual ('87, 82 pages); scoring service offered by publisher.
Special Edition: Audiotape edition available.
Time: (45–55) minutes.
Comments: Self-administered; computer-scored.
Authors: Robin E. Inwald.
Publisher: Hilson Research, Inc.
Cross References: The review by Allen K. Hess originally appeared in 11:161.

Review of the Hilson Adolescent Profile by ALLEN K. HESS, Professor and Department Head, Auburn University at Montgomery, Montgomery, AL:

The Hilson Adolescent Profile (HAP) is a 310-item true-false inventory intended to screen adolescents "at risk" for personality, behavior, and adjustment problems. The items are grouped into four domains; the first domain is a validity scale, Guarded Responses (21 items); the second is an Acting Out Behavior with subdomains consisting of "External Behavior," which has scales regarding Alcohol Use (13 items), Drug Use (15 items), Educational Adjustment Difficulties (19 items), and Law/Society Violations (21 items), and an Attitudes and Temperament with subdomains consisting of scales concerning Frustration Tolerance (23 items), Antisocial/Risk Taking (19 items), and Rigidity/Obsessiveness (21 items). The third domain is titled Interpersonal Adjustment and consists of scales labelled Interpersonal/Assertiveness Difficulties (26 items), Homelife Conflicts (33 items), and Social/Sexual Adjustment (22 items). The fourth domain is called "Internalized Conflict" and is composed of scales focussed on Health Concerns (14 items), Anxiety/Phobic Avoidance

(25 items), Depression/Suicide Potential (25 items), Suspicious Temperament (17 items), and Unusual Responses (10 items).

Fourteen items appear on more than one scale, avoiding the heavy item-scale contamination problem that plagues some other inventories. By contrast, the Millon Clinical Multiaxial Inventory has over 90% item overlap, precluding differential validity, differential diagnosis, and any research based on correlation due to the collinearity problem. The HAP avoids this problem.

Section One of the test manual describes the rationale for the HAP, citing the tumultuous nature of adolescence and the large number of youth enmeshed in emotional turmoil, substance abuse, and legal trouble.

Section Two describes the scales' content, and Section Three provides clear directions for test administration. Scoring can be done by subscribing to The Hilson Mail-In Service, or purchasing software for scoring by one's own computer. Handscoring keys are unavailable. A tape-recorded version of the HAP is available for those unable to read this test, scaled for the fifth grade reading level.

Section Four describes psychometric properties of the HAP. The norming sample of 465 males and 251 females ranged from 10 to 19 years of age with a mean of 15 years, 9 months. Norms for the sample, plus subsamples of delinquents, psychiatric inpatients and outpatients, and college students are presented.

Internal consistency (KR 20) coefficients range from .67 to .90 for the 16 HAP scales. Two- to four-week test-retest reliabilities for the scales range from .74 to .95 for 33 students in one study, and .60 to .86 for a sample of 72 high school dropouts in a second 2- to 4-month test-retest study.

Factor analytic research for the 716-adolescent normative study reveals a three-factor solution with an "Internalized Difficulty" factor, an "Acting Out" factor, and a minor factor best characterized as gross disturbance.

Finally, criterion validity is addressed via a set of discriminant function analyses in which six groups were defined with problems of suicide, drug, alcohol, substance or sexual abuse, or conduct disturbance. Each group was contrasted with the remainder of the norm group. "Hits" or correct classifications ranged in the .70s, a modest level of prediction. These results require cross-validation and the coefficients will likely shrink in such studies. Moreover, false positives and negatives in classification applications have drastically different consequences, an issue not addressed in the manual.

Section Five presents several cases to show the HAP in action. The authors duly note that no inventory should be used in isolation.

So what does one make of all this description? The HAP addresses an important group, adolescents, with a set of obvious content items grouped in meaningful scales of decent reliability. Yet, the HAP, developed over the decade of the 1980s, is incipient in such areas as the correlation of items to scales, development of a national norm base, and criterion validity of the concurrent and predictive types. Although the HAP is supposed to be behavioral, the only criterion studies presented concern factor structure and classification. There are no studies, for example, on whether those scoring high on Frustration Tolerance (FT) differ on tasks tapping that quality when contrasted with low FT scorers. Specific, behavioral validity studies are needed.

Similarly, before the HAP can be useful in clinical settings where dissimulation may be a problem, studies concerning response distortion are needed. We simply do not know how the Guarded Response scale works, though we do know that youth, particularly troubled ones, are prone to exaggerations.

In sum, the HAP is akin to a hypothesis that is yet to be tested. There seems to be a set of obviously stated, readable items that cluster in three areas, and have some reasonable reliabilities and modestly representative norms groups. The intrepid test user may wish to use the HAP in concert with other information sources and inventories, and develop local norms. The HAP, however, is an inventory in search of validity.

[2.17]
Hilson Career Satisfaction Index.

Purpose: To aid in employee "fitness-for-duty" evaluations, promotion, and special assignment decisions.
Population: Public safety/security officers.
Publication Date: 1989.

Acronym: HCSI.
Scores, 13: Stress Patterns, Stress Symptoms, Drug/Alcohol Abuse, Interpersonal Support, Anger/Hostility Patterns, Disciplinary History, Excusing Attitudes, Aggression/Hostility, Dissatisfaction with Career, Dissatisfaction with Supervisor, Relationship with Co-Workers, Dissatisfaction with Job, Defensiveness.
Administration: Group.
Price Data, 1993: $60 per complete starter kit including test booklet, 3 computer-scorable answer sheets, and manual ('89, 40 pages); $2 per test booklet; $2.50 per 10 Scantron/standard answer sheets; $3 per 10 Sentry answer sheets; $15 per manual; scoring services offered by publisher at $10–$12.75 per test (volume discounts available).
Time: (25–35) minutes.
Author: Robin Inwald.
Publisher: Hilson Research, Inc.
Cross References: See T4:1166 (1 reference).

This test has not been reviewed in *The Mental Measurements Yearbook*.

[2.18]
Inwald Personality Inventory [Revised].

Purpose: "To aid public safety/law enforcement and security agencies in selecting new officers."
Population: Public safety, security and law enforcement applicants (post-conditional job offer only).
Publication Dates: 1980–1992.
Acronym: IPI.
Scores, 26: Guardedness, Externalized Behavior Measures (Actions [Alcohol, Drugs, Driving Violations, Job Difficulties, Trouble with the Law and Society, Absence Abuse], Attitudes [Substance Abuse, Antisocial Attitudes, Hyperactivity, Rigid Type, Type A]), Internalized Conflict Measures (Illness Concerns, Treatment Programs, Anxiety, Phobic Personality, Obsessive Personality, Depression, Loner, Unusual Experiences/Thoughts), Interpersonal Conflict Measures (Lack of Assertiveness, Interpersonal Difficulties, Undue Suspiciousness, Family Conflicts, Sexual Concerns, Spouse/Mate Conflicts).
Administration: Group.
Price Data, 1993: $60 per complete starter kit including test booklet, 3 computer-scorable answer sheets, and manual ('92, 78 pages); $2 per test booklet; $2.50 per 10 Scantron/standard answer sheets; $3 per 10 Sentry answer sheets; $15 per manual; scoring service offered by publisher at $10–$12.75 per test; (all prices may be adjusted for volume discounts).
Time: (30–45) minutes.
Author: Robin Inwald.
Publisher: Hilson Research, Inc.
Cross References: Reviews by Brian Bolton and Richard I. Lanyon originally appeared in 12:194; see also T4:1275

(1 reference); for reviews of an earlier edition by Samuel Juni and Niels G. Waller, see 11:183 (2 references); for reviews of an earlier edition by Brian Bolton and Jon D. Swartz, see 9:530.

Review of the Inwald Personality Inventory [Revised] by BRIAN BOLTON, University Professor, Arkansas Research and Training Center in Vocational Rehabilitation, University of Arkansas, Fayetteville, AR:

Recent allegations of police corruption; unwarranted use of force, including brutality and murder; and other forms of misbehavior have brought to public attention the importance of careful selection of police officer candidates. The Inwald Personality Inventory (IPI) was developed 12 years ago for the express purpose of improving the effectiveness of the law enforcement officer selection process. After a decade of experience in candidate evaluation and the accumulation of considerable evidence for predictive validity, it is appropriate now to rereview the IPI.

My first review of the IPI was published in the *Ninth Mental Measurements Yearbook* (Bolton, 1985). Since then the IPI computer report has been expanded and the IPI technical manual has been revised, with the results of recent validity studies added, along with other changes. For the convenience of readers who would like to refer to the original review, the psychometric issues are addressed below in the same order as in the first review. However, the current review can also be read independently of the initial review.

The IPI booklet and the scored scales have not been modified. The 26 scales are grouped into five types of measures: Validity (i.e., Guardedness), Acting-Out Behavior (e.g., Drugs, Trouble with the Law and Society), Attitudes and Temperament (e.g., Hyperactivity, Rigid Type), Internalized Conflict (e.g., Anxiety, Obsessive Personality), and Interpersonal Conflict (e.g., Interpersonal Difficulties, Family Conflicts).

Dr. Inwald did not explain how she selected or developed the 26 scales, except to say that the scales were designed using a "common sense" approach to the measurement of behavioral patterns relevant to successful performance in a stressful occupation. She generated the 310 IPI items from a review of over 2,500 pre-employment interviews with public safety officer candidates. No specific guidelines were followed; the author simply depended on her "best judgment" to identify the items for the inventory.

Several comments about the construction of the IPI are warranted. First, because Dr. Inwald is a psychologist, it must be assumed that she relied, in part, on the results of several decades of personality assessment research to develop the IPI scales. And although it is true that the rational (or deductive) approach to test construction has been demonstrated to be as effective as sophisticated statistical strategies, this does not relieve test authors of the responsibility for providing an outline of the instrument development plan.

I am sure that Dr. Inwald had a tentative map of the behavioral domain that she wanted to measure firmly in mind when she initiated work on the IPI, but that plan should have been made explicit for users. What was the specific rationale for the various scales? Where did the ideas for the scales originate? At the very least, the manual should include a table showing the items that are keyed on each of the 26 scales. This information would provide literal (content) definitions of the scales.

The data presented in the manual do not permit an accurate evaluation of the dimensionality of the IPI. Tabled factor analytic results include fewer than half of the 26 scales. These incomplete data suggest that one factor accounts for about 60% of the variability in the IPI scales. This finding is not unreasonable, considering the relatively high proportion of multiply keyed items (i.e., more than half of the items are scored on two or more scales). With all of the data that have been collected, there is really no excuse for not publishing a definitive factor analysis of the IPI.

The IPI can be scored only by the publisher. The computer-generated IPI report includes six sections. The narrative section provides one brief interpretive paragraph for each of the 26 scales. These are previously prepared or "canned" statements that correspond to score intervals on the scales. The author repeatedly cautions users not to quote these interpretive statements in psychological reports. The second section lists "critical items" for follow-up evaluation and converts the total to a standard score. It was not explained how the critical responses were identified; presumably, the author's clinical judgment was the criterion applied.

The third section of the IPI report presents a statistical prediction of the risk rating (low, moderate, high) assigned by a psychologist after conducting a comprehensive assessment based on other tests and an interview. The fourth section includes statistical predictions of four performance criteria: tardiness, absences, disciplinary actions, and termination. The fifth section is a standard normative profile of the 26 scale scores in a graphical form. The final section contains a printout of the examinee's responses to the 310 items.

The description of the IPI computer report contains a statement that separate norms for males and females are used, but a short section at the end of the manual indicates that a combined norm group is employed. The current normative sample is apparently composed of 1,512 male and 873 female public safety officer applicants. No other demographic information is provided. An analysis of the recommended decision rule for designating "high risk" candidates identified equal proportions of males and females in the normative sample. Interestingly, an earlier study of sex difference found IPI results consistent with "stereotypical behavior patterns of males and females" (manual, p. 44).

Although the normative sample is not adequately described, the normative data tabled in the manual suggest that females and minority candidates may be overrepresented. Without presenting any supporting data, the author indicates in a short sentence that "National norms on the IPI have remained stable over the past decade, with the exception of the DV (Driving Violations) scale" (p. 12). Considering the enormous amount of data that have been collected during the last 12 years, it should be a straightforward task to construct a large normative sample that is representative in terms of sex, race, age, location, position, and other relevant demographic variables. This information should be detailed in the manual.

The only reliability statistics presented for the IPI scales are the original figures. Median test-retest coefficients with a 6- to 8-week interval for male and female correction officer candidates were .72 and .70, respectively. Almost all coefficients were between .60 and .80. Four of the scales are rather short, with just three, five, six, and eight items. Although the reported reliabilities for the

IPI scales are adequate, it should be noted that the coefficients would be somewhat higher with a more appropriate interval of 1 to 2 weeks.

The strongest feature of the IPI is the program of ongoing validation research. Since 1982, two dozen studies of the predictive validity of the IPI have been carried out. The typical investigation of law enforcement officer candidates compared the IPI with the MMPI (Minnesota Multiphasic Personality Inventory) in predicting a variety of performance criteria. The outcomes usually analyzed were termination and disciplinary reviews, with lateness, absences, and supervisory ratings often included. Various other criteria were also studied, such as psychologists' risk ratings, derelictions, results of urinalysis, psychiatric illness, and examination scores.

The outcomes were typically assessed between 6 and 12 months after the IPI was administered, but two investigators obtained follow-up data on hired candidates 5 and 7 years later. The research samples included police officer applicants, correction officer candidates, government security personnel applicants, and candidates for other law enforcement positions. Samples were divided by sex and occasionally separated by race/ethnicity (White, Black, Hispanic). The results of cross-validated statistical analyses demonstrated that the IPI consistently predicted the performance criteria more accurately than the MMPI, but that the two instruments in combination produced the most accurate predictions.

The latter result is consistent with the findings of a redundancy analysis of the IPI and MMPI. These two instruments have a rather small overlap, suggesting that the IPI generally measures nonpathological characteristics and behavior patterns. It is unfortunate the results of the validity investigations are presented only in nonstandardized abstracts in the manual. A tabulation consisting of the samples, procedures, and findings of each study, with an overall statistical integration, would be an excellent way to summarize the predictive validity of the IPI. Ironically, the manual does include a nice summary table for a dozen "selected" predictive studies that is not referred to in the validity section!

The final section of the manual contains a discussion of the implications of the Americans with Disabilities Act when using the IPI as a psychological screening instrument. Two issues are critical: the IPI has empirically documented job-relatedness and it has never been recommended for use in diagnosing specific mental disorders. After reviewing the opinions of several professional organizations, the author concluded that the IPI can be appropriately used in the assessment of police officer candidates, but should be administered only after a conditional job offer has been made.

SUMMARY. The IPI was developed to assist psychologists in the assessment of police officer candidates.

The revised IPI has an expanded computer report and is supported by additional validity evidence. The manual does not present the rationale for the development of the instrument, nor is the normative sample adequately described. The manual is poorly organized and should be revised again. During the past decade two dozen studies of the predictive validity of the IPI against a variety of outcome criteria have been conducted. The research results support the value of the IPI in assessing the suitability of law enforcement officer applicants. Despite the deficiencies noted above, it can be concluded that the IPI has been demonstrated to be useful for its intended application.

REVIEWER'S REFERENCE

Bolton, B. (1985). [Review of the Inwald Personality Inventory]. In J. V. Mitchell, Jr. (Ed.), *The ninth mental measurements yearbook* (pp. 711–713). Lincoln, NE: Buros Institute of Mental Measurements.

Review of the Inwald Personality Inventory [Revised] by RICHARD I. LANYON, Professor of Psychology, Arizona State University, Tempe, AZ:

This is the third *MMY* review for the Inwald Personality Inventory (IPI), and it is occasioned by the appearance of the revised edition of the manual in 1992. The IPI is a 310-item, 26-scale, true/false inventory intended "to aid public safety/law enforcement agencies in selecting new officers who will be able to satisfy job requirements" (technical manual, p. 2). Scoring is available only through Hilson Research, Inc., by mailing back the answer sheet or by computer linkage. A computerized narrative report is provided to the user; however, the manual author warns the user not to utilize statements from the report unless independent information has been obtained to verify the accuracy of the statements.

The manual author states the IPI scales were designed "to measure specific behavioral patterns or characteristics judged appropriate and necessary in the evaluation of a job candidate's "suitability" to perform in a stressful occupation" (p. 5). Representative examples of scale names include Rigid Type, Alcohol, Job Difficulties, Phobic Personality, Depression, and Undue Suspiciousness. The manual author points out that the bars on the computer-generated profile graph are divided into three areas: Externalized Behavior Measures, Internalized Conflict Measures, and Interpersonal Conflict Measures. In fact, they are divided into four areas, plus the Guardedness scale as a fifth area, and the computerized narrative is also divided into four areas. Eight sets of norms for males and eight for females, with sample sizes ranging from 15 to more than 2,000 are presented. It is not indicated which normative group or groups are used in the preparation of the computerized report, or if they differ according to the person being tested.

The test itself appears to be basically unchanged from its original publication in 1982. Its development at that time employed procedures that have been obsolete for many years. Essentially, there was no development at all. On the basis of clinical experience with employment interviewing, items were written and fitted, using the author's "best judgment," into scale categories that were apparently also created subjectively. The extensive available technology of test construction appears to have been completely ignored. The essential components of this technology, as demonstrated in the development of tests such as the NEO Personality Inventory (Costa & McCrae, 1986; 330) and the Personality Assessment Inventory (Morey, 1991; 290), include the formulation of concepts based on a systematic plan, development of a definition and universe of content for each concept, preparation of items that map each universe, and psychometric procedures that include the computation of item reliabilities, skewness, relationship to social desirability, item correlations within each preliminary scale and with other scales, and exploratory and/or confirmatory factor analyses. The purpose of this tedious but necessary work is, of course, to build into each scale the potential for the greatest possible validity in prac-

tical use. Indeed, each step contributes to the potential for predictive accuracy in a unique way.

The use of no more than common sense in putting a test together practically guarantees a low ceiling on predictive accuracy, and the validity research reported in the manual confirms this expectation. An overall analysis of reported studies that give cross-validated figures for predicting job success show an overall hit rate of only about 60%. A further difficulty is that most of the studies use discriminant function analyses, which yield the "statistically best" prediction. It is unlikely that either the computerized narrative report or the test user's subjective analysis of the profile could achieve even this level of accuracy.

Examination of the several exploratory factor analyses presented in the manual indicates that a single factor consistently accounts for about two thirds of the common variance in the IPI scales. This factor is represented by the scales Rigid Type, Type "A," and Undue Suspiciousness. The second factor represents substance abuse/impulsiveness/hyperactivity, and the content of the third factor varies among the analyses. However, the relatively few studies listing the actual scales that carry the greatest predictive power for job success versus failure show that two entirely different concepts are relied on to make these predictions: a "mental health problems" concept and a "previous legal and job difficulties" concept. Thus, it is likely that a test assessing the latter concepts, developed in a methodologically adequate manner, would have better success than the IPI in making relevant predictions in the public safety personnel area.

The major difficulties with the IPI and the 1982 manual, as identified in Bolton's (1985) review, remain in the 1992 edition. In addition to those discussed above, the computer-generated report has no demonstrated empirical basis, and the manual author instructs the user to all but disregard it. Thus, there appears to be no supportable reason to continue offering it. Also, the profile form incorrectly displays a zero through 100 range for the *T*-scores that represent each scale, giving the impression that they are percentiles.

OVERVIEW. Although the manual emphasizes that the IPI is to be used as only one of a number of sources of information in making a personnel decision, it is difficult to believe that enough useful information is added by such low hit rates to justifying using it. It is commendable that a significant amount of research has been done on the ability of the IPI to make useful predictions, and those data give the beginnings of an empirical basis for understanding what predictors might be most relevant. Thus, a partial foundation is laid for a new and properly constructed instrument that would be potentially useful.

REVIEWER'S REFERENCES

Bolton, B. (1985). [Review of the Inwald Personality Inventory.] In J. V. Mitchell, Jr. (Ed.), *The ninth mental measurements yearbook* (pp. 711–713). Lincoln, NE: Buros Institute of Mental Measurements.

Costa, P. T., Jr., & McCrae, R. R. (1986). *NEO Personality Inventory: Manual.* Odessa, FL: Psychological Assessment Resources.

Morey, C. C. (1991). *Personality Assessment Inventory: Manual.* Odessa, FL: Psychological Assessment Resources.

[2.19]

The Lawrence Psychological Forensic Examination.

Purpose: "A guide for comprehensive psychological assessments and report writing with clients in the criminal, juvenile and civil justice systems."

Population: Juvenile, criminal, and civil justice clients.

Publication Dates: 1978–1983.

Acronym: LAW-PSI.

Scores: No scores as such; ratings and judgments.

Administration: Individual.

Price Data: Available from publisher.

Comments: Ratings by mental health professional; handbook contains descriptive legal information for report writing, and 3 tests.

Author: Stephen B. Lawrence.

Publisher: Lawrence Psychological Center.

a) LAWRENCE PSYCHOLOGICAL FORENSIC EXAMINATION.

Comments: Guided forensic interview to determine precise mental states of mind, life history, or prediction of future client behavior.

b) LAWRENCE MENTAL COMPETENCY TEST.

Acronym: LAW-COMP.

Comments: To aid clinicians in making judgments needed to determine a client's present legal mental competency to stand trial.

c) LAWRENCE PSYCHOLOGICAL FORENSIC EXAMINATION REPORT EVALUATION.

Acronym: LAW-PSI/EVAL.

Comments: A rating instrument for evaluating written forensic reports.

Cross References: The review by Samuel Roll originally appeared in 10:171.

Review of The Lawrence Psychological Forensic Examination by SAMUEL ROLL, Professor of Psychology and Psychiatry, University of New Mexico, Albuquerque, NM:

The Lawrence Psychological Forensic Examination is, in reality, not a test or even an examination in the sense of a psychological examination. It is, rather, a compilation of a broad variety of suggestions, information, checklists, guides to administering other tests and compiling information from other test data, legal definitions, excerpts from California jury instructions, and guidelines for probation. It even contains a model of a predeposition agreement for the psychologist to use in working with an attorney, estimated potential blood alcohol concentration depending on type and number of drinks and body weight, sections of DSM-III, a description of the author's own version of personality traits and a sample professional resume. It might more correctly be labeled "Thoughts, checklists, and sundry materials which may be useful in a forensic practice." Its worst general feature is that it is almost unedited and varies in quality from material that is ready for publication to rather poorly xeroxed and unintegrated material from unidentified sources.

One part of the vast amount of information presented is Lawrence's own version of a mental status exam which, like most mental status exams, contains guidelines for the evaluation of general appearance, speech, mood, sensorium, symptoms, etc. It also contains an outline for a life history, a developmental history, a family history, an educational history, a military history, an occupational history, criminal-legal history, medical history, etc. It is more lengthy than most guidelines for a mental status exam and, as expected, more geared to data of value in a forensic setting. As is the case with most mental status exams, it is a guideline for collecting data rather than a psychological test. As such, there are no norms, no reliability data, no validity data, and certainly no indications of conceptual validity or theoretical orientation.

Another component of the Lawrence is the Lawrence Present Mental Competence Test. As is the case with the mental status exam in the Lawrence, it also is not a test in the sense that there are no norms or other psychometric information available describing it to potential users. It does, unlike the mental status exam, have a conceptual orientation because it tries to capture in a structured interview format the legal criteria for mental competency offered by the California penal code. The California criteria match those of most states. Based on those criteria (e.g., that the person can understand the proceedings and can cooperate in the defense) the structured interview aims at collecting two different kinds of information. The first is referred to as "Factual Criterion" and taps the patient's capacity to understand his or her current legal situation, the charges, legal rights, legal issues and procedures, the role of defense counsel, of prosecuting attorney, judge, etc., and the range and nature of possible pleas. The second kind of information, referred to as "Inferential Criterion," includes capacity to cooperate with counsel, understand the need to provide counsel with information, need to maintain a consistent legal strategy, comprehend counsel's instruction and advice, follow court testimony for contradictions, testify relevantly and protect himself or herself by using available legal safeguards, identify defense witnesses, and avoid mental deterioration throughout the legal proceedings. Based on the information from the interview the psychologist ranks each area as to whether the patient had good or adequate knowledge, no knowledge, or inadequate knowledge. A numerical scale is provided but only as a rough outline or summary of the data. The Competence Test is not designed to be used in conjunction with supporting norms or other psychometric aids.

The companion Lawrence Psychological Forensic Examination Reports is a collection of sample forensic evaluation reports written by Lawrence using the outlines, checklists, interviews, and suggestions that are contained in the Lawrence Psychological Forensic Examination.

In sum, the Lawrence is a kind of outline for an applied textbook in the area of forensic psychology. It certainly would be useful to almost all beginners and to a great many experienced professionals in the area of forensic psychology. None of the material approaches being a "test" with acceptable psychometric properties. Researchers and practitioners looking for a more standardly defined and supported test of competency should check the Competency Screening Test (Lipsitt, Lelos, &

McGarry, 1971) with the caution the instrument is appropriate only for subjects who are literate.

REVIEWER'S REFERENCE
Lipsitt, P. D., Lelos, D., & McGarry, A. L. (1971). Competency for trial: A screening instrument. American Journal of Psychiatry, 128, 105-109.

[2.20]
Lifestyle Assessment Questionnaire.

Purpose: Provides individuals with a measurement of their lifestyle status in various wellness categories, offers a health risk appraisal component that lists the individual's top ten risks of death, projects an achievable health age, makes suggestions for lifestyle improvement, and offers a stimulus for positive lifestyle change by providing a guide to successful implementation of that change.
Population: Adults with a minimum of 10th grade education.
Publication Dates: 1978–1991.
Scores, 16: Physical (Exercise, Nutrition, Self-Care, Vehicle Safety, Drug Usage), Social/Environmental, Emotional (Emotional Awareness and Acceptance, Emotional Management), Intellectual, Occupational, Spiritual, Actual Age, Appraised Health Age, Achievable Health Age, Top 10 Risks of Death, Lifestyle Improvement Suggestions.
Administration: Group.
Price Data, 1993: $3 per literature set including questionnaire, results folder, Behavior Change Guide, and scannable answer sheet; $.25 per scannable answer sheet; $10 per individual National Wellness Processing Center scoring; $1,995 per software program and license.
Time: (45–60) minutes.
Comments: Computer scoring or scoring by National Wellness Institute available; information on up to four wellness areas included in scoring report; individual and group reports available.
Authors: Dennis Elsenrath, Bill Hettler, and Fred Leafgren.
Publisher: National Wellness Institute.
Cross References: Reviews by Michael B. Brown and William E. Martin, Jr. will appear in the 13th MMY; see also T4:1461 (3 references).

Review of the Lifestyle Assessment Questionnaire by MICHAEL B. BROWN, Assistant Professor of Psychology, East Carolina University, Greenville, NC:

The Lifestyle Assessment Questionnaire (LAQ) is a tool for evaluating an adult's habits and knowledge on a number of health and wellness dimensions. The questionnaire requires the respondent to answer 227 questions about demographics, lifestyle, and health risks. An additional 43 questions allow for the respondent to request additional information on a wide variety of health-related topics. Responses are made on an optical scanning sheet, which can be scored on site through a single site software license or through a scoring and interpretation service offered through the publisher.

Computer-generated individual and group reports are available. The individual report includes a wellness report, health-risk appraisal, and resources for further information on the topics requested by the user. The wellness report is considered an assessment of the individual's lifestyle in six life areas including occupational, emotional, intellectual, physical, social, and spiritual dimensions. Percentage scores are provided for the individual, the average scores of individuals in the organization with whom the individual is taking the assessment, and the average score of the same age/sex reference group. The health-risk appraisal provides an assessment of an individual's risk of death over the next decade and provides suggestions for lifestyle improvements. Results are presented for risk of death, life expectancy, and life expectancy if suggested changes are made. A behavior change guide called Making Wellness Work For You provides a systematic guide for making a specific behavior change. The personal growth resource list provides bibliographic resources for further information on specific health and wellness topics. The management group report provides a summary of lifestyle and health-risk status of the individuals in an organization. This report is intended to serve as both an organizational wellness needs assessment and an evaluation of the organization's wellness programming.

MANUAL. The LAQ software package comes with a ring-bound user's guide that is devoted to installation and use of the software package, interpretation of results, and a description of its technical characteristics. Several pages of technical information were provided in addition to that in the manual. Sample individual and group reports are also available with the manual. There are no guidelines on qualifications of users or overall strategy for the use of the instrument.

TECHNICAL CHARACTERISTICS. There are significant limitations with both the types and adequacy of technical data. Although the reference group includes a large sample of over 47,000 persons, descriptive data are provided only for age and sex. No data are provided for other relevant descriptors of the norm group, such as socioeconomic status or level of education. Although the reference group includes persons from 15 years of age and older, 23% of the sample were 18 years old. With the exception of those identified as college students, the method of selection and identification of the remainder of the reference group is not specified. Based upon these limitations, it is unclear how representative the reference group is or how well the group may represent persons of different ethnic and socioeconomic groups. Information on the derivation of health-risk data is also limited. Health risk is said to be based on data from the most recent U.S. Centers for Disease Control epidemiological data, although the exact year of the data is not specified. No information is provided for how life expectancy scores are computed, or how forecast life expectancy was calculated.

Reliability data are reported for test-retest reliability over 2-week periods for the wellness scale. Test-retest reliabilities of the wellness categories ranged from .57—.87, with an average coefficient of .76. Test-retest reliability for the subscales ranged from .81–.97. However, the two studies reported in the manual included only 15 and 39 subjects, which is an inadequate number of subjects from which to ascertain reliability. The internal consistency of the wellness subscales ranged from .67–.94. However, no information was provided from which to identify the size of the group used to determine internal consistency.

Content validity is said to have been established by a panel of experts, who are not identified further in the manual. Later in the manual, content validity was said to be ascertained by two experts in measurement and health promotion. Factor analysis was said to be used to determine construct validity, but no data are provided that identify the factors utilized, resulting factor structure, or factor scores. Two studies are cited that are said to establish criterion validity. The first study reports that the LAQ emotional subscales can differentiate college students who are receiving psychotherapy from those who are not. Few additional details are provided on this study. The other criterion-validity study investigated the relationship between the LAQ wellness scales and objective physiological indicators of health. No relationship was found in the college students studied, although a relationship was found between the scores taken "as a whole" and "general health." There is a section that provides research citations for a number of health risks. Another section follows listing research studies that used the LAQ. Its placement here is potentially misleading, as the research cited does not study the technical characteristics of the LAQ, but uses the LAQ only as a measurement tool for research on wellness intervention.

OVERALL EVALUATION. The Lifestyle Assessment Questionnaire has inadequate technical data to support its use as a norm-referenced measurement tool. The reference group, although large, is not sufficiently described to allow a test user to be certain that users of various socioeconomic and ethnic groups are represented in the reference group. In addition, the reference group is heavily weighted to persons of college age. Reliability studies, although encouraging, are not large enough to demonstrate reliability. Validity data are not sufficiently described in the manual, and do not illuminate the meaning or predictive power of the scales. The scale scores for the wellness portion of the inventory have only face validity. The health-risk appraisal portion may be based on adequate epidemiological data, but this is not clear from the information provided. There is no information supporting the forecast life expectancy. This could be misleading to clients and unsophisticated users. The Health Risk Appraisal may be useful, although its suggestions for reducing risk are very generic and somewhat unimaginative. For example, suggestions to reduce risk of motor vehicle accidents include "obey all rules of the road" and "don't drive while tired." The Making Wellness Work For You behavior change guide is a thorough and well-constructed device that could be very helpful to persons who are motivated to change.

Review of the Lifestyle Assessment Questionnaire by WILLIAM E. MARTIN, JR., Professor of Educational Psychology, Northern Arizona University, Flagstaff, AZ:

According to an information pamphlet provided by the National Wellness Institute, Inc., "The Lifestyle Assessment Questionnaire (LAQ)

is a powerful wellness tool developed in 1976 by the Board of Directors and Cofounders of The National Wellness Institute." The LAQ is intended to serve a dual purpose for assessment and education. The assessment purpose of the LAQ is to provide individuals with a measurement of their lifestyle status in the following six wellness dimensions: occupational, intellectual, spiritual, social, physical, and emotional. The measurement information generated from the LAQ provides an educational stimulus for individuals to change their lifestyles.

The LAQ is divided into four primary sections. The first of the four sections, Personal Data, comprises 12 multiple-choice questions related to age, sex, etc. The second section is the Lifestyle Inventory. The Lifestyle Inventory has 11 subsections that relate to the six wellness dimensions. However, it is not clear to me how some of the subsections would be grouped with the six wellness dimensions (i.e., self-care, vehicle safety, and drug usage and awareness). This section has 185 statements formatted with a 5-point Likert-type response ranging from *Almost never* (less than 10% of the time) to *Almost always* (90% or more of the time). The number of questions per subsection varies from 10 to 31 questions.

The third section of the LAQ is Health Risk Appraisal and consists of interlocked questions: 33 for men and 38 for women. For this section, both multiple-choice and short answer questions are used. The final section, Topics for Personal Growth, is a listing of 43 lifestyle topics. In this section, the examinee is instructed to select four lifestyle topics for which they would like to receive additional information.

The Lifestyle Inventory of the LAQ is used to generate individual reports that compare an individual's score to those of the group with which the test was taken and to group scores for all those who have taken the LAQ since 1978. The Health Risk Appraisal scores are compared to national averages for individuals of the same sex and age. Group reports are also generated to provide direction to organizations for developing wellness programs.

DEVELOPMENT OF THE SCALES. The authors state that when the LAQ was initially developed, it was reviewed by a panel of health promotion and wellness professionals to verify the validity of the instrument's content. The 11 assessment categories of the LAQ's Lifestyle Inventory were reviewed by professionals working in each of the six wellness dimensions and the Health Risk Appraisal section was developed using research data from the Carter Center at Emory University and the Center for Disease Control.

RELIABILITY AND VALIDITY. A two-page National Wellness Institute, Inc. flyer briefly described two studies that have generated test-retest reliability and internal consistency coefficients and two studies that were intended to reflect test validity of the LAQ. The first test-retest study was conducted in 1982 with 39 parents of incoming university students. For this sample, the 2-week test-retest reliability coefficients on the Lifestyle Inventory scales ranged from .57 to .87 with an "overall" coefficient of .76. The Personal Growth section yielded a .87 coefficient and a .90 test-retest reliability coefficient was reported for the Health Risk Appraisal section. A 1985 study of 15 female university students demonstrated test-retest reliability coefficients ranging from .81 to .97; however, no time interval was identified. Additionally, coefficients of internal consistency ranging from .67 to .94 were reported as part of this study. The discussion presented relative to validity studies was too brief and unclear to report with any accuracy. For example, a result of one of the studies was "there is considerable support for external validity of the physical scales." The use of the term external validity is confusing because it is a concept related to research design not measurement. It appears that the authors meant to use the term criterion-related validity.

ADMINISTRATION, SCORING, AND INTERPRETATION. Lifestyle Assessment Questionnaires are given to the individual to self-administer and can be taken in an individual or group setting. Either way, it is not necessary for a test administrator to be present. Directions are provided throughout the questionnaire and test takers respond to questions using scannable answer sheets. Completed questionnaires can be scored either by sending the materials to the National Wellness Institute Processing Center or by purchasing a software program and license. Individual and group reports (where appropriate) are gener-

ated that provide numerical information and narrative interpretation. Scores on the individual report range from 0 to 100 and represent the percent of possible points for each area. Scores and bar charts are given for wellness dimensions and subcategories. An individual's LAQ scores are compared to those of the group (when applicable) with which the test was taken and to individuals who have taken it since 1978. The individual's Health Risk Appraisal scores are compared to a national population average for individuals of the same age and sex. Additionally, the individual report presents information concerning suggestions on increasing expected years of life, health-risk appraisal forecast information, and available resources related to various health-related topics. When a group of individuals from a shared organizational setting take the LAQ as a group, a group report is generated. The report reflects group frequency and percentage scores by dimensions and subcategories.

SUMMARY. Although the LAQ has functional use appeal, is attractively packaged, and has been used since 1978, there are technical weaknesses that must be considered in using the instrument. The first concern relates to the instrument's construct validity. Established methods in test construction appear not to have been used in the development of the LAQ scales including: (a) a theoretical grounding of the construct of wellness, (b) empirically derived factors and items, and/or (c) evidence of homogeneity in relation to the construct. Do the six dimensions of the LAQ accurately represent the construct of wellness? Do the items accurately reflect the dimensions of wellness? The validity and reliability studies presented appear weak partially because they are difficult to understand due to limited information and a lack of clarity on what is presented. Additionally, there were several methodological problems reported in the studies such as using only 15 subjects for test/restest reliability estimates and establishing content validity of the LAQ "with evaluation by two experts in measurement and health promotion." Second, there have been significant changes in knowledge of wellness since 1978. There is no evidence that the authors have adapted the LAQ to evolving research and changing knowledge about wellness. Based upon the first two concerns, it is highly recommended that a thorough literature review covering the last 20 years be completed and a factor analytic study be conducted to generate a wellness construct that is empirically derived. Then, the established steps for test construction can be followed. There is no doubt that a psychometric instrument that soundly measures a construct of wellness would be beneficial in promoting healthful practices by individuals. Accurate measurement of a valid and stable construct must, however, be demonstrated for users to have confidence in the LAQ.

[2.21]
London House Personnel Selection Inventory.

Purpose: "Helps identify individuals who are likely to be honest and have positive attitudes toward work, safety and customer service."
Population: Job applicants.
Publication Dates: 1975–1980.
Acronym: PSI.
Scores: 14 scales: Honesty, Supervision Attitudes, Tenure, Employee/Customer Relations, Drug Avoidance, Work Values, Safety, Math, Emotional Stability, Nonviolence, Productivity, Responsibility, Applicant Employability Index, Detailed Personal and Behavioral History.
Administration: Group.
Forms: 19 versions available including non-integrity test versions.
Price Data: Available from publisher.
Time: Administration time not reported.
Author: SRA/London House.
Publisher: SRA/London House.
Cross References: The review by William I. Sauser originally appeared in 9:631; see also T3:1339 (2 references).

Review of the London House Personnel Selection Inventory by WILLIAM I. SAUSER, JR., Associate Professor and Head, Department of Management, Auburn University at Montgomery, Montgomery, AL:

According to its manual, the London House Personnel Selection Inventory (PSI) is intended to evaluate "attitudes, opinions, and experiences of job applicants in three critical areas: Dishonesty, Violence, and Drug abuse." The PSI is administered to job applicants, either individually or in groups, on the premises of the employing company. Test booklets are then mailed to London House for coding and scoring, and a standardized Test Analysis Report is mailed back to the company. For faster turnaround, the PSI may be coded in the employment office; these codes are then transmitted by telephone to London House, the data are key-entered and analyzed, and the nine scores are provided while the caller is still on the line. Follow-up written reports are mailed to the employing company when the test booklets are returned to London House. To maintain test security, all test booklets, even those damaged or partially used, must be returned to London House. Directions for administering and coding the PSI are very clear; no special training is required to use it.

The test booklet itself is 16 pages long and contains, in addition to the test questions, instructions to the test-taker, a compliance notice regarding equal employment opportunity, a consent form, a short survey about the employing company, and a lengthy, detailed survey of the applicant's personal and employment history. The PSI items take a variety of forms, including rating scales, checklists, and open-ended questions. Only the rating scale items are coded and scored; thus the reason for including many of the questions is unclear to this reviewer. The items themselves are straightforward, but the response options do not always seem to fit the question stems. The PSI is not a timed test and no estimates of administration time are provided in the manual. However, given the length and detail of the survey, it appears that many respondents would require an hour or more to complete the PSI.

Interpreting the nine scores is a straightforward matter. The percentile scores simply rank the applicant in relation to the normative sample. The risk category scores rate the applicant as either low, borderline, or high risk based on past behavior, and the low risk confidence scores predict the probability that the applicant will avoid future problems in each area. The manual provides no information regarding the precision of these predictions.

Although no scoring keys or technical data are reported in the test manual, it does include abstracts of 21 cited studies of the PSI's reliability, validity, and fairness. A comparison of these abstracts with the full-length reports of each study (provided to this reviewer) reveal that the abstracts are accurate and are based on statistically significant research findings. The PSI appears to be a reliable and fair instrument; moreover, validity studies with a variety of designs, samples, and criteria have established that the PSI provides meaningful scores in all three areas.

A shortcoming of the PSI manual is that it does not warn the user of possible misuses of the test. The PSI elicits very sensitive information, and test administrators and coders should be told to keep all responses strictly confidential. The manual should also warn users not to make copies of test responses to place in application files, nor to base any decisions on individual item responses, since these have not been validated. The manual includes letters from an attorney attesting to the legality of using the PSI for selection purposes, but users should not be misled regarding the need to establish, through their own local studies, that the scores obtained by the PSI are job related, and/or that the PSI has no adverse impact on employment opportunities for protected groups.

In summary, the PSI appears to be a useful instrument for evaluating the risks, in terms of potential for dishonesty, violence, and drug abuse, associated with hiring job applicants. Although lengthy, the PSI is easy to administer and code, and its results can be obtained quickly and interpreted easily. Users of the test should, however, be given more explicit warning in the manual regarding potential misuses of the PSI.

[2.22]
Millon Adolescent Clinical Inventory.

Purpose: Designed to assess "an adolescent's personality, along with self-reported concerns and clinical syndromes."
Population: Ages 13–19.
Publication Date: 1993.
Acronym: MACI.
Scores: 27 scales: Personality Patterns (Introversive, Inhibited, Doleful, Submissive, Dramatizing, Egotistic, Unruly, Forceful, Conforming, Oppositional, Self-Demeaning, Borderline Tendency), Expressed Concerns (Identify Diffusion, Self-Devaluation, Body Disapproval, Sexual Discomfort, Peer Insecurity, Social Insensitivity, Family Discord, Childhood Abuse), Clinical Syndromes (Eating Dysfunctions, Substance Abuse Proneness, Delinquent Predisposition, Impulsive Propensity, Anxious Feelings, Depressive Affect, Suicidal Tendency), and 3 Modifying Indices (Disclosure, Desirability, Debasement).
Administration: Individual or group.
Price Data, 1994: $80 per Mail-In Preview Package; $80 per MICROTEST Q Preview Package; $18.60 per Prepaid Interpretive mail-in answer sheet; $18.60 per Prepaid Hispanic Interpretive mail-in answer sheet; $11 per prepaid Profile mail-in answer sheet; $11 per Prepaid Hispanic profile mail-in answer sheet; $12 per 25 MICROTEST Q answer sheets; $12 per 25 Hispanic MICROTEST Q answer sheets; $17.60 per Interpretive MICROTEST Q Administrations; $10 per Profile MICROTEST Q administrations; $41.50 per audio cassette (specify English or Hispanic); $23 per 10 handscoring test booklets; $32 per manual (123 pages); $200 per handscoring starter kit including manual, handscoring user's guide, 10 test booklets, 50 handscoring answer sheets, 50 handscoring work sheets, and 50 profile forms and handscoring keys; $100 per handscoring reorder kit including 50 handscoring answer sheets, 50 worksheets, and 50 profile sheets.
Time: (30) minutes.
Comments: Self-report personality inventory replacing the Millon Adolescent Personality Inventory (9:707); available in paper-and-pencil and on-line administration; MICROTEST Q, mail-in scoring, and handscoring available.
Authors: Theodore Millon with Carrie Millon and Roger Davis.
Publisher: NCS Assessments.
Cross References: Reviews by Paul Retzlaff and Richard B. Stuart originally appeared in 12:236 (6 references); see also T4:1633 (14 references); for reviews by Douglas T. Brown and Thomas A. Widiger of the Millon Adolescent Personality Inventory, see 9:707.

Review of the Millon Adolescent Clinical Inventory by PAUL RETZLAFF, Associate Professor of Psychology, University of Northern Colorado, Greeley, CO:

The Millon Adolescent Clinical Inventory (MACI) is a revision of the Millon Adolescent Personality Inventory (MAPI) (see MMY 9:707). The change in name is indicative of the very major revision that was undertaken. For the most part the changes are appropriate, useful, and welcome.

The MACI has 27 content scales and 4 response bias scales. It is intended for "disturbed" adolescents who have come to the attention of clinical professionals. It is not appropriate for screening or for the assessment of "normal" personality. The 160 sixth grade reading level items should be finished by most adolescents in 20 minutes.

The Personality Patterns scales (Introversive, Inhibited, Doleful, Submissive, Dramatizing, Egotistic, Unruly, Forceful, Conforming, Oppositional, Self-Demeaning, and Borderline Tendency) parallel the DSM-III-R/IV personality disorders in the order of their presentation in the Millon Clinical Multiaxial Inventory—II (MCMI-II/III) (see MMY 11:239). Specifically, Introversive is viewed as an adolescent equivalent of Schizoid, Inhibited as Avoidant, Doleful as Depressive, etc. The MACI includes a number of patterns/disorders that were not included in the MAPI including Doleful (Depressive), Forceful (Sadistic), Self-Demeaning (Self-Defeating), and Borderline Tendencies.

The expressed Concerns scales include Identity Diffusion, Self-Devaluation, Body Disapproval, Sexual Discomfort, Peer Insecurity, Social Insensitivity, Family Discord, and Childhood Abuse. Here Academic Confidence has been dropped from the MAPI and Childhood Abuse has been added. Also, the scale names have been changed to reflect high scores on the domains appropriately. For example, Self Concept has been changed to Identity Diffusion and Body Comfort to Body Disapproval.

The last section of the test has been changed from Behavioral Correlates to Clinical Syndromes. These include Eating Dysfunctions, Substance-Abuse Proneness, Delinquent Predisposition, Impulsive Propensity, Anxious Feelings, Depressive Affect, and Suicidal Tendency. Most of these are new to the MACI and represent the more clinical focus of this instrument. The inclusion of the Anxiety and Depression scales are of particular clinical importance.

The response bias scales are referred to as Modifying Indices and include Reliability, Disclosure, Desirability, and Debasement. The Reliability scale is a low level screen to determine if the patient could or did read the items. The first of the two items is, "I have not seen a car in the last ten years." With the typical motivational problems of an adolescent in treatment this is an important screen and, perhaps, three or four items should have been included. The Disclosure scale is similar to the Disclosure scale on the MCMI-II/III. It represents a linear combination of scale scores that are indicative of over- or under-reporting psychopathology. It should be fairly effective (Retzlaff, Sheehan, & Fiel, 1991). The final two indices are Desirability and Debasement. These, unfortunately, did not enjoy the very sophisticated domain construction model that the rest of the test did.

The construction of the test followed the domain theory construction model. It included face-valid pools of initial items, internal structural-statistical methods, and, finally, external empirical keying. As such, it encompasses most of the traditional methods of construction and should have high reliabilities and strong (cross) validities. The initial item pool was 331 items including the MAPI item set and newly written items. These items faced subsamples of a total subject pool of 1,017. After item-total homogeneity procedures, final validities were against clinician judgments. The Base Rate scores represent this underlying criterion referencing. On the basis of these construction procedures, items are weighted in the scoring of the test. This has been shown to be unnecessary (Retzlaff, Sheehan, & Lorr, 1990).

The Cronbach alpha reliabilities are excellent, ranging from .73 to .91. Most of these internal consistencies are in the .80s. The correlations against clinician judgments are not impressive and are largely between .10 and the .20s. They do not seem much worse though than the interrater reliability kappa statistics in the field trials of the DSMs. Finally, from a psychometric perspective, the interscale, intercorrelation matrix has far too many scales correlating with each other in the .70s. There seems to be a lack of specificity of the scales above and beyond what should be clinically expected.

This lack of scale specificity is the largest problem with the MACI and is a manifestation of the largest construction problem with the test. The 160 items are insufficient to score the 30 (Disclosure is a formula) scales. Indeed, the 160 items are keyed 923 times. Each item, on average, is keyed on six scales. As part of this problem, each scale has too many items keyed to it with most scales having 30 or more items out of the 160. To correct this, the test should have more items, fewer scales, and/or fewer items per scale. The intent was noble but so few items cannot be stretched that far.

The computer scoring and interpretation of the MACI is easy to use. The MACI is one of the first tests on National Computer System's new "Q" platform for Microsoft Windows. The software can be loaded on any number of computers and security is maintained by a small firmware device inserted in the printer port. There are a number of input, output, and utility options. The interpretations are informative and clinically useful. There should be a Macintosh version though.

The problems of too few items for too many scales aside, this is a good test. It includes personality variables mapped to DSM personality disorders, expressed concerns appropriate to adolescents, and clinical syndromes of significance. No other test even attempts this. In practice, the test works and works much better than the MAPI. There is no better test available.

REVIEWER'S REFERENCES

Retzlaff, P., Sheehan, E., & Lorr, M. (1990). MCMI-II scoring: Weighted and unweighted algorithms. *Journal of Personality Assessment, 55*, 219–223.

Retzlaff, P., Sheehan, E., & Fiel, A. (1991). MCMI-II report style and bias: Profile and validity scales analysis. *Journal of Personality Assessment, 56*, 466–477.

Review of the Millon Adolescent Clinical Inventory by RICHARD B. STUART, Professor Emeritus, Department of Psychiatry and Behavioral Sciences, School of Medicine, University of Washington, Seattle, WA:

The Millon Adolescent Clinical Inventory (MACI) is a revision of the Millon Adolescent Inventory (MAI), developed in 1974, and the Millon Adolescent Personality Inventory (MAPI), developed in 1982, which is identical to its predecessor in item content, but differs in its norms and intended uses. The original MAPI was written in two forms: the MAPI-C, designed for use by mental health workers assessing teenagers who exhibited emotional or behavioral disorders and who were in a diagnostic or treatment setting at the time of testing; and the MAPI-G, designed for use by guidance personnel in school settings in their efforts to determine which students would benefit from further psychological assessment. The MACI was developed to serve both purposes, taking advantage of suggestions from those who had used its predecessors for a decade, to make it more reflective of developments in its guiding theory, and to make it more consonant with recent developments in DSM-IV. In addition to adding new personality scales and weighting items differently, the MACI retains only 49 items used in its predecessors, adding 111 new ones.

The MACI consists of 160 items which are scored to yield 12 Personality scales, 8 Expressed Concerns scales, 7 Clinical Syndrome scales, and 4 modifying indices (Disclosure, Desirability, Debasement, and Reliability). From 2 to 48 items comprise each scale. Although not all items are used equally, a total of 923 items are included in the 32 varied scales, an average of 5.77 applications per item. Although Millon has surely anticipated this problem, there is a risk that adolescents who carelessly answer a few items may bias their scale scores in several areas. The justification, however, for this multiple use of items is its contribution to the brevity of the MACI.

The MACI is available in two pencil-and-paper formats, one for handscoring and one for computer scoring, as well as in English and Spanish audiocassettes. Its items are written at a sixth grade reading level and were easily comprehended by the adolescents to whom I administered the MACI as a test. Test administration took an average of 30 minutes, in contrast to the 20 minutes stipulated in the manual. Computer scoring can be done either on-site or by mailing protocols to NCS Assessments. The manual contains instructions for handscoring, with the admonition that this is a very complex process. The complexity stems from the need for the test scorer to make base rate transformations of raw scores, and then to adjust these scores for the age of the adolescent, as well as further adjustments for disclosure, anxiety/depression, desirability/debasement, and denial/complaint. In effect, the MACI cannot be handscored in an efficient manner, although those who intend to use it extensively are well advised to handscore at least a few protocols in order to better understand the ways in which subjects' responses are used.

Millon did not use projectable or population proportionate samples to establish norms for the MACI. Instead, norms were developed from a primary sample of 579 adolescents and two cross-validation samples of 139 and 194 each. Subjects in these three groups were subsequently pooled in a combined sample for the development of norms. All of the subjects were in treatment programs. Adolescents who were not identified as patients were not included in the normative sample, thus limiting the utility of the MACI for use as a screening tool with general adolescent populations. The three samples were 78.8% white, somewhat limiting the applicability of the norms to populations of nonwhite adolescents. An even more serious limitation stemming from the validating sample is the fact that although the test is recommended for use by adolescents ages 13–19, 18-year-olds comprised only 3.2%, and 19-year-olds only .03% of the development and cross-validating samples. At this time use of the MACI with 18- and 19-year-olds is ill-advised. If the MACI enjoys the wide use of its sister adult measure, the Millon Clinical Multiaxial Inventory-II (MCMI-II; T4:1635), Millon will surely be able to fill in the demographic gaps in his normative sample, enhancing the validity of using the MACI with the broader range of adolescents for which it was intended.

Items were selected for inclusion in the scales using the very careful criteria one has come to expect of Millon. Base rates were then developed for each item through an unfortunately arcane process which is difficult to follow in the manual. The value of this type of item weighting has not necessarily been established, and the process potentially threatens the validity of conclusions drawn from the MACI. Given the importance of base rates in scoring the MACI, its use with groups not included in its development should be undertaken with caution.

Reliability of the MACI is estimated in terms of its internal consistency, with alphas ranging between .73 and .91 for the various scales. Test-retest reliability was found to range from .57 to .92 when the test was readministered at 3- to 7-day intervals with two of the samples. Given the fact that only two state-dependent scales, Introversive and Peer Insecurity, fell below the very satisfactory range of .70 to .90, responses to the MACI can be accepted as quite stable over short intervals. Data on test-retest scores across a longer interval of perhaps 2 months would lend greater confidence in the reliability of the MACI with a population which, by definition, experiences very rapid change.

The content validity of the MACI is somewhat assured by its congruence with the underlying theory of personality, which has been well developed in the writings of its creator. Its concurrent validity was assessed first by contrasting its results with the judgments of the clinicians through whom the validation samples were created. The resulting correlations tended to be generally modest. Of 49 comparisons in two samples, only five exceeded the level of .35. Responses to the MACI were intercorrelated with a range of other measures including the Beck Depression Inventory (BDI), Beck Hopelessness Scale (BHS), Beck Anxiety Inventory (BAI), and Eating Disorder Inventory. Because sample sizes are unknown, it is not possible to determine the clinical significance of these statistical correlations. In a number of instances, many scales of the MACI correlated above the moderate level of .25 with responses to the other measures. For example, 20 of its 27 scales had such correlations with total scores of the BDI and BHS, and 16 of its scales correlated at this level with the BAI. In the array of correlations presented in the manual it is possible to pinpoint some which support the interinstrument validity of the MACI (e.g., correlations of .75 and .88 respectively between the Eating Dysfunction Scale of the MACI and the Drive for Thinness and Body Dissatisfaction measures on the Eating Disorder Inventory-2, or correlations of .59 between the Depressive Affect Scale of the MACI and both the BDI and the BHS). But it is also possible to find some discordant associations. For example, the correlation between the Body Disapproval scale of the MACI and a bulimia measure was only .25 and the correlation between the Peer Insecurity Scale of the MACI and a measure of social insecurity was -.02. These correlation charts should be taken as a starting point for examining the relationship between the MACI and other measures. It remains to be seen whether the instrument redundantly overlaps other tests or correlates highly enough with other measures to offer a meaningful overview of their results through administration of a single instrument.

Printouts of responses include a cover sheet, a histographic display of scale scores, an average of six pages of narrative, and a complete list of respondents' answers. The responses of NCS was quick and flawlessly accurate in the test protocols. Clinicians are very likely to find its list of Axis I and II entities to be a very useful source of diagnostic hypotheses, although one major presenting problem was not detected in one of the protocols studied for this review. Those who use the MACI extensively may be disturbed by the amount of boiler-plate redundancy across printouts. It seems that as much as 75% of the word-count was identical across protocols. This is a necessary characteristic of computer-scored instruments in which different responses to a small number of items trigger prepared blocks of text. Presenting the ideographic information in bold type would help to minimize this problem. Clinicians may also be uneasy about the forcefulness with which some of the conclusions and treatment recommendations are expressed. In general, these recommendations go beyond assessment per se and one aspect of the development of the MACI assessed respondents' ability to benefit from varied treatment approaches. If these printouts were placed in an adolescent's school file, nonpsychologists who have not been trained to use test results to formulate rather than validate diagnostic hypotheses, might construe their contents as firm conclusions rather than as suggestive diagnostic impressions. Clinicians may also regret the fact that contrary to the manual's assertion that the MACI assesses adolescents' strengths and weaknesses, the printouts generated make few if any strength-oriented statements, leaving therapists to infer assets from the absence of pathological indications.

In summary, although the MACI has a 20-year history, it is best to regard its present iteration to be a new instrument. It holds great promise for use as a screening instrument to assess a broad spectrum of adolescent problems, and as a means of generating DSM-IV diagnostic categories in clinical settings. Confidence in these uses, however, must await validating studies by clinicians working independently of Millon.

[2.23]
Millon Clinical Multiaxial Inventory—II.

Purpose: "Provides a profile of the scale scores and a detailed analysis of personality and symptom dynamics as well as suggestions for therapeutic management."
Population: Adults receiving "mental health services stemming from genuine emotional, social, or interpersonal difficulties."
Publication Dates: 1976–1987.
Acronym: MCMI-II.
Scores, 25: Modifier Indices (Disclosure, Desirability, Debasement), Clinical Personality Pattern (Schizoid, Avoidant, Dependent, Histrionic, Narcissistic, Antisocial, Aggressive/Sadistic, Compulsive, Passive-Aggressive, Self-Defeating), Severe Personality Pathology (Schizotypal, Borderline, Paranoid), Clinical Syndrome (Anxiety Disorder, Somatoform Disorder, Bipolar-Manic Disorder, Dysthymic Disorder, Alcohol Dependence,

Drug Dependence), Severe Syndrome (Thought Disorder, Major Depression, Delusional Disorder).
Administration: Individual or Group.
Price Data, 1994: $99 per mail-in preview package; $99 per MICROTEST Q preview package; $30.35 per prepaid interpretive mail-in answer sheet; $30.35 per prepaid Hispanic interpretive mail-in answer sheet; $11.40 per prepaid profile mail-in answer sheet; $11.40 per prepaid Hispanic profile mail-in answer sheet; $12 per 25 MICROTEST Q answer sheets; $12 per 25 Hispanic MICROTEST Q answer sheets; $29.35 per interpretive MICROTEST Q administrations; $10.40 per profile MICROTEST Q administrations; $43.50 per audio cassette (specify English or Hispanic); $24 per 10 handscoring test booklets; $29 per manual ('87, 123 pages); $190 per handscoring starter kit including manual, hanscoring user's guide, 10 test booklets, 50 handscoring answer sheets, 50 handscoring work sheets, and 50 profiel forms and handscoring keys; $55 per handscoring reorder kit including 50 handscoring answer sheets, 50 worksheets, and 50 profile sheets.
Time: [25–30] minutes.
Comments: Designed to coordinate with DSM III-R categories of personality disorders and clinical syndromes; revision of the Millon Clinical Multiaxial Inventory (9:709).
Author: Theodore Millon.
Publisher: NCS Assessments.
Cross References: Reviews by Thomas M. Haladyna and Cecil R. Reynolds originally appeared in 11:239 (74 references); for reviews by Allen K. Hess and Thomas A. Widiger of an earlier edition, see 9:709 (1 reference); see also T3:1488 (3 references).

Review of the Millon Clinical Multiaxial Inventory—II by THOMAS M. HALADYNA, Professor of Educational Psychology, Arizona State University West, Phoenix, AZ:

INTRODUCTION AND OVERVIEW. The second edition of the Millon Clinical Multiaxial Inventory—II (MCMI-II) intends to assist clinicians in diagnosing psychopathology in patients. The original version (MCMI-I) had 175 items and 20 clinical scales and 2 validity scales. The new version (MCMI-II) also has 175 items and yields 22 clinical scales and 3 validity scales, including ones reflecting "response style." The MCMI-II greatly improves on its predecessor in many ways. The new manual documents these improvements. This review will begin with a summary of the past and the present, and then look toward its future.

ITS PAST. The 1977 MCMI-I version was viewed as a promising instrument but not a worthy rival of the vaunted Minnesota Multiphasic Personality Inventory (MMPI; Hess, 1985; Widiger, 1985). These reviewers have collectively stated that (a) the MCMI-I manual tends to oversell the virtues of the test, (b) the test is experimental, (c) the test results are very complex, and (d) that more validation research is needed on the test. Despite these limitations, both reviewers were positive about the existence of a theoretical basis for the test, the relationship to the American Psychiatric Association's DSM-III-R diagnostic categories and labels, and the formidable effort in test development and validation that had begun in the late 1960s. Clearly, the MCMI-I had a future.

ITS PRESENT. The MCMI-II is the product of an evolutionary pattern spanning the 1970s and 1980s. The new manual, published in 1987, is impressive both in size and scope when compared to the previous manual. For instance, the earlier manual has grown from 73 pages to the present 249-page version. The virtues of the test are numerous: (a) The author has developed a theory to guide the development of the test, and both the theory and the test have been modified as a result of continued research; (b) the test results continue to be keyed to the DSM-III-R diagnostic categories and labels; (c) extensive validation research has been completed, much of it in recent years; and (d) the MCMI-I has provided a strong foundation for the current, revised version.

However, it would be remiss not to discuss some limitations. First, the basis for test validation is dated. A more modern view can be drawn from the work of Messick (1988, 1989) and incorporates the broader conception of validity under the rubric "construct validation." There are many facets of construct validation that would be easily satisfied by the work of Millon and other researchers, but the technical detail in the manual is centered more around traditional correlational and reliability studies.

Some technical difficulties persist. Foremost is the overlap of items to scales, which affects interscale correlations. Much discussion is given to this issue and problem, but lamentably more work is needed. The factor analytic work is not well described or documented, but recent advances in multivariate statistics should lead researchers to use confirmatory factor analysis as a technique of choice instead of traditional exploratory methods used in this validation effort.

The manual is written in highly technical language that will challenge most readers. The large amount of technical data is supported by many references in the literature. That this research appears in journals is laudable. The author gives sensible advice about how to use the test, based on the Standards for Educational and Psychological Testing (American Educational Research Association, American Psychological Association, & National Council on Measurement in Education, 1985). The mass of data presented could have been synthesized to be more readable. Periodic summaries communicate much more effectively than the lengthy prose passages punctuated with graphs or tables of data. Much of this could appear in appendices with chapters providing shorter, more insightful summaries of the impressive array of findings.

ITS FUTURE. During and since the time of these earlier reviews, the test has matured. Computerized reporting has improved, and validation research has mushroomed. For example, 46 validation studies were published in 1985 or later. The fact that the author, his colleagues, and others seem to be actively pursuing additional validation research and also that a brief research agenda is offered in the manual give an indication that the MCMI-II will continue to improve.

SUMMARY. The MCMI-II has grown impressively from its promising beginning. The theory base and extensive and growing validation research contribute to a growing respect for the instrument and its applications for the author's stated purposes. Although its chief competitor, the MMPI, will probably continue to be widely used instead of the MCMI-II, the manual offers impressive evidence for why clinicians should consider trying the MCMI-II.

REVIEWER'S REFERENCES

American Educational Research Association, American Psychological Association, & National Council on Measurement in Education. (1985). *Standards for educational and psychological testing.* Washington, DC: American Psychological Association, Inc.

Hess, A. K. (1985). [Review of the Millon Clinical Multiaxial Inventory]. In J. V. Mitchell, Jr. (Ed.), *The ninth mental measurements yearbook* (pp. 984-986). Lincoln, NE: Buros Institute of Mental Measurements.

Widiger, T. A. (1985). [Review of the Millon Clinical Multiaxial Inventory]. In J. V. Mitchell, Jr. (Ed.), *The ninth mental measurements yearbook* (pp. 986-988). Lincoln, NE: Buros Institute of Mental Measurements.

Messick, S. (1988). Validity. In R. L. Linn (Ed.), *Educational measurement* (3rd ed., pp. 13-104). New York: American Council on Education and MacMillan Publishing.

Messick, S. (1989). Meaning and values in test validation: The science and ethics of assessment. *Educational Researcher, 18*(2), 5-11.

Review of the Millon Clinical Multiaxial Inventory—II by CECIL R. REYNOLDS, Professor of Educational Psychology, Texas A&M University, College Station, TX:

The Millon Clinical Multiaxial Inventory—II (MCMI-II) is a revision of the original 175-item MCMI that includes an updating of item content (45 items were replaced), the addition of two new personality disorder scales, additional modification indexes to correct distortions in responding, an item-weighting system for scoring, and substantial changes in the interpretive text in its accompanying computerized scoring and interpretive system. The MCMI-II can be completed by individuals with at least an eighth grade reading level in 20-30 minutes.

The MCMI-II is divided into a complicated array of 22 clinical scales with frequent item overlap and variable item weighting across scales. This obfuscates scoring and interpretation to the point that the only practical choice for most clinicians is to use the computerized interpretive system. At this writing, hand scoring is not available for the MCMI-II although templates are in preparation by the publisher. The array of 22 clinical scales reflects Millon's decades of work in the development of personality theory and its links to psychopathology (e.g., Millon, 1969, 1981, 1986). This is at once a major strength of the MCMI-II and a serious practical limitation. Intelligent and compassionate use of the MCMI-II requires a working knowledge of Millon's approach to personality but also mastery of an extensive, impressive manual. Unfortunately, the manual, like the MCMI-II, is far more abstruse than necessary.

As one example of the latter, the differential item weighting and scale overlap (items typically appear on three scales with differential weighting on the three scales) complicates scoring tremendously and also makes certain of the internal validity studies more difficult—and to what end? The use of differential item weights has long been controversial in the measurement literature, principally because they fail to improve reliability or validity over unit weights. Despite arguments to the contrary in the MCMI-II manual (pp. 86-93), evidence for enhancement of key psychometric characteristics is not convincing. The case for overlapping items is a better one even if limited to the utility of this approach in generating a narrative report for MCMI-II results. Eliminating these complexities probably would require a 30-50% increase in the length of the MCMI-II, which should be tolerated easily, given its present brevity, and much simplify its use.

The norming of the MCMI-II also varies from prototypical practice. Rather than use population proportionate sampling techniques, Millon chose to attempt to sample the population of referred individuals who are typically administered the MCMI-II. A sample of 1,292 individuals was obtained and demographic data are made available for the variables of: gender, age, marital status, religion, ethnicity (Black, White, Hispanic, Other), setting, patient's stated major problem (from the front of the MCMI-II protocol list), and duration of most recent episode of patient's problem. This is a controversial approach to norming with many potential problems. Further, its superiority to population proportionate sampling of the entire United States population has not been demonstrated and must be considered suspect until shown otherwise. On certain key demographic variables, the MCMI-II norms are problematic. Only 6.1% of the sample is age 56 or higher, thus its use with older Americans, the most rapidly growing segment of the population, may raise concerns, especially because scores are not age based. Ethnicity is another problem as is the stability of parameter estimates for scaling the raw scores of Blacks and Hispanics (with separate norms and all Ns<100). The MCMI-II sample is 87.7% White with only 6.9% Black and 4.3% Hispanic representation. Level of education and other measures of socioeconomic status are not provided and the method of sampling seems to assure that the higher socioeconomic groups are the most strongly represented. As an analog to understanding the sampling problems inherent to this approach, consider the reaction to standardization of the Wechsler Adult Intelligence Scale—Revised (9:1348) if conducted only as a sampling of individuals typically administered the WAIS-R in clinical practice. Other assumptions and problems related to such sampling approaches have been discussed also by Reynolds, Gutkin, Elliott, and Witt (1984).

Scaling the MCMI-II 22 clinical scales presents some complex problems and, as accomplished by Millon, relies heavily on the estimation of base rates of various DSM-III-R Axis I and Axis II diagnoses. To the extent these estimates are in error, scaling of the MCMI-II will have distortion, especially at the upper end of the distribution, the most important range of scores in relation to the diagnosis of psychopathology. Considerably more information on the precise techniques of scaling would be of more than a passing or mere academic interest but would assist many clinicians in evaluating performance on the MCMI-II.

Reliability data are reported for the total sample by subscale using the well-known Kuder-Richardson formula 21 estimates, which with dichotomous scoring such as on the MCMI-II, is equivalent to coefficient alpha. However, this straightforward approach is not appropriate when differential item weighting is employed. The calculation of internal consistency reliability is more complex because the total score is an unequally weighted composite of the item scores and reliability must be determined based on the differential item weights. This is not difficult to do but is computationally quite laborious. The MCMI-II manual is unclear about whether the proper procedures were followed.

Considerable thought and decades of research and writing have gone into the conceptualization of the MCMI-II. Its greatest strengths lie in the relative validity of Millon's theories of personality and psychopathology. Millon's theory is a strong one and the evidence for construct validation of the MCMI-II is equally strong. Traditionally, as validity has been arbitrarily presented in its tripartite conceptualization, construct validity is considered of greatest importance for measures of personality and this is where the MCMI-II is at its best. True to Millon's approach, the MCMI-II provides a strong survey of a lengthy array of personality problems and emphasizes personality deficiencies, an approach, the efficacy of which deserves debate elsewhere, the MCMI-II accomplishes better than any other existing scale.

The computerized interpretive report also strongly emphasizes the problematic aspects of the patient's personality and fails to identify strengths that may be useful in the context of therapy. The printout contains appropriate cautions that are real and meaningful, and clinicians must take these cautions seriously or they will almost certainly overinterpret the MCMI-II profile.

The MCMI-II is a conceptual gem and psychometrically somewhere between a nightmare and an enigma. If carefully considered, the MCMI-II has a potentially key role to play in assessing personality and psychopathology and in clinical practice. Data on how nonreferral populations respond to the MCMI-II and its role in viewing normal variations in personality, especially in the very low range of scoring (T<30), will be important in its future. Clinicians must be extremely careful in using the MCMI-II with nonclinical populations such as in child custody evaluations, foster-parent studies, employment testing in all settings but especially in police agencies, security, and nuclear energy settings where one might be strongly tempted to use the MCMI-II, and in criminal forensic work where one is presumed innocent and mentally healthy—the latter not being the assumption of the MCMI-II. This interesting scale deserves far more research attention by clinicians other than Millon who, with his students and colleagues, has been the primary source of key research to date. The MCMI-II has a unique role in providing the most thorough, most well-conceptualized evaluation of Axis II disorders available but much remains to be understood about its psychometrics and how its complex profile might be interpreted best.

REVIEWER'S REFERENCES

Millon, T. (1969). *Modern psychopathology*. Philadelphia: Saunders.
Millon, T. (1981). *Disorders of personality: DSM-III, Axis II.* New York: Wiley.
Reynolds, C. R., Gutkin, T. B., Elliott, S. N., & Witt, J. C. (1984). *School psychology: Essentials of theory and practice* New York. John Wiley & Sons.
Millon, T. (1986). A theoretical derivation of pathological personalities. In T. Millon & G. Klerman (Eds.), *Contemporary directions in psychopathology: Toward the DSM-IV* (pp. 639-670). New York: Guilford.

[2.24]
Minnesota Multiphasic Personality Inventory—2.

Purpose: "Designed to assess a number of the major patterns of personality and emotional disorders."
Population: Ages 18 and over.
Publication Dates: 1942–1990.
Acronym: MMPI-2.
Scores, 75: 7 Validity Indicators: Cannot Say (?), Lie (L), Infrequency (F), Correction (K), Back F (FB), Variable Response Inconsistency (VRIN), True Re-

sponse Inconsistency (TRIN) (last 3 are supplementary validity scales); 10 Clinical Scales: Hypochondriasis (Hs), Depression (D), Conversion Hysteria (Hy), Psychopathic Deviate (Pd), Masculinity—Femininity (Mf), Paranoia (Pa), Psychasthenia (Pt), Schizophrenia (Sc), Hypomania (Ma), Social Introversion (Si); 15 Supplementary Scales: Anxiety (A), Repression (R), Ego Strength (Es), MacAndrew Alcoholism Scale—Revised (MAC-R), Overcontrolled Hostility (O-H), Dominance (Do), Social Responsibility (Re), College Maladjustment (Mt), Gender Role—Masculine (GM), Gender Role—Feminine (GF), 2 Post-Traumatic Stress Disorder Scales (PK & PS); 15 Content Scales: Anxiety (ANX), Fears (FRS), Obsessiveness (OBS), Depression (DEP), Health Concerns (HEA), Bizarre Mentation (BIZ), Anger (ANG), Cynicism (CYN), Antisocial Practices (ASP), Type A (TPA), Low Self-Esteem (LSE), Social Discomfort (SOD), Family Problems (FAM), Work Interference (WRK), Negative Treatment Indicators (TRT); 3 Si subscales: Shyness/Self-Consciousness (Si$_1$), Social Avoidance (Si$_2$), Alienation-Self and Others (Si$_3$); 28 Harris-Lingoes Subscales: Subjective Depression (D$_1$), Psychomotor Retardation (D$_2$), Physical Malfunctioning (D$_3$), Mental Dullness (D$_4$), Brooding (D$_5$), Denial of Social Anxiety (Hy$_1$), Need for Affection (Hy$_2$), Lassitude-Malaise (Hy$_3$), Somatic Complaints (Hy$_4$), Inhibition of Aggression (Hy$_5$), Familial Discord (Pd$_1$), Authority Problems (Pd$_2$), Social Imperturbability (Pd$_3$), Social Alienation (Pd$_4$), Self-Alienation (Pd$_5$), Persecutory Ideas (Pa$_1$), Poignancy (Pa$_2$), Naivete (Pa$_3$), Social Alienation (Sc$_1$), Emotional Alienation (Sc$_2$), Lack of Ego Mastery, Cognitive (Sc$_3$), Conative (Sc$_4$), Defective Inhibition (Sc$_5$), Bizarre Sensory Experiences (Sc$_6$), Amorality (Ma$_1$), Psychomotor Acceleration (Ma$_2$), Imperturbability (Ma$_3$), Ego Inflation (Ma$_4$).

Administration: Group.

Price Data, 1989: $17.70 per 10 reusable softcover test booklets; $24.60 per reusable hardcover test booklet; $39.30 per 100 hand-scorable answer sheets (select hardcover or softcover); Basic Service Profile Report: $15.05 per 25 Arion II or MICROTEST answer sheets; $36.30 per set of Basic Scales softcover scoring stencils; $32.30 per set of Basic Scales hardcover scoring stencils; $35.30 per set of Supplementary Scales scoring stencils (select hardcover or softcover); $44 per set of Content Scales scoring stencils (select hardcover or softcover); $45 per set of Harris-Lingoes Subscales scoring stencils (select hardcover or softcover); $35.40 per set of Wiener—Harmon Subtle—Obvious Subscales scoring stencils (select hardcover or softcover); $39.30 per 100 profiles (select scales); $57.20 per audiocassette; $23 per manual for administration and scoring ('89, 166 pages); $10 per Adult Clinical System User's Guide ('89, 71 pages); $10 per Personnel Selection System User's Guide ('89, 76

pages); price data available from publisher for IBM compatible microcomputer edition based on type of score or interpretive report desired; price data available from publisher for scoring service by publisher based on type of score or interpretive report desired.

Time: (90) minutes.

Comments: Revision of the Minnesota Multiphasic Personality Inventory; publisher recommends use of original MMPI for adolescents until norms become available for this group; may be administered by audiocassette or microcomputer.

Authors: S. R. Hathaway, J. C. McKinley, and James N. Butcher (user's guides).

Publisher: Published by University of Minnesota Press; distributed by National Computer Systems, Inc.

Cross References: See T4:1645; reviews by Robert P. Archer and David S. Nichols originally appeared in 11:244 (637 references); see also 9:715 (339 references) and T3:1498 (749 references); for reviews of the original version by Henry A. Alker and Glen D. King, see 8:616 (1,188 references); see also T2:1281 (549 references); for reviews by Malcolm D. Gynther and David A. Rodgers, see 7:104 (831 references); see also P:166 (1,066 references); for a review by Arthur L. Benton, see 4:71 (211 references); for reviews by Arthur L. Benton, H. J. Eysenck, L. S. Penrose, and Julian B. Rotter, and an excerpted review, see 3:60 (76 references).

Review of the Minnesota Multiphasic Personality Inventory—2 by ROBERT P. ARCHER, Professor of Psychiatry and Behavioral Sciences, Eastern Virginia Medical School, Norfolk, VA:

Stark Hathaway reported that he encountered substantial difficulty, including several rejections, before successfully finding a publisher for the Minnesota Multiphasic Personality Inventory (MMPI) in the early 1940s (Dahlstrom & Welsh, 1960). From this humble beginning, the MMPI's climb in popularity was nothing less than phenomenal. Surveys of test usage conducted in 1946 listed the MMPI among the 20 most widely used psychological tests (Louttit & Browne, 1947). A survey conducted in 1959 showed the MMPI to be among the 10 leading tests, and the only objective personality assessment instrument included in this group (Sundberg, 1961). By 1982, a national survey of patterns of psychological test usage found the MMPI to rank second overall (behind the Wechsler Adult Intelligence Scale) among clinicians' reports of tests they had used, and first overall when ratings were adjusted for frequency of usage (Lubin, Larsen, & Matarazzo, 1984). Despite its primary focus in the assessment of adults, the MMPI is also the most popular objective personality measure used with adolescents (Archer, Maruish, Imhoff, & Piotrowski, 1991). Beyond issues of clinical popularity, the MMPI has been the focus of extensive research interest. Butcher and Owen (1978), for example, have estimated that 84% of all research conducted in the personality inventory domain has been centered on the MMPI. Butcher (1987) has estimated that over 10,000 articles and books have documented the use of the MMPI. Much of this research involves the use of MMPI results as a means of increasing the understanding of clinical phenomena (e.g., alcohol and substance abuse) or special groups of interest to researchers (e.g., parents of psychiatrically disturbed offspring). A very important component of this research, however, has centered on the test instrument in studies of the external correlates and validity of the MMPI.

The MMPI-2 represents the first revision of the test since its original publication in 1943. Given the phenomenal success of the MMPI, it was likely that any effort to revise this instrument would have generated some controversy. Conservative revision efforts which minimized changes to the original instrument might be criticized by those who viewed the MMPI as an anachronistic measure with many undesirable psychometric properties. On the other hand, efforts to undertake a substantial revision of this highly successful instrument would run the risk of alienating many strong supporters of the original test. As Butcher and Owen (1978) have observed, "If modifications [in the MMPI] are too drastic, the instrument may be unacceptable to present users . . . They may continue to use the present MMPI because it is a known entity" (p. 507). In short, the original MMPI was destined to be a "tough act to follow" for those attempting to set revision goals and directions.

The MMPI Restandardization Project began in the summer of 1982 and resulted in the publication of the MMPI-2 in August 1989. The University of Minnesota Press, represented by Beverly Kaemmer, appointed a Restandardization Committee to advise on the development of the MMPI-2. This Committee consisted of Drs.

James Butcher and Auke Tellegen of the University of Minnesota, W. Grant Dahlstrom of the University of North Carolina, and John Graham of Kent State University. The major goals of the MMPI restandardization project have been summarized by Butcher, Graham, Williams, and Ben-Porath (1990) as follows: (a) Obtaining a contemporary normative sample; (b) Undertaking a revision of the original instrument which preserved sufficient continuity to allow for the generalizability of the massive MMPI research literature to the revised instrument; and (c) Creation of new items to address areas of behavior not adequately covered by the original MMPI, and the deletion or revision of offensive, outdated, or antiquated item content. When the MMPI-2 was published in August 1989, extensive test materials were also released including the MMPI-2 Test Manual (Butcher, Dahlstrom, Graham, Tellegen, & Kaemmer, 1989), hand-scoring templates, and a variety of computer-scoring options. Several computer-based test interpretation (CBTI) products have been marketed for the MMPI-2.

The MMPI-2 differs from the original test instrument in a variety of ways. Although the total lengths of the MMPI (566 items) and MMPI-2 (567 items) are almost identical, substantial changes have occurred on the item level. Levitt (1990) has stated that 394 unaltered items were carried over from the MMPI to the MMPI-2, as well as 66 items that were modified/rewritten. Thus, 84% of the MMPI items appear in the MMPI-2 in an original or modified form. The major reasons for item rewordings included replacing obsolete or idiomatic language with more contemporary wording, elimination of sexist language, and modifications designed to simplify or improve sentence structure. Ben-Porath and Butcher (1989) administered the MMPI and MMPI-2 to college students, in a counterbalanced design, in order to compare responses to the original and rewritten version of items. They concluded that the rewritten items did not significantly alter test response patterns and were psychometrically equivalent to the original items.

In addition to modified items, 90 items were deleted from the original MMPI, of which 13 came from a standard validity or clinical scale. The standard scales losing the most items were F and

Mf, each scale losing four items. The deleted items often involved potentially offensive content concerning sexual adjustment, bodily functions, or religious views or attitudes. These types of items were particularly intrusive/inappropriate when the MMPI was used in personnel screening applications. In addition to these 90 item deletions, the 16 duplicate items that appear in the original MMPI, and which have been utilized in the Test-Retest (TR) Index, have also been deleted in the MMPI-2. In place of these original items, the MMPI-2 contains 107 new items, most of which are found on the new MMPI-2 scales in the latter half of the test booklet.

The standard validity and clinical scales of the MMPI have been carried over, or protected, into the MMPI-2. No efforts were made to reevaluate the external validity of these measures, or to reexamine the K-correction weights traditionally assigned to five of the standard clinical scales. Additionally, MMPI-2 profile sheets and scoring programs provide for the derivation of 18 supplementary scales, 15 content scales, the Harris-Lingoes Subscales, and the Subtle-Obvious Subscales. An important effect of the creation of the MMPI-2 may be in the area of standardizing the use of a specific body of special scales that will be widely used with this instrument. This may be contrasted with the use of the original MMPI, in which test users often combined standard scale data with individualistic (and often idiosyncratic) special scale selections from the body of several hundred such measures which had been developed over the past five decades.

Of the 18 MMPI-2 supplementary scales, 8 are carried over from the original MMPI, typically with some item modifications. For example, the popular MacAndrew Alcoholism Scale (1965) has been incorporated into the MMPI-2 with four item replacements as MAC-R. Other popular special scales that were retained in the MMPI-2 include Anxiety (A), Repression (R), Ego Strength (Es), and Overcontrolled Hostility (O-H). Several less widely used special scales were also carried over, including College Maladjustment (Mt), Social Responsibility (Re), and Dominance (Do). The MMPI-2 supplementary scales also include two separate but overlapping measures of posttraumatic stress disorder based on contrasting development methodologies. These measures are the Pk

Scale, developed by Keane, Malloy, and Fairbank (1984), and the Ps Scale by Schlenger and Kulka (1987).

Several new validity scales have been developed for the MMPI-2 including the F-b (Back F) Scale, the Variable Response Inconsistency Scale (VRIN), and the True Response Inconsistency Scale (TRIN). The F-b Scale consists of infrequently endorsed items which occur in the latter stages of the MMPI-2 test booklet, therefore allowing for the possibility of identifying individuals who adopt random response patterns during the latter portion of the test. The VRIN and TRIN are inconsistency scales, similar to the Carelessness Scale developed by Greene (1978) for the original MMPI, which allow for an evaluation of the degree to which a subject responded to items in an inconsistent or contradictory manner. Also included in new supplementary scales are Masculine Gender Role (GM) and Feminine Gender Role (GF) Scales, and three new subscales for the Si standard scale which are Shyness/Self Consciousness (Si-1), Social Avoidance (Si-2), and Alienation-Self and Others (Si-3).

In addition to the supplementary scales, a series of 15 content scales were developed by Butcher, Graham, Williams, and Ben-Porath (1990) based on content dimensions identifiable within the MMPI-2 item pool. In contrast to the criterion group method employed by Hathaway and McKinley in the development of the original MMPI scales, the MMPI-2 content scales employ what is described as a deductive scale construction method. This later approach combines the use of empirical, theoretical, and rational criteria in the construction of these MMPI-2 measures (Butcher, Graham, Williams, & Ben-Porath, 1990). The end result of this process was the development of a series of face-valid, narrow-band scales with high levels of internal consistency. Much work on the validity of the scales remains for future researchers. The focus of the MMPI-2 content scales varies widely, from traditional measurement constructs including Anxiety (ANX) and Depression (DEP), to innovative scales including Work Interference (WRK) and Negative Treatment Indicators (TRT). Many of the MMPI-2 content scales appear similar to, and share items with, content scales developed by Wiggins (1966) for the original MMPI.

The development of the content scales may have also contributed to a resurrection of the debate concerning the utility of subtle items. Because the MMPI-2 content scales consist of obvious items (i.e., items bearing an easily discerned relationship to the constructs being measured), opponents and proponents of the use of subtle items are likely to have different views of the usefulness of the MMPI-2 content scales. Ambivalence concerning the use of subtle items may be reflected in the MMPI-2 manual statement concerning the use of the Weiner and Harmon (1946) Subtle-Obvious Subscales: "These scales are included in the manual because we recognize that some authorities recommend their use and because we wish to facilitate further research. Their inclusion does not represent the committee's endorsement of the scales. We urge that they be interpreted with caution" (Butcher et al., 1989, p. 47).

In addition to changes that have occurred on the item and scale levels, the MMPI-2 is based on a new normative sample. The MMPI-2 norms are based on responses of 1,138 males and 1,462 females between the ages of 18 and 84. In comparison with the ethnic, geographic, and sample size restrictions present in the norms developed for the original instrument, the MMPI-2 norms offer very substantial improvements. Normative data were collected for the MMPI-2 primarily in seven sites involving the west coast (California and Washington), the midwest (Minnesota and Ohio), and the eastern region of the United States (North Carolina, Pennsylvania, and Virginia). The ethnic origins of the MMPI-2 restandardization sample compare reasonably well to the data from the 1980 U.S. Bureau of the Census. Similarly, the age sampling of restandardization subjects, although somewhat underrepresenting the extreme ends of the age distribution, is reasonably well done. It is in the area of the educational and occupational levels of MMPI-2 normative subjects that substantial controversy has been focused. Roughly 50% of males and 42% of females included in the MMPI-2 restandardization sample reported an educational level of a bachelor's degree or higher. This may be compared with 20% of males and 13% of females in the 1980 U.S. Census data, which reported comparable educational levels. Similarly, approximately 42% of males and 40% of females reported

occupations in professional groups, in contrast to a 16% Census figure for this category. Debate is still occurring concerning what effects, if any, this educational skewing might have on MMPI-2 interpretation. In the April 1990 issue of the APA Monitor, several MMPI experts raised concerns regarding the suitability of the MMPI-2 norms in interpreting test respondents from lower socioeconomic status levels. In contrast, Butcher (1990a) has argued that educational level has a minimum impact on MMPI-2 scores, and that MMPI-2 norms "appear to work quite well for all levels of education even when K-correction is involved" (p. 3).

Independent of this debate, it is clear that the response patterns of subjects in the MMPI-2 normative sample differ substantially from those produced by the subjects for the original MMPI (i.e., the "Minnesota normals"). This is most apparent in T-score elevations differences found between the two instruments. The MMPI-2 clinical scale profiles are typically lower in elevation than profiles produced for the original instrument. This shift is reflected in a reduction of the demarcation point for clinical range elevations from $T >/= 70$ on the original instrument to $T >/= 65$ on the MMPI-2 profile sheet. This aspect of the MMPI-2 is likely to surprise many individuals in the initial stages of making the conversion from the original instrument to the revised test. First-time users may find the MMPI-2 profiles for clinical patients appear "too normal." As experience is gained with the MMPI-2 profile, however, most test users rapidly acclimate to the differences in "calibration." Many have erroneously attributed these elevation differences to the use of uniform T-scores in the MMPI-2. Uniform T-scores represent composite or averaged linear T-scores which serve to standardize the percentile equivalents represented by a given T-score across MMPI-2 clinical and content scales (Tellegen, 1988). Uniform T-scores do not, however, have major effects on the underlying distribution of raw scores and were not a substantial factor in the reduction of T-score elevation in the MMPI-2. Research by Pancoast and Archer (1989) suggests that part of these MMPI versus MMPI-2 elevations differences may reflect longstanding problems in the original MMPI norms. These authors observed that samples of normal adults have consistently shown substantial T-score elevations on the original instrument since its publication.

The major area of controversy and debate concerning the MMPI-2 has centered on the degree to which the profiles produced by this instrument are comparable to, or congruent with, test findings from the original MMPI. More broadly stated, this issue relates to the degree to which the MMPI and the MMPI-2 are equivalent measures. This concern has received substantial focus because it determines the degree to which the vast research literature available on the traditional MMPI can be generalized to the MMPI-2.

Empirical research is slowly accumulating on this crucial issue. The MMPI-2 manual provides congruence data for 2-point high-point codes using MMPI-2 norms and the original test norms in a sample of 232 male and 191 female psychiatric patients. These data indicate a congruence rate of 70% for males and 65% for females when high points are defined as the most elevated scale regardless of the magnitude of that elevation. Graham, Timbrook, Ben-Porath, and Butcher (in press) have reexamined these data and report that when 2-point codetype elevations were "well defined," as reflected in at least a 5 T-score point difference between the second and third most elevated scale in the clinical codetype, the congruence rate increased to 81.6% for males and 94.3% for females. Honaker (1990) investigated the congruence issue in an independent sample of 101 adults receiving either inpatient or outpatient psychological treatment who received both the MMPI and MMPI-2 in counterbalanced administrations. Results indicated that single-point and 2-point codetype similarity was lowest between the MMPI and MMPI-2, in comparison with MMPI-2/MMPI-2 comparisons and MMPI/MMPI comparisons. Honaker concluded that it would be erroneous to assume that the MMPI clinical research literature may be generalized to MMPI-2 test findings for all patients.

At the present time, many individuals who are beginning to use the MMPI-2 have elected to create profiles based on MMPI-2 norms as well as T-score values generated from Appendix K of the manual using the original (Minnesota normals) norms. These test users feel more comfortable when being able to examine the ways in which the

MMPI and MMPI-2 produce comparable, or divergent, findings for a specific patient, and believe that this approach facilitates learning about the new test instrument. Clinicians working from an MMPI-2 manual generated in the first printing, however, should consult the Appendix K erratum sheet which has been distributed by the University of Minnesota Press. Others have elected to profile and interpret the MMPI-2 based exclusively on MMPI-2 norms, preferring a "clean break" with the original instrument. Both approaches appeared reasonable and defensible, given the current state of our knowledge concerning the MMPI-2.

An extensive literature will develop for the MMPI-2 over the next few years. The MMPI-2 manual (Butcher et al., 1989) provides a solid overview of the instrument, including administration and interpretive guides and 11 appendices providing a wide variety of data concerning the instrument. A specialized text has been published on the use of MMPI-2 content scales (Butcher, Graham, Williams, & Ben-Porath, 1990) and general guides to the MMPI-2 have been provided by Butcher (1990b), Graham (1990), and Greene (1991). The MMPI text by Friedman, Webb, and Lewak (1989) contains a chapter providing information on the MMPI-2. A growing research literature is also rapidly evolving including studies of the use of the MMPI-2 in populations of college students (Butcher, Graham, Dahlstrom, & Bowman, 1990), substance abusers (Greene, Arredondo, & Davis, 1991), and active duty military personnel (Butcher, Jeffrey, Cayton, Colligan, DeVore, & Minnegawa, 1990).

In conclusion, the MMPI-2 is a new instrument closely related to the original MMPI. The MMPI-2 and MMPI are not, however, equivalent measures. Until a substantial correlate literature is published for the MMPI-2, the issue of the generalizability of findings from the original test will be very important. It is likely that the generalizability of findings will vary depending on variables including gender, codetype definition or "crispness," and other factors to be determined by future researchers. As the MMPI-2 ultimately amasses its own independent research base, this issue will assume decreasing emphasis. The MMPI-2 is a reasonable compromise of the old and the new; an appropriate balance between that which required change (norms) and that which required preservation (standard scales). It should prove to be a worthy successor to the MMPI.

REVIEWER'S REFERENCES

Weiner, D. N., & Harmon, L. R. (1946). *Subtle and obvious keys for the MMPI: Their development.* (Advisement Bulletin No. 16). Minneapolis: Regional Veterans Administration Office.

Louttit, C. M., & Browne, C. G. (1947). The use of psychometric instruments in psychological clinics. *Journal of Consulting Psychology, 11,* 49-54.

Dahlstrom, W. G., & Welsh, G. S. (1960). *An MMPI handbook: A guide to use in clinical practice and research.* Minneapolis: University of Minnesota Press.

Sundberg, N. D. (1961). The practice of psychological testing in clinical services in the United States. *American Psychologist, 16,* 79-83.

MacAndrew, C. (1965). The differentiation of male alcoholic outpatients from nonalcoholic psychiatric outpatients by means of the MMPI. *Quarterly Journal of Studies of Alcohol, 26,* 238-246.

Wiggins, J. S. (1966). Substantive dimensions of self-report in the MMPI item pool. *Psychological Monographs, 80* (22, Whole No. 630).

Butcher, J. N., & Owen, P. L. (1978). Objective personality inventories: Recent research and some contemporary issues. In B. Wolman (Ed.), *Clinical diagnoses of mental disorders* (pp. 475-546). New York: Plenum.

Greene, R. L. (1978). An empirically devised MMPI carelessness scale. *Journal of Clinical Psychology, 34,* 407-410.

Keane, T. M., Malloy, P. F., & Fairbank, J. A. (1984). Empirical development of an MMPI subscale for the assessment of combat-related posttraumatic stress disorder. *Journal of Consulting and Clinical Psychology, 52,* 888-891.

Lubin, B., Larsen, R. M., & Matarazzo, J. D. (1984). Patterns of psychological test usage in the United States: 1935-1982. *American Psychologist, 39,* 451-454.

Butcher, J. N. (1987). Computerized clinical and personality assessment using the MMPI. In J. N. Butcher (Ed.), *Computerized psychological assessment: A practitioner's guide* (pp. 161-197). New York: Basic Books.

Schlenger, W. E., & Kulka, R. A. (1987, August). *Performance of the Keane-Fairbank MMPI scale and other self-report measures in identifying posttraumatic stress disorder.* Paper presented at the 95th Annual Convention of the American Psychological Association, New York, NY.

Tellegen, A. M. (1988, August). *Derivation of uniform T-scores for the restandardized MMPI.* Symposium presentation at the 96th Annual Convention of the American Psychological Association, Atlanta, GA.

Ben-Porath, Y. S., & Butcher, J. N. (1989). Psychometric stability of rewritten MMPI items. *Journal of Personality Assessment, 53,* 645-653.

Butcher, J. N., Dahlstrom, W. G., Graham, J. R., Tellegen, A., & Kaemmer, B. (1989). *Minnesota Multiphasic Personality Inventory-2: Manual for administration and scoring.* Minneapolis: University of Minnesota Press.

Friedman, A. R., Webb, J. T., & Lewak, R. (1989). *Psychological assessment with the MMPI.* Hillsdale, NJ: Lawrence Erlbaum Associates.

Pancoast, D. L., & Archer, R. P. (1989). Original adult MMPI norms in normal samples: A review with implications for future developments. *Journal of Personality Assessment, 53,* 376-395.

Butcher, J. N. (1990a). Educational level and MMPI-2 measured psychopathology: A case of negligible influence. In J. N. Butcher (Ed.), *MMPI-2 News and Profiles: A Newsletter of the MMPI-2 Workshops & Symposia* (Vol. 1, No. 2, p. 3). Minneapolis: University of Minnesota Department of Psychology.

Butcher, J. N. (1990b). *MMPI-2 in psychological treatment.* New York: Oxford University Press.

Butcher, J. N., Graham, J. R., Dahlstrom, W. G., & Bowman, E. (1990). The MMPI-2 with college students. *Journal of Personality Assessment, 54,* 1-15.

Butcher, J. N., Graham, J. R., Williams, C. L., & Ben-Porath, Y. S. (1990). *Development and use of the MMPI-2 content scales.* Minneapolis: University of Minnesota Press.

Butcher, J. N., Jeffrey, T., Cayton, T. G., Colligan, S., DeVore, J., & Minnegawa, R. (1990). A study of active duty military personnel with the MMPI-2. *Military Psychology, 2,* 47-61.

Graham, J. R. (1990). *MMPI-2: Assessing personality in psychopathology.* New York: Oxford University Press.

Honaker, L. M. (1990, August). MMPI and MMPI-2: Alternate forms or different tests? In M. Maruish (Chair), *The MMPI and MMPI-2 comparability examined from different perspectives.* Symposium conducted at the annual conference of the American Psychological Association, Boston, MA.

Levitt, E. E. (1990). A structural analysis of the impact of MMPI-21 on MMPI-1. *Journal of Personality Assessment, 55,* 562-577.

Archer, R. P., Maruish, M., Imhof, E. A., & Piotrowski, C. (1991). Psychological test usage with adolescent clients: 1990 survey findings. *Professional Psychology: Research and Practice, 22,* 247-252.

Greene, R. L. (1991). *The MMPI-2/MMPI: An interpretive manual.* Boston: Allyn & Bacon.

Greene, R. L., Arredondo, R., & Davis, H. G. (1991). *MMPI and MMPI-2 MacAndrew Alcoholism Scales: Comparability of classification rates.* Manuscript submitted for publication.

Graham, J. R., Timbrook, R. E., Ben-Porath, Y. S., & Butcher, J. N. (in press). Code-type congruence between MMPI and MMPI-2: Separating fact from artifact. *Psychological Assessment: A Journal of Consulting and Clinical Psychology.*

Review of the Minnesota Multiphasic Personality Inventory—2 by JUDITH CLEMENTSON, Clinical Psychologist, Lincoln General Hospital Independence Center, Lincoln, NE:

Historically, the Minnesota Multiphasic Personality Inventory (MMPI) has been the most highly respected psychological assessment instrument in the field of substance abuse. Research on MMPI profiles of alcoholics was published as early as 1943 (Hewitt). Similar research continues to this day (e.g., Wasyliw, Haywood, Groosman, & Cavanaugh, 1993; Windle, 1994). During the past 50 years the MMPI has been the most widely used instrument to assess personality characteristics of individuals being evaluated for the presence of addiction and those being treated for addiction (Butcher, 1991). Butcher suggested the MMPI had been chosen as a result of its effectiveness as a screening device for psychopathology, its success in assessing long-standing personality problems that could be related to outcomes of rehabilitation, and a lack of comparable instruments.

The publication of the MMPI—2 in 1989 addressed many shortcomings of the original test (see Archer, 1992; see also MMPI—2 manual for administration and scoring). It also provided the opportunity to enhance the instrument's richness and utility through the addition of scales. Two scales of particular interest for the substance abuse field were developed in 1992 (Weed, Butcher, McKenna, & Ben-Porath, 1992), the Addiction Potential Scale (APS) and the Addiction Admission Scale (AAS). The existing substance abuse scale, the MacAndrew Alcoholism Scale (MAC), was revised as part of the restandardization.

In substance abuse treatment and research, the MMPI and MMPI—2 have been used primarily for two purposes: (a) to screen for the probable presence of substance abuse; and (b) to assess personality style and psychopathology to aid in treatment planning. The effectiveness of the MMPI—2 in accomplishing these tasks will be examined in the context of current standards for addiction assessment and demands for highly specific diagnostic information on which to base treatment planning decisions.

SUBSTANCE ABUSE SCREENING. The MacAndrew Alcoholism Scale (MAC; MacAndrew, 1965) was frequently used to identify individuals as alcoholics. Today, however, it is far less likely that this or any other MMPI scale will be used for this purpose. The use of all self-report measures of addiction is being questioned (Carroll, 1995) due to enhanced awareness of the numerous factors that may lower the reliability and validity of such instruments, including direct and indirect results of recent and chronic substance abuse, motivation to describe the self honestly, and frequent desire to avoid consequences of a substance abuse diagnosis. Biological markers, collateral information, and documented life history are seen as holding greater promise for accurate detection of such problems (Carroll, 1995; Donovan & Marlatt, 1988). If self-report measures are used to screen for the presence and/or nature of substance abuse disorders, one of the many brief, behavioral, and reasonably well-validated inventories and interview schedules that have been developed for this purpose is typically chosen (see Bohn, Babor, & Kranzler, 1995; Carroll, 1995; and Cooney, Zweben, & Fleming, 1995 for reviews of instruments such as the ASI, AUDIT, CAGE, MAST, POSIT, and SASSI).

The MMPI—2 is, in fact, far superior to the MMPI as a screening tool, as a result of the addition of the Addiction Admission Scale (AAS) and the Addiction Potential Scale (APS; Weed et al., 1992). Thus, it may be useful in those situations in which personality assessment is necessary and there is no desire to administer additional screening tools or interview questions related to substance abuse.

The MMPI—2 contains three scales designed to identify individuals who abuse substances. Two of the scales, the MAC-R and the APS, are indirect and empirically derived. The third, the AAS, is a rationally designed measure composed of items that directly assess substance abuse behaviors. The strongest scale is the AAS (Weed, Butcher, & Ben-Porath, 1995).

The AAS consists of 11 items directly related to substance abuse problems and 2 items highly correlated with the 11 obvious items. Weed et al. (1995) describe the AAS as a measure of willingness to report substance abuse problems directly. As a direct measure of self-reported substance abuse, the AAS is the MMPI—2 scale most similar to commonly used brief screening instruments.

The APS was designed to identify empirically "personality and lifestyle patterns specifically associated with alcohol and drug use" (Weed et al., 1995). The scale is highly correlated with measures of tension and self-criticism. Factor analysis indicates a primary component of harmful habits and significant dissatisfaction with self. Component 2 appears to be indicative of positive treatment attitudes including a belief in the possibility of change and a desire to trust others to help.

The MAC-R is the revised form of the 1965 MacAndrew Alcoholism Scale, which was developed to discriminate alcoholics from other psychiatric patients. The scale was originally developed on an all male, primarily Caucasian sample of alcoholic and nonalcoholic psychiatric outpatients. This scale has been very widely used in spite of serious questions regarding its validity (Gottesman & Prescott, 1989). The revised scale (MAC-R) differs from the original only in the replacement of four items, necessitated by the test revision. The new items were selected on the basis of their ability to discriminate between groups. The new scale appears to tap into the same personality dimensions as did its predecessor. These dimensions include impulsivity, high energy levels, boldness, and a high level of psychological maladjustment (Greene, 1991). Weed et al. (1995) cite the first four MAC-R components to be cognitive impairment, school maladjustment, interpersonal competence, and risk taking.

Reliability analyses (Weed et al., 1992) show the AAS to have the highest internal consistency and test-retest reliabilities of the three scales. As the only rationally derived, essentially homogeneous scale, greater internal reliability would be expected, but the higher stability estimate is somewhat surprising. Alpha coefficients range from .70 for females on the AAS to .51 for females on the MAC-R. Test-retest coefficients were higher, ranging from .89 for males on the AAS to .62 for males on the MAC-R. These figures are similar to the MMPI—2 clinical scales. The test-retest figures on the MAC-R for males are, however, low enough to be of some concern.

Validation studies demonstrate the ability of the AAS to discriminate between those individuals who engage in patterns of substance abuse and those who do not with a fairly high degree of accuracy. Neither the APS nor the MAC-R has consistently shown similar utility. In the original validation study (Weed et al., 1992), the MAC-R was found to discriminate between the substance abuse sample and the normative sample, but not between the substance abuse sample and the psychiatric sample. However, in that study, the AAS accounted for over twice the amount of variance in group membership than did the MAC-R. In a 1992 study (Greene, Weed, Butcher, Arredondo, & Davis, 1992), the AAS and the APS were shown to be able to discriminate statistically between substance abuse and psychiatric samples, though the APS resulted in a unacceptably high false positive rate of .39. Svanum, McGrew, and Ehrmann (1994) found that only the AAS could effectively identify college students with substance use disorders, as defined by *DSM-III-R*.

ASSESSMENT OF PERSONALITY STYLE AND PSYCHOPATHOLOGY. Three major questions must be addressed in determining the value of the MMPI for use as a personality and psychopathology assessment tool for treatment planning and clinical research: (a) Of what value is the MMPI system of personality classification and interpretation in current substance abuse settings? (b) Is there a well-validated empirical basis for interpretation of results of the MMPI—2? and (3) Do results meet the current needs of substance abuse clinicians and researchers for information that is useful in diagnosing and treating patients and in measuring outcomes of treatment?

In understanding the personality style of substance abusers, the MMPI—2 profile has much to offer clinicians, as did its predecessor. Both easily respond to the need to identify the specific defensive patterns of substance abusers. Common profiles, such as those of the antisocial, histrionic, anxious, and passive-aggressive personality types have been useful in choosing an appropriate therapeutic approach, determining likely prognosis for treatment, and anticipating ancillary treatment needs. Specific interpretative materials for use with substance abuse populations are available (e.g., Graham & Strenger, 1988; Penk, 1981; Tosi,

Eshbaugh, & Murphy, 1993), though these materials rely on MMPI rather than MMPI—2 interpretive databases. A computer-generated narrative report developed specifically for patients in substance abuse treatment is available for the MMPI—2 (Butcher, 1991).

The validity scales added to the MMPI—2, the Back F (FB) scale, the True Response Inconsistency scale (TRIN), and the Variable Response Inconsistency scale (VRIN), provide considerable assistance in identifying invalid profiles, which are especially common in resistant individuals. The FB detects deviant responses to items in the later portion of the item pool, which might indicate a change in response set as a result of fatigue or escalating resistance. The TRIN may reflect a response bias toward True or False responses, and the VRIN provides a strong measure of random or inconsistent responses.

Content and supplementary scales have been shown to add significantly to interpretive validity of the MMPI—2 clinical scales (Ben-Porath, McCully, & Almajor, 1993). In substance abuse treatment, several of the new scales can be especially useful, including the negative treatment indicators (TRT), which identify low motivation for change and attitudes counterproductive to treatment success. Social Discomfort (SOD), Anxiety (ANX), Fears (FRS), and Obsessiveness (OBS) can assist in determining more specifically the nature of a generally anxious person. Bizarre Mentation (BIZ) can, with the assistance of the Harris-Lingoes subscales, delineate more clearly the meaning of an elevated Scale 8 (Schizophrenia). As most MMPI-2 interpretive literature continues to rest very heavily on the MMPI empirical database, these homogeneous scales developed with the MMPI-2 population, designed to be interpreted in a very straightforward manner, can be especially helpful in clarifying unusual or puzzling MMPI-2 profiles.

Administratively, the MMPI-2 is identical to the MMPI. Though its length continues to be daunting for many substance abuse patients, the reading level should not present problems for most. A taped version is available, as is a Spanish translation.

DEVELOPMENT OF NEW INTERPRETIVE DATABASE. Since the restandardization of the MMPI in 1989, two lines of research have been actively encouraged to develop an empirical basis for MMPI-2 profile interpretation: studies of the correspondence between MMPI and MMPI-2 profiles and studies that establish external correlates for MMPI-2 profiles. There has also been a general call to go beyond merely looking at code-types in developing an interpretative base, given the richness of the new content and supplementary scales (Ben-Porath & Tellegen, 1995).

Comparability of MMPI and MMPI-2 profiles has been an active and highly contentious research area since 1989 (see Tellegen & Ben-Porath, 1993, and Ben-Porath & Tellegen, 1995 for reviews). This issue is of special importance to those in the field of substance abuse, given the strong tradition of MMPI assessment and the broad-based familiarity with the meaning and implications of common MMPI profiles (e.g., spike 4 and 2-7-8).

Much of the controversy stems from differences in the data chosen for comparison (e.g., high point codes or full clinical scale *t*-scores; profiles with clear high point codes or all profiles including those with no discriminable high points and those entirely within normal limits). It appears there is a reasonably high level of comparability for sharply defined code types (e.g., Graham, Timbrook, Ben-Porath, & Butcher, 1991), though not consistently for less clearly delineated profiles.

Published studies of comparability of profiles for substance use disorder populations have been slow in coming, perhaps as a result of commitment to ongoing research protocols using the MMPI or to an initial reluctance to change to the new instrument. Thus, several recent articles on use of the MMPI with substance abuse populations, or those with a high base rate of such disorders, used only MMPI data, sometimes not even mentioning the existence of the MMPI-2 (e.g., Greene, Adyanthaya, Morse, & Davis, 1993; Gripshover & Dacy, 1994; Tosi et al., 1993; Wasyliw et al., 1993; Windle, 1994). Husband & Iguchi (1995) did find a reasonably high degree of similarity in MMPI and MMPI-2 profiles in methadone maintenance clients. High-point similarity ranged from 61% to 92% of the subjects, depending on the definition of similarity used.

The conclusion of Ben-Porath and Tellegen (1995) that although practitioners can use the empirical database of the MMPI with "reasonable confidence" on MMPI-2 profiles, there is still a need to develop a new and more inclusive data base for the MMPI-2, appears to be an apt summary of the issue at this time. However, there is a special need for further studies of correspondence in substance use disorder populations due to the differences between these populations and the psychiatric populations on which this conclusion was based, and the consequently reduced certainty with which it can be applied to these populations.

EXTERNAL CORRELATE RESEARCH. Numerous researchers have called for the development of an MMPI-2 external correlate literature (see Archer, Griffin, & Aiduk, 1995), but in the 6 years since publication of the MMPI-2, few such studies have appeared. Archer and colleagues (1995) accurately describe their examination of clinical correlates for 10 common profile types in a sample of psychiatric inpatients as representing an "initial step in the creation of an MMPI-2 correlate literature" (p. 391). One study of MMPI-2 correlates in male substance abusers was found (Ward, 1995). In this factor analytic study, MMPI-2 and Millon Clinical Multiaxial Inventory—II (MCMI-II) profiles were compared and found to show a high degree of correspondence, in contrast to earlier comparisons of the MMPI and MCMI. Ward attributed the difference largely to the contribution of MMPI-2 special and content scales.

A correlate literature specific to substance use disorders is unlikely to be developed rapidly. Researchers are increasingly questioning the nature, timing, and role of personality assessment in substance abuse populations (Callahan & Pecsok, 1988; Carroll, 1995), or choosing to use other measures that provide greater behavioral specificity and/or are more directly related to current diagnostic categories (Carroll, Ball, & Rounsaville, 1993; Connors et al., 1994; Rounsaville, Tims, Horton, & Wowder, 1993). References to the MMPI-2 are quite rare in recent volumes of the *Journal of Studies on Alcohol, Psychology of Addictive Behaviors,* and *Alcoholism: Clinical and Experimental Research.*

In treatment settings there is a very clear trend away from the use of broad-band personality assessment instruments and toward use of short, highly specific measures of diagnostically significant behaviors or behavioral measurement. The

MMPI has not, in recent years, been proposed as a diagnostic tool, though it has been used in practice to suggest diagnoses, and most automated MMPI-2 profiles include "diagnostic impressions." Its scales clearly do not lend themselves to such use, as the instrument was developed long before current diagnostic systems. A 1993 study found that with even a classic disorder (unipolar depression), the MMPI-2 could not predict its presence or absence among male alcoholics (Elwood, 1993).

CURRENT SUBSTANCE ABUSE ASSESSMENT NEEDS. The purposes of psychological assessment are rapidly being confined to formulation of the initial diagnosis, measurement of evolving response to treatment, and measurement of eventual treatment outcome (Bindler & Shapiro, 1995; Ficken, 1995; Oss, 1995). Schlosser (1995) refers to traditional testing as a "dinosaur," which lacks the "here-and-now focus" needed for brief therapy. To be financially reimbursed, most assessment must be precertified by the managed care provider, and such precertification often rests on proving that testing is "medically necessary" (Sipkoff & Oss, 1995). Although this trend is fueled largely by managed care providers, questions have been raised for some time as to the validity of personality measures, especially when administered to substance abuse patients with a current or very recent history of heavy abuse (Callahan & Pecsok, 1988; Carroll, 1995). With increasingly short treatment programs, any assessment conducted must be done very quickly after admission to be of any use in treatment planning.

SUMMARY. The MMPI-2 appears to possess considerably greater utility than did the MMPI for predicting the presence of a substance abuse disorder. This is due to the superior validity of the new Addiction Admission Scale (AAS) that has been added to the widely used screening scale on the MMPI, the MacAndrews Alcoholism Scale (MAC). However, many other methods are available to screen for the presence of such disorders, and the AAS would likely not be the instrument of choice in most settings unless administration of the MMPI-2 was necessary for other reasons.

The MMPI-2 holds great promise for more comprehensive assessment of personality and psychopathology than was possible with the MMPI as a result of the addition of the new content and supplementary scales. The personality classification system of the MMPI-2 is one that can continue to provide the kind of information on which substance abuse clinicians have long depended, although the development of an interpretive MMPI-2 database is imperative.

As substance abuse treatment and research trends continue to move toward the use of assessment tools that can more easily be linked to outcome measures, the MMPI-2, even with its advantages over the MMPI, may hold a far less central place than did its predecessor.

REVIEWER'S REFERENCES

Hewitt, C. C. (1943). A personality study of alcohol addiction. *Quarterly Journal of Studies on Alcohol, 4,* 368–386.

MacAndrew, C. (1965). The differentiation of male alcoholic outpatients from nonalcoholic psychiatric outpatients by means of the MMPI. *Quarterly Journal of Studies on Alcohol, 26,* 238–246.

Penk, W. E. (1981). Assessing the substance abuser with the MMPI. In J. Butcher, G. Dahlstrom, & W. Schoefield (Eds.), *Clinical notes on the MMPI, Number 7* (pp. 3–17). Minneapolis, MN: NCS Professional Assessment Services.

Callahan, E. J., & Pecsok, E. H. (1988). Heroin addiction. In D. M. Donovan & G. A. Marlatt (Eds.), *Assessment of addictive behaviors* (pp. 390–418). New York: Guilford Press.

Donovan, D. M., & Marlatt, G. A. (Eds.). (1988). *Assessment of addictive behaviors.* New York: Guilford Press.

Graham, J. R., & Strenger, V. E. (1988). MMPI characteristics of alcoholics: A review. *Journal of Consulting and Clinical Psychology, 56,* 197–205.

Gottesman, I. I., & Prescott, C. A.. (1989). Abuses of the MacAndrew MMPI Alcoholism Scale: A critical review. *Clinical Psychology Review, 9,* 223–242.

Butcher, J. N. (1991). *User's guide: The Minnesota Report: Alcohol and drug treatment.* Minneapolis: University of Minnesota Press.

Graham, J. R., Timbrook, R. E., Ben-Porath, Y. S., & Butcher, J. N. (1991). Code-type congruence between MMPI and MMPI-2: Separating fact from artifact. *Journal of Personality Assessment, 57,* 205–215.

Greene, R. L. (1991). *The MMPI-2/MMPI: An interpretative manual.* Needham Heights, MA: Allyn & Bacon.

Archer, R. P. (1992). [Review of the Minnesota Multiphasic Personality Inventory—2.] In J. J. Kramer & J. C. Conoley (Eds.), *The eleventh mental measurements yearbook* (pp. 546–562). Lincoln, NE: Buros Institute of Mental Measurements.

Greene, R. L., Weed, N. C., & Butcher, J. N., Arrendondo, R., & Davis, H. G. (1992). A cross-validation of MMPI-2 substance abuse scale. *Journal of Personality Assessment, 58,* 405–410.

Weed, N. D., Butcher, J. N., McKenna, T., & Ben-Porath, Y. S. (1992). New measures for assessing alcohol and drug abuse with the MMPI-2: The APS and AAS. *Journal of Personality Assessment, 58,* 389–404.

Ben-Porath, Y. S., McCully, E., & Almajor, M. (1993). Incremental validity of the MMPI-2 content scales in the assessment of personality and psychopathology by self-report. *Journal of Personality Assessment, 61,* 557–575.

Carroll, K. M., Ball, S. A., & Rounsaville, B. J. (1993). A comparison of alternate systems for diagnosing antisocial personality disorder in cocaine abusers. *Journal of Nervous and Mental Disease, 181,* 436–443.

Elwood, R. W. (1993). The clinical utility of the MMPI-2 in diagnosing unipolar depression among male alcoholics. *Journal of Personality Assessment, 60,* 511–521.

Greene, R. L., Adyanthaya, A. E., Morse, R. M., & Davis, L. J., Jr. (1993). Personality variables in cocaine- and marijuana-dependent patients. *Journal of Personality Assessment, 61,* 224–230.

Rounsaville, B. J., Tims, F. M., Horton, A. M., & Wowder, B. J. (Eds.). (1993). *Diagnostic source book on drug abuse research and treatment.* (NIH Publication No. 93-0363-P). Rockville, MD: National Institute on Drug Abuse.

Tellegen, A., & Ben-Porath, Y. S. (1993). Code-type comparability of the MMPI and MMPI-2: Analysis of recent findings and criticisms. *Journal of Personality Assessment, 61,* 489–500.

Tosi, D. J., Eshbaugh, M. A., & Murphy, M. A. (1993). *A clinician's guide to the personality profiles of alcohol and drug abusers: Typological descriptions using the MMPI.* Springfield, IL: Charles C. Thomas.

Wasyliw, O. E., Haywood, T. W., Grossman, L. S., & Cavanaugh, J. S., Jr.. (1993). The psychometric assessment of alcoholism in forensic groups: The MacAndrew Scale and response bias. *Journal of Personality Assessment, 60,* 252–266.

Conners, G. J., Allen, J. P., Cooney, N. L., DeClemente, C. C., Tonigan, J. S., & Anton, R. F. (1994). Assessment issues and strategies in alcoholism treatment matching research. *Journal of Studies on Alcohol.* (Supplement, 12), 92–100.

Gripshover, D. L., & Dacy, C. M. (1994). Discriminative validity of the MacAndrew scale in settings with a high base rate of substance abuse. *Journal of Studies on Alcohol, 55,* 303–308.

Svanum, S., McGrew, J., & Ehrmann, L. (1994). Validity of the substance abuse scales of the MMPI-2 in a college student sample. *Journal of Personality Assessment, 62,* 427–439.

Windle, M. (1994). Characteristics of alcoholics who attempted suicide: Co-occurring disorders and personality differences with a sample of male Vietnam era veterans. *Journal of Studies on Alcohol, 55,* 571–577.

Archer, R. P., Griffin, R., & Aiduk, R. (1995). MMPI-2 clinical correlates for ten common codes. *Journal of Personality Assessment, 65,* 391–407.

Ben-Porath, Y. S., & Tellegen, A. (1995). How (not) to evaluate the comparability of MMPI and MMPI-2 profile configurations: A reply to Humphrey and Dahlstrom. *Journal of Personality Assessment, 65,* 52–58.

Bindler, P. R., & Shapiro, R. (1995). Psychological testing in brief psychotherapy. *Behavioral Health Management, 15,* 18–20.

Bohn, M. J., Babor, T. F., & Kranzler, H. R. (1995). The Alcohol use disorders identification test (AUDIT): Validation of a screening instrument for use in medical settings. *Journal of Studies on Alcohol, 56,* 423–432.

Carroll, K. M. (1995). Methodological issues and problems in the assessment of substance use. *Psychological Assessment, 7,* 349–358.

Cooney, N. L., Zweben, A., & Fleming, M. F. (1995). Screening for alcohol problems and at-risk drinking in health-care settings. In R. K. Hester & W. R. Miller (Eds.), *Handbook of alcoholism treatment approaches: Effective alternatives* (2nd ed.) (pp. 45–60). Needham Heights, MA: Allyn & Bacon.

Ficken, J. (1995). New directions for psychological testing. *Behavioral Health Management, 15,* 12–14.

Humphrey, D. H., & Dahlstrom, W. G. (1995). The impact of changing from the MMPI to the MMPI-2 on profile configuration. *Journal of Personality Assessment, 64,* 428–439.

Husband, S. D., & Iguchi, M. Y. (1995). Comparison of MMPI-2 and MMPI clinical scales and high-point scores among methadone maintenance clients. *Journal of Personality Assessment, 64,* 371–375.

Oss, M. E. (1995). Psychological testing: Does it have a future? *Behavioral Health Management, 15,* 2.

Schlosser, B. (1995). Psychological testing: Past and future. *Behavioral Health Management, 15,* 8–10.

Sipkoff, M., & Oss, M. E. (1995). Value Behavioral Health's protocols for psychological testing. *Behavioral Health Management, 15,* 27–29.

Ward, L. C. (1995). Correspondence of the MMPI-2 and MCMI-II male substance abusers. *Journal of Personality Assessment, 64,* 390–393.

Weed, N. C., Butcher, J. N., & Ben-Porath, Y. S. (1995). In J. N. Butcher & C. D. Spielberger (Eds.), *Advances in personality assessment* (vol. 10, pp. 121–145). Hillsdale, NJ: Lawrence Erlbaum Associates.

Review of the Minnesota Multiphasic Personality Inventory-2 by DAVID S. NICHOLS, Supervising Clinical Psychologist, Department of Psychology, Dammasch State Hospital, Wilsonville, OR:

The original Minnesota normal sample consisted of 724 relatives and other visitors at the University of Minnesota Hospitals. The data from this sample provided the needed contrast for the original criterion groups from which the clinical scales of the Minnesota Multiphasic Personality Inventory (MMPI) were developed. But this use made the normal sample unsuitable for the establishment of test norms. Unfortunately, funds that would have been required to gather a normative sample of adequate size and representation were unavailable. By making the Minnesota Normals serve as both a source of contrast for pathological samples and the reference for normative standards, the latter function was compromised. Forcing the Normals to perform this double duty in effect purged them of their normal levels of abnormality. The consequence of this bias became evident as data from subsequent normal groups became available. Plotted on the standard profile form, these groups appear overpathologized, their scores tending to hover at about 5 T-scores of elevation above the mean (Colligan, Osborne, Swenson, & Offord, 1983; Pancoast & Archer, 1989). Thus, the need for the restandardization of the MMPI has been present from the beginning.

But the pressures to revise came less from problems with the original norms than from developments that followed the test's release. Foremost among these was the overwhelming success of the MMPI in assisting clinical work, a success vastly underanticipated by the test's founders. The lack of a nationally representative normative sample began to stand out as the applications of the MMPI expanded outside the psychiatric ward to include general medicine, personnel screening and selection, forensic and child custody evaluations, outpatient psychotherapy, assessment of disability, and a host of others. The phrase "Minnesota farmers" became the standard term of opprobrium for this largely rural, eighth-grade educated, skilled or semiskilled, northern midwestern group of Scandinavian origins. The geographic, cultural, educational, and occupational atypicality of the normative sample grew increasingly conspicuous with the passage of half a century and the availability of competing instruments with broader based normative samples such as the Basic Psychological Inventory (Jackson, 1989), the Clinical Analysis Questionnaire (9:232), the Millon Clinical Multiaxial Inventory (11:239), and the NEO Personality Inventory (11:258).

There were internal problems as well. The lack of percentile equivalence among the linear T-distributions for the basic clinical scales, although not compromising interpretation from actuarially derived profile types, confounded inferences based on scale-by-scale comparisons because greater elevations did not necessarily correspond to greater statistical deviance. Many items suffered from ambiguous, awkward, agrammatical, or overly complex phrasing. Others employed sexist wording or language that has fallen into disuse: streetcars, sleeping powders, acid stomach, cutting up, cross, the funnies, trifling, hooky. In other cases obscurity surrounded the item as a whole: "I used to like drop-the-handkerchief." For some items, endorsement frequencies had drifted over time, or they had been found objectionable and represented potential violations of Equal Employment Opportunity Commission guidelines if included in testing for personnel decisions. Items covering bowel and bladder functioning, sexual adjustment, and religious beliefs might fall into this category.

THE RESTANDARDIZATION. Funded by the test's copyright holder, the University of Minnesota Press, the restandardization is based on a sample of 2,600 paid volunteer adults, recruited from newspaper advertisements and random mailing solicitations, and tested under supervision at prearranged sites in seven states. Collateral data included biographical information and recent stressful life events. Behavior ratings were collected from 928 couples with each spouse rating the other. The sample exceeds 1980 census values for education and occupational status but approximates them in terms of age and income ranges, ethnic diversity, and marital status. The consequences of census disparities appear minor. The effect of the educational bias, for example, is limited to scores on scales F and MF for men and K for both sexes.

Deviations from the norm for the basic clinical scales (excluding Mf & Si) and the Minnesota Multiphasic Personality Inventory-2 (MMPI-2) content scales, to be discussed below, are represented in uniform T-scores such that the positive skew of the original scale distributions is preserved but a given T-score corresponds to nearly identical percentile values across the scales. For each sex and scale set, scores were represented in a composite distribution. Scales were then individually transformed to conform to the composite. The procedure reduced the skewness of Scales 1, 7, and 8, and augmented it for Scales 3, 4, 6, and 9 (the skew of Scale 2 was reduced for men, augmented for women). Compared with the normative shifts observed from the original to the restandardization sample, the effects of making uniform the new scale distributions are small. It is the normative differences that will require some getting used to. Scales 4 and 8, for example, will be less prominent in MMPI-2 profiles than in the original MMPI; Scale 6, more so. T-scores on Scale MF for men are 11 points lower throughout the raw score range. The F Scale that a consensus of expert opinion has viewed as elevating too fast now goes up even faster, partly as a consequence of eliminating high F protocols from the restandardization sample. This effect is especially dramatic for women: T-scores of 70, 80, and 90 on the MMPI become 79, 92, and 109 on the MMPI-2, respectively. The L Scale, however, long considered sluggish by MMPI experts, now elevates much more briskly on the MMPI-2.

From the beginning, normal and pathological groups have been most reliably discriminated on the MMPI by a point 1.5 standard deviations above the mean. On the original MMPI, a T-score of 70 reflected this amount of deviation *plus* an additional increment that can be traced to three major causes: (a) the hypernormalizing effect on the original normative sample of their service as the controls for clinical scale development (Pancoast & Archer, 1989), (b) the failure to discourage the use of the Cannot Say (?) category in the earlier work, and (c) the decision to exclude from the normal sample anyone "under a physician's care" (Hathaway & McKinley, 1980, p. 10). None of these three factors were operative in the restandardization, hence the movement of the line of demarcation between normals and patients from T-70 to T-65 on the MMPI-2 represents less a change than a point of continuity.

Considerable controversy has surfaced over the concordance between MMPI and MMPI-2 codetypes. Rates reported thus far cluster around 67%, about twice the value reported for 1–2-week codetype stabilities. The effect of the lack of complete concordance between the original MMPI and the MMPI-2 on clinical prediction/description will be unclear for some time, but sweeping claims for the superiority of the codetypes of either version, when the two disagree, should be viewed skeptically.

REVISED ASPECTS AND NEW FEATURES. One hundred fifty-four new items were written for the restandardization of which 107 appear in the MMPI-2. Others were rewritten for reasons given above. Although the new items expand clinically important areas of content like substance use, marital relations, and suicide, their phrasings do not always reflect the smooth, worn quality of common speech. The three new suicide statements, for example, employ the fixed operative expression, "kill(ing) myself," in preference to more varied and less violent locutions like "want to die," "end it all," "commit suicide," "get it over with." Most of the hundreds of scales developed from the original item pool are relatively intact unless they included significant religious content or were drawn mainly from the last 200 items of the original MMPI. In order to be scored, however, the older keys must be translated into MMPI-2 item numbers, a process aided by an appendix in the manual (Butcher, Dahlstrom, Graham, Tellegen, & Kaemmer, 1989).

Item order has been rearranged to permit the basic validity and clinical scales to be scored from the first 370 items. Permitting the inventory to be discontinued at this point is a practice to be deplored, however, because it sacrifices the assessment of consistency (VRIN) and the content scales that amount to conceptually (though not statistically) independent self-ratings of symptoms and attitudes.

The availability of the Harris-Lingoes subscales continues, but those for Scale 4 were altered by dropping the off scale items. The Serkownek subscales for Scales 5 (*Mf*) and 0 (*Si*) have been abandoned, though those for Scale 0 have been replaced by three new, internally consistent subscales (Ben-Porath, Hostetler, Butcher, & Graham, 1989). The first two of these nicely distinguish the subjective (visibility discomfort, ease of embarrassment, self-consciousness; the feeling component of shyness) from the objective (social withdrawal, avoidance of groups and crowds; the public component) aspects of introversion. The third subscale is a residual dominated by neuroticism. An attempt to develop new Scale 5 subscales reportedly failed (Hostetler, Ben-Porath, Butcher, & Graham, 1989), but this failure owed more to unrealistic internal consistency hurdles than to the lack of independent subdimensions.

Of many supplementary scales listed in the manual, Peterson's *GM* (Masculine Gender Role) and *GF* (Feminine Gender Role) scales are among those new on the MMPI-2. These scales tap independent dimensions related to gender identity and, by implication, to sex role differentiation or rigidity on the one hand, and "androgyny" or a lack of sex role differentiation on the other. Three scales, *Mt* (College maladjustment), *PK* (Post Traumatic Stress Disorder-Keane), and *PS* (PTSD-

Schlenger) are experimental and of doubtful utility in the clinical arena, but may have value in epidemiological research. All are saturated with nonspecific variation, and none has demonstrated adequate discriminative validity. The use of any of these in clinical settings will result in an explosion of false positives. The manual section describing *PK* and *PS* contains the only howler I was able to find: "These two scales appear to be largely independent of each other" (p. 41). With 26 items in common, the scales neither appear independent, nor are they (rs about .90).

Two new features are especially noteworthy. The MMPI-2 permits a much more comprehensive and reliable ascertainment of protocol validity. A new inconsistency scale (VRIN) has been added, as has a content-free acquiescence scale (TRIN). Both consist of paired items and hand scoring for both is complicated and taxing. A new infrequency scale F-Back (F_B) takes over as items scored on F become exhausted midway through the test. Like F, the new scale is sensitive to flagging cooperation, negative dissimulation, reading difficulties, cognitive disorganization, and carelessness.

Expanding the item pool to include new areas such as suicide and substance use created an occasion for reassessing dimensions of content. Three of the 13 content scales developed by Wiggins (1966) lost 20% or more of their items in the revision. The development of the 15 MMPI-2 content scales is described in Butcher, Graham, Williams and Ben-Porath (1990). Half of these scales are essentially MMPI-2 versions of their Wiggins predecessors but show somewhat higher internal consistencies. New scales address anxiety, antisocial attitudes and behavior, anger, low self-esteem, work interference, obsessiveness, health concerns, Type A personality, and negative treatment indicators. Most of these scales are destined to become useful in their own right and as aids to interpreting the standard profile. An internally consistent anxiety scale to stand beside an internally consistent depression scale has been needed for years. The MMPI-2 has them. The low self-esteem scale is one of similar value. The Type A and negative treatment indicators scales, however, have a significant potential for misinterpretation and misuse, and should probably be ignored pending adequate evidence for their construct and discriminative validity. Subscales for most of the new content scales are under development and these should enhance the interpretation of the content and clinical scales.

DOCUMENTATION. The MMPI-2 manual is five times the size of its predecessor, and is divided between text and appendices in a ratio of 1:2. It is clearly written and strikes an appropriate balance between clinical and psychometric values. The restandardization is well described and tables are provided that compare the normative sample against 1980 census data. For the clinician, there are scoring keys and interpretative information for each scale mentioned in this review, a section on protocol validity, and a pair of interpreted protocols. Tables are provided that give interpretative implications of four or five levels of elevation for the standard scales. This feature serves a very useful orienting purpose, but these tables may be quite misleading when moderate to extreme response sets are present. Tables for converting raw scores to linear or uniform T-scores are provided for the standard scales, with and without K-corrections. For the psychometrician, there are test-retest and internal consistency values, itemmetric and codetype concordance data, and external correlates for most scales. Conversion tables for translating MMPI item numbers into MMPI-2, and vice versa, are provided. Three scoring key and a few other errors have been discovered so far and will be noted in forthcoming errata. A final appendix, K-1 and K-2, is given for converting K-corrected and non-K-corrected T-scores on MMPI-2 profiles into MMPI values. By an unfortunate oversight, the T-score values reported in these tables did not reflect the adjustments to the original normative data made by Hathaway and Briggs (1957). Corrected tables will appear in the next manual revision.

A second basic document, *Development and Use of the MMPI-2 Content Scales* (Butcher, Graham, Williams, & Ben-Porath, 1990), contains a more leisurely and comprehensive description of the MMPI-2 restandardization than that given in the manual, and describes the construction, psychometric characteristics, preliminary validation, and interpretive guidelines for this new set of scales. More extensive reviews of this monograph are available (Caldwell, 1991; Nichols, in press).

THE LIMITS OF REVISION. Some critics of the MMPI-2 will complain that the revision did not go far enough. The nosology of *fin de siecle* psychiatry persists in the clinical scales. Why not develop new scales based on new pathological criterion groups defined by *DSM-III-R* criteria? The 50 years of research devoted to the MMPI have contributed to the very definition of the test. To have abandoned the original clinical scales would have been to decouple the revision from a body of validating evidence that could require another half-century to replace. But there were three other reasons for stopping short of a thoroughgoing revision: Criterion samples for many of the original scale constructs are simply no longer available. The pervasive use of psychotropic medications in contemporary psychiatry, and judicial rulings covering the right to treatment have virtually eliminated access to unmedicated criterion cases needed for reconstituting the clinical scales. Second, even if unmedicated criterion cases were available, a new set of basic clinical scales developed from them would not necessarily be justified. The recent acceleration in the rate at which the defining criteria for mental disorders are revised would render such scales ephemeral, thereby defeating any hope of repeating the incremental but cumulatively massive elaboration of scale constructs that has occurred with the original scales. A final reason for preserving the original constructs was the discovery in the late 1940s that high-point pairs and triads (codetypes) were often associated with distinct and sometimes unanticipated homogeneities in the patients that produced them. Thus, to abandon these constructs would have been to hamper the means by which the covariation among the personal and symptomatic characteristics common to specific code patterns could be identified and studied in the future.

SUMMARY. So far as the standard validity and clinical scales are concerned, the statistical properties of the MMPI-2 with respect to reliability, validity, and standard error are those of its predecessor, for better or worse. The provision of uniform T-scores is a significant advance, the immediate benefit of which is to simplify the comparison of scale elevations against a fixed percentile standard. In the longer term, this change may enhance the understanding of common configural patterns. As in the past, the interpretive implications of the clinical scales and codetypes are significantly augmented by reference to subscales, content scales, and supplementary scales.

In general, the new features incorporated in the MMPI-2 are genuine improvements. The new validity scales will greatly aid the ascertainment of validity, something the original validity scales were never very good at. The restandardization was appropriately executed and provides a normative sample of suitable size and ethnic diversity. Some of the shortcomings in representativeness (few Hispanics, Asian-Americans, older women, unrepresentative Native Americans) appear unlikely to compromise the test in most settings. Other divergences from the census such as the limited number of subjects at the lowest educational and occupational levels, and the generally higher socioeconomic status of the restandardization sample are of uncertain consequence at present. In psychiatric contexts, the higher educational and occupational attainment of the normative group may well increase the discrimination of psychopathology over the original version (W. G. Dahlstrom, personal communication, 1991).

The University of Minnesota Press and the Restandardization Committee wisely chose to rehabilitate the MMPI at a time when it had never been more vigorous, well before it began to cackle and wheeze. The revision breathes new life into a test the utility and excellence of which have made it the most widely used device for personality measurement in the world. The accustomed user will find that most of what was broke was fixed, most of what was not broke was left alone, and that the iatrogenic disfigurements are few and mostly minor. The psychodiagnostician selecting a structured inventory for the first time will find that no competing assessment device for abnormal psychology has stronger credentials for clinical description and prediction. As an inventory of normal range personality attributes, the MMPI-2 retains all the weaknesses of its predecessor and will, for most purposes, prove less satisfactory than instruments like the NEO Personality Inventory.

REVIEWER'S REFERENCES

Hathaway, S. R., & Briggs, P. F. (1957). Some normative data on new MMPI scales. *Journal of Clinical Psychology, 13,* 364-368.
Wiggins, J. S. (1966). Substantive dimensions of self-report in the MMPI item pool. *Psychological Monographs, 80*(22, Whole No. 630).
Hathaway, S. R., & McKinley, J. C. (1980). Construction of the schedule. In W. G. Dahlstrom & L. E. Dahlstrom (Eds.). *Basic readings on the MMPI: A new selection on personality measurement* (pp. 7-11). Minneapolis: University of Minnesota Press.
Colligan, R. C., Osborne, D., Swenson, W. M., & Offord, K. P. (1983). *The MMPI: A contemporary normative study.* New York: Praeger.
Ben-Porath, Y. S., Hostetler, K., Butcher, J. N., & Graham, J. R. (1989). New subscales for the MMPI-2 Social Introversion (Si) scale. *Psychological Assessment, 1,* 169-174.
Butcher, J. N., Dahlstrom, W. G., Graham, J. R., Tellegen, A., & Kaemmer, B. (1989). *Minnesota Multiphasic Personality Inventory-2 (MMPI-2): Manual for administration and scoring.* Minneapolis: University of Minnesota Press.
Hostetler, K., Ben-Porath, Y. S., Butcher, J. N., & Graham, J. R. (1989, April). *New MMPI-2 subscales.* Paper presented at the annual meeting of the Society for Personality Assessment, New York, NY.
Jackson, D. N. (1989). Basic Personality Inventory. Port Huron, MI: Sigma Assessment Systems, Inc.
Pancoast, D. L., & Archer, R. P. (1989). Original adult MMPI norms in normal samples: A review with implications for future developments. *Journal of Personality Assessment, 53,* 376-395.
Butcher, J. N., Graham, J. R., Williams, C. L., & Ben-Porath, Y. S. (1990). *Development and use of the MMPI-2 content scales.* Minneapolis: University of Minnesota Press.
Caldwell, A. B. (1991). MMPI-2 content scales: What you say is what you get? *Contemporary Psychology, 6,* 560-561.
Nichols, D. S. (in press). *New MMPI-2 content scales.* Journal of Personality Assessment.

[2.25]
Minnesota Multiphasic Personality Inventory—Adolescent.

Purpose: Designed for use with adolescents to assess a number of the major patterns of personality and emotional disorders.

Population: Ages 14–18.

Publication Date: 1992.

Acronym: MMPI-A.

Scores, 68: 16 Basic Scales [6 Validity Scales (Cannot Say (?), Lie, Infrequency, Defensiveness, Variable Response Inconsistency, True Response Inconsistency); 10 Clinical Scales (Hypochondriasis, Depression, Hysteria, Psychopathic Deviate, Masculinity-Femininity, Paranoia, Psychasthenia, Schizophrenia, Hypomania, Social Introversion); 28 Harris-Lingoes Subscales (Subjective Depression, Psychomotor Retardation, Physical Malfunctioning, Mental Dullness, Brooding, Denial of Social Anxiety, Need for Affection, Lassitude-Malaise, Somatic Complaints, Inhibition of Aggression, Familial Discord, Authority Problems, Social Imperturbability, Social Alienation, Self-Alienation, Persecutory Ideas, Poignancy, Naivete, Social Alienation, Emotional Alienation, Lack of Ego Mastery-Cognitive, Lack of Ego Mastery-Conative, Lack of Ego Mastery-Defective Inhibition, Bizarre Sensory Experiences, Amorality, Psychomotor Acceleration, Imperturbability, Ego Inflation); 3 Si Subscales (Shyness/Self-Consciousness, Social Avoidance, Alienation); 15 Adolescent Content Scales (Anxiety, Obsessiveness, Depression, Health Concerns, Alienation, Bizarre Mentation, Anger, Cynicism, Conduct Problems, Low Self-Esteem, Low Aspirations, Social Discomfort, Family Problems, School Problems, Negative Treatment Indicators); 6 Supplementary Scales (Anxiety, Repression, MacAndrew Alcoholism Scale, Alcohol/Drug Problem Acknowledgment, Alcohol/Drug Problem Proneness, Immaturity)].

Administration: Group.

Price Data, 1992: Microtest Reports ($20 per Adolescent Interpretive System, $14 per Extended Score Report, $8 per Basic Service Profile); Prepaid Mail-In Reports ($21 per Adolescent Interpretive System; $15 per Extended Score Report; $9 per Basic Service Profile); $40 per manual; $15 per Adolescent Interpretive System User's Guide; $25 per 10 softcover test booklets; $25 per hardcover test booklet; $75 per audiocassette; $60 per 100 Content/Supplementary Scales Profile Forms; $60 per 100 Harris-Lingoes Subscales Profile Forms; $50 per Basic Scales answer keys; $50 per Content/Supplementary Scales answer keys; $50 per Harris-Lingoes Subscales answer keys; $385 per hand-scoring starter kit including manual, test booklets, Basic Scales keys, Harris-Lingoes Subscales keys, Content/Supplementary Scale keys, 100 hand-scoring answer sheets, 100 Basic Scale Profile Forms, Harris-Lingoes Profile Forms, 100 Content/Supplementary Profile Forms.
Time: Administration time not reported.
Comments: May be administered by audiocassette or microcomputer.
Authors: James N. Butcher, Carolyn L. Williams, John R. Graham, Beverly Kaemmer, Robert P. Archer (manual); Auke Tellegen (manual), Yossef S. Ben-Porath (manual), S. R. Hathaway (test booklet), and J. C. McKinley (test booklet).
Publisher: University of Minnesota Press (distributed by National Computer Systems).
Cross References: Reviews by Charles D. Claiborn and Richard I. Lanyon originally appeared in 12:238; see also T4:1646 (4 references).

Review of the Minnesota Multiphasic Personality Inventory—Adolescent by CHARLES D. CLAIBORN, Professor, Division of Psychology in Education, Arizona State University, Tempe, AZ:

Nearly 50 years after the development of the Minnesota Multiphasic Personality Inventory (MMPI), years during which it became without doubt the most widely used inventory for assessing psychopathology, the MMPI was extensively revised and restandardized as the MMPI-2 (T4:1645). The MMPI-2, like its predecessor, was designed for use with adults. More recently, a second, largely parallel inventory, the Minnesota Multiphasic Personality—Adolescent (MMPI-A), was designed for use with adolescents, ages 14 to 18. Given its parallel development and structure, the MMPI-A shares many strengths and a few weaknesses with the MMPI-2; however, it has a number of unique features as well, as appropriate to its intended use with adolescents.

The development of the MMPI-A so resembles that of the MMPI-2 and is so clearly described in the MMPI-A Manual for Administration, Scoring, and Interpretation that a few comments about it will suffice here. First, the normative sample is admirably diverse and, with a few acknowledged exceptions, probably representative of the adolescent population of the United States. Adolescent norms are essential because adolescents tend to score higher on the MMPI than adults and, if adult norms are used, adolescents may appear more disturbed than they actually are. The clinical sample is less representative than the normative sample: All are from settings in Minneapolis, and the majority are from drug and alcohol treatment. Further work with other, specific clinical samples will strengthen the empirical base of the inventory.

Second, many items from the MMPI and MMPI-2 have been reworded for or omitted entirely from the MMPI-A, and items unique to the MMPI-A have been added (see Appendix E of the manual). The language of MMPI-A items is generally suitable for contemporary adolescents, and item content appropriately reflects adolescent personality and psychopathology. The length of the inventory has been shortened, as well, to 478 items (compared with the MMPI's 566 items), and some of the validity scales and all of the basic clinical scales may be completed in the first 350 items. Length changes, like item changes, make the MMPI-A more accessible to adolescents than the MMPI.

Third, MMPI-A developers employed uniform, rather than linear, T scores for most of the basic clinical scales (Scales 1 to 4 and 6 to 9) and all of the content scales. Uniform T scores, an innovation carried over from the MMPI-2, preserve the positively skewed distributions of these scales but at the same time correct for differential skewness across scales, so that the percentile scores of the different scales are comparable.

User qualifications, administration, and scoring of the inventory are clearly described in the manual. A large part of the manual is devoted to conceptual and psychometric information about each scale and guidelines for scale interpretation. Although users will, of course, consult research reports and texts in making interpretations, the overview to interpretation provided in the manual is excellent. In addition to the text descriptions of the scales, Tables 12 and 24 of the manual contain general interpretive guidelines for the basic clinical and content scales, respectively. These guidelines include cutoff scores for high (or "clinically significant") and moderate evaluations on the scales and describe the degree of confidence one might have in interpretations at each elevation. The clear and uniform guidelines provided in these tables make MMPI-A interpretation more straightforward than interpretation of the original MMPI. Nevertheless, interpretation is still a complex process.

Throughout the text suggestions for interpretation are specific, appropriately tentative and flexible, and empirically based. The tables in Appendix D of the manual, which contain specific behavioral correlates of the validity and basic clinical scales for the normative and clinical samples, are particularly helpful in interpreting those scales. Table 23 in the text has similar information for the content scales but in narrative, rather than statistical, form. Finally, the manual contains two extended case illustrations that are extremely helpful in demonstrating the interpretive process and highlighting features of the inventory. (The only unfortunate aspect of the case illustrations is that although we learn that Joyce, the subject of Case 1, is "attractive," we never discover how Scott, in Case 2, rates on this variable.)

Like the MMPI-2, the MMPI-A has four sets of scales: validity scales, basic clinical scales (several of which have subscales to aid in their interpretation), content scales, and supplementary scales. The authors of the MMPI-A manual helpfully point out the relation between MMPI-A scales and their MMPI-2 and MMPI counterparts, both in terms of the items they comprise and the personality constructs they measure. With respect to validity, the K scale of the MMPI-A is not used as a correction factor for some of the basic clinical scales, as it is with adults, and indeed is hardly interpretable for adolescents. Otherwise, the validity scales of the MMPI-A feature the innovations found in the MMPI-2. The F scale is divided into subscales, F_1 and F_2, that appear in the first and second halves of the inventory, respectively. F_1 may thus serve as a validity indicator for the basic clinical scales, and F_2 for the content and supplementary scales. The old problem with F—

that it may indicate validity problems (exaggeration of symptoms) or serious disturbance—remains; however, helpful suggestions for sorting this out are contained in the manual. The MMPI-A also contains the valuable response set indicators, VRIN (Variable Response Inconsistency) and the TRIN (True Response Inconsistency), which assess indiscriminate and acquiescent/nonacquiescent responding, respectively. The use of these indicators in interpreting the traditional validity scales, particularly F, is well demonstrated in the manual.

The basic clinical scales, despite the wealth of information they provide about client symptomatology, are the most problematic for the inventory. Because they are intended to measure multifaceted psychopathological constructs and because they were developed for this purpose using an empirical criterion method, the clinical scales range widely in internal consistency. Alpha coefficients for the 10 clinical scales are presented in Table 14 of the manual, by sample (normative and clinical) and gender. Of the 40 alpha coefficients, 17 (43%) range from .75 to .91; 18 (45%) range from .55 to .68; and the remaining 5 (13%) range from .35 to .53. Internal consistencies like these make scale interpretation difficult, but the use of the Harris-Lingoes subscales in interpreting Scales 2, 3, 4, 6, 8, and 9 and the Si subscales for interpreting Scale 0 ameliorates this problem somewhat.

Intercorrelations among the clinical scales range widely, as well, from .00 to .85 in the normative sample, as reported in Table C-1 in Appendix C of the manual. There is considerable overlap in what the scales measure. Factor analysis of the clinical and validity scales supports this notion, with a familiar (within the MMPI family) four-factor solution: The first factor, described as "general maladjustment," includes positive loadings by Scales 1 to 4 and 6 to 9, which are the clinical scales most concerned with psychopathology. Scale 9 also loads positively on the second factor, "overcontrol," which is otherwise influenced by the validity scales. The third and fourth factors are represented by Scales 0 and 5, respectively; these are the two clinical scales less concerned with psychopathology. The intercorrelation and factor analytic data simply confirm that interpretation of the clinical scales is going to be a complicated affair.

The clinical scales have retained the labels given to their original MMPI counterparts. This is unfortunate because some of the labels (Hypomania, Psychasthenia) are archaic and others (Hysteria, Psychopathic Deviate) are offensive. A better approach might have been to retain only the scale numbers, because these are widely used and recognized, and to have used the more accurate of the scale labels, such as Depression, only within the scale descriptions. The authors of the manual have actually done this to some extent, for example, in their description of Scale 7 as "originally designed to measure psychasthenia, a neurotic syndrome most closely related to the currently used category of obsessive-compulsive disorder" (p. 48).

The biggest mystery—and interpretive problem—among the clinical scales is Scale 5, which purports to measure Masculinity—Femininity. Why is this scale in the inventory? How is it to be interpreted? Unlike the other clinical scales, with the possible exception of Scale 0, Scale 5 has nothing to do with psychopathology, nor indeed personality. It is an interest measure, and its scores address the clinically (and otherwise) uninteresting question of whether one has stereotypically masculine or feminine interests. The interpretation of the scale is understandably troublesome. It has the lowest internal consistency of the clinical scales, ranging from .35 to .44 in the normative and clinical samples, and the scale correlates are few and contradictory across studies. In addition, interpretive descriptors have nothing explicitly to do with gender or gender identity. The MMPI-A's developers themselves seem puzzled about this scale, as evidence by the odd, inappropriately causal statement in the manual, "Having Scale 5 as the highest scale … seems to have an inhibitory effect on acting-out behaviors in both genders" (p. 47). The developers have a challenge ahead of them if they hope to justify the retention of Scale 5 in the inventory.

The content scales and the new supplementary scales represent probably the most important innovation of the MMPI-A. The content scales were developed using the "rational and statistical" approach that was used for the MMPI-A and that is described in Table 20 of the manual. They have generally higher and less variable internal consistencies than the basic clinical scales. Many of the content scales have MMPI-2 counterparts, though some are unique to the MMPI-A. Even when conceptually similar scales are found on both instruments, they may share only a portion of their items; for example, the Adolescent—Family Problems scale of the MMPI-A has only 15 of its 35 items in common with the Family Problems scale of the MMPI-2. Table 23 of the manual contains information on the relation between the content scales of the MMPI-A and MMPI-2, as well as interpretive information for the MMPI-A scales.

The content scales measure constructs relevant to adolescent symptomatology—for example, anger, low self-esteem, and school problems—and assess symptomatology more specifically and straightforwardly than the basic clinical scales do. The constructs measured by the content scales seem to be more unitary than those measured by the clinical scales, and the content scales themselves seem more homogeneous than the clinical scales. The content scales are clinically interesting in their own right, given the range of symptoms they cover, and they are likely to be helpful, as well, in interpreting the clinical scales.

The MMPI-A contains three unique supplementary scales in addition to supplementary scales found in the MMPI-2. The unique scales measure acknowledgment of alcohol and drug problems, likelihood of having alcohol and drug problems, and (in an unusual step for an MMPI) a theoretically based construct of psychological maturity. Like the content scales, the supplementary scales are clearly relevant to understanding adolescent development and symptomatology; they are interesting in themselves and as adjuncts to clinical scale interpretation.

In conclusion, the MMPI-A is an impressive inventory, sure to become a preeminent tool for assessing adolescent psychopathology. Its flaws are relatively minor, correctable, and enormously outweighted by the strengths of the inventory. Clearly, the MMPI-A was developed with a great deal of care, expertise, and sensitivity to the problems of adolescents and the needs of practitioners who work with them. Practitioners will find MMPI-A materials easy to use, and they may satisfy themselves that despite the complexities involved in interpretation (complexities hardly surprising given the nature of adolescent behavior itself), the considerable and expanding empirical base of the inventory will support their efforts.

Review of the Minnesota Multiphasic Personality Inventory—Adolescent by RICHARD I. LANYON, Professor of Psychology, Arizona State University, Tempe, AZ:

The Minnesota Multiphasic Personality Inventory—Adolescent (MMPI-A), published in 1992, is a revision of the MMPI for use with adolescents of age 14 through 18. It can be considered as parallel to the MMPI-2 (T4:1645), the revision of the MMPI for adults, that was published in 1989. Previous authors have documented the need for these revisions, or restandardizations, of the MMPI: the lack of nationally representative norms; the presence of obsolete and otherwise objectionable items; the lack of percentile equivalence of the T-scores for the clinical scales; and, particularly for adolescents, the lack of item content and scales to assess problems of specific relevance to this population.

DEVELOPMENT. The challenge faced in producing both the MMPI-2 and the MMPI-A was to keep them similar enough to the MMPI so that its vast collection of empirical findings would also apply to the new tests, while correcting as many as possible of the deficiencies. This goal is judged to have been achieved for the MMPI-2 (Archer, 1992), and it is this reviewer's opinion that it has also been achieved for the MMPI-A. Because the MMPI-2 was done first, most of the technical and policy decisions that needed to be made in regard to the MMPI-A had already been worked through, and the basic strategy for revision was the same. An experimental Form TX was created with 704 items: the 550 MMPI items, plus the 58 new items written for the MMPI-2 (to expand the item pool for treatment compliance, attitudes toward self-change, amenability to therapy, alcohol and drug use, eating problems, and suicide potential), plus 96 items specific to adolescence (in the areas of identity formation, negative peer-group influence, school and teachers, relationships with parents and families, and sexuality).

The end-product is a test for which the format is virtually identical to that of the MMPI-2. There are the original three "validity" scales (L, F, and K) and three new ones (F_2, VRIN, and TRIN), the

original 10 basic scales, 15 new content scales, and 6 supplementary scales. All the items on the basic scales appear in the first 350 of the 478 items.

NORMS. Credit is due to the seminal work of Marks, Seeman, and Haller (1974), who discovered that separate adolescent norms were needed for the MMPI, and that omitting the K-correction resulted in better validities. To develop norms for the MMPI-A, subjects were obtained through schools in eight states (California, Minnesota, New York, North Carolina, Ohio, Pennsylvania, Virginia, and Washington), with the goal of obtaining a balanced sample of subjects according to geographic region, urban-rural residence, and ethnic background. These balances were satisfactorily achieved; however, like the MMPI-2, the MMPI-A normative sample is quite heavily skewed in the direction of higher education and occupational level. The significance of these imbalances, although minimized in the manual, is unknown at the present time. The intended age range for the MMPI-A is 14–18, although bright, mature 12- and 13-year-olds can also be tested, and 18-year-olds who have completed high school should be given the MMPI-2.

SUPPLEMENTARY SCALES. Of the six supplementary scales, A (Anxiety), R (Repression), and MAC-R (Alcoholism) are revised and shortened versions of the corresponding MMPI scales. Three additional scales are included: ACK (Alcohol/Drug Problem Acknowledgment), PRO (Alcohol/Drug Problem Proneness), and IMM (Immaturity). These scales focus specifically on adolescents, and each was constructed using a different series of psychometric steps. The manual includes somewhat variable test-retest reliabilities for these scales.

CONTENT SCALES. Based on the premise of the primacy of content in underpinning the validity of personality assessment devices, and on the success of the Wiggins' (1966) content scales for the MMPI, a great deal of effort was expended in developing and validating a set of 15 content scales for the MMPI-A. This work is documented in a separate, book-length report (Williams, Butcher, Ben-Porath, & Graham, 1992). Although the scale constructs partially overlap with those of the 15 MMPI-2 content scales, the item sets are different in all cases.

VALIDITY. Although the procedures used in the original development of the MMPI were technically advanced for their time, they are simplistic by today's standards. Specifically, state-of-the-art test construction technology involves the use of many psychometric steps in the development and final selection of the items. All of these steps are geared toward ensuring that the scale will be valid for its intended uses; in other words, they can be viewed as procedures for *building into* an instrument the foundation for its validity. Scales that are not based on such work are simply collections of items, whose validity is more-or-less unknown and must be established entirely through subsequent research. Although such research is also necessary for state-of-the-art scales, it is much more likely to be successful because of the extensive item development procedures.

As with other tests of its era, the original MMPI could be considered valid only to the extent that it was supported by subsequent empirical research. Fortunately, there is a huge quantity of such work, presented in many sources, including landmark works by Lachar (1974) and Marks, Seeman, and Haller (1974). Thus, to the extent that the MMPI-A retains the essence of the MMPI, the basic clinical scales come complete with demonstrated validity.

The validity of the 15 new content scales must be examined separately. Fortunately for MMPI-A users, the development of these scales involved extensive psychometric procedures, and although experts might disagree as to a particular strategy or sequence of steps, there can be no doubt that the potential of these scales for clinical utility is very high. Initial research toward the establishment of external validity for the content scales is presented in the volumes by Butcher and Williams (1992) and Williams et al. (1992), and is summarized in the manual. Thus, the future of the MMPI-A as an empirically valid device seems assured.

OVERVIEW. How wise was it to expend such a huge amount of time and energy in "cleaning up" the MMPI for more satisfactory use with adolescents, rather than simply building a new test? The answer, as with the MMPI-2, is that the life of the MMPI has thereby been enhanced and significantly extended, and it is a safe prediction that further empirical validity studies will appear rather quickly to facilitate the adaptation of the existing MMPI adolescent interpretive research for use with the MMPI-A. Overall, in surveying the available test instruments for assessing psychopathology in adolescents, the MMPI-A would appear to have no serious competition.

REVIEWER'S REFERENCES

Wiggins, J. S. (1966). Substantive dimensions of self-report in the MMPI item pool. *Psychological Monographs, 80*(20, Whole No. 630).

Lachar, D. (1974). *The MMPI: Clinical assessment and automated interpretation.* Los Angeles: Western Psychological Services.

Marks, P. A., Seeman, W., & Haller, D. L. (1974). *The actuarial use of the MMPI with adolescents and adults.* Baltimore: Williams and Wilkins.

Archer, R. P. (1992). [Review of the Minnesota Multiphasic Personality Inventory-2.] In J. J. Kramer & J. C. Conoley (Eds.), *The eleventh mental measurements yearbook* (pp. 558–562). Lincoln, NE: Buros Institute of Mental Measurements.

Butcher, J. N., & Williams, C. L. (1992). *Essentials of MMPI-2 and MMPI-A interpretation.* Minneapolis: University of Minnesota Press.

Williams, C. L., Butcher, J. N., Ben-Porath, Y. S., & Graham, J. R. (1992). *MMPI-A content scales: Assessing psychopathology in adolescents.* Minneapolis: University of Minnesota Press.

[2.26]
People Performance Profile.

Purpose: Designed to determine how employees perceive their organization, their work team, and themselves.

Population: Organization members.

Publication Date: 1985.

Acronym: PPP.

Scores, 20: Organizational Performance (Planning, Management Procedures, Motivational Climate, Physical Environment, Organizational Stress Factors), Work—Team Performance (Supervision, Role Clarity, Communications, Conflict Management, Problem Solving, Meeting Effectiveness, Job Satisfaction, Group Productivity), Personal Fitness (Health, Exercise, Nutrition, Alcohol and Drug Use, Interpersonal Support, Time Management, Personal Stress Management).

Administration: Group.

Price Data: Available from publisher.

Time: Administration time not reported.

Authors: Bob Crosby, John Scherer (survey, leader's guide), and Gil Crosby (work-team guide).

Publisher: Pfeiffer & Company International Publishers.

Cross References: Rreviews by Seymour Adler and Larry Cochran originally appeared in 10:274.

Review of the People Performance Profile by SEYMOUR ADLER, *Associate Professor of Applied Psychology, Department of Management, Stevens Institute of Technology, Hoboken, NJ:*

The People Performance Profile (PPP) is an organizational survey instrument designed to diagnose organizational effectiveness across 20 dimensions that are presumed to have impact on productivity and employee satisfaction. The authors have designed the instrument to be used as the basis of an organizational development process. A Leader's Guide and a Work-Team Guide are provided to structure the intervention process meant to accompany administration, analysis, and feedback of the PPP.

The instrument itself contains 190 items, divided into three sections, and takes from 30-45 minutes to complete. Completed forms are submitted to the test publisher for analysis. Results are presented on both an organizational level and on a subgroup level. To protect the anonymity of respondents, subgroups must contain at least four members in order to be separately analyzed.

Section I of the questionnaire addresses the organization-level factors of planning, management procedures, motivational climate, and physical environment. In addition, an organizational stress score is calculated from some unspecified subset of items in this section. Section II addresses the work-team factors of supervision, role clarity, communications, conflict management, problem-solving, meeting effectiveness, job satisfaction, and group productivity. Section III, which organizations may or may not want to include in the survey, addresses personal fitness and includes subsections on health habits, exercise, nutrition, alcohol and drug use (the only dimension excluded from the survey feedback provided to participants), interpersonal support, time management, and personal stress management. In addition, respondents indicate those dimensions they would be interested in seeing improve. Finally, many of the 20 subsections described above are in fact comprised of even more detailed multi-item subscales from which separate scores are calculated.

In sum, then, the PPP appears to be comprehensive in scope while measuring organizational attitudes and perceptions at a detailed level. As such, researchers and practitioners might find the PPP useful in exploratory research.

Unfortunately, technical documentation for the PPP is inadequate to address basic questions concerning the reliability and construct validity of the 20 dimension scores derived from the PPP, let alone the more detailed subscores provided as output. Consequently, at this point the PPP cannot

be recommended as an instrument of demonstrated value. In the one study cited, 40 employees in four work groups—two effective and two ineffective—completed the PPP on two occasions, 1 month apart. The correlation between the two administrations of the survey is reported as $r = .95$. Presumably, "total PPP score" was correlated over two administrations, although no mention is made anywhere in the support materials, or in the computer analysis of the PPP, of an overall score, nor is it clear what such a score would mean. No reliability analysis of any sort—internal consistency or stability—is provided for any of the PPP dimension or subscale scores.

Users might also like to know the extent to which the scales on the PPP are intercorrelated, especially because some of the items included as work-team level items appear to address organization-level factors. For example, among the items presumably relating to communication within the immediate work group are those that address organization-wide communication from top management. Unfortunately, an overall correlation matrix is not provided.

The only validity data reported are from a concurrent study which showed, for a sample of 40 employees in four work groups, that—on an overall profile basis—group effectiveness related significantly to PPP responses. On the whole, then, the publishers provide wholly inadequate data to support their claim that the instrument "has the highest reliability and validity achievable" (PPP Research and Validity Summary, undated).

Some potential users might find the very title of this instrument objectionable, because it implies that the attitudinal and perceptual dimensions measured help determine performance in organizations. This implication is strengthened by the opening sentence of the introduction to the survey, which refers to employee productivity. Unfortunately, this approach perpetuates the myth held by many managers that the organizational climate and attitudinal dimensions measured on the PPP have a demonstrated impact on productivity. More suitable is the description provided in the accompanying Guides that describes the PPP as a survey of the work environment.

Finally, those considering the PPP for exploratory research might want to revise the response scale utilized in the instrument. Virtually all 190 items are rated on a 5-point frequency scale (from "never" to "always") although the vast majority of items are more suitably rated on an agreement Likert-type scale.

Review of the People Performance Profile by LARRY COCHRAN, Associate Professor of Counselling Psychology, The University of British Columbia, Vancouver, British Columbia, Canada:

Apparently, the People Performance Profile is designed to be used as a part of a pre-set organizational effectiveness program for working teams within organizational settings. Members of a working team first complete an 11-page survey. The answer sheets are then computer scored. When the scores for the group are returned to the organization, two meetings are held for the working team, conducted by a guide in accordance with a 30-page guidance manual. Using the tabulated responses the working team is oriented toward improving the work situation rather that blaming personalities, and becomes acquainted with the interpretive scale by identifying group strengths and weaknesses. Items with low scores suggest problem areas. The team is then led to exemplify problems, brainstorm solutions, and make recommendations to their supervisor. Essentially, it is a test-referenced program for increasing the productivity and quality of life of a working team.

The survey is composed of 190 items such as "my supervisor coordinates the work of my team well." Each item is rated on a 5-point scale ranging from always, frequently, occasionally, seldom, to never. The survey has three major sections with subsections under each. Organizational performance indicators include subsections on planning, management procedures, motivational climate, physical environment, and organizational stress. Work-team performance indicators include supervision, role clarity, communications, conflict management, problem solving, meeting effectiveness, job satisfaction, and group productivity. Personal fitness indicators include health habits, exercise, nutrition, alcohol and drug use, interpersonal support, time management, and personal stress management. The items are transparent with an obvious positive or negative answer. Indeed, subsection instructions are educational, indicating what, for

instance, good supervision is. For truthful answers, the authors rely upon the test rationale, which is that the test provides a way "to determine what needs to be done to make your organization a healthier, happier, better place." Individual profiles are not returned. Rather, team scores are returned for each item, subsection, and section, along with frequencies of response for scale points. The scoring scale ranges from 0 to 6 with labels of critical, marginal, functional, good, excellent, and superior.

The test items are clear, seem well-constructed, and appear to have content validity. The survey of issues is broad and reasonably conceived, although it would be desirable if a manual presented a theory that suggested the items or described free responses of workers to determine if coverage is as broad as it appears.

Unfortunately, there is no test manual. There is no indication of how scores were derived, why responses require computer scoring, or what the scores mean with reference to a norm group. There is no indication of how the test was constructed, nor any evidence for reliability and validity. The survey has the appearance of a test, but no substance whatever in the sense that no standards for tests are satisfied.

Without reliability, validity, and norming group evidence, the survey is more of a checklist than a test. It might be argued that this is enough for the use envisioned. That is, it organizes team member responses so the team can concentrate upon problematic issues for correction. However, there are two difficulties with this position. First, if the survey is posed as a test, it should meet acceptable standards or at least provide evidence of an attempt to meet them. Second, the responses are returned as scores and there is no evidence that these scores accurately represent what they are purported to mean. For example, how would one know if a team characterized as functional by this test actually was functional, whatever functional might mean in this context? Would an improvement of scores reflect an improvement in work productivity, worker satisfaction, or what? Are some sections more important than others? Do the sections really measure different things? There are no answers to these and other questions, and no research context to know how to interpret the scores or gauge their significance.

The survey has such strong face validity and fits so well as a basis for the work-team meetings that one can almost be lulled into thinking that the lack of evidence does not matter. That is, the test items provide a focus for problem-solving discussions. What could be clearer? However, it does matter. For example, suppose that with further evidence, one found that a functional score for, say, role clarity was actually very low with reference to norms for productive and satisfied work teams. The work team would no doubt miss it, concentrating instead upon presumably very low scores from other sections. In short, they could be distracted away from areas that might really make a difference in their setting. Norms, along with other statistics, provide a way to highlight areas upon which to focus with some degree of confidence and a way to interpret the meaning of the aggregated scores. The People Performance Profile is woefully lacking in this very basic and essential information.

[2.27]

Personal Adjustment and Role Skills Scale.

Purpose: Constructed to evaluate the community adjustment of adults.
Population: Mental health patients and clinic clients.
Publication Dates: 1974–1981.
Acronym: PARS Scale.
Scores, 8: Interpersonal Relations, Alienation, Anxiety, Confusion, Alcohol—Drug Use, House Activity, Child Relations, Work.
Administration: Individual.
Price Data, 1990: $9 per 25 scales including profile; $10 per manual ('81, 27 pages); $11 per specimen set.
Time: Administration time not reported.
Comments: Pre- and posttreatment ratings by significant others.
Authors: Robert B. Ellsworth and Shanae L. Ellsworth.
Publisher: Consulting Psychologists Press, Inc.
Cross References: Reviews by Robert H. Deluty and David R. Wilson originally appeared in 9:936 (1 reference); see also T3:1765 (8 references); for a review by William J. Eichman of an earlier edition, see 8:638 (6 references).

Review of the Personal Adjustment and Role Skills Scale by ROBERT H. DELUTY, Assistant Professor of Psychology, University of Maryland Baltimore County, Baltimore, MD:

Several versions of the Personal Adjustment and Role Skills (PARS) Scale have been developed over the past 10 years for use by significant others (Ellsworth, 1975, 1981). In the most current version (Ellsworth, 1981), the significant other evaluates a given person's behavior during the past month on 31 items representing eight adjustment dimensions.

Throughout the development of the earlier PARS Scales, five criteria were utilized for item selection: (1) sensitivity to differences among clinic, hospital, and "non-client" samples; (2) sensitivity to pre-post treatment change; (3) internal consistency; (4) test-retest reliability; and (5) high factor loadings. In constructing the present version of the scale, factor consistency across four groups—men, women, clinic clients, and hospitalized patients—was used as an additional item-selection criterion. The internal consistency of those items meeting this criterion was then assessed; only those items contributing to high factor score internal consistency were retained.

Unfortunately, the samples used by Ellsworth to develop the current PARS Scale were the same samples utilized to assess its internal reliability and criterion validity. The validity coefficients are, therefore, spuriously high, since they capitalize on random sampling errors within those particular samples (Anastasi, 1982). The internal reliabilities for the PARS factor scores (which range from .83 to .92) were obtained only on samples of clinic clients and hospitalized patients; whether comparable reliability coefficients would be obtained with non-client groups or with other clinical samples has not been assessed. In addition to the absence of cross-validation and the failure to assess internal consistency for samples other than those used in item-selection, there are several other major flaws in the scale's reliability and validity research.

Although Ellsworth reports that the factor test-retest reliabilities of earlier versions of the PARS Scale were between .80 and .98, no data are provided concerning the temporal consistency of the present version. Data bearing on the scale's criterion validity were reported by LaFerriere (1979), who found modest correlations (.22 to .45) between ratings on particular PARS factors and self-ratings by outpatients, at both intake and 6-month follow-up, on the Brief Symptom Inventory, a modified version of the SCL-90 (Derogatis, Lipman, & Covi, 1973). In addition, PARS Scale ratings showed mild to moderate agreement with self-ratings of clinic clients on Ellsworth's Profile of Adaptation to Life-Clinical (PAL-C) Scale. These correlations were generally high for overt forms of adjustment and maladjustment (e.g., "closeness" between spouses, alcohol/drug use), but were substantially lower, and typically non-significant, when internal states were assessed (e.g., negative emotions, sense of well-being). Unfortunately, the Brief Symptom Inventory has been shown not to possess construct validity for men (LaFerriere, 1979), the criterion validity of the PAL-C Scale has not been demonstrated adequately (Deluty, in press), and the vast majority of the above correlations are either modest or non-significant. Thus, the evidence for the PARS Scale's criterion validity is quite unimpressive.

The major problem with the scale, however, involves the determination of adjustment ranges and pre-treatment-post-treatment change norms. These change norms were established from the pre- and post-treatment PARS ratings of clinic clients and hospitalized patients, while the adjustment ranges were based on the average post-treatment scores of these individuals. The lack of information concerning the nature of these outpatient and inpatient samples is astounding. No data are provided concerning their age ranges, sex, presenting problems, or the nature of treatment they received. Although the diagnoses of the inpatient and outpatient samples are reported, only three diagnostic categories were used: neurotic, psychotic, and organic. Absolutely no information is provided regarding the differential diagnostic criteria employed, and it is unknown whether all outpatients and inpatients were "forced" into one of these three categories or whether patients not suffering from neurotic, psychotic, or organic disturbances (e.g., those with personality or substance use disorders) were excluded from the study. Even if patients with other disorders were excluded, the variety of disturbances subsumed under the broad labels "neurotic," "psychotic," and "organic" is so large that being assigned such a diagnosis tells us very little about the patient. Furthermore, the decision to base the adjustment ranges on the average ratings of post-treatment clients, as opposed to those of non-clinical samples with clearly demonstrated high levels of adjustment, is particu-

larly odd given Ellsworth's failure to assess objectively how well adjusted the post-treatment clients actually were. Thus, in view of the dearth of information regarding the inpatients' and outpatients' demographic characteristics, diagnoses, and treatments, one cannot use or interpret with confidence Ellsworth's adjustment ranges or pre-post treatment change norms.

On a positive note, the intercorrelations among factor scores provide some construct validity for certain factor dimensions. One would predict that interpersonal relationship scores should be highly related; indeed, the correlation between Close Relations and Child Relations ratings was .54 for men and .48 for women. In addition, one would expect that the intercorrelations of the three dimensions of Personal Adjustment (Alienation, Anxiety, and Confusion) should be higher than their correlations with the other dimensions; this, too, was shown to be the case for men, although not for women (for men, the three intercorrelations ranged from .54 to .56; for women, from .31 to .49).

To summarize, evidence for the criterion validity of the 31-item PARS Scale is quite weak. Temporal consistency has not been evaluated, and internal consistency of the PARS factor scores has only been assessed for the clinical samples used to develop the scale. The lack of information regarding the clinical samples' demographic dimensions, diagnoses, and treatments render the scale's adjustment ranges and change norms largely useless. Internally-valid studies using samples which are described thoroughly and diagnosed differentially (according to well-established behavioral criteria) are, therefore, strongly encouraged in order to assess the PARS Scale's reliability, convergent and discriminant validity, adjustment-maladjustment ranges, and clinical sensitivity.

REVIEWER'S REFERENCES

Derogatis, L. R., Lipman, R. S., & Covi, L. SCL-90: An outpatient psychiatric rating scale. PSYCHOPHARMACOLOGY BULLETIN, 1973, 9, 13-28.

Ellsworth, R. B. Consumer feedback in measuring the effectiveness of mental health programs. In M. Guttentag & E. L. Struening (Eds.), HANDBOOK OF EVALUATION RESEARCH (Vol. 2). Beverly Hills, CA: Sage Publications, 1975.

LaFerriere, L. The validity of a self-report instrument for evaluating mental health treatment outcomes. Unpublished doctoral dissertation, Michigan State University, 1979.

Ellsworth, R. B. PARS SCALE: MEASURING PERSONAL ADJUSTMENT AND ROLE SKILLS. Palo Alto, CA: Consulting Psychologists Press, Inc., 1981.

Anastasi, A. PSYCHOLOGICAL TESTING (5th Ed.). New York: Macmillan, 1982.

Deluty, R. H. Profile of Adaptation to Life-Clinical Scale. In J. V. Mitchell (Ed.), THE NINTH MENTAL MEASUREMENTS YEARBOOK. Lincoln: Buros Institute of Mental Measurements, in press.

Review of Personal Adjustment and Role Skills Scale by DAVID R. WILSON, Coordinator of Psychology Services and Research & Evaluation, Brewer-Porch Children's Center, The University of Alabama, University, AL:

The Personal Adjustment and Role Skills (PARS) is a brief (31-item), easily administered scale designed to be filled out by significant others regarding the personal adjustment and the instrumental performance of adult psychiatric patients. The manual provides a thorough discussion of the rationale for using ratings made by significant others as compared to the use of ratings by staff, or by the patients themselves. PARS is designed to be filled out at the time the patient enters treatment, and then again soon after discharge. The manual also includes suggestions for ways to reduce information loss, a major problem with this type of data.

There have been several previous versions of the PARS with the number of items ranging from 120 to 50. The 31-item current version with 8 factors was chosen based on five criteria: (1) item test-retest reliability; (2) item contribution to the factor's internal consistency; (3) pre-post T-test differences; (4) the ability of the item to discriminate clinic, hospital and non-client populations; and (5) factor loadings. This version also differs from the most recent version (previously reviewed 8:638) in that the same form and factors are used for males and females. The sample used in the item selection phase consisted of 248 outpatients and 204 inpatients. Only sketchy information is provided about these samples.

The manual indicates that the factors are "relatively uncorrelated" even though there are some intercorrelations in the .50s. The fact that some of the scales do correlate in an expected fashion is used as evidence of validity. Acceptable levels of test-retest reliability (factor test-retest reliabilities ranged from .80 to .98) and internal consistency (alphas from .83 to .92) have been demonstrated.

The question of the validity of PARS was approached in several ways. First, ratings by relatives were found to correlate with self-rated PARS of hospital patients. Significant correlations with various scales of the developer's PAL scale are also cited as evidence for validity. Discriminant validity is demonstrated by virtue of the fact that the PARS scores differentiated between the pre-treatment adjustment of clinic clients and hospitalized patients. It is commendable that there has been an attempt to establish discriminant validity, but the methods used here are questionable. One of the criteria for including items in the PARS was the ability of these to discriminate between clinic and hospitalized patients. It is not legitimate to then cite this as evidence of discriminant validity unless cross-validation occurs through the use of other subjects.

The manual provides clear instruction for administration of the PARS, as well as suggestions for maximizing the return of these questionnaires. The procedures for scoring and profiling are also simple. In order to interpret the PARS, the factor scores are transferred to a profile sheet on which there are T-scores based on the average post-treatment scores of people who had received mental health services. This reviewer wonders why there are not two profiles, so the average pre-treatment scores could also be considered. Another potentially helpful feature of the PARS is the inclusion of change norms. These are standardized residual scores which take into account the fact that post-treatment scores significantly correlate with pre-treatment scores. This type of score is highly preferable to reliance on change scores, because of this statistical association; making clinicians and program evaluators more aware of this may be the major contribution of this scale. Change norms are referenced by the simple procedure of consulting a table for each factor. In this table, the vertical axis contains the post score and the horizontal axis the pre score, and by looking at the intersection of these two, the standardized change score is read. These scores have a mean of 50 and a standard deviation of 10, so they are interpreted like T-scores. The norms for these tables came from the combined sample of outpatients and hospitalized psychiatric patients, and the test developer states that separate tables were not necessary since the slope of the regression line of these two samples did not differ significantly.

The PARS does achieve its objective of being an easily administered instrument to be used in determining the outcome of mental health services. There are many reasons to recommend its use, especially for program evaluations. The main caveat to be offered here would be for the user to be cautious in relying too heavily on the profiles and the change norms that are provided in the manual. The rationale for these norms is that patients can be compared to some standard based on a sample which has undergone similar treatment. Because of the diversity of mental health treatment and institutions, however, interpretations based on a sample of 248 outpatients (treatment unspecified) and 204 inpatients (treatment unspecified) should be considered tentative and speculative. Anyone who is using this scale (especially in a large scale program involving a substantial sample of patients) should consider developing local norms. It is overly optimistic to expect that norms which are gathered on this restrictive a sample should generalize to all mental health populations. Other than this potential for interpretive overgeneralization, the PARS is a very worthwhile instrument.

[2.28]
Personality Assessment Inventory.

Purpose: Designed to provide information relevant to clinical diagnosis, treatment planning, and screening for psychopathology.
Population: Ages 18–adult.
Publication Date: 1991.
Acronym: PAI.
Scores, 54: Inconsistency, Infrequency, Negative Impression, Positive Impression, Somatic Complaints (Conversion, Somatization, Health Concerns, Total), Anxiety (Cognitive, Affective, Physiological, Total), Anxiety-Related Disorders (Obsessive-Compulsive, Phobias, Traumatic Stress, Total), Depression (Cognitive, Affective, Physiological, Total), Mania (Activity Level, Grandiosity, Irritability, Total), Paranoia (Hypervigilance, Persecution, Resentment, Total), Schizophrenia (Psychotic Experiences, Social Detachment, Thought Disorder, Total), Borderline Features (Affective Instability, Identity Problems, Negative Relationships, Self-Harm, Total), Antisocial Features (Antisocial Behaviors, Egocentricity, Stimulus-Seeking, Total), Alcohol Problems, Drug Problems, Aggression (Aggressive Attitude, Verbal Aggression, Physical Aggression, Total), Suicidal Ideation, Stress, Nonsupport, Treatment Rejection, Dominance, Warmth, Total.
Administration: Individual or group.
Price Data, 1995: $135 per comprehensive kit including professional manual (193 pages), 2 reusable item booklets, 2 administration folios, 25 Form HS handscorable answer sheets, 25 adult profile forms, and 25 critical items forms; $30 per professional manual; $17 per reus-

able item booklet; $24 per 25 Form HS handscorable answer sheets; $15 per 25 profile forms; $17 per 25 critical items forms; $17 per administration folio.
Time: (40–50) minutes.
Comments: Self-report inventory of adult psychopathology.
Author: Leslie C. Morey.
Publisher: Psychological Assessment Resources, Inc.
Cross References: Reviews by Gregory J. Boyle and Michael G. Kavan originally appeared in 12:290 (8 references); see also T4:1997 (3 references).

Review of the Personality Assessment Inventory by GREGORY J. BOYLE, Associate Professor of Psychology, Bond University, Gold Coast, Queensland, Australia:

The Personality Assessment Inventory (PAI) has been developed as a multidimensional alternative to the Minnesota Multiphasic Personality Inventory (MMPI) for assessing abnormal personality traits. According to Morey (manual, p. 5), the PAI was designed "to provide information relevant to clinical diagnoses, treatment planning and screening for psychopathology." The PAI is a self-report questionnaire consisting of 344 items (scored on a 4-point ordinal scale: F = False, Not At All True; ST = Slightly True; MT = Mainly True; VT = Very True). Some 22 nonoverlapping scales include 4 validity scales, 11 clinical scales, 5 treatment scales, and 2 interpersonal scales (10 scales are further subdivided into 31 conceptually distinct subscales). Most scales consist of 8, 12, or 24 items with an average grade 4 reading level. Validity scales measure response Inconsistency, Infrequency, Negative Impression, and Positive Impression. The clinical scales are Somatic Complaints, Anxiety, Anxiety-Related Disorders, Depression, Mania, Paranoia, Schizophrenia, Borderline Features, Antisocial Features, Alcohol Problems, and Drug Problems. Treatment scales are Aggression, Suicidal Ideation, Stress, Nonsupport, and Treatment Rejection. Interpersonal scales are Dominance and Warmth.

Psychopathological syndromes measured by the PAI were selected in view of contemporary nosology and diagnostic practice. Answers can be scored by hand (HS Answer Sheet), or optical scanning (SS Answer Sheet). Profile forms (Adults; College Students) allow quick conversion of raw scale scores into linear T-scores. A Critical Items Form provides specific information as to Delusions and Hallucinations, Potential for Self-Harm, Potential for Aggression, Substance Abuse, Potential Malingering, Unreliability/Resistance, and Traumatic Stressors. The test author recommends that positive responses to any critical items should be investigated further.

The PAI was developed in the USA for use with individuals aged 18 and older, using an adult normative standardization sample (stratified on gender, race, and age according to 1995 U.S. Census projections); adult clinical patients; and college students (all samples comprised at least 1,000 individuals). The PAI manual contains descriptive characteristics for each sample, including scale and subscale means and standard deviations by gender, race, and age, as well as detailed specimen profiles.

The PAI contains a number of items concerning sexual and bodily functions that may be objectionable to some individuals, such as Item 315 ("I have little interest in sex"), and Item 312 ("I frequently have diarrhea"). Item 40 ("My favorite poet is Raymond Kertezc") assumes specific knowledge.

Moderator variables (age and sex) appear to have some effects on the discriminative validity of PAI scales (Boyle & Lennon, 1994). For the normative group, differences in scale scores between males and females are negligible, except for the Antisocial and Alcohol Problems scales (higher incidence of antisocial disorder and alcoholism in males). Differences due to race are also small. Age is important, as younger individuals obtain higher scores on Anxiety, Paranoia, Borderline Features, and Antisocial Features. For adults aged 60 or over, mean scores generally are below those for the entire sample. Also, years of education are directly related to PAI scale scores, with more highly educated individuals usually obtaining lower mean scores.

Use of the pathognomic sign approach for the Schizophrenia scale may be problematic (cf. Newmark, Falk, Johns, Borer, & Forehand, 1976). The limited scope of the 12-item Alcohol Problems scale may not be sufficiently sensitive in view of the occurrence of distinct alcoholic subgroups (cf. Corbisiero & Reznikoff, 1991). The implicit assumption of comparability across scales may be unwarranted, as linear T-scores do not take account of differing distributions of scale scores.

The manual author suggests adequate scale and subscale reliabilities. Alpha coefficients of internal consistency for the 22 scales range from .45 to .90 (median .81); from .22 to .89 (median .82); and from .23 to .94 (median .86) for the normative, college, and clinical samples. Item homogeneity is low (median .22, .21, .29 respectively), so that item redundancy is minimal and breadth of measurement good, with most items within each scale contributing new information to the particular construct being measured (cf. Boyle, 1991).

Median alphas for Whites and Nonwhites are .77 and .78; for Men and Women .79 and .75; and for Under Age 40 vs. Age 40 and Over .79 and .75, respectively. Subscale median alphas are .71, .73, and .80 for the normative, college, and clinical samples, whereas median item homogeneities are .27, .28, and .35, respectively.

Test-retest reliabilities (retest interval 3–4 weeks) ranged from .31 to .92 (median .82). Low test-retest coefficients were obtained for Inconsistency (.31) and Infrequency (.48), two of the validity scales. Subscale test-retest reliabilities ranged from .68 to .85 (median .78). Boyle and Lennon (1994) reported test-retest coefficients (retest interval 28 days) for the PAI scales ranging from .62 to .86 (median .76), with several scales exhibiting inadequate stability (some less than .7). For trait scales, stabilities should be .8 or higher (cf. Boyle, 1985).

A short-form of 160 items is available, but the 22 scales have insufficient items (mean of 8 items/scale) to achieve adequate reliability. Application of the Spearman-Brown prophecy formula (Crocker & Algina, 1986) suggests that even an adequate stability coefficient of .8 would reduce to .65 for the 160-item version of the PAI. Consequently, use of the short form is not recommended.

Concurrent validity correlations of the PAI validity, clinical, treatment, and interpersonal scales with several other personality instruments (e.g., MMPI, STAI, Beck Scales, Wahler Physical Symptoms Inventory, Fear Survey Schedule) reveal many small to moderate coefficients, suggesting only relatively modest common variance. Exploratory factor analyses based on the scale and subscale intercorrelations for the standardization and clinical samples are methodologically questionable (using the inadequate "Little Jiffy" procedure—cf. McDonald, 1985). Consequently, the four higher-order personality trait factors reported are almost certainly inaccurate. The confirmatory factor analyses are apparently based on the same data sets ("standardization clinical subjects") used in the exploratory factor analyses (Breckler, 1990). Application of cluster analysis (using a subsample of only 300 clinical subjects) to discover modal profiles in clinical samples would be expected to yield unstable clusters (cf. Cuttance & Ecob, 1987, p. 243).

On the positive side, the PAI includes current items, and avoids colloquial and slang expressions. Items considered potentially biased (on gender, ethnic, economic, religious or other grounds) were excluded. Furthermore, the PAI manual is both comprehensive and informative. Detailed information is provided on psychometric issues, including reliability and concurrent validity data, for each of the scales and subscales across several samples. One notable exception is the lack of concurrent validity correlations between the PAI and the Clinical Analysis Questionnaire or CAQ (Krug, 1980)—a factor analytically derived measure of abnormal personality dimensions.

Boyle and Lennon (1994) reported a significant multivariate main effect across normal, alcoholic, and schizophrenic groups after age and gender effects were partialled out, and significant differences between alcoholic and control groups, and between alcoholic and schizophrenic groups, supporting the discriminative validity of the new PAI instrument. Although the PAI may comprise too many scales with insufficient numbers of items for greatest practical utility, undoubtedly, it will serve a very useful role in both research and applied psychological applications.

Further studies into psychometric properties of the PAI instruments should be encouraged, especially into its construct validity and factor structure. It is important to know whether or not the existing scale and subscale structure of the instrument will stand up in the light of new confirmatory factor analyses, based on appropriately large and independent samples of normal and clinical adult populations (cf. Boyle, Ward, & Lennon, 1994). In addition, development of normative data for use of the PAI overseas (e.g., Australia or Britain)

would greatly enhance the utility of the instrument. As compared with other multidimensional measures of abnormal personality such as the MMPI or CAQ, the PAI appears to make an exciting new contribution in its own right, pending further investigations along the lines suggested above.

REVIEWER'S REFERENCES

Newmark, C. S., Falk, R., Johns, N., Boren, R., & Forehand, R. (1976). Comparing traditional clinical procedures with four systems to diagnose schizophrenia. *Journal of Abnormal Psychology, 85*, 66–72.

Krug, S. E. (1980). *Clinical Analysis Questionnaire manual.* Champaign, IL: Institute for Personality and Ability Testing.

Boyle, G. J. (1985). Self-report measures of depression: Some psychometric considerations. *British Journal of Clinical Psychology, 24*, 45–59.

McDonald, R. P. (1985). *Factor analysis and related methods.* Hillsdale, NJ: Erlbaum.

Crocker, L., & Algina, J. (1986). *Introduction to classical and modern test theory.* Chicago: Holt, Rinehart & Winston.

Cuttance, P., & Ecob, R. (1987). *Structural modeling by example: Applications in educational, sociological, and behavioral research.* New York: Cambridge University Press.

Breckler, S. J. (1990). Applications of covariance structure modeling in psychology: Cause for concern? *Psychological Bulletin, 107*, 260–273.

Boyle, G. J. (1991). Does item homogeneity indicate internal consistency or item redundancy in psychometric scales? *Personality and Individual Differences, 12*, 291–294.

Corbisiero, J. R., & Reznikoff, M. (1991). The relationship between personality type and style of alcohol use. *Journal of Clinical Psychology, 47*, 291–298.

Boyle, G. J., & Lennon, T. J. (1994). Examination of the reliability and validity of the Personality Assessment Inventory. *Journal of Psychopathology and Behavioral Assessment, 16*, 173–187.

Boyle, G. J., Ward, J., & Lennon, T. J. (1994). Personality Assessment Inventory: A confirmatory factor analysis. *Perceptual and Motor Skills, 78*, 1441–1442.

Review of the Personality Assessment Inventory by MICHAEL G. KAVAN, Director of Behavioral Sciences and Associate Professor of Family Practice, Creighton University School of Medicine, Omaha, NE:

The Personality Assessment Inventory (PAI) is a self-administered, objective inventory designed to measure adult (ages 18 and over) personality. Specifically, it is meant to yield information related to the screening, diagnosis, and treatment planning for psychopathology. Three-hundred and forty-four items make up 22 nonoverlapping full scales (i.e., 4 validity, 11 clinical, 5 treatment, and 2 interpersonal scales). Ten of these full scales contain conceptually derived subscales that are meant to more completely cover each clinical construct and facilitate interpretation. The clinical syndromes measured by the PAI were selected based on their historical importance within the nosology of mental disorders and their current significance in diagnostic practice.

ADMINISTRATION AND SCORING. The PAI is designed to be administered to adults in either individual or group testing situations. A fourth grade reading level (Flesch-Kincaid) is necessary to complete the PAI. Upon administration, respondents are requested to first complete basic demographic information on the answer sheet and then to follow the directions within the test item booklet. Unlike many other objective personality inventories, the PAI does not use "true/false," "yes/no," or forced-choice response formats. Instead, it uses a 4-point Likert-type response format (i.e., *false, not at all true, slightly true, mainly true*, or *very true*). The inventory is available in English, Spanish, and audiotape versions. A software system for administration, scoring, and interpretation may also be purchased from the publisher. Answer sheets are available for both handscoring and optical scanning. Typical administration times range between 40–50 minutes.

In order to hand score the PAI one must peel away the top answer sheet to reveal a self-carbon page that has item scores (ranging from 0 to 3) for all 344 items. Items belonging to each full scale or subscale, which are designated by ruled and color-shaded boxes, are summed and transferred to a profile sheet. Although most of this is done with ease, some difficulty occurs in the calculation of the Inconsistency (ICN) scale because it requires one to determine the absolute value of the difference in scores for 10 pairs of items.

PAI full scale and subscale raw scores are then plotted onto the profile sheet and converted to linear T-scores. These scores may then be compared to both the standardization sample and a "representative *clinical* sample" (p. 11) that is noted by a blue profile line on the form. For the adult form, this blue profile line is two standard deviations above the mean for 1,246 patients selected from "a variety of clinical settings." Interpretation proceeds by using single scale interpretation and then examining the configuration or pattern of elevations. Cluster analysis was used to determine 10 modal profiles that can serve as a foundation for interpretation; however, assigning a particular profile to one of these groups is both complicated and laborious. Finally, 27 critical items, which are distributed across seven content areas, may be examined for further inquiry.

RELIABILITY. Internal consistency (coefficient alpha) values are presented within the manual for full scales and subscales for the census-matched normative sample (N = 1,000), college student sample (N = 1,051), and the clinical sample (N =

1,246). Median alphas for the 22 full scale scores for the three groups are .81 (range of .45 to .90), .82 (range .22 to .89), and .86 (range .23 to .94), respectively. Whereas most of these alphas are in the .70s to .90s range, coefficients for the Inconsistency (ICN) and Infrequency (INF) full scales tend to be low for each sample. The alpha ranges for the 31 subscales are .51 to .81 for the census sample, .57 to .85 for the college sample, and .55 to .89 for the clinical sample. Alpha coefficients for the full scales are also presented by race, gender, and age for the census-matched standardization sample.

Test-retest correlations for a community sample (n = 75) ranged from .29 to .94 for the full scales and from .67 to .90 for the subscales over a 24-day period. Test-retest correlations for a college sample (n = 80) ranged from .32 to .90 for the full scales and from .54 to .86 for the subscales over a 28-day period. Mean T-scores for the combined samples are also provided for the two administrations for full and subscale scores. Whereas most of the test-retest subscale correlations are respectable given their length, the ICN and INF full scale correlations are considerably lower (i.e., range is .31 to .48) for the combined sample. Rogers, Flores, Ustad, and Sewell (1995) administered the English and Spanish versions of the PAI to monolingual and bilingual clients and found considerable variability in the correlations between the Spanish and English PAI validity scales. The mean correspondence correlation between these versions for the 11 full scales was r = .71. Slightly lower correlations existed between these versions on the five treatment and two interpersonal scales (mean r = .68). The median test-retest correlation was r = .58 for the validity scales and r = .78 for the clinical scales (median interval was 14 days).

VALIDITY. Extensive validity data are provided for the validity and clinical scales. For the validity scales, several subject samples and computer-generated responses were used to examine issues of random responding, impression management, and various item/response sets. In addition, correlational studies were performed using the four PAI validity scales and the L, F, and K scales of the Minnesota Multiphasic Personality Inventory (MMPI) and the Marlowe-Crowne Social Desirability scale to determine convergent and discriminant validity. The Negative Impression (NIM) and Positive Impression (PIM) scales demonstrated moderate correlations in the expected direction; however, the INF scale had negligible correlations with these measures and the ICN scale demonstrated only a weak, negative correlation with the Marlowe-Crowne. In another study, Rogers, Ornduff, and Sewell (1993) found that the NIM cutoff score (i.e., >8) was highly effective with feigned schizophrenia, marginally effective with feigned depression, and ineffective with feigned generalized anxiety disorder.

Data regarding scale intercorrelations, factor analyses, confirmatory factor analyses, and cluster analyses are presented within the manual. For most scales, small to moderate intercorrelations existed in the expected direction. Factor analyses have typically resulted in two to four factors being generated including: (a) subjective distress and affective disruption, (b) behavioral acting-out, (c) egocentricity and exploitiveness in interpersonal relationships, and (d) validity/carelessness (for the clinical groups) and social detachment/sensitivity (for normal subjects). As noted previously, 10 clusters emerged through the use of Ward's method of cluster analysis.

Convergent and discriminant validity data are also provided for three broad classes of disorders (i.e., neurotic [Somatic Complaints, Anxiety, Anxiety-Related Disorders, and Depression], psychotic [Mania, Paranoia, and Schizophrenia], and behavior disorder [Borderline Features, Antisocial Features, Alcohol Problems, and Drug Problems] scales). The manual also includes mean profiles for different diagnostic groups. In addition, correlations between PAI subscales and MMPI scales and subscales, NEO-PI scales, and other measures are included in the manual. Research by Schinka (1995) has also provided support for the generalizability of the PAI to a sample of mostly male alcohol-dependent inpatients.

NORMS. Means and standard deviations for full scales and subscales are available for the complete census-matched standardization ($n = 1,000$), clinical ($n = 1,246$), and college student ($n = 1,051$) samples. Projected U.S. Bureau of the Census projections for the year 1995 were used for the census-matched group. The clinical sample was recruited from 69 clinical sites and appears to be quite representative in its coverage of various diagnostic groups. The college student sample consists of psychology students in seven universities across the U.S. Means and standard deviations are presented for full scales and subscales by gender, race (i.e., whites, blacks, and "other"), age (i.e., 18–29, 30–49, 50–59, and 60+ years), and education level (i.e., 4–11, 12, 13–15, and 16+ years of education). For most scales, differences among the demographic groups are generally small.

SUMMARY. Overall the PAI is an impressive inventory. The manual contains clear and comprehensive discussions of scale development, reliability, and validity data. The inventory itself is relatively easy to use, score, and interpret. Some difficulty occurs in attempting to assign a respondent's profile to one of the modal profiles contained within the manual; however, the available software system can facilitate this process. Except for previously mentioned weaknesses associated with the validity scales, the instrument has decent reliability and validity. Unlike the MMPI-2 and Millon Clinical Multiaxial Inventory—II, the PAI contains nonoverlapping scales that enhance its discriminant validity. Its major flaw appears to be its relative novelty. As further research and clinical information are collected on the PAI, it should prove to be a worthy competitor to the MMPI-2, which remains the dominant objective personality inventory.

REVIEWER'S REFERENCES

Rogers, R. Ornduff, S. R., & Sewell, K. W. (1993). Feigning specific disorders: A study of the Personality Assessment Inventory (PAI). *Journal of Personality Assessment*, 60, 554–560.

Rogers, R., Flores, J., Ustad, K, & Sewell, K. W. (1995). Initial validation of the Personality Assessment Inventory—Spanish version with clients from Mexican American communities. *Journal of Personality Assessment*, 64, 340–348.

Schinka, J. A. (1995). Personality Assessment Inventory scale characteristics and factor structure in the assessment of alcohol dependency. *Journal of Personality Assessment*, 64, 101–111.

[2.29]

Profile of Adaptation to Life—Clinical Scale.

Purpose: "Measures 7 areas of psychological adjustment and functioning, and physical health."

Population: Counseling or mental health or medical services clients.

Publication Dates: 1978–1981.

Acronym: PAL-C.

Scores, 7: Negative Emotions, Psychological Well Being, Income Management, Physical Symptoms, Alcohol/Drug Use, Close Interpersonal, Child Interpersonal.

Administration: Group.

Price Data, 1990: $9 per 25 scales including profile; $10 per manual ('81, 25 pages); $11 per specimen set.

Time: (10) minutes.

Comments: Self-report questionnaire pre- and post-treatment.

Author: Robert B. Ellsworth.

Publisher: Consulting Psychologists Press, Inc.

Cross References: The review by Robert H. Deluty originally appeared in 9:995.

Review of Profile of Adaptation to Life—Clinical Scale by ROBERT H. DELUTY, Assistant Professor of Psychology, University of Maryland Baltimore County, Baltimore, MD:

The Profile of Adaptation to Life—Clinical (PAL-C) Scale was developed for use by mental health professionals to assess a wide range of positive and symptomatic aspects of psychological adjustment and physical health. In contrast to the vast majority of self-report adjustment inventories, which focus exclusively on the negative aspects of adjustment (e.g., depression, anxiety, hostility), the PAL-C Scale assesses both negative aspects (e.g., physical symptoms, alcohol/drug use, negative emotions) AND positive aspects of adjustment (e.g., enjoying and trusting others, feeling needed and useful).

In developing the PAL-C Scale, Ellsworth selected only those items which were: (1) sensitive to pre-post treatment change; (2) able to distinguish between groups he assumed to be different in adjustment; and (3) salient for measuring various adjustment domains, as estimated by their factor loadings. Unfortunately, the population employed to develop the inventory was the same population used to assess its validity. As noted by Anastasi (1982), validity coefficients obtained on the same sample used for item-selection purposes are spuriously high, since they capitalize on random sampling errors within that sample. Indeed, in the absence of cross-validation, high validity coefficients may be found even when the test has no validity whatsoever in predicting particular criteria (Anastasi, 1982).

Even if the PAL-C Scale had been cross-validated, many problems would still remain regarding its reliability and criterion validity. No information is provided regarding the sample used to assess the scale's internal consistency, and the reliability coefficients are presented imprecisely (i.e., three PAL-C dimensions are reported by Ellsworth as having reliabilities "in the .80's"). The test-retest correlations for the seven PAL-C dimen-sions are, likewise, described very vaguely (i.e., as exceeding .80). Furthermore, temporal consistency was assessed over a 1-week interval exclusively on a group of people in an alcohol treatment program. Why such an atypical group was chosen to assess test-retest reliability is unspecified, as is any information about the group's size and demographic characteristics.

Ellsworth attempted to validate the PAL-C Scale by demonstrating that its scores differentiated among groups "known to differ in adjustment." Ellsworth's groups included (among others) 678 clinic clients seeking mental health services, 121 people being trained in Transcendental Meditation (TM), 96 Community College students, and 435 persons responding to a National Enquirer article on psychic experiences. Ellsworth provides extraordinarily little information regarding the composition of these groups; for example, there are no data concerning the clinic clients' reasons for referral, diagnoses, and length and nature of treatment. The only information that is provided leads one to question the comparability of these groups on dimensions other than adjustment which might influence PAL-C performance: there were substantial group differences in terms of age, sex, educational level, and marital status.

At no point does Ellsworth account for how he "knew" these groups differed in adjustment; it appears that he simply assumed that persons seeking mental health counseling or TM training SHOULD differ in adjustment from "normal" persons. And whom did Ellsworth choose as the norm group? Remarkably, he selected the persons who responded to the National Enquirer article on psychic experiences. Ellsworth's only rationale for choosing this group as "normal" was that they performed significantly better on six of the seven adjustment dimensions than did the clinic clients, and that they represented a "broad range of educational, age, and geographical characteristics." Given Ellsworth's failure to assess actual (as opposed to assumed) levels of adjustment and "normalcy," his failure to control for critical demographic differences among his groups, and the lack of any information regarding the diagnoses and nature of treatment received by the clinic clients, both the normative scores and the pre-post treatment change norms reported by Ellsworth are largely useless.

On a positive note, scores on the PAL-C Scale showed mild to moderate agreement with Ellsworth's Personal Adjustment and Role Skill (PARS) Scale, an adjustment index consisting of ratings by significant others. The correlations between PAL-C scores of clinic clients and PARS ratings by their significant others were particularly high for overt forms of adjustment (e.g., measures of "closeness" between spouses) and overt forms of maladjustment (e.g., alcohol/drug use). Correlations were substantially lower between PAL-C scores and PARS ratings when internally felt states were assessed (e.g., negative emotions, sense of well-being). In addition, significant differences were found on five PAL-C dimensions when comparisons were made between clinic clients' pretreatment vs. posttreatment scores. Unfortunately, a no-treatment control group was not included in the latter study, so it is unknown whether PAL-C scores changed merely as a function of time or as a function of actual changes in adjustment.

Ellsworth also assessed the intercorrelations among the seven PAL-C dimensions. With the exception of the Alcohol/Drug Use dimension, the intercorrelations were quite high, thereby demonstrating the interrelatedness of physical health, a sense of psychological well-being, sound income management, and close relations with one's spouse, parents, and/or children.

In conclusion, Ellsworth is to be commended for trying to develop an inventory which assesses adjustment and maladjustment (i.e., health AND illness) in intrapersonal, social, and physical spheres. Nevertheless, due to (1) the dearth of information regarding the samples used in the reliability and validity studies, (2) the failure to cross-validate, (3) the untested assumptions regarding actual differences in adjustment among clinical and non-clinical subgroups, and (4) the absence of a control group in the pretreatment-posttreatment study, one cannot utilize or interpret with confidence the reliability and validity coefficients, normative scores, or pre- posttreatment change norms provided. The PAL-C Scale's correlations with observer ratings are encouraging, however, and it is therefore strongly recommended that internally valid investigations, employing clearly-delineated samples and appropriately-matched subgroups, be conducted to assess the scale's reliability, convergent and discriminant validity, and clinical sensitivity.

REVIEWER'S REFERENCE
Anastasi, A. PSYCHOLOGICAL TESTING (5th Ed.). New York: Macmillan, 1982.

[2.30]
Profile of Adaptation to Life—Holistic Scale.

Purpose: Designed to assess personal lifestyle and spiritual awareness.
Population: Counseling or mental health or medical services clients.
Publication Dates: 1978–1981.
Acronym: PAL-H.
Scores: 7 scores: Negative Emotions, Psychological Well Being, Income Management, Physical Symptoms, Alcohol/Drugs, Close Interpersonal Relationships, Child Relationship, plus 5 life style areas correlated with good adjustment: Social Activity, Self Activity, Nutrition and Exercise, Personal Growth, Spiritual Awareness.
Administration: Group.
Price Data, 1990: $9 per 25 scales including profile; $10 per manual ('81, 21 pages); $11 per specimen set.
Time: (10) minutes.
Comments: Self-report questionnaire pre- and posttreatment.
Author: Robert B. Ellsworth.
Publisher: Consulting Psychologists Press, Inc.
Cross References: The review by Robert H. Deluty originally appeared in 9:996.

Review of the Profile of Adaptation to Life—Holistic Scale by ROBERT H. DELUTY, Assistant Professor of Psychology, University of Maryland Baltimore County, Baltimore, MD:

The Profile of Adaptation to Life—Holistic (PAL-H) Scale was developed for counselors, ministers, and staff working in "Holistic" healing centers to assess psychological adjustment and physical health, as well as life style behaviors and beliefs associated with health and adjustment. The PAL-H Scale consists of the seven dimensions of adjustment found in Ellsworth's Profile of Adaptation to Life—Clinical (PAL-C) Scale, as well as items pertaining to nutrition, exercise, meditation, and beliefs in mysticism and parapsychological phenomena.

The sample utilized by Ellsworth to develop the seven clinical adjustment dimensions was the same sample used to assess its validity. This failure to cross-validate results in validity coefficients which are spuriously high, since these coefficients capitalize on random sampling errors within the selected sample (Anastasi, 1982). In addition to the critical absence of cross-validation, studies assessing the reliability and validity of the adjustment dimensions of the PAL-H Scale suffer from a variety of other shortcomings.

There is a striking lack of information regarding the nature of the samples used in the reliability and validity investigations. Although the internal consistency and temporal reliabilities of the seven adjustment dimensions are quite acceptable (all coefficients exceed .80), no data are provided concerning the size and demographic characteristics of the samples used to assess reliability. In the major validation study of the seven adjustment dimensions, Ellsworth compared the scores of clinic clients seeking mental health services, trainees in Transcendental Meditation (TM), students from a community college, and persons responding to a National Enquirer article on psychic experiences, among others. Subjects in these groups were not matched for age, sex, educational level, marital status, or any other demographic dimension; no information is provided regarding the clinic clients' reasons for referral, diagnosis, or treatment. Ellsworth assumed that the clinical samples would have poorer adjustment scores than the non-clinical samples, but did not assess in an objective manner actual differences in adjustment among his subgroups. In addition, Ellsworth chose the National Enquirer sample as his "normal" group simply because they outperformed the clinic clients on all seven adjustment factors and because they represented a wide range of educational, age, and geographical dimensions. As a consequence of Ellsworth's failure to assess actual (rather than assumed) levels of adjustment and normalcy, to control for critical demographic differences among the groups, and to clearly delineate and describe the diagnoses and treatments received by his clinical sample, the normative scores, validity coefficients, and pre-post treatment change norms provided cannot be used or interpreted with confidence.

The life style and spiritual belief items on the PAL-H Scale were selected solely on the basis of their correlations with four of the adjustment dimensions; more specifically, those 18 items which correlated significantly with Negative Emotions, Physical Symptoms, Psychological Well Being, and Close Relations became part of the PAL-H Scale. The internal consistency and test-retest reliabilities of these life style and belief items have not been assessed. Furthermore, with the exception of their significant correlations with the above-mentioned adjustment dimensions, no data are provided by Ellsworth pertaining to the validity of these items.

The fact that these items correlated significantly with the four adjustment dimensions is hardly cause for excitement, however. First of all, many of the correlations (although significant) are of rather low magnitude (e.g., Physical Symptoms correlated only -.19 with Social Activity and -.28 with Self Activity). Second, it must be remembered that the criterion-related validity of the four adjustment dimensions themselves has yet to be demonstrated adequately. Third, although the "normal" group tended to endorse particular life style activities and beliefs more often than did the clinical samples, it should be recalled that the "normal" group consisted of persons responding to a National Enquirer article on psychic phenomena. It is not surprising, therefore, that these persons were more likely to meditate (item #41), to believe that spiritual or psychic healing is often as effective as medical treatment (item #48), or to regard mental telepathy as a reality (item #49). It is remarkable that these latter activities and beliefs were judged indicative of good adjustment merely because they were endorsed by a sample of persons whose PAL-C scores differed from those of clinic clients, a sample whose own adjustment, normalcy, and representativeness are, themselves, extremely questionable.

In conclusion, the internal consistency, temporal reliability, and convergent and discriminant validity of the entire PAL-H Scale have yet to be demonstrated. It is strongly recommended that the scale be administered to groups which have well-documented differences on objective measures of adjustment and which are carefully matched on such critical dimensions as age, sex, socioeconomic and educational levels, and marital status. In addition, the clinical sensitivity of the PAL-H Scale should be assessed by administering it to differentially diagnosed samples before and after clearly specified treatments are provided, and then comparing their change scores to those of no-treatment controls.

REVIEWER'S REFERENCE

Anastasi, A. PSYCHOLOGICAL TESTING (5th Ed.). New York: Macmillan, 1982.

[2.31]
Psychiatric Diagnostic Interview—Revised.

Purpose: "Designed to determine if an individual is suffering, or has ever suffered, from a major psychiatric disorder."

Population: Ages 18 and older.

Publication Date: 1989.

Acronym: PDI-R.

Scores, 21: 17 basic syndromes: Organic Brain Syndrome (OB), Alcoholism (Al), Drug Abuse (Dr), Depression (De), Mania (Ma), Schizophrenia (Sc), Antisocial Personality (As), Somatization Disorder (So), Anorexia Nervosa (AN), Bulimia (Bu), Post-Traumatic Stress Disorder (PS), Obsessive-Compulsive Disorder (OC), Phobic Disorder (Ph), Panic Disorder (Pa), Generalized Anxiety (GA), Mental Retardation (MR), Adjustment Disorder (Ad), and 4 derived syndromes: Polydrug Abuse (Poly), Schizoaffective Disorder (Sc-Af), Manic-Depressive Disorder (Ma-De), Bulimarexia (Bu-AN).

Administration: Individual.

Price Data, 1993: $100 per complete kit including reusable administration booklet, 25 recording booklets, and manual (174 pages); $45 per administration booklet; $17.50 per 25 recording booklets; $42.50 per manual; $195 per microcomputer disk (IBM).

Time: (15–30) minutes for normals; (60) minutes for those with 2 or more syndromes.

Comments: Computer-assisted interview is available along with scoring and recording instructions.

Authors: Ekkehard Othmer, Elizabeth C. Penick, Barbara J. Powell, Marsha R. Read, and Sieglinde C. Othmer.

Publisher: Western Psychological Services.

Cross References: Reviews by Brian Bolton and Peter F. Merenda originally appeared in 11:316 (3 references).

Review of the Psychiatric Diagnostic Interview— Revised by BRIAN BOLTON, Professor, Arkansas Research and Training Center in Vocational Rehabilitation, University of Arkansas, Fayetteville, AR:

The revised Psychiatric Diagnostic Interview (PDI-R) is a structured interview that evaluates 17 basic syndromes and four derived syndromes. Its purpose is to determine whether an examinee is suffering or has ever suffered from a major psychiatric disorder. The questions that compose each of the 17 basic syndromes are organized into four sections that are administered sequentially. If the critical symptoms in any section are not present, the remaining sections are omitted. Because the PDI-R is a criterion-referenced instrument, there are no norms. However, base rates for the syndromes and diagnoses are given for various populations.

The administrative format of the PDI-R parallels the strategy used by skilled clinicians, beginning with very general questions and moving to increasingly specific questions, but only if earlier questions suggest the presence of a disorder. The four levels of assessment in the PDI-R are: Cardinal questions, Social Significance questions, Auxiliary questions, and Time Profile questions. The Time Profile questions identify the age of onset and the duration of the symptoms. After all 17 basic syndromes are reviewed, a current diagnosis and a lifetime diagnosis are established.

The PDI-R is based on the traditional assumption that psychiatric disorders are discrete categories. It follows that diagnosis is a classification problem, rather than a measurement task. The hierarchical ordering of the 21 basic and derived syndromes, which assumes that certain syndromes take precedence over others, and the time profile information provide the foundation for differential diagnosis with the PDI-R. Comparative studies support the validity of the PDI-R diagnostic strategy.

The median number of questions in each of the four sections forming the 17 basic syndromes are: Cardinal (2), Social Significance (7), Auxiliary (20), and Time Profile (4). Clearly, a substantial reduction in administration time may result if the questioning for any syndrome is terminated after the Cardinal section or the Social Significance section. Considering the small number of positive syndromes that actually occur in samples of hospitalized medical patients ($M = .26$), psychiatric outpatients ($M = 1.85$), and hospitalized psychiatric patients ($M = 2.51$), it is apparent that the PDI-R's process of contingent questioning provides a comprehensive evaluation with great economy of effort.

The original PDI was constructed to operationalize the Feighner diagnostic criteria developed by a team of researchers at the Washington University School of Medicine in the late 1960s. Publication of the third edition of the *Diagnostic and Statistical Manual of Mental Disorders (DSM-III)* in 1980 necessitated a revision of the PDI. Two of the original syndromes were deleted (Homosexuality and Transsexualism) and four syndromes were added (Bulimia, Post-Traumatic Stress Disorder, Generalized Anxiety, and Adjustment Disorder). To further increase the correspondence between the PDI-R and *DSM-III* diagnostic categories, the criteria used to define PDI-R syndromes were modified and interview questions were added. Because the validity of the PDI-R depends in good part on studies conducted with the original PDI, all changes should be specified in the manual.

The PDI-R was designed to be administered by a carefully trained and supervised graduate student or psychiatric technician. Using either the paper-and-pencil version or the computer-assisted version, the PDI-R can be readily administered to most examinees. Like all structured interviews, the PDI-R is essentially a self-report assessment, thus requiring considerable judgment by the examiner. Thorough training including supervised practice is especially critical with an interview that uses a "skip out" or contingent procedure, because evaluation of syndromes may be prematurely terminated if the decision is wrong. The manual properly advises continuation to the next section when in doubt.

With the paper-and-pencil version of the PDI-R, scoring is accomplished simultaneously with the administration of the syndromes. The manual provides detailed guidelines with examples for scoring each of the 17 syndromes. A series of tables may be used to translate PDI-R results into *DSM-III* and Revised *DSM-III* diagnoses. The computer-assisted interview, which includes automatic branching, scores all syndromes, generates current and lifetime diagnoses, and converts PDI-R responses to *DSM-III* and *DSM-III-R* diagnoses.

Because the reliability and validity of the PDI-R could be inferred from relevant studies of the original PDI-R, if the two instruments were determined to be measuring the same constructs, it was important to establish the diagnostic concordance of the two editions. The median agreement for the 13 basic syndromes common to both interviews was 96% and identical diagnoses were obtained in 80% of cases. In another study, seven expert judges rated the PDI-R's implementation of the *DSM-III*'s diagnostic criteria for comparable disorders to be uniformly good for all syndromes except Organic Brain Syndrome.

Reliability studies of the original PDI produced the following results: (a) six judges agreed perfectly on the current and lifetime diagnoses and syndrome scoring for four patients; (b) four of the judges were in perfect agreement 3 months later with their earlier diagnoses and scoring and with each other; (c) test/retest agreement for syndrome identification with a 6-week interval between interviews was 93%; diagnostic agreement ranged from 67% to 93%, depending on whether categories were combined; and (d) syndrome identification agreement of between 66% to 92% and diagnostic agreement ranging from 70% to 100% against an extended or complete administration (i.e., all questions were asked) supported the reliability of the PDI "skip out" or branching format.

Because the PDI-R was developed to implement previously established diagnostic guidelines in a standardized format, the validity of the instrument is a function of the correspondence between the symptomatic criteria and the interview questions constituting the PDI-R syndromes. In other words, validity depends upon how accurately the clinical standards were translated into PDI-R questions. Research indicates substantial diagnostic agreement between the PDI-R and psychiatrists using conventional examination procedures.

Four validity investigations of the original PDI produced these findings: (a) the PDI diagnoses for psychiatric inpatients agreed (78% to 82%) with the diagnoses given by a psychiatrist, (b) the PDI diagnoses for outpatients agreed (63% to 84%) with those rendered by psychiatric residents, (c) the PDI correctly identified 90% of the cases in eight diagnostic reference groups, and (d) the PDI and the Diagnostic Interview Schedule agreed on syndrome identification (91%) and current diagnosis (79%). Because of the demonstrated similarity between the PDI and the PDI-R, these data by extension strongly support the diagnostic validity of the PDI-R.

SUMMARY. The PDI-R is a carefully developed structured interview for evaluating psychiatric patients. Its goal is to establish the presence or absence of 17 major psychiatric disorders. The PDI-R provides a comprehensive, standardized assessment that may be converted to *DSM-III* and *DSM-III-R* diagnostic categories. The manual is exemplary, with thorough explanations of the rationale, construction, and technical studies conducted, as well as detailed directions for administration and scoring. The reliability and validity evidence support the clinical utility of the instrument. It can be concluded that the PDI-R is a highly efficient screening procedure that generates diagnostic information potentially useful in treatment planning.

Review of the Psychiatric Diagnostic Interview—Revised by PETER F. MERENDA, Professor Emeritus of Psychology and Statistics, University of Rhode Island, Kingston, RI:

The Psychiatric Diagnostic Interview—Revised (PDI-R) was originally published in 1981 and revised in 1989. The accompanying revised manual, which is both comprehensive and extensive (155 pages) was prepared by only one of the three original coauthors, Elizabeth C. Penick. The PDI-R is a structured diagnostic interview technique designed to complement a clinician's use of the Diagnostic and *Statistical Manual of Mental Disorders, 3rd Edition (DSM-III)*. The current revised form includes several modifications in the number and kinds of syndromes reviewed by the instrument as compared to the original PDI. There have also been changes in the criteria used to define the various syndromes as well as the addition of specific items or questions. However, the basic underlying theoretical rationale and format of the instrument remain unchanged. The modifications and the theoretical foundations appear to have a sound basis, and for these the authors are to be complimented. It is also heartening to realize that the major work, original and revisional, was accomplished twice within a decade.

Because the instrument has been designed to determine whether an individual is suffering or has ever suffered from a major psychiatric disorder, its use is limited to highly sophisticated and well-trained (generally speaking) clinicians as well as those who have also been trained specifically in its application and limitations. Although the manual does explain the steps that should be taken for the reliable and ethical applications of the PDI-R, there is no indication that either the authors or the publisher are making any significant effort to restrict sales only to those persons who have demonstrated competence in its use. In fact, in the publisher's order form, the only pertinent information regarding a purchaser's qualifications is "highest academic degree." Furthermore, so much information is given in the manual regarding scoring and interpretation of the instrument, and case studies as well, that unqualified buyers could use the manual as a "cook book." A computer-assisted version, complete with a microcomputer test report, is available to anyone, presumably, who states on the order form that he or she possesses a master's or doctoral degree in any field!

Regarding standardization procedures and the psychometric properties possessed by the PDI-R, it is difficult to evaluate these from the information and data given and not given in the manual. For instance, were the items and questions tried out on representative samples of adults, 18 years or older? If so, who were these persons; how many were there; how representative were the samples?

Reliability is claimed through results reported from several studies conducted over a 10-year period. These measures of reliability include interrater, intrarater, and test-retest reliabilities. However, they are all based on inadequately small samples, overwhelmingly males (4–6 judges; 4–67 patients). Retest intervals were relatively short ranging from 11 days to 3 months, with an average interval of approximately 6 weeks. More importantly, however, these studies were all conducted with the PDI and none with the PDI-R. The distinction between the PDI and PDI-R is significant because the revised version includes substantial modifications and additions. It is therefore not possible to evaluate the reliability of the PDI-R.

The demonstration of validity is claimed through the reporting of several validation studies with the PDI and two with the PDI-R. All were conducted on samples that are considered quite small for validation purposes. One study conducted with the PDI was based on a rather large sample ($N = 485$). However, it was a "naturalistic" study, not an empirical one. Hence, it does not support evidence of validity as required by the *Standards for Educational and Psychological Testing* (AERA, APA, & NCME, 1985). There is also the question as to whether there has been proper statistical treatment of the data in these studies. For example, inspection of the data in Tables 5 and 6, without further explanation in the text on pages 102-103, suggests that a 3 x 2 analysis of variance was performed on percentages. If so, this would have been highly irregular and incorrect. And the statistical results reported in Table 6 would be uninterpretable. In any event, the paucity of validity studies with positive results, reported by the authors or others over the 10-year period of the operational use of the PDI and PDI-R, fails even to approach the APA standard of validity as a "unitary concept." This standard, which has become widely accepted by psychometricians, states that validity is demonstrated only through substantial supportive evidence over long periods of time of the inferences made by scores yielded by psychometric instruments.

In addition to the ethical concerns expressed by the authors in the manual (pp. 3-4) there are two additional ones that arise to this reviewer: (a) The introduction of computer administration, scoring, and reporting of the PDI-R without apparent or evident compliance with APA Guidelines (APA, 1986); and (b) unwarranted claims by the publisher regarding the usefulness of the instrument to clinicians. It is stated in a promotional piece that "clinicians find the PDI-R useful because: It provides a reliable record . . . . It reduces the chance of diagnostic error . . . . It provides a systematic and efficient approach to diagnosis." Such claims require substantiated unequivocal evidences of reliability and validity of the PDI-R. In this reviewer's judgment, these important psychometric properties have yet to be convincingly demonstrated for this instrument.

In summary, the authors and their collaborators are to be commended for their 10-year effort in producing both an instrument and manual that could prove to be useful to well-qualified and trained clinicians in making effective psychiatric diagnoses. However, before the PDI-R is deemed ready for operational use, considerably more and better evidence of its reliability and validity than exists at present must be demonstrated. The authors and publisher are also admonished to heed the standards made explicit in the references to this review; to monitor more carefully who can gain access to the instrument; and to be more restrained in the claims made of the PDI-R until such time that they can support these with the necessary documentation.

REVIEWER'S REFERENCES

American Educational Research Association, American Psychological Association, & National Council on Measurement in Education. (1985). *Standards for educational and psychological testing.* Washington, DC: American Psychological Association, Inc.

American Psychological Association. (1986). *Guidelines for computer-based tests and interpretations.* Washington, DC: American Psychological Association.

[2.32]
Psychiatric Evaluation Form.

Purpose: Designed "to record scaled judgments of a subject's functioning during a one week period" on dimensions of psychopathology.
Population: Psychiatric patients and nonpatients.
Publication Dates: 1967–1968.
Acronym: PEF.
Scores, 28: 20 psychopathological scores in Part I (Narcotics-Drugs, Agitation-Excitement, Suicide-Self Mutilation, Grandiosity, Somatic Concerns, Anti-Social Attitudes-Acts, Speech Disorganization, Hallucinations, Social Isolation, Belligerence-Negativism, Disorientation-Memory, Alcohol Abuse, Anxiety, Inappropriate, Suspicion-Persecution, Daily Routine-Leisure Time, Denial of Illness, Depression, Retardation-Lack of Emotion, Overall Severity of Illness), 3 occupational roles and 2 social roles; 3 admission scores (Duration, Stress, Reason for Admission).
Administration: Individual.
Price Data, 1994: $3.50 per booklet including score sheet and instruction manual; $1 per teaching tape/key; additional price data available from publisher.
Time: (2–4) minutes.
Authors: Robert L. Spitzer, Jean Endicott, Alvin Mesnikoff, and George Cohen.
Publisher: Department of Research Assessment and Training, New York State Psychiatric Institute.
Cross References: See T4:2153 (9 references); the reviews by Goldine C. Gleser and Jerome D. Paulker originally appeared in 7:126 (1 reference); see also T3:1922 (15 references) and T2:1339 (4 references).

Review of the Psychiatric Evaluation Form by GOLDINE C. GLESER, Professor of Psychology and Director, Psychology Division, University of Cincinnati College of Medicine, Cincinnati, OH.

The Psychiatric Evaluation Form consists of an optical scanning form for computer recording of ratings on 19 dimensions of psychopathology, an overall evaluation, and five areas of possible role impairment, in addition to other data such as identification, date, age, sex, diagnosis, duration of illness, and the like, needed for both clinical and research files. Severity ratings are made on six-point scales ranging from "none" to "extreme." There is also a space for indicating that a particular scale is inapplicable or unratable.

The PEF is normally used in conjunction with an interview guide conveniently arranged so that the scale definitions and appropriate questions are opposite the scale being rated. The time period on which the judgments are based is the week up to and including the day of evaluation. Both "intensity and duration" of symptoms are considered in making judgments but inferences are avoided. Questions may be added or omitted to obtain the desired information from the interview and supplementary records may be consulted.

A salient aspect of the manual is the emphasis placed by the authors on the importance of training in obtaining reliable and valid judgments. Two case histories are presented and rated to indicate what evidence is used for each scale and how it is interpreted quantitatively. In addition, a tape is available with two interviews that can be rated and compared to the key. It would be desirable if even more practice material were made available, particularly in the form of examples of responses classified as mild, moderate, severe, etc., on each of the scales. Unless such objectification can be accomplished, ratings are not likely to be highly comparable from one center to another.

The current version of the manual has no psychometric data on these scales for various clinical populations. However, additional information was provided by the authors. Two reliability studies have been undertaken. In the first study, 64 newly admitted psychiatric inpatients were interviewed by two first-year medical students who had had three weeks of intensive training in the use of the PEF. It was not indicated whether both were present at each interview or whether tape recordings were employed. The intraclass correlations ranged from .51 to .95, with a median of .74. Another study of 31 inpatients in which four raters were paired in various combinations yielded intraclass correlation coefficients ranging from .69 to 1.00, with a median of .90. Minimal agreements were obtained in both studies for ratings of "inappropriate affect" and "anxiety." The lower coefficients obtained by the medical students would certainly indicate the advisability of obtaining raters with adequate psychiatric training and experience. One wonders, however, whether the design of the second study might not have tended to result in inflated coefficients, since variance attributable to difference in interviewers was confounded with subject effects. The inadequate attention paid to

rater main effects is a weakness of these and other such rating scales.

Intercorrelations among the 19 rating scales are available on 433 patients. These have been factored to yield six clusters or syndromes, namely: disorganization, grandiosity-externalization, withdrawal, antisocial, depression, anxiety. Some evidence is available that the rating scales can differentiate inpatient, outpatient, and nonpatient samples, and among various diagnostic groups.

The PEF form and interview guide is much easier to handle and administer than the *Mental Status Schedule* by the same authors. It remains to be seen, however, which type of scaling will yield the more meaningful results. Certainly the rating form will appeal more to psychiatrists and is potentially useful for a broader range of patients.

Review of the Psychiatric Evaluation Form by JEROME D. PAUKER, Associate Professor of Psychiatry (Medical Psychology) and Psychology, University of Missouri, Columbia, MO:

The PEF is one of several related rating instruments to come out of Biometrics Research of the New York State Department of Mental Hygiene. It is a means for evaluating the functioning of a subject over a short period of time; the authors recommend one week as the target period but also allow for studies involving special time periods. Seven days is seen by them as being long enough to cover a reasonable sampling of the person's behavior and short enough to be handled in a manageable rating scale. The information on which the ratings are based can come from a variety of sources, including interviews with the patient, interviews with other informants, hospital records, and other documents. Judgments are made about 19 dimensions of psychopathology called the Comprehensive Psychopathology Scales, plus an additional scale called Overall Severity of Illness. The other scales carry such titles as Agitation-Excitement, Hallucinations, Belligerence-Negativism, and Daily Routine-Leisure Time. Each dimension is given a definition which the rater must follow. If the subject meets specified criteria for the roles of wage earner, housekeeper, student or trainee, mate, or parent, his degree of role impairment is also rated.

Ratings are made on a six-point scale ranging from "none" to "extreme." The score sheet upon which the ratings are marked consists of an original and two self-marking duplicates. Another clever device is a reusable scoring booklet into which the score sheet is placed. The booklet is set up in such a way that the definition of a dimension is next to the place where it is to be marked, with the opposite page providing a guide to aid in eliciting information appropriate to that dimension when an interview is used. A second part of the PEF is used if the subject is a new admission to a psychiatric facility. This part deals with the duration of the most recent illness or episode, the stress of precipitating events, and the primary reason for admission.

Unfortunately, there is relatively little information to which a potential user can refer if he wishes to evaluate the PEF. It appears that the content of the PEF dimensions is derived for the most part from factored and other scales which are a part of other psychiatric rating methods developed by these authors or their associates, but there is little to show how well the scales fare in the transformation. There is a manual of instructions, which describes the PEF and provides some material for practice, but there is no manual which presents data about scale construction, reliability, or validity, nor are there as yet any other publications in which such material is presented. A section in an unpublished progress report provided by the authors presents some of the results of interrater reliability studies (demonstrating reasonable reliability), intercorrelations among scales, factor analyses among the psychopathology scales (resulting in six summary scales), data concerning differentiation among psychiatric populations, and expected changes in psychopathology as a function of time. The information is sketchy, however, with respect to such crucial information as population characteristics, research design, and significance levels.

Personal communication with one of the authors reveals that further information will be published, and that the results of additional factor analyses and reliability and validity studies are in preparation. This is fortunate, because it is apparent that a good deal of effort has gone into the development of the PEF. Until such time as much more background and pertinent research results are available, however, the PEF will have to be rated as a potentially useful instrument which is worthy of further investigation. At the present time, if you are looking for a rating scale which has considerable overlap with the PEF dimensions, you might consider the *Inpatient Multidimensional Psychiatric Scale*, which uses ratings based on an interview.

[2.33]

The Psychiatric Status Schedule: Subject Form, Second Edition.

Purpose: Designed to evaluate social and role functioning as well as mental status.
Population: Psychiatric patients and nonpatients.
Publication Dates: 1966–1968.
Acronym: PSS-2.
Scores, 43: 18 symptom scores (Inappropriate Affect—Appearance—Behavior, Interview Belligerence—Negativism, Agitation—Excitement, Retardation—Lack of Emotion, Speech Disorganization, Grandiosity, Suspicion—Persecution—Hallucinations, Reported Overt Anger, Depression—Anxiety, Suicide—Self-Mutilation, Somatic Concerns, Social Isolation, Daily Routine—Leisure Time Impairment, Antisocial Impulses or Acts, Alcoholic Abuse, Drug Abuse, Disorientation Memory, Denial or Illness), 5 role functioning scores (Wage Earner, Housekeeper, Student or Trainee, Mate, Parent), 5 summary symptom and role scales (Subjective Distress, Behavioral Disturbance, Impulse Control Disturbance, Reality Testing Disturbance, Summary Role), 20 supplemental scores (Anxiety, Auditory Hallucinations, Catatonic Behavior, Conversion Reaction, Delusions—Hallucinations, Depression—Suicide, Disassociation, Elated Mood, Guilt, Lack of Emotion, Obsessions—Compulsions, Persecutory Delusions, Phobia, Psychomotor Retardation, Sex Deviation, Silliness, Somatic Delusions or Hallucinations, Visual Hallucinations, Miscellaneous, Validity Check).
Administration: Individual.
Price Data: Available from publisher.
Time: (30–50) minutes.
Comments: Most sections dealing with signs and symptoms of psychiatric disorder are from Mental Status Schedule.
Authors: Robert L. Spitzer, Jean Endicott, and George M. Cohen.
Publisher: Department of Research Assessment and Training, New York State Psychiatric Institute.
Cross References: See T4:2154 (14 references); see T3:1923 (18 references); see also T2:1340 (6 references); the review by Hans H. Strup originally appeared in 7:127 (5 references).

Review of The Psychiatric Status Schedule: Subject Form, Second Edition by HANS H. STRUPP,

Professor of Psychology, Vanderbilt University, Nashville, TN:

HISTORY AND USE. The PSS is one of an integrated group of instruments. Its specific role is "to improve the research value of clinical judgments of psychopathology and role functioning based on data collected during a psychiatric interview." Although the procedure can be used for the clinical evaluation or description of an individual subject, its major use is in the research comparison of groups of patients or nonpatients. The schedule is appropriate for a single evaluation but can also be administered repeatedly to evaluate change. Investigators have used the PSS in such areas as rehabilitation of mental patients, psychiatric evaluation, cross-cultural and cross-group comparisons, community assessment of care facilities, subject selection, instructional aid, psychiatric research, and epidemiological studies. The authors have utilized these research findings to improve the existing schedule and to construct related instruments and services.

CONTENT AND FORMAT. Information of demonstrated relevance was culled from the professional literature, textbooks, available scales, and hospital records before preliminary forms were constructed and submitted to experienced clinicians and researchers for their critical opinion. The items, calling for dichotomous (true/false) judgments, "are brief, non-technical descriptions of small units of observed or reported overt behavior." Each item to be judged contains only words or phrases explicitly defined within the context of the measure. All judgments are made and recorded during the interview. This task is facilitated by the cofeatures in the design of the interview schedule and answer sheet.

ADMINISTRATION. The interviewer need not be an experienced clinician, but he must be trained to use the PSS. The interview schedule format is best suited for situations where the assessor has no clinical responsibility for the subject. The manual provides explicit and complete directions covering all aspects of the interview interaction and judgment-making processes. Training tapes provide essential practice and demonstrate proper techniques. Accompanying keys present a supporting discussion for the "correct" scoring, based on the judgments of experienced observers.

SCORING. The basic scoring system yields scales at either of two levels of summarization. Level one provides the 23 symptom and role functioning scales. The scales are based on a range of 6 to 38 items, and most are derived from factor analytic studies performed on data from 2,000 subjects. Level two provides the summary role scale, scored "by averaging the standard scores of those occupational role scales which are applicable for the subject," and the four summary symptom scales, scored by summing the raw scores of their constituent scales. The latter were achieved through applying a principal component-varimax factor analysis to the correlations among the symptom scales, based on data from 1,760 subjects from 11 studies. The user can select the level of summarization most appropriate for his purposes; however, the use of the summary scales is recommended when more detail is not needed. The supplementary scoring procedure yields 19 additional scales which are used in presenting a detailed, clinical portrait of psychopathology along traditional diagnostic lines and in providing input for the computer program, DIAGNO I.

All PSS raw scores are converted to standard scores to facilitate comparisons across different scales. No item is included in more than one scale, and some items are weighted to increase their fidelity to clinical judgments of severity. The item ratings are conservative, so errors fall in the direction of greater health rather than in assigning a symptom on little or infrequent evidence.

COMPUTER PROGRAMS. Available subroutines are RECORD, providing the "subject's standard scale scores, the items judged true with their weights, and . . . a computer diagnosis"; PROFILE, which "displays the subject's scale scores graphically"; and GRAPH, which visually shows group comparisons on scales.

DIAGNO I is a branch analysis program which utilizes data from the PSS to approximate the diagnoses arrived at by psychiatrists in the usual clinical procedure. A later version, DIAGNO II, considers data based on any source of information, using as input age, sex, and 94 scales derived from the six-point scales of the *Current and Past Psychopathology Scale* (CAPPS) covering current state over a one-month period and past history after age 12. The agreement with hypothetical cases is .60 for DIAGNO I and .61 for DIAGNO II. The mean agreement with clinicians on real cases is .28 for DIAGNO I and .45 for DIAGNO II. The greater validity of DIAGNO II is probably attributable to the addition of historical information. DIAGNO II is able to boast an "agreement between computer diagnoses and clinical diagnoses equal to the diagnostic agreement between clinicians given the same information" and has "been shown to have substantial agreement with diagnoses made by psychiatrists functioning in a setting where they knew the subject well."

PSYCHOMETRIC PROPERTIES. *Internal Consistency.* The K-R 20 reliabilities range from .80 to .89 for the four summary symptom scales; .43 to .93 (median .74) for the 17 symptom scales; and .65 to .80 for the six role scales.

Interjudge Reliability. Intraclass correlation coefficients for a single rater, for 46 newly admitted patients, ranged from .90 to .98 for the four summary symptom scales; .57 to .99 (median .89) for the symptom scales; .94 for the summary role scale; and .66 to .98 for the role scales. In a separate study, the average coefficient was .86.

Test–Retest Reliability. Different interviewers assessed 25 newly admitted psychiatric patients twice within a week's time. Scale score coefficients ranged from .30 to .85 (median .57). "Generally the scales based on verbal content [were] more stable than the scales based on overt physical behavior."

Intercorrelations Among the Scales. For the standardization sample, the correlations among the symptom scales within each summary scale tended to be higher than the correlations among symptom scales included in different summary scales. Subjective Distress, Behavioral Disturbance, and Impulse Control were virtually independent of each other; while Reality Testing Disturbance was correlated with both Subjective Distress and Behavioral Disturbance; and Summary Role was correlated with Subjective Distress and Impulse Control Disturbance.

Concurrent Validity Studies. A series of concurrent validity studies have demonstrated the PSS to be an effective instrument in differentiating contrasting populations of inpatients, outpatients, and nonpatient community residents; differentiating contrasting diagnostic groups of organic brain syndrome, schizophrenia, and neurosis, drug addiction and alcoholism, and the four common schizophrenic subtypes; and the measurement of change in 40 newly admitted psychiatric patients, interviewed on admission and again four weeks later, who showed the expected improvements on all but two scales, and 12 manic-depressive patients who, when interviewed during the three phases of their illness, showed specific changes in scale scores.

STRENGTHS. Some advantages of the PSS are (a) an interview format which eliminates error variance due to response sets, failure to understand questions, or inability to perform the task; provides information on personal appearance, speech, delusions, etc.; allows probes into areas of uncertainty; and maintains sufficient flexibility for establishing rapport; (b) a standardized procedure; (c) judgments based on specific, defined, small units of behavior; and (d) a wide range of coverage.

LIMITATIONS. The role scales appear to be of limited value in assessing role impairment in highly disorganized patients, as they show almost no correlation with Behavioral Disturbance and Reality Testing. Their greatest value is for patients primarily disturbed in the area of subjective distress.

RECOMMENDATION. To increase the value of the PSS for the researcher, it would be desirable to compile in a single manual a unitary and concise presentation of all the background and supporting information which now appears in diverse places.

CONCLUSION. The PSS provides researchers with an interview schedule which does a fine job of combining clinical flexibility with systematic, comprehensive, and standardized assessment. Its psychometric properties are sound, with reliability and validity well documented. Users of the PSS will find the investment of time and training necessary for optimum use of the schedule to be amply rewarded if their research needs are consonant with the purposes for which the instrument was designed. The scale construction is a model of excellence in both conception and execution. A close study of the PSS should aid anyone engaged in psychiatric interviewing, whether or not he elects to use the instrument for research purposes.

[2.34]
Quickview Social History.

Purpose: Assists in the collection and reporting of client information.
Population: Ages 16 and older.

Publication Dates: 1983–1992.
Administration: Individual.
Price Data, 1994: $45 per preview package including user's guide ('92, 33 pages), hardcover test booklet, and 3 answer sheets; $24.95 per hardcover test booklet; $2.40 per soft cover test booklet; $8 per computer-scored report.
Time: (30–90) minutes
Author: Ronald A. Giannetti.
Publisher: NCS Assessments.
a) BASIC REPORT.
Scores: 8 areas of inquiry: Demographic Data, Developmental History, Family of Origin, Educational History, Marital History, Occupational History/Financial Status, Legal History, Military History.
Comments: The report also has a follow-up summary that includes contradictory responses, indeterminate responses, and client-requested follow-up sections.
b) CLINICAL SUPPLEMENT.
Scores: Includes 8 areas of inquiry listed in Basic Report, plus Physical and Psychological Symptom Screens including: Adult Problems (Substance Use, Psychotic Symptoms, Mood Symptoms, Anxiety Disorders, Somatoform Symptoms, Psychosexual Disorders, Sleep and Arousal, Antisocial Personality, Other Current or Past Potential Adult Problems/Stressors), Developmental Problems (Activity Level/Lability, Conduct Problems, Anxious/Avoidant, Eating/Weight, Tic/Elimination/Sleep, Other Disorders/Delays, Other Potential Developmental Problems/Stressors).
Cross References: The review by Edward R. Starr will appear in the 13th MMY.

Review of the Quickview Social History by EDWARD R. STARR, Assistant Professor of Counseling Psychology, State University of New York at Buffalo, Buffalo, NY:

In these latter days of increasing concern for making psychological services more economical and amenable to external evaluation, the Quickview Social History is introduced as a reasonable way to respond to the demands imposed by managed care that has at least the potential actually to improve the quality of care. Although not a psychological measure per se, the Quickview Social History is a comprehensive psychosocial inventory that assists clinicians in collecting and reporting routine social history data. Self-report data provided by clients on a computer scan sheet are compiled into a narrative report that not only organizes information pertinent to initial client interviews, but indicates potential issues for follow-up. According to the manual, it is appropriate for use with clients at least 16 years old and with at least a 6th grade level reading ability, making it fairly widely applicable to most adult clinical settings.

The Quickview is intended as an adjunct to an initial clinical interview, allowing the therapist more opportunity to use the initial contact to establish rapport with clients. It is divided into two discrete sections: the Basic Report, yielding a comprehensive general social history; and a Clinical Supplement, consisting of information pertaining specifically to psychological and medical concerns. This feature allows for greater flexibility in its use. The Basic Report section can be administered without the Clinical Supplement, if desired, but the Clinical Supplement items must always accompany the Basic Report.

The Basic Report includes sections related to general Demographic Data, Developmental History, Family of Origin, Educational History, Marital History, Occupational History and Financial Status, Legal History, and Military History. The report also includes a Contradictions section as a check on internal validity, indicating any client responses that are logically incompatible. These are recommended as areas for further investigation.

The Clinical Supplement comprises sections dealing with Adult Problems (subsections include Substance Use and Abuse, Psychotic Symptoms, Mood Symptoms, Anxiety Disorders, Somatoform Symptoms, Psychosexual Disorders, Sleep and Arousal, Antisocial Personality, and Other Current or Past Potential Adult Problems/Stressors), and Developmental Problems (subsections include Activity Level/Lability, Conduct Problems, Anxious/Avoidant, Eating/Weight, Tic/Elimination/Sleep, Other Disorders/Delays, and other Potential Developmental Problems/Stressors). Items in these sections, although not grouped according to any particular diagnostic scheme, relate to various categories of psychopathology in the *DSM-III*. The author cautions against overreliance on this data for purposes of diagnosis, advising diagnosticians to obtain additional information. Data from the Clinical Supplement also enrich the information in the Developmental History and Family of Origin sections and append an additional Symptom Screen to the Basic Report.

A convenient Follow-Up Interview Summary, not considered part of the actual report, is provided at the end of the narrative as a clinician's reference to issues pertinent to future interviews. It essentially flags client responses to the Basic Report and Clinical Supplement sections that may require clarification. This summary consists of Indeterminate Responses (i.e., items endorsed as "other") and Client-Requested Follow-Up details (i.e., issues or concerns that clients indicated they would like to discuss with the therapist).

The Quickview Social History reflects fairly extensive research on reliable and valid methods of computerized psychosocial assessment. It was developed based on refinements to the GOLPH (Giannetti On-Line Psychosocial History) and GOLPH 2.0 psychosocial histories (Giannetti, 1987; Giannetti, Klinger, Johnson, & Williams, 1976), one of the first reliable on-line assessment systems. The on-line option is an economical and very convenient means of accomplishing a task that can otherwise consume inordinate amounts of clinicians' time and energy. When used on an institution-wide basis, it has the potential to help clinics realize what may amount to substantial financial savings.

The manual is clear and informative, although fairly brief in its discussion of the development of the inventory and lacking in detail with respect to the dimensions of assessment reflected in the various sections. The several illustrative narrative reports provided give a clear example of how client data are compiled and what actual outputs look like.

Because, unlike most other approaches to history taking, it comprises a standardized set of items in a consistent format, the Quickview also has the advantage of allowing for descriptive and comparative analyses of client characteristics. Analyses can be conducted for program planning, resource allocation, quality assurance evaluations, and other research purposes. It can also be immensely valuable for reporting to funding sources, external evaluators, accrediting bodies, and third-party reimbursers. This is a clear improvement over laborious chart reviews by hand.

Another strength of the Quickview Social History is its inclusion of a section dealing with military experience. This, in my experience, is a frequently overlooked yet often important dimension of initial history taking. It also makes the Quickview an especially invaluable aid to psychological and psychiatric units in Veteran's Administration and other veteran's services programs.

Although the major strength of the Quickview Social History is that it can be used on-line, this is also, unfortunately, its primary limitation. Despite the apparent ubiquity of computer applications in contemporary clinical settings, not all clinics have this advantage. Many other clinics face severe limitations in computer resources. Still others may not be convinced of the advantages of providing computer support to clinical personnel. Although users of the Quickview are provided the option of a mail-in service, this option is likely to compromise the real cost and time advantages that accrue to on-line users.

REVIEWER'S REFERENCES

Giannetti, R. A., Klinger, D. E., Johnson, J. H. & Williams, T. A. (1976). The potential for dynamic assessment systems using on-line computer technology. *Behavior Research Methods and Instrumentation, 8,* 101–103.

Giannetti, R. A. (1987). The GOLPH psychosocial history: Response-contingent data acquisition and reporting. In J. N. Butcher (Ed.), *Computerized psychological assessment* (pp. 124–144). New York: Basic Books, Inc.

[2.35]

Reid Report.

Purpose: "The Report consists of a customized set of scales and questionnaires which focus on key, business-related employee behaviors. Measures attitudes toward conscientiousness and counterproductivity in the workplace and predicts overall work performance and counterproductive acts (turnover, absenteeism, tardiness, theft and inappropriate substance use)."

Population: Job applicants.

Publication Dates: 1969–1992.

Scores: 1 of 4 possible evaluations (Recommended, Qualified, Not Recommended, No Opinion) in 4 parts (Integrity Attitude, Antisocial History, Recent Drug Use, Work History) and overall evaluation.

Administration: Group.

Price Data: Price information available from publisher for test materials including examiner's manual ('89, 39 pages).

Time: (15–60) minutes.

Comments: Overall evaluation established by client organization, based upon specific organizational requirements.

Authors: Reid Psychological Systems, Paul Brooks (manual), and David Arnold (manual).

Publisher: Reid Psychological Systems.

Cross References: Reviews by George Domino and Kevin R. Murphy originally appeared in 12:324 (2 references); see also T4:2243 (1 reference); for a review by Stanley L.

Brodsky, see 8:658 (3 references); for integrated version of Reid Report/Reid Survey, see T2:1353 (1 reference) and 7:132 (1 reference).

Review of the Reid Report by GEORGE DOMINO, Professor of Psychology, University of Arizona, Tucson, AZ:

The Reid Report (RR) is said to measure "attitudes toward honesty and integrity" and aims to "predict dishonest acts on the job" (manual, p. 1). The test booklet consists of four parts for a total of 320 items (oddly enough the first item is numbered 101), but it is only Part 1, made up of 80 yes-no items (only 70 are scored) and comprising the Integrity Attitude Inventory, that is scored and for which there is psychometric information available.

The Examiner's Manual is well written and presents considerable reliability and validity data, but does not seem to be written for the psychometrically sophisticated reader. The manual is perhaps more noteworthy for what is absent than what is presented.

There is in the manual no distinction made between the RR in its totality and Part 1, with Part 1 typically labelled as the RR. The manual indicates the RR contains 80 items, but the test booklet contains 83. For this reader there was considerable confusion over how scores are generated. The test information indicates that a four-fold evaluation is given (recommended, qualified, not recommended, no opinion), but most of the manual information indicates a two-fold evaluation (recommended vs. not recommended) with a cutoff score of 49–50. No indication is given how this particular score was selected. Although scores are reported as raw scores, as percentiles, and as probability (that the applicant will commit theft) scores, there is no table or other information that allows the reader to equate raw scores with percentiles. There is a table (Table 16) that equates "percent rank" with probability, but nowhere is there information on how the probability scores were computed, nor their degree of validity. The nature of the table strongly suggests that these probabilities are not empirically based, but were calculated "statistically."

The manual authors recommend the RR be administered only to applicants for positions "in which honesty and integrity are major job requirements" and where "dishonest behavior could cause significant economic, organizational or personal harm" (manual, p. 2). The RR has, however, been administered to over 5 million individuals, and what job descriptions are given suggest that many applicants were for relatively low-level positions such as parking lot attendants, laborers, assemblers, as well as salespersons, stock clerks, and warehouse workers.

The manual indicates that 18 internal consistency studies have been carried out, but Table 1 gives results for 14 samples, and it is not clear how the samples and the studies interface. Five of the coefficients are given as Cronbach's alphas, which is puzzling given the dichotomous nature of the item responses.

These aspects, like the misspelling of psychological on the inside frontispiece of the manual, are minor and only slightly irritating. There are, however, a number of more major and frustrating aspects to the RR. First, there is no discussion of the development of the test other than to indicate the authors. The conclusion is that the test was developed by "fiat" rather than by empirical procedures, and that internal consistency analyses or other item selection procedures were not followed. A few of the items are nearly identical with MMPI-CPI (Minnesota Multiphasic Personality Inventory—Californial Psychological Inventory) items, but no mention of this is made.

Secondly, given the aim of the test, its self-report format, and item transparency, faking is of central concern. The manual indicates that there is "extensive research on its resistance to faking" (p. 4), but what is presented does not support this claim. In one study, 51 college students were instructed to fake good, but the obtained mean was not significantly different from that obtained by a randomly selected group of employment applicants. Only when the two samples were "equated" for college education did a significant (but miniscule) difference appear. Incidentally, no means, standard deviations, or ANOVA results are presented in the manual, and of the 30 references cited only 9 are to publications in the public domain. In two other sets of studies the effects of different attitudes toward test-taking and different instruction conditions are explored. Attitudes are related to RR scores but instructions are not. Finally, one study is presented comparing incarcerated felons with randomly selected job applicants, with none of the felons earning a "recommended" score. The evidence presented on faking is neither convincing nor complete.

Two studies of the factorial structure of the RR are reported, suggesting four separate factors, but there is no evidence given for the separate validity (or lack) of these factors. Despite these results, the manual suggests that "integrity" (not one of the four factors) is what is being measured, and two studies are presented in which RR results are compared to multivariate personality inventories, showing that high scorers on the RR are better adjusted than low scorers. Somehow the leap between integrity and adjustment is made without specifying their equivalence.

Several predictive and concurrent validity studies are reported, most utilizing a self-report criterion. The results indicate substantial correlations between RR scores and self-reported criteria of honesty (those who say they are "honest" on the test say they are "honest" outside of the test), but low to marginal correlations when the criterion is not a self-report.

Cunningham, Trucott, and Wong (1990) studied employed college students in an experimental situation where the students were overpaid for their participation in the study, and could retain or return the overpayment. Those who returned the overpayment scored higher on the RR ($r = .33$). However, scores on the RR also correlated significantly with Mach IV scores ($r = -.34$), with the tendency to impress others ($r = .55$), and with the tendency to deny undesirable qualities ($r = .38$). Note that all these coefficients are greater in magnitude than the criterion one.

In summary, the RR has an impressive potential—it has been administered to over 5 million individuals, has apparently no adverse impact on minorities, and addresses an important issue in the workplace. The available evidence, however, provides more questions than answers, and leaves much to be desired from a psychometric point of view.

REVIEWER'S REFERENCE

Cunningham, M. R., Trucott, M., & Wong, D. T. (1990). *An experimental investigation of integrity: Testing the predictive validity of the Reid Report.* Unpublished manuscript.

Review of the Reid Report by KEVIN R. MURPHY, Professor of Psychology, Colorado State University, Fort Collins, CO:

The Reid Report is designed to predict acts of dishonesty in the workplace (e.g., employee theft) on the basis of respondents' attitudes toward theft and dishonesty and their admissions of past misdeeds. Various versions of the inventory have been in use for over 40 years; according to Brodsky (1978), at least 19 revisions were undertaken in the first 30 years of its existence. The current Reid Report includes an 80-item Integrity Attitude Inventory, together with up to three optional supplements designed to assess work history, drug and alcohol abuse, and antisocial history. The Attitude Inventory includes 80 items measuring punitiveness toward self and others and projections of one's own honesty and others' dishonesty (Cunningham & Ash, 1988). The supplements include a variety of items, including many that request direct admissions of previous misdeeds, job dismissals, etc. For example, the antisocial history supplement inquires about committing and being convicted of a number of crimes and misdemeanors.

Each section of the test leads to one of four evaluations: (*a*) recommended, (*b*) qualified (i.e., recommended with qualifications), (*c*) not recommended, and (*d*) no opinion (e.g., if examinee does not complete the form). The overall evaluation resulting from the test is based on the least favorable recommendation from any part. Furthermore, evaluations of "qualified" on two or more parts lead to an overall evaluation of "not recommended." Test reports typically include the overall evaluation, evaluations on each part, and information about specific admissions made on each of the supplemental parts. Approximately 75% of those who complete the inventory receive evaluations of "recommended."

Percentile ranks are reported for the sections of the test on which an evaluation of "not recommended" is recorded. The examiner's manual reports normative data from a total sample of over 200,000 that links these percentile ranks to the probability of on-the-job theft. It is not clear how these probabilities were derived; given the evidence of differences in theft rates across occupations (Hollinger & Clark, 1983), it is not clear that these results could be generalized, even if we assume that they are approximately correct for at least some occupations.

Evidence of relatively high reliability (internal consistency and test-retest coefficients of approximately .90 and .70, respectively) and of criterion-related validity, in terms of correlations with theft admissions, inventory shortfalls, and self-reports of time theft and substance abuse is reviewed in the manual. Given the fact the three supplements contain many questions that themselves call for these same admissions, these "validity" coefficients seem conceptually more similar to test-retest reliability coefficients than to independent demonstrations of the predictive power of the test. Nevertheless, they do provide some evidence to support the hypothesis that test scores are related to dishonest behavior.

Correlations between scores on the Reid Report and scores on several personality inventories (e.g., the Minnesota Multiphasic Personality Inventory [MMPI]) are presented as evidence of construct validity (Kochkin, 1987). Because no clear definition of the construct this test is designed to measure is ever presented, this type of evidence is hard to evaluate. It is useful to know that individuals who receive unfavorable recommendations on the Reid Report also show elevated scores on a number of personality and psychopathology scales, but until the construct is more clearly defined, it is difficult to sort supportive evidence from evidence *against* the construct validity of this measure.

In 1991, a task force of the American Psychological Association carried out an evaluation of integrity tests. Although the evaluation was on the whole more positive than negative, the use of categorical scoring systems in integrity testing (e.g., recommended vs. not recommended) was strongly criticized. The scoring system employed by the Reid Report presents a number of potentially serious problems, notably the use of the least favorable of the four possible evaluations as the determinant of the overall evaluation reported for each examinee. Although the test manual warns consumers not to use the Reid Report as the sole basis for hiring decisions, the fact that the test labels a person as "not recommended" if *any* of four scores falls below a cutting point that seems arbitrary does not seem likely to encourage the optimal use of information from the test.

On the whole, the Reid Report is representative of a growing class of tests that are used to make inferences about the trustworthiness of job applicants and incumbents. As the APA task force pointed out, this class of tests should be evaluated according to the same standards as other psychological tests, in which case the Reid Report appears to have demonstrated more than adequate reliability, as well as some evidence (independent of admissions similar to those on the test itself) of criterion-related validity. The scoring system and normative data for the test are both far from optimal, but if the limitations of tests of this type (particularly those that report categorical scores) are kept firmly in mind, this test can provide a potentially useful component of a personnel selection program.

REVIEWER'S REFERENCES

Brodsky, S. L. (1978). [Review of the Reid Report]. In O. K. Buros (Ed.), *Eighth mental measurements yearbook* (pp. 1025–1026). Highland Park, NJ: Gryphon Press.

Hollinger, R. C., & Clark, J. P. (1983). *Theft by employees*. Lexington, MA: Lexington Books.

Kochkin, S. (1987). Personality correlates of a measure of honesty. *Journal of Business and Psychology, 1*, 236–247.

Cunningham, M. R., & Ash, P. (1988). The structure of honesty: Factor analysis of the Reid Report. *Journal of Business and Psychology, 3*, 54–66.

APA Task Force. (1991). *Questionnaires used in the prediction of trustworthiness in pre-employment selection decisions: An A.P.A. Task Force report*. Washington, DC: American Psychological Association.

[2.36]
Schedule for Affective Disorders and Schizophrenia, Third Edition.

Purpose: "To record information regarding a subject's functioning and psychopathology."

Population: Adults.

Publication Dates: 1977–1988.

Acronym: SADS.

Administration: Individual.

Price Data, 1993: $.50 per SADS/SADS-L suggested procedures; $2 per SADS/SADS-L instructions and clarifications ('85, 24 pages).

Time: Administration time not reported.

Authors: Robert L. Spitzer, Jean Endicott, Jo Ellen Loth (SADS-LB, SADS-LI), Patricia McDonald-Scott (SADS-LI), and Patricia Wasek (SADS-LI).

Publisher: Department of Research Assessment and Training, New York State Psychiatric Institute.

a) SCHEDULE FOR AFFECTIVE DISORDERS AND SCHIZOPHRENIA.

Scores, 24: Current Syndromes (Depressive Mood/Ideation, Endogenous Features, Depressive-Associated Features, Suicidal Ideation/Behavior, Anxiety, Manic Syndrome, Delusions-Hallucinations, Formal Thought Disorder, Impaired Functioning, Alcohol or Drug Abuse, Behavioral Disorganization, Miscellaneous Psychopathology, GAS [worst period], Extracted Hamilton); Past Week Functioning (Depressive Syndrome, Endogenous Features, Manic Syndrome, Anxiety, Delusions-Hall-Disorganization, GAS rating, Extracted Hamilton, Miscellaneous Psychopathology); Past Other than Diagnosis (Social Functioning, Suicidal Behavior). **Price Data:** $3 per SADS booklet; $.50 per SADS score sheet; $1.50 per SADS summary scales scores; $.25 per editing and coding instructions; $2 per instructions/clarifications.

b) SCHEDULE FOR AFFECTIVE DISORDERS AND SCHIZOPHRENIA LIFETIME (VARIOUS VERSIONS).

1) *SADS-L.*

Purpose: To record information regarding a subject's functioning and psychopathology; includes current disturbance.

Price Data: $2 per SADS-L booklet; $.50 per SADS-L score sheet.

2) *SADS-LB.*

Purpose: To record information regarding a subject's functioning and psychopathology; includes current disturbance and additional items related to bipolar affective disorder.

Price Data: $2 per SADS-LB booklet; $.50 per SADS-LB score sheet.

3) *SADS-LI.*

Purpose: To record information regarding a subject's functioning and psychopathology; specifies follow-up interval.

Price Data: $2 per SADS-LI booklet; $.50 per SADS-LI score sheet.

Cross References: Reviews by Paul A. Arbisi and James C. Carmer originally appeared in 12:343 (414 references); see also T4:2340 (152 references).

Review of the Schedule for Affective Disorders and Schizophrenia, Third Edition by PAUL A. ARBISI, Assessment Clinic Director, Psychology Service, Minneapolis VA Medical Center, Minneapolis, MN:

The Schedule for Affective Disorders and Schizophrenia (SADS) was developed in the mid-1970s primarily as a research instrument designed to obtain homogeneous groups of subjects defined by functional psychiatric illness. The introduction of a semistructured interview that supplied established criteria and allowed for the description of the clinical features of the episode provided a means by which researchers could lend coherence to the field and opened the way for a better understanding of both the social and biological basis of psychopathology. Prior to the advent of

the SADS, there was tremendous disparity in the rate of diagnoses of particular disorders across research centers that differed geographically as well as philosophically (Cooper et al., 1972). To a great extent, this was a result of the nonsystematic gathering of information during an unstructured clinical interview. The interview was often driven by the biases of the interviewer, and hence, reached an unreliable diagnosis. Consequently, the development of clinically meaningful and reliable diagnostic categories was hindered by the use of unstructured interviews. The SADS was one of the first systematic attempts to address the two major sources of clinician unreliability, information variance and criterion variance, by use of an organized progression of questions based on established criteria. In so doing, the SADS revolutionized the way in which information regarding mental illness was obtained during the interview and deserves to be recognized as a major force in the evolution and refinement of psychiatric diagnosis.

The SADS is divided into two parts and takes approximately 1.5 to 2 hours to administer. Part I provides a detailed description of the clinical features of the current episode when it is most severe, and during the week prior to the interview. Part II focuses on historical information required to obtain a lifetime diagnosis. Further, the SADS provides estimates of severity by rating each symptom along a behaviorally anchored dimension of impairment or frequency of occurrence. The organization of the instrument was designed to mimic a clinical interview bent on differential diagnosis based on the Research Diagnostic Criteria (RDC) (Spitzer, Endicott, & Robins, 1975) by providing a suitable progression of questions along with appropriate rule-in and rule-out criteria. The SADS contains relevant information necessary to make diagnoses defined in the RDC, both currently and over the course of the subject's life time. Further, some, but not all, DSM-III-R diagnoses can be extracted. The failure to address questions relating to most personality disorders as well as Post Traumatic Stress Disorder (PTSD) is noteworthy and limits the applicability of the interview. There are several versions of the SADS differing primarily in terms of the time period that is the focus of assessment. Additionally, investigators have modified the instrument to add coverage of additional areas of function or for use in specialized populations. The SADS-L version is similar to Part II except that the time period covered is not limited to the past and includes any current disturbance. Consequently, information regarding the current episode is less well detailed when obtained with the SADS-L. Therefore, it is more suitable to studies where there is no need for detailed information regarding the current episode or the subject is currently asymptomatic. The SADS-LB is similar to the SADS-L, but contains additional items related to the diagnosis of bipolar illness. There are two versions designed to assess change in psychiatric status subsequent to an initial assessment, the SADS-C (change) and the SADS-I (interval) versions corresponding to Parts I and II, respectively. Score sheets are provided for each version that allow for coding and entry into a computer data base.

Test-retest and joint reliabilities for major RDC diagnoses obtained across separate research centers range from excellent to good. For example, the diagnosis of Mania was generally reliably obtained, yet the diagnosis of hypomania or cyclothymia was considerably less reliable and consensus diagnosis was more difficult to achieve. Rationally constructed summary dimensions of psychopathology demonstrate internal consistency ranging from excellent (.97) for manic syndrome, to poor (.47) for formal thought disorder. The validity of a diagnostic instrument not only hinges on the reliability of the instrument, but also on the validity of the adopted diagnostic criteria. The RDC served as the basis for many diagnostic categories in DSM-III-R (American Psychiatric Association, 1987), but does not always directly correspond to DSM-III-R, and now DSM-IV, criteria. A discussion of the validity of psychiatric diagnosis exceed the scope of this review; however, suffice it to say, as is the case with DSM-III-R, some RDC diagnoses do a better job of capturing a real nosological entity than do others. Finally, the SADS gives short shrift to the personality disorders and does not allow for certain prominent DSM diagnoses such as PTSD. On the other hand, if the investigator is interested in particular aspects of Affective Disorder, the SADS-L provides a detailed description of severity, intensity, and frequency of occurrence as well as lifetime history of the disorder. The SADS also shows utility in making reliable lifetime diagnoses in nonpatient populations.

The SADS semistructured format presupposes prior knowledge of psychiatric concepts and the manual designates raters such as psychiatrists, clinical psychologists, or psychiatric social workers as appropriate users. Extensive additional training is recommended in the use of the SADS to include viewing of videotapes of SADS interviews conducted by master interviewers and joint interviews with more experienced SADS interviewers. This level of mastery is in contrast to fully structured diagnostic interviews such as the SCID (Spitzer, Williams, Gibbon, & First, 1990) or the DIS (Robins, Helzer, Croughan, & Ratcliff, 1981) that do not require as much prior background or training in the administration of the respective interviews, and can be successfully administered by trained lay interviewers. The manual and supplementary instructions for the use of the SADS and SADS-L are straightforward, but the interview format itself can be somewhat confusing and requires study and practice before an accomplished, unstilted style of delivery can be achieved. Again, the purpose of the SADS is to obtain homogenous groups of subjects who meet specific, reliable diagnostic criteria. This level of precision can only be achieved through intensive training and practice with the SADS.

The SADS was designed as a research tool and not as an aid for clinicians in reaching diagnoses. Given that premise, the SADS, in general, performs well and does an excellent job at providing reliable RDC based current and lifetime diagnoses. In sum, good diagnostic reliability is achieved for all major diagnoses with the SADS, but in order to reach an acceptable level of interrater reliability, a highly educated rater is required to undergo extensive training in the administration of the SADS. On principle, this degree of scrupulous attention to rater reliability is certainly desirable, yet many investigators do not have the resources necessary to achieve this level of expertise and will want to rely on a more rigidly structured interview, such as the SCID (Spitzer et al., 1990) or the DIS (Robins et al., 1981). Finally, if reliable DSM-III-R diagnosis is the goal or there is a need to systematically address character pathology, then the more accessible SCID is the structured interview of choice.

REVIEWER'S REFERENCES

Cooper, J. E., Kendell, R. E., Gurland, B. J., Sharpe, L., Copeland, J. R. M., & Simon, R. (1972). *Psychiatric diagnosis in New York and London: A comparative study of mental hospital admissions.* London: Oxford University Press.

Spitzer, R. L., Endicott, J., & Robins, E. (1975). Research Diagnostic Criteria (RDC). New York: Biometrics Research, New York State Psychiatric Institute.

Robins, L. N., Helzer, J. E., Croughan, J., & Ratcliff, K. S. (1981). National Institute of Mental Health diagnostic interview schedule: Its history, characteristics, and validity. *Archives of General Psychiatry, 38,* 381–389.

American Psychiatric Association. (1987). *Diagnostic and statistical manual of mental disorders* (3rd ed., rev.). Washington, DC: American Psychiatric Association.

Spitzer, R. L., Williams, J. B. W., Gibbon, M., & First, M. B. (1990). *User's guide for the Structured Clinical Interview for DSM-III-R: SCID.* Washington, DC: American Psychiatric Press.

Review of the Schedule for Affective Disorders and Schizophrenia, Third Edition by JAMES C. CARMER, Clinical Psychologist, Lincoln, NE:

The Schedule for Affective Disorders and Schizophrenia (SADS) consists of a structured interview and rating form pertaining to symptoms of major psychiatric disorders. The SADS was developed out of the multicentered National Institute of Health Collaborative Study of the Psychobiology of Depression. This ambitious project prompted the development of widely standardized interview techniques, which could facilitate the kind of data collection necessary to conduct large scale epidemiological studies involving large numbers of subjects in divergent geographical locations and across generations. A companion diagnostic rating scale, the Research Diagnostic Criteria, relates to the SADS items, resulting in suggested diagnostic classifications for the subject of the interview. The Research Diagnostic Criteria was the forerunner of the DSM-III.

The SADS interview process consists of two parts. Part I involves rating the subject's symptoms *at their most severe* during the past week, or if the focus of the study is on the current episode of illness, the Part I ratings pertain to the week of the current episode of illness when the symptoms were at their most severe. Part II of the SADS focuses on historical information. It is expected that a rater familiar with the SADS could complete the interview in less than 2 hours. An advantage of the structure and focus of the SADS is that the interview process is not necessarily time limited and information can be gathered over the course of several days.

Four versions of the SADS are described in the accompanying materials. The SADS-L is similar to Part II of the SADS and is focused on rating the subject's symptoms over the individual's lifetime. The SADS-LI is based on the SADS-L and is designed to be administered following specified intervals or events to individuals previously administered the SADS-L. The SADS-C is a modification of the SADS which emphasizes current symptoms. With its emphasis on present symptoms, the SADS-C is potentially useful for treatment outcome studies and ongoing monitoring of targeted symptom relief. Because the SADS relies on the clinical judgment of the interviewer to shape the detail of the questions asked, the SADS should be administered by clinicians familiar with diagnostic issues who have been specifically trained in the SADS. The authors offer support in training interviewers.

The SADS interview structure permits the clinician to use all sources of information available, including records and the reports of family members, using clinical judgment in instances where sources conflict. Depending on the focus of the study, the SADS also can be used "blind," with only the interview data available.

The interview forms are well laid out, with general instructions and recommended queries for the interviewer to make. Reference help comes in the form of various updates and journal article reprints included with the testing materials. Scoring of the SADS results in 24 scales including various symptom groupings, an extracted Hamilton Depression Rating Scale score, and a Global Assessment Scale.

Reliability data for the SADS are reported through the inclusion of reprints of several different studies reporting reliability across time, interviewer, geographical location, and diagnostic category. The reliabilities reported are acceptable, although, because it is an interview technique, studies utilizing the SADS should assess and report at least interrater agreement. Additional studies have demonstrated acceptable reliability for joint interview and test-retest conditions, as well as internal consistency.

Studies included with the test material comparing diagnoses obtained with the SADS with diagnoses obtained with the Diagnostic Interview Schedule (DIS) indicate that agreement of diagnoses obtained by the two instruments is unexpectedly weak. This finding has not yet been explained. The value of the SADS does not rest in the diagnoses obtained with it; the SADS is a powerful research tool in the investigation of psychiatric symptomatology independent of diagnosis over time and across generations and cultures. Researchers should carefully evaluate which instrument is best suited for their study, as diagnoses obtained with the SADS are not necessarily equivalent to diagnoses obtained with the DIS.

The authors urge potential researchers to contact them for assistance in interviewer training, scale modifications, and referral and support for the instrument. It is emphasized that the SADS and its related scales are to be utilized only by trained interviewers and researchers. This instrument is not for general use by clinicians untrained specifically in its administration and scoring. Fortunately, the authors are available for consultation and assistance in maintaining the coherence of the body of research which utilizes the SADS. The authors offer assistance in the training of raters, and offer themselves as resources for both audio and video recordings of interviews to promote the reliability of SADS ratings.

The SADS has found almost universal acceptance in research which focuses on epidemiological perspectives, and, as such, has been frequently used in studies assessing the impact of political and physical events on affected groups worldwide. The SADS has been translated into several languages, and has been revised repeatedly to sharpen its applicability to each new target group investigated. Somewhat independently, numerous revisions of the SADS have been developed to target different ages and developmental levels. For example, the Kiddie-Schedule for Affective Disorders and Schizophrenia (K-SADS) is a modification of the SADS targeting school-age children (Ambrosini, Metz, Prabucki, & Lee, 1989).

A disadvantage of the SADS is that its terminology relates to diagnostic classification as conceptualized in the 1970s, during the time of the development of the DSM III. Diagnostic classification has changed with the advents of the DSM III, DSM III-R, and DSM IV. Terminology and diagnostic entities used in the DSM IV now differ significantly from that used in the SADS. However, because the SADS is focused on determining the presence of symptoms in individuals, rather than determining a psychiatric diagnosis, its usefulness throughout ongoing changes in diagnostic classification is assured. Using the SADS in research involving diagnostic entities will require some conversion of SADS results into the diagnostic classification utilized.

The SADS lacks a clear, coherent manual. The testing packet includes various reprints, mimeographed monographs, and revised instructions which are not integrated. Given the enormous utilization of the SADS, a comprehensive and cogent manual should be developed.

The SADS obviously meets an almost overwhelming need for a standardized instrument for documenting the presence of various indications of psychopathology. With the SADS it is possible for multiple researchers to investigate a wide range of real world situations affecting individuals, groups, and even societies. The SADS provides a stable human perspective from which it is possible to comprehend the subjective impact of biological, physical, and political events. The rapidly growing body of research utilizing the SADS is forming the foundation for long-term studies that previously have been impossible to conduct. The SADS is a potentially powerful treatment outcome assessment instrument for all modalities of psychological and psychiatric treatment.

REVIEWER'S REFERENCE

Ambrosini, P. J., Metz, C., Prabucki, K., & Lee, J. (1989). Videotape reliability of the third revised edition of the K-SADS. *Journal of the American Academy of Child and Adolescent Psychiatry, 28*(5), 723–728.

[2.37]
Search Institute Profiles of Student Life.

Purpose: Designed to "assist ... school officials ... in monitoring a series of indicators related to student well-being."

Population: Grades 6–12.

Publication Dates: 1988–1990.

Scores: 3 Group Summary Areas: Social and Personal Resources, Behavior Patterns, Opportunities for Helping Your Youth.

Administration: Group.

Editions, 3: Alcohol and Other Drugs, Sexuality, Attitudes and Behaviors.

Price Data, 1991: $1,400 per survey service for the first 800 participating students, $1.25 per student thereafter.

Time: (30–40) minutes.

Authors: Search Institute.

Publisher: Search Institute.

Cross References: Reviews by Ernest A. Bauer and Sharon Johnson-Lewis originally appeared in 11:350.

Review of the Search Institute Profiles of Student Life by ERNEST A. BAUER, Research, Evaluation, and Testing Consultant, Oakland Schools, Waterford, MI:

The Search Institute Profiles of Student Life includes three separate surveys: Attitudes and Behaviors, Alcohol and Other Drugs, and Sexuality. They were developed as the result of several studies the Search Institute conducted for various clients in business, education, social service agencies, and religious organizations. The authors claim the surveys are useful as needs assessment devices or evaluation instruments. Respondents are anonymous, so only summary data are available.

The four-page Administration Manual consists of directions for administering and returning the surveys. The manual contains no information about content or concurrent validity, internal consistency, readability, test development procedures, or norming. There are no references of any kind. Personal correspondence from the Search Institute assured this reviewer that, "items stem from research projects we have conducted in the past; again, validity and reliability have been established through the field testing and extensive analyses associated with these in-depth projects." Unfortunately, information about those analyses is unavailable.

A brochure for each of the surveys contains broad claims with no references to any research or other literature. This reviewer sought additional information about the surveys and was provided with the computerized "Sample Report" available for the Alcohol and Other Drugs survey (described below) and the book-sized report based on 46,799 6th through 12th grade students who took the Behavior Patterns survey as a component of the RespecTeen project of the Lutheran Brotherhood.

This reviewer, then, had two computer-generated sample reports that the company provides users and the surveys themselves to examine. (He was informed that a similar report for the Sexuality survey was not available.) Each report shows the distributions of grade level, gender, and race/ethnicity. Some items have national norms because they are taken from the national Monitoring the Future Project. The Sample Report for the Alcohol and Other Drugs survey contains Wisconsin norms for nine items about substance usage rates. Each report uses an inadequately described process to eliminate respondents who made inconsistent responses, reported unrealistically high use of drugs, or had high levels of nonresponse.

The Behavior Patterns report is organized into three major parts: Social and Personal Resources (11 subareas with 1-10 items each), Behavior Patterns (10 subareas with 3-13 items each), and Opportunities for Helping Your Youth (9 items). The survey attempts to cover a very broad range of student experiences and, consequently, the coverage is skimpy in several of the areas (e.g., "sexuality" is measured with three items). The other surveys go into greater detail in these areas, but many of the items are redundant if more than one of the surveys were to be used in a single school.

Generally, all of the items relating to a subarea are reported on the top of one page with "Key Findings" for the area reported at the bottom of the page. For example, "Frequent TV watching is highest in grade 6." This message (and others like it) appears to be triggered by some statistical analysis which is not described. A footnote refers to "a technical appendix with scale composition and confidence intervals" but this reviewer was unable to acquire it. Most Key Findings appears to be percentages from the item data put into prose; some appear to be based on more than one item.

In one case, "Values as Behavior Determinants," a one-item subarea, a whole page is devoted to reporting how students respond to: "It is against my values to have sex while I am a teenager." The Key Findings area cites their own research which showed that, "Values, therefore, are more powerful than even peer pressure in determining intentions concerning intercourse." No references are provided. If responses to this item are so predictive of behavior, perhaps the area deserves a few more items.

The definitions used sometimes seem idiosyncratic. For example, in the 20-factor "at-risk index," "Gang Fights: twice or more in last 12 months" and "Used knife, gun, or club to get something from someone, twice or more in last 12 months" are treated as equivalent to "Cigarettes: 1 or more cigarettes per day" and "School Absence: skipped school 2 or more days in last month." It is not surprising that 85% of seniors report they experienced at least one of the indicators and 58% report three or more.

The very readable reports present percentages of respondents who used the top two choices (or bottom two on negatively worded items) by grade, gender (not simultaneously), and total group. Users are cautioned that self-reported alcohol and drug use data are "consistent with other methods of collecting chemical use data" (no reference), but that, "The validity of other kinds of self-reported data (e.g., sexual activity, physical abuse, sexual abuse) is less clearly understood."

Each survey is printed in its own eight-page, scannable, professionally designed booklet. The surveys have a reasonable amount of eye appeal. They seem to provide broad coverage of the areas for which they are intended. They are reported to be the result of in-depth work in a variety of areas. The computerized scoring program generates reports that are readable. Unfortunately, none of the technical characteristics of the surveys are documented. They are relatively expensive. They may be useful as needs assessment devices for some organizations or as evaluation devices for some programs if local survey design capabilities are limited or if program goals and definitions of terms happen to match those of the authors.

Review of the Search Institute Profiles of Student Life by SHARON JOHNSON-LEWIS, Director of Research, Evaluation, and Testing, Detroit Public Schools, Detroit, MI:

The Search Institute Profiles of Student Life consists of three instruments designed to provide information about students' (a) attitudes and behaviors in general, as well as their attitudes and behaviors related to (b) alcohol and other drugs, and (c) sexuality.

Each instrument is priced separately at $2,500 per survey service ($1,000 if only computer output is required) plus $1.25 per student.

At first glance, the price appears high. However, after conducting a thorough examination of the materials and the scoring package, one can certainly conclude that the money is well spent.

The Profiles are extremely comprehensive and very well developed. However, for use with small groups of students, the cost may still be prohibitive, in spite of the quality. For example, to administer one of the three instruments to a group of 400 students, and receive full service, would cost $3,000 or $7.50 per pupil, for 300 students a total of $2,875 or $9.58 per pupil. Of course, these prices would multiply if more than one profile is administered.

A small number of core questions appear in each of the three instruments. For example, each has a few questions related to drug use and non-use, peer and parent relationship, and sexuality. In addition, the demographic probes for each are similar. However, each instrument contains specialty items.

ALCOHOL AND OTHER DRUGS. This survey specializes in questions designed to assess the degree to which students participate in alcohol and drug use. The survey asks questions about student attitudes and frequency of use related to drinking alcohol, cigarette and marijuana smoking, and use of LSD, PCP, and smokeless tobacco.

The instrument also asks questions concerned with how students think their parents would react to their alcohol and drug use, student's knowledge of school rules, behaviors of friends, and knowledge of community or school support groups, religious beliefs, and school expectations.

ATTITUDES AND BEHAVIORS. The Attitudes and Behaviors Profile asks students questions related to recreation, being popular, having money, religious preference, helping people, school likes and dislikes, skipping school and classes, self-concept, sex, love, decision making, and relationships with people, parents, and friends. Items also assess the degree in which students are involved in extracurricular activities, and use of alcohol, cigarettes, and drugs. In addition, the survey attempts to assess the quality of parent/child interaction, how much, if any, physical and sexual abuse exists, and how much students worry about the future.

SEXUALITY. The Sexuality Profile is designed to ascertain where students learned about sex, if they are interested in learning more about sex-related issues, concerns about sexism, and sexually transmitted diseases. Students indicate to whom they would talk about sex, how often they have engaged in sexual intercourse, and their knowledge of body changes during puberty.

Students also rate the quality of conversations they have had with their parents about sex, and indicate if statements such as "Males have stronger sex drives than females" or "Using birth control makes having sex less romantic" are facts or myths.

Because of the explicit nature of these questions, it is strongly recommended that a thorough review of the survey items be conducted prior to use.

SURVEY ADMINISTRATION. Survey administration times range from 30 to 40 minutes. The questions are multiple choice and students can respond quite rapidly to the fixed answer choices. The test format and layout allows for easy reading.

The user can administer the survey to the total student population or a sample of students. The scoring service includes consultation on how to select an appropriate sample.

The survey directions are clear and concise and are quite explicit. For instance, on the Sexuality Profile the directions state, "The words 'having sex' or 'had sex' mean the act of having sexual intercourse, that is, a male's penis going into a female's vagina."

The manual also contains suggestions for testing students arriving late to do the survey.

SUMMARY. The Search Institute Profiles of Student Life is a battery of three instruments—Alcohol and Other Drugs, Sexuality, and Attitudes and Behaviors. Although the surveys contain a common core of items they also have "speciality" items.

The surveys are well constructed and are comprehensive. Because of the explicit nature of the questions, the potential user should review the Sexuality Profile prior to purchase.

The reports are also well designed and comprehensive, providing the user with a thorough understanding of the results through the use of tables and graphics. National norms are seldom used for comparison purposes.

The major weakness is the cost, which is extremely high especially for small groups of students.

REPORTING. Report forms for the Attitude and Behavior Profile were provided for review. Survey results are reported in the percents of students responding positively or negatively to each item. Data are disaggregated by grade and gender. Data are combined for groups of students smaller than 30.

The results are divided into three parts: Social and Personal Resources, Behavior Patterns, and Opportunities For Helping Your Youth. Each part comprises tables and graphs which profile the given subheading. The subheadings are composed of several characteristics:

Part I: Social and Personal Resources—Family Characteristics, Attitudes Toward School, Parent Involvement in Schooling, Use of Time, Involvement in Youth Activities, Access to Positive Adult Influence, Peer Influence, Student Values, Values as Behavior Determinants, Self-Concept, and View of the Future.

Part II: Behavior Patterns—Prosocial Behavior, Alcohol Use, Other Alcohol Issues, Tobacco Use, Other Drug Use, Alcohol and Drug Use Patterns, Comparisons to National Norms (seniors—alcohol and drug use), Sexuality, Anti-social Behavior, Days School Skipped, Physical and Sexual Abuse, At-risk Indicators and Stress, Depression and Suicide.

Part III: Opportunities for Helping Youth—Interests, Factors related to at-risk behaviors and a comprehensive discussion of how, based on research and data, the school, family, and community might help students. The commentary also provides data sources that can be used to develop strategies for helping students prosper. This section encourages a multilevel approach to helping students involving families, schools, churches, government, businesses, and community organizations.

The Sexuality brochure indicates that the items were normed on a sample of 1,800 students in four major cities. A major flaw in the reporting is that national norms for comparison purposes are seldom used.

[2.38]
Socio-Sexual Knowledge & Attitudes Test.

Purpose: Designed to assess sex knowledge and attitudes of individuals with development disabilities.
Population: Developmentally disabled ages 18–42 and non-retarded persons of all ages.
Publication Dates: 1976–1980.
Acronym: SSKAT.
Scores: 14 topic areas: Anatomy Terminology, Menstruation, Dating, Marriage, Intimacy, Intercourse, Pregnancy and Childbirth, Birth Control, Masturbation, Homosexuality, Venereal Disease, Alcohol and Drugs, Community Risks and Hazards, Terminology Check.

Administration: Individual.
Price Data, 1994: $150 per complete kit including stimulus picture book, manual ('80, 59 pages), and 10 record forms; $44.50 per 10 record forms including student profile and response summary; $25 per manual.
Time: Administration time not reported.
Comments: Criterion-referenced.
Authors: Joel R. Wish, Katherine Fiechtl McCombs, and Barbara Edmonson.
Publisher: Stoelting Co.
Cross References: The review by Edward S. Herold originally appeared in 9:1152; see also T3:2237 (1 reference).

Review of the Socio-Sexual Knowledge & Attitudes Test by EDWARD S. HEROLD, Associate Professor of Family Studies, University of Guelph, Guelph, Ontario, Canada:

The test items of this instrument adequately reflect the concerns and issues caregivers have regarding the socio-sexual functioning of the mentally handicapped. The test is easy to administer and requires little verbalization by the respondent.

The stimulus picture book is an essential component of the test and makes it easy for the subjects to respond to the questions. The pictures are black and white. Colored pictures would have provided more effective stimuli. The meaning of some pictures is ambiguous. In none of the pictures is a vagina shown and this may result in some confusion for the subjects.

The 261 test questions require 2 or more hours to administer. Given the lengthiness of the test, test administrators would need to decide ahead of time which items were to be given priority for testing. There are too many items to be covered at one time.

Experimental testing was done with 100 males and females from an institutional population and 100 males and females from a community population. One-half of the subjects were retested. For knowledge items the mean percentage test-retest agreement on the items in each subject area ranged from 78.2% to 89.7%. For the attitudinal items the mean test-retest item agreements for each subject area ranged from 76% to 91.5%. These statistics were obtained prior to changes being made in the test. It would be more enlightening if test-retest measures were done with the revised material. Also it would be helpful to know which specific items had the lowest test-retest agreement. It

should be noted that during the experimental testing an item sampling procedure was used rather than having the subjects complete all of the items on the test. The Kuder-Richardson reliabilities ranged from .53 to .83. The author, in defending these moderately low reliabilities, states that it is more important to know a subject's response to a particular question than it is to know how his/her response to one question relates to his/her responses to other questions.

Validity data are lacking. There are no data available, for example, relating knowledge and attitude test scores to actual sexual practices. The author refers to "curricular validity" in describing that the test items were based on a review of literature and subjects were rated as relevant by 50 individuals. However, it does not appear that specific test items were evaluated by outside experts.

Despite these shortcomings, the test is worthwhile and should be of considerable assistance in helping educators and clinicians to determine the socio-sexual knowledge and attitudes of the mentally handicapped.

[2.39]
Symptom Scale—77.
Purpose: "Designed to reflect specific symptom changes … capable of modification by psychotherapy or neuropharmacology."
Population: Adolescents and adults.
Publication Dates: 1992–1995.
Acronym: SS—77.
Scores: 10 scales: Somatic Complaints, Depression, Alcohol and Other Drug Abuse, Anxiety, Obsessive—Compulsive Symptoms, Panic Disorder Without and With Agoraphobia, Traumatic Stress, Minimization of Symptoms, Magnification of Symptoms, Guardedness Index.
Administration: Individual or group.
Price Data, 1996: $110 per complete kit including professional manual ('95, 50 pages), user manual ('95, 14 pages), and 3.5-inch diskettes.
Time: (15–20) minutes.
Comments: Computer administration requires IBM-compatible with at least 4 MB RAM and 1.4 MB disk drive and mouse and Windows 3.1.
Author: Judith L. Johnson.
Publisher: The Psychological Corporation.

This test has not been reviewed in *The Mental Measurements Yearbook.*

INDEX OF TITLES

This title index lists all the tests included in this Buros Desk Reference. *Citations are to test entry numbers, not to pages (e.g., 1.4 refers to Test 4 in Section 1). Test numbers along with test titles are indicated in the running heads at the top of each page, and page numbers, used only in the Table of Contents and not in the indexes, appear at the bottom of each page.*

INDEX OF ACRONYMS

This *Index of Acronyms* refers the reader to the appropriate test in the *Buros Desk Reference*. In some cases tests are better known by their acronyms than by their full titles, and this index can be of substantial help to the person who knows the former but not the latter. Acronyms are only listed if the author or publisher has made substantial use of the acronym in referring to the test, or if the test is widely known by the acronym. There is some danger in the overuse of acronyms, but this index, like all other indexes in this work, is provided to make the task of identifying a test as easy as possible. All numbers refer to test numbers, not page numbers.

PUBLISHERS DIRECTORY
AND INDEX

This directory and index gives the addresses and test entry numbers of all publishers for in-print tests represented in this Buros Desk Reference. *Please note that all numbers in this index refer to test entry numbers, not page numbers. Publishers are an important source of information about catalogs, specimen sets, price changes, test revisions, and many other matters.*

New Standards, Inc., 1080 Montreal Avenue, Suite 300, St. Paul, MN 55116, 1.31, 1.38

NFER-Nelson Publishing Co., Ltd., Darville House, 2 Oxford Road East, Windsor, Berkshire SL4 1DF, England, 2.3

NIDA Addiction Research Center (Attn. Charles A. Haertzen, Ph.D.), c/o Baltimore City Hospital, Bldg., D-5E, 4940 Eastern Avenue, Baltimore, MD 21224, 1.1

Person-O-Metrics, Inc. [No reply from publisher; status unknown], 1.30

Pfeiffer & Company, 350 Sansome St., 5th Floor, San Francisco, CA 94104, 2.26

PRO-ED, Inc., 8700 Shoal Creek Blvd., Austin, TX 78757-6897, 2.4

Psychological Assessment Resources, Inc., P.O. Box 998, Odessa, FL 33556-9908, 1.16, 1.3, 1.35, 2.1, 2.11, 2.28, 2.6

Psychologists and Educators, Inc., Sales Division, P.O. Box 513, Chesterfield, MO 63006, 1.12, 1.15

Reid Psychological Systems, 200 South Michigan Avenue, Suite 900, Chicago, IL 60604-2401, 2.35

RENOVEX Corporation, 1421 Jersey Avenue N., Minneapolis, MN 55427, 1.11

Rocky Mountain Behavioral Science Institute, Inc., P.O. Box 1066, Fort Collins, CO 80522, 1.9

The SASSI Institute, P.O. Box 5069, Bloomington, IN 47407, 1.37

Nina G. Schneider, Ph.D., Psychopharmacology Unit, VA Medical Center, Brentwood T350, Mail Code: 691/B151D, Los Angeles, CA 90073, 1.34

Search Institute, 700 South 3rd Street, Suite 210, Minneapolis, MN 55415-1138, 2.37

Melvin L. Selzer, M.D., 6967 Paseo Laredo, LaJolla, CA 92037, 1.24

Slosson Educational Publications, Inc., P.O. Box 280, East Aurora, NY 14052-0280, 1.36

SRA/London House, 9701 West Higgins Road, Rosemont, IL 60018-4720, 2.21

Stoelting Co., Oakwood Center, 620 Wheat Lane, Wood Dale, IL 60191, 2.38

University of Minnesota Press, Mill Place, Suite 290, 111 Third Avenue South, Minneapolis, MN 55401-2520, 2.24, 2.25

Western Psychological Services, 12031 Wilshire Blvd., Los Angeles, CA 90025-1251, 1.2, 1.23, 1.26, 1.27, 1.28, 1.39, 1.4, 2.13, 2.31

Dale E. Williams, Ph.D., Department of Psychology, John Carroll University, University Heights, OH 44118, 1.14

The Wilmington Institute [No reply from publisher; status unknown], 2.10

Wonderlic Personnel Test, Inc., 1509 N. Milwaukee Avenue, Libertyville, Il 60048-1387, 2.12

World Health Organization, Programme on Substance Abuse, 1211 Geneva, Switzerland, 1.7

SCORE INDEX

This Score Index lists all the scores, in alphabetical order, for all the tests included in this Buros Desk Reference. *Because test scores can be regarded as operational definitions of the variable measured, sometimes the scores provide better leads to what a test actually measures than the test title or other available information. The Score Index is very detailed, and the reader should keep in mind that a given variable (or concept) of interest may be defined in several different ways. Thus the reader should look up these several possible alternative definitions before drawing final conclusions about whether tests measuring a particular variable of interest can be located in this volume. If the kind of score sought is located in a particular test or tests, the reader should then read the test descriptive information carefully to determine whether the test(s) in which the score is found is (are) consistent with reader purpose. Used wisely, the Score Index can be another useful resource in locating the right score in the right test. As usual, all numbers in the index are test numbers, not page numbers.*